MW01504315

The
Specter
of Babel

The Specter of Babel

A Reconstruction of Political Judgment

MICHAEL J. THOMPSON

Published by State University of New York Press, Albany

For information, contact State University of New York Press, Albany, NY
www.sunypress.edu

Library of Congress Cataloging-in-Publication Data

Names: Thompson, Michael, 1973– author.
Title: The specter of Babel : a reconstruction of political judgment /
    Michael J. Thompson.
Description: Albany : State University of New York, 2020. | Includes
    bibliographical references and index.
Identifiers: LCCN 2020000966 (print) | LCCN 2020000967 (ebook) | ISBN
    9781438480350 (hardcover : alk. paper) | ISBN 9781438480374 (ebook)
Subjects: LCSH: Critical theory. | Social sciences—Philosophy. | Ontology. |
    Political sociology.
Classification: LCC HM480 .T463 2020 (print) | LCC HM480 (ebook) |
    DDC 306.2—dc23
LC record available at https://lccn.loc.gov/2020000966
LC ebook record available at https://lccn.loc.gov/2020000967

10 9 8 7 6 5 4 3 2 1

For the seekers of true justice
ὁμοθαμνεῖν μέν, μὴ ὁμοδογματεῖν δέ

Contents

Preface

This book is technical in nature, but its subject matter is far from scholarly or obscure. It concerns the problem of judgment—that activity of discerning those forms of politics and society that are worthy of our rational obligations and those that warrant our disobedience. It concerns our capacity to think through defective and pathological forms of our social world and how they shape our individuality and the kinds of lives we live. I contend that modern political societies are losing their collective capacity for judgment, and that the ideal of the individual as an agent of conscience and reason is in peril. Regaining critical judgment through a more coherent and more radical conception of ethics and value is the central subject of my investigation, one that I hope will spark renewed interest in the paradigm of critical social ontology and its relation to critical reason.

For many years, I have been troubled by the remarkable lack of critical consciousness and judgment displayed by modern citizens, especially during the early decades of the present century. Reckless wars, senseless material consumption, the toleration of staggering economic inequality, utter passivity in the face of human-generated climate change, the loss of thousands of animal and plant species, new forms of populism, the resuscitation of old prejudices, and a new penchant for authoritarianism, among so much more, all point toward a crisis in the ethical and political culture of modern societies. Conformity (no less than indifference) marks the modern personality as autonomy and critical reason have receded as cultural values. As a partisan of the Enlightenment and critical reason, I see it as essential that we question how contemporary philosophy has engaged the question of political judgment in particular and practical reason in general.

My firm conviction is that the dominant approach to ethical questions that pervades contemporary philosophy and culture is misguided and cannot serve as the basis for a critical fulcrum against the imperatives and forces of technological, administrative-capitalist society. I mean *critical* in the sense that reason has more than a capacity to be reasonable, it must also, as Marx emphasized, go to the root of social phenomena, that is, the features and dynamics of human social being.

As such, I assert that our ideas about practical reason, about ethics itself, have lost their way. Because of this, I believe something new is required. A new paradigm for thinking about practical reason in critical terms and granting to our critical capacities a kind of ethical coherence and vision for a more just, more emancipated society. The political and ethical crises of the first half of the twentieth century gave rise to a renewed project to establish a form of practical reasoning that would no longer rely on "metaphysics," established truths that were posited as transcendent to human life and action. At the same time, an emerging liberal social contract meant that radical ideas rooted in human emancipation from an alienating and dehumanizing social order no longer served as a valid political aspiration. A move toward language, pragmatism, intersubjectivity, identity, pluralism, and the "political" were articulated in this period. The symbolic took center stage, and the premise was put forth that social change and social critique should be grounded in the intersubjective, noumenal layer of human praxis rather than the actual structures of power that were constitutive of society.

Now with economic problems of distribution largely viewed as solved by the welfare states of Western capitalist democracies, we were free to formulate theories of practical reason, where the exchange of reasons and the recognition of the identity of the "other" were of paramount importance. Gone was the need to thematize the totality as a reifying process; gone, too, was the idea that the "working class" could be the political agent for social transformation. But recent changes in our political economy have made evident that this was indeed only a temporary phase. The rise of neoliberalism has revealed once more the exploitative nature of capitalist accumulation and the antidemocratic impulses of a social order based on technical-administrative institutional control even as the reactions to its extractive and managerial logics have spawned a new phase of populism and social unreason.

In short, the mainstream philosophical project that effected a shift toward postmetaphysics and nonfoundationalism has been, in my view, a wrong turn in our thinking about judgment and practical reason as a whole. As we witness the inflammation of the neoliberal social order, where a rise in identity politics, racism, neo-authoritarianism, and other antidemocratic forces are becoming prevalent, the need for critical judgment is even more crucial. The temptation to follow the group, to allow the experiences of ego-threat to impel us into the confines of some group identity is further eroding the practice of judgment and critique. We can see, I maintain, that the lack of foundations and grounding for our ethical life pushed by the postmetaphysical turn has left us with little armature for this struggle. My suggestion in what follows is that we reground our ideas about judgment and practical reason in a critical social ontology; that we look at ethical value not as a matter of discursive concern but as rooted in the forms of social reality we inhabit and how these social forms either promote or debase the development and flourishing of our capacities. In short, a return to an ontological conception of the species as a basis for ethics can be achieved and, I believe, grant us a more critical theory of consciousness and ethics, one dearly needed in times of rising nihilism and ethical incoherence.

Critique requires both breaking down encrusted forms of power and ideological conformity and a vision of what ought to replace it. This "ought" should not be seen in neo-idealistic or postmetaphysical terms but as an expression of what can potentially unfold from us if we were to live in a rational society—in a society shaped *for* the concrete, common purpose of the development of each member of the community and self-consciously *by* those members. We cannot ignore that there are certain species-specific needs and potentialities that can be enhanced or frustrated by the forms of life we inhabit and that we actively reconstitute in everyday life. The key project of critical reason is to reveal the pathological norms, institutions, and purposes that our lives are put to and by which our community as a whole is constituted. I hope that this book can at least alert readers to the importance of rethinking the dominant trends in current philosophy and engage a more critical and rational way of thinking about the concerns of the *res publica*.

What I hope to accomplish is therefore an entrée to a more robust form of practical reason and ethics. As I see it, the project of articulating an objective ethics can be achieved once we are able to keep in view the shapes that our social reality takes. This means judging our world according to the various ways it shapes our relations with others, articulates norms and practices, and realizes certain ends, purposes, and goods. We have to judge these realities not through some illusory form of deliberative discourse but according to parameters about what kind of needs and relational goods are requisite for the good life, for a modern form of freedom. The Enlightenment's project of modernity is in peril. Despite its best efforts to do otherwise, it has wedded its fate to the imperatives of capitalism: variables of production, consumption, and growth of material affluence as criteria for the success of modern society. But this is showing itself more and more to be a vapid and impoverished form of life. Under the pressures of neoliberalism, the prospects for a more rational and committed form of ethical life has withered to the point of nihilism. A new theory of ethics, rooted in our distinctive capacities and features as social and practical beings, will be able to open up new ways of thinking about social critique and social transformation. In this spirit, this book is offered, and I can only hope that it will foster some fresh reflection on these questions for future labors.

Acknowledgments

The bulk of this book was initially drafted in Berlin in the summer of 2018 during a lengthy stay at the Literatur Hotel in Friedenau, steps from the former homes of Rosa Luxemburg, Karl Liebknecht, and Karl Kautsky, among others—intimidating inspiration, indeed. It was completed about a year later in New York City late in the summer of 2019. Many of the ideas developed in these pages were worked out in different conference papers and symposia over the past several years. These took place at the University of Cambridge; the Symposium on New Critical Social Theory at the University of Iowa; a meeting of the Marx and Philosophy Society at University College, London; York University in Toronto; the Inter-University Center for Advanced Studies in Dubrovnik; the New York German Idealism Workshop; and annual meetings of the Southern Political Science Association, Mid-Western Sociological Society, Pacific Sociological Association, Western Political Science Association, Southern Sociological Society, Northeastern Political Science Association, Midwestern Political Science Association, International Sociological Association, American Political Science Association, American Sociological Association, the Annual Symposium on Self and Society, and the highly fruitful, intellectually stimulating annual meetings of the International Social Theory Consortium.

I have debated and discussed these ideas with many people whose insights deserve mention: Bob Antonio, Jim Block, Stephen Eric Bronner, Mike Brown, Daniel Brudney, Tom Bunyard, Andrew Chitty, Joel Crombez, Harry Dahms, Andrew Feenberg, Harrison Fluss, Jeff Halley, Neal Harris, Dick Howard, Axel Honneth, Peter Hudis, Reha Kadakal, Konstantinos Kavoulakos, Rafael Khatchaturian, Dan Krier, Lauren Langman, Christian Lotz, Toby Lovat, Darrow Schecter, Dirk

Michel-Schertges, Patrick Murray, Steve Panageotou, Nathan Ross, Volker Schmitz, Jean Schuler, David Smith, Tony Smith, Heinz Sünker, Mark Worrell, and Greg Zucker. My wife, Elena Mancini, has also been an insightful and provocative interlocutor on my ideas as they have developed and, sometimes rightly, fallen to the ground. I owe her more than words can say. Although all of these people helped deepen my ideas, none of them can be held responsible for what unfolds in the pages that follow.

Introduction

Cybernetic Society and the Crisis of Modernity

Seen from the point of view of its supporters over the course of the past two centuries, the project of modernity was always centered on the premise that rational, self-legislating individuals were capable of generating self-government and cultivating moral personhood. Even for those who took the view that each person is essentially a social and cooperative being, the individual was still the crucible for any understanding of modern, rational forms of politics and ethics. Modernity was to create a world where the powers of irrational tradition, superstition, and illegitimate authority would be questioned, where public reason could generate binding norms and institutions. At the center of this Enlightenment project was the concept of *judgment*, or the capacity to discern which norms, laws, institutions, and social ends were rational, worthy of justification and obligation, and which did not deserve this endorsement and even those which warranted dissent and disobedience.

This project is now seriously in question. This book proceeds from the premise that modern society is quickly losing its sense of vision of the purposes and potentialities of political life, that it is in fact losing its capacity for critical judgment. Concepts such as the common interest have been all but banished from the realm of modern political philosophy and consigned to the abstract preferences of the individual. In its place, we have been asked to accept a theory of politics that rests on consensus, agreement, and intersubjectivity; a theory of politics and judgment that seeks out sociality with others as a matter of the exchange of reasons rather than an object with its own dynamics and features. This theory is based on pluralism, tolerance, and mutual

1

understanding. Although codified in volume after volume of contemporary political philosophy, it is profoundly detached from the actual dynamics of power that shape the contours of the real world. In a more philosophical sense, it fails as a guide for human societies seeking to judge and even transform their collective ethical life. Even more, I believe it has distracted us from more pressing questions about the nature of political life and practical reason, from the deep structures of our social world that generate personal and social pathologies, and from a tradition of thought that saw the structure of society as a whole, as a totality, as the primary object of concern for political thought and emancipatory critique. The collapse of Western humanistic ideas that accompanied the destructive events of the first half of the twentieth century have led to a fear of discussing any kind of concrete nature of the good, freedom, or justice. Instead, we are now asked to commit to a more cautious, more academic model of ethics and politics. It is a model of democratic reason that, as I see it, is not up to the task of critical reason and is instead an unwitting legitimating logic for the most subtle and yet pervasive forms of social power.

From its origins in the Enlightenment, the concept of modern democratic life was seen to be based on the capacity of agents to reflect rationally on their world and the kinds of norms and institutions that constituted it. As religion and other forms of traditional authority were gradually displaced in terms of political power by an alternative rational agency, the modes of thought and life that bound humans to rigid authority structures and hierarchies seemed to be collapsing. What essentially destroyed the social basis for premodern forms of authority, however, was also the soil for a new form of social power and dominance. The destruction of premodern ethical life was not replaced with a thorough, rational alternative. The gradual erosion of religion's capacity for serving as a cohesive ground for ethical life was sensed by thinkers like Rousseau, Kant, and Hegel, among others. They saw that a more rational alternative for ethics and value was possible: one that would be rooted in a concept of social reason where each member was able to think in terms of a rational, general will and freedom would be found in the self-consciousness of this new, expanded conception of personhood. What they could not have anticipated was the technological transformation of economic life oriented toward generating surplus and the repatterning of society and self that came with it. This set the stage for the derailment of the project to construct a viable alternative to premodern, pre-Enlightenment ethical life and value systems.

The search for such an alternative nevertheless continued in different forms—some rational and progressive, others reactionary—well into the present. But our time has been shaped by a structure of thought that was constructed largely in the post–World War II period. This way of thinking can be characterized by a noumenal model of sociality where individuals exchange reasons and justify their normative commitments to one another. The model is built off of the scaffolding of the eighteenth-century Enlightenment mixed with twentieth-century philosophies of language. What has resulted is a dominant approach to ethics that misses any concrete conceptualizations of the good and ethical judgment. My central thesis in this book is that this project has failed to provide an adequate theory of ethics and judgment and that a more critical conception of political judgment is in fact necessary. It is necessary because the prevailing theoretical ideas and figures that have dominated the past several decades in academic discourse have become increasingly sealed off from the mechanisms of the real world and how power, consciousness, and society have been transformed by a resurgent form of administration and a technological form of capitalism. The fate of the individual and of individual judgment have been at the mercy of the formative pressures of social integration that undermine the capacity to think outside of the parameters of this integration. What has resulted is a withered form of critical reason and a denatured moral agency rapidly losing the capacity to protest the imperatives of cybernetic mechanisms of conformity and control.

One of the core theses of this book is that modern citizens are losing the capacity for critical political judgment understood as the ability to grasp and dissent from the dominant logics of power relations the make up modern society. Even more, the eroding capacity for judgment contributes to a new kind of politics and culture, one where democratic ideas of solidarity, the common good, and democratic equality are replaced by identity with one's group membership. The ideas that dominate what passes for political judgment in the literature are not equipped for restoring this capacity or a culture of it in modern politics because it remains caught in a theoretical paradigm that cannot account for how the ontological structures of society deplete our critical capacity to comprehend it and judge it. This is not meant to imply that we have all become automata, lacking ethical values or capacity for evaluative reason. Rather, I suggest that we have lost a basic form of ethical coherence with respect to how the power structures of our world have been shaped. We lack not simply judgment but *critical* judgment: the capacity to question the social totality and how it shapes and patterns the world we experience phenomenologically. Critical judgment, as I reconstruct it, must have in view some sense of what forms of human sociality promote self-development and freedom and which ones do not. Critical judgment must be able to penetrate the appearances of our inherited world and grasp the essence of our species-specific dynamics. Only then can we shatter the reifying pull of the highly technical, administrative mass society that seeks to fold each of us into its manifold logic.

Central to my thesis is that two forces have shaped modern society from the middle of the nineteenth century through today. First is the gradual technical patterning of the world, originating in the constant search for efficiency in production logics and the management of large-scale production and consumption regimes. These logics become ever more deeply constitutive of the individual as they colonize what were previously distinct spheres of culture and life. Second is a reaction, in many ways, to this trend: the increasing subjectification and particularization of ethical values and concepts of the "good." With the phrase "specter of Babel," I am denoting the potential reality of a society fragmenting along the lines of identity, culture, religion, ethnicity (or whatever axis we wish to insert) that generates a particularist field of ethical value—a society that no longer has self-understanding of its collective good and that allows each particular subgroup to turn inward and lose sight of the importance of the common interest. As a result, each individual increasingly comes to see the world in terms of their particular worldviews rather than in terms of common social patterns that affect all members of society. Whereas the project of postwar liberalism was to construct a moral-political framework for a pluralistic society in the face of modernity's collapse of a common ethical life and substantive political vision, it has instead given rise to a dearth of critical consciousness in the face of an increasingly powerful cybernetic society that has expanded the powers of private wealth and capital.

Although, on one hand, there has been an increasingly cohesive knitting together of our lives under the auspices of technical and administrative institutional logics, each person searches for meaning in a world increasingly devoid of any meaning. Two forces exert pressure on our practical reasoning: the increasing technical mastery of our lives by the rationalized logics of power, and an increasing subjectification of value even as our powers of critical and moral reasoning are flattened by technical integration. The search for a common life with others, a kind of society that could realize a common good, is undermined by the atomized individual seeking their own conception of the good. The more that these mutually reinforcing trends increase in their potency, the more that critical judgment loses contact with the emancipatory goals of the Enlightenment and reflects the defective reality principle of the present. I see the tension between these two forces of modern life as the essential problematic of modern culture and modern philosophy. Let me explore these forces in turn.

The increasing search for efficiency in production and social stability in modern capitalist societies has manifested a deepening of the social logics of administrative-rational authority and extended technical logics that have had deep effects on the nature of subjectivity. These social changes have only led to an increasing tendency of subjectivity to be routinized into power relations and forms of authority that are largely internalized but resonant with the imperatives and normative structures of production and consumption. Substantive cultural differences in terms of value orientations and worldviews become eroded as people become guided more by external logics, norms, and rule-following. The result has been less and less use of the individual is evaluative and cognitive capacities and an increasing reliance on external, indeed, heteronomous systems for social action.[1] This has been the result of how the productive powers of the machine have been able to pattern the life of human beings. Not just the machine as a concrete object but also the socially autonomous logic of capital seeks its own expansion of surplus extraction and the instrumentalization of all social, natural, and cultural entities for that purpose.

I refer to this sociological transformation of social systems and culture as the *cybernetic society* because it manifests the characteristics of a self-regulating, governing system. The problem with this image of modern society is that it represses the true nature of our social order.

---

1. I have explored this phenomenon elsewhere as a form of alienation. See Michael J. Thompson, "Alienation as Atrophied Moral Cognition and its Impact on Social Behavior." *Journal for the Theory of Social Behaviour*, vol. 43, no. 3 (2013): 301–21.

Far from being "self-regulating" and "autonomous" from individual human will, it exists and persists due to the socialized conformity and absorption of the individual into the collective processes and logics of the social system as a whole—a social system that is steered and organized as much as possible by elites with economic power and increasingly oligarchic control over material and institutional resources. The individual is in effect "piloted" through much of their substantive social activities by the internalized norms that have been articulated by highly rationalized forms of institutional authority, crowding out nonformal structures of life. The word "cybernetic" is derived from the Greek verb κυβερνάω, which means "to pilot" or "to steer," which in Latin was translated as *gubernare*, from which we get the term "to govern." Resonant in the semantics of this term is the idea that "cybernetics" refers to the means by which the components of complex systems are directed and steered. Applied to modern society, this entails the spread of instrumental logics that subsume noninstrumental spheres of life, action, and consciousness. As capital and technical reason widen their scope of subsumption of subjective patterns of thought and feeling and make them resonant with their own ends and means, cybernetic society can be seen to emerge.

This transformation of modern society has had deleterious effects on the structure of the individual and the capacity of critical consciousness to resist the pressures of conformity that emanate from the cybernetic patterns of social reality. More crucially, the individual becomes alienated from the processes that dominate the life-world and, as a result, seeks refuge in one's "particularity." Ideas like this go back to the origins of mass society. Georg Simmel, writing in the early twentieth century, formulated the outlines of such a description of society as a "culture which outgrows all personal life." He continues:

> Here in buildings and educational institutions, in the wonders and comforts of space-conquering technology, in the formations of community life, and in the visible institutions of the state, is offered such an overwhelming fullness of crystallized and impersonalized spirit that the personality, so to speak, cannot maintain itself under its impact. . . . They carry the person as if in a stream, and one needs hardly to swim for oneself. On the other hand, however, life is composed more and more of these impersonal contents and offerings

which tend to displace the genuine personal colorations and incomparabilities. This results in the individual's summoning the utmost in uniqueness and particularization, in order to preserve his most personal core.[2]

Simmel's thesis of what he called the crisis of culture was that the powers of modern society were outstripping a person's capacity to comprehend the whole. As such, as the "hypertrophy" of technologically complex society increased, so did the "atrophy" of the subject's individual cognitive and moral-evaluative powers. Key to this is the rise of a certain kind of technical-instrumental reason that has become constitutive of the institutional and administrative life of modern subjects. It is a centripetal force that socializes our subjectivity to its own objectivity. Its norms colonize our practices, and as a result, ethical reflection and judgment begin to wither. The cybernetic society therefore must be seen as more than the communicative model of information exchange to capture a new form of administrative governance, a new kind of highly integrated, patterned form of behavior and consciousness. As Norbert Wiener, one of the founders of cybernetics, once put it:

> When I give an order to a machine, the situation is not essentially different from that which arises when I give an order to a person. In other words, as far as my consciousness goes I am aware of the order that has gone out and of the signal of compliance that has come back. To me, personally, the fact that the signal in its intermediate stages has gone through a machine rather than through a person is irrelevant and does not in any case greatly change my relation to the signal. . . . It is the purpose of Cybernetics to develop a language and techniques that will enable us indeed to attack the problem of control and communication in general, but also to find the proper repertory of ideas and techniques to classify their particular manifestations under certain concepts.[3]

---

2. Georg Simmel, *The Sociology of Georg Simmel*, trans. Kurt H. Wolff (New York: Free Press, 1950), 422.

3. Norbert Wiener, *The Human Use of Human Beings: Cybernetics and Society* (New York: Da Capo Press, 1954), 16–17.

Social power now becomes a function of *compliance*—compliance to a system that has its own autonomous logic within which human culture becomes embedded. Wiener's conflation of the person and the machine, which he took to be a fear of the future rather than a prescription for it, is no exaggeration. The development of modern techniques of power, production, and consumption now become tracks for the development of the subject's cognitive, evaluative, and cathectic ego-structure. The highly patterned, machine-like construction of administered institutional life socializes even the most recalcitrant among us into its fields of operation. The result of this has been an acute decline in the capacity for critical judgment—practical and political. The intense cybernetic patterning of social life is accompanied by an intensification of the reification of consciousness—not only its cognitive and epistemic capacities but also its moral-evaluative powers.

The cybernetic society is therefore only possible once technical means of control and command have become routinized and rational authority has become reified in consciousness as the routinization of technical forms of control and administrative operationality has saturated socializing institutions. Indeed, Jacques Ellul saw this occurring in what he called "automatism of technical choice":

> When everything has been measured and calculated mathe-
> matically so that the method which has been decided upon
> is satisfactory from the rational point of view, the method is
> manifestly the most efficient of all those hitherto employed
> of those in competition with it, then the technical movement
> becomes self-directing, I call the process of *automatism*.[4]

As the institutional context of society becomes more automatic and self-regulating, so do the structures of the self and subjectivity. As Kenneth Thompson has insightfully pointed out: "The more socialization into institutions is effective, the more predictable and controlled conduct will be."[5] The implications of this transformation and intensification of technical manipulation and control on the individual is immense.

---

4. Jacques Ellul, *The Technological Society* (New York: Vintage Books, 1964), 79–80.

5. Kenneth Thompson, "Organizations as Constructors of Social Reality," in Graeme Salaman and Kenneth Thompson (eds.), *Control and Ideology in Organizations* (Cambridge, MA: MIT Press, 1980), 218.

Particularly important is the effect it has on our practical lives. With the regularity and efficiency of the internalization of institutionalized norms generated by administrative-capitalist society comes the erosion of personal spontaneity and critical thought. Emile Durkheim correctly saw the problem: "If we live amorally for a good part of the day, how can we keep the springs of morality from going slack on us? . . . The unleashing of economic interests has been accompanied by debasing of public morality."[6]

Perhaps one of the most pervasive effects of the gradual emergence of the cybernetic society is that a new kind of integration between the self and the institutions of the techno-administrative apparatus of modernity has taken place. It is not only in the suppression of critical-evaluative faculties of the person but also the problem that the essential reality of what human sociality is has become increasingly hidden from view. Our social world more and more takes on the shape of an autonomous machine separate from the actual human practices and relations that constitute it. Even more, as hierarchies of wealth and technical knowledge ramp up, the control of various social system becomes wrested from democratic and popular control and increasingly co-opted by economic and technical elites. Add to this the fact that the purposes and legitimate ends of the polity, economy, and culture are becoming recoded by the imperatives of a cybernetic society fused to surplus accumulation at all costs. We are witnessing a great reversal of the Enlightenment project where society would finally be emancipated from superstition and autocracy and become the legitimate manifestation of the common interest of a free citizenry. It is not some dialectic of the Enlightenment that has effected this historical shift but a failure of its most mature and developed humanistic and democratic principles to transform consciousness and society.

The crucial thing to keep in mind is that despite this increasing social integration at the systematic level of society, this does entail a uniformly conformist culture. The second, centrifugal force in modern society, as I pointed out, is the reaction spawned by the increasing tendencies of the centripetal force of the cybernetic society. We can see this as the turn inward and the search for meaning and identity—but a form of meaning and identity that, as Simmel had already observed, is particular in nature, which means that it is detached from

---

6. Emile Durkheim, *Professional Ethics and Civic Morals* (Glencoe, IL: Free Press, 1958), 12.

the social world and a construct of one's fragmented worldview. As the institutions governing society become more saturated by technical and cybernetic mechanisms of socialization, control, and social reproduction, the individual has increasingly sought refuge in the self. Hence we see the postmodernist's attack against modern rationalism, the retreat into identity as a search for meaning and "authenticity," the narcissistic exploration of self, return to religious traditions, and other expressions of anti-Enlightenment impulse. This leads me to the second force to which I alluded: the tendency for atomized individuals to search for their own conceptions of the good and moral meaning. With the erosion of traditional and conventional collective forms of meaning, Enlightenment rationality had attempted to provide a rational philosophical alternative for practical reasoning and subjective meaning. But the crisis of this project was already evident by the end of the nineteenth century and the beginning of the twentieth. Max Weber lamented what he saw to be the eclipse of the possibility for an "authentic modernity," or a kind of secularized Protestant notion of conscience grounded in rational, evaluative self-reflection.

What has declined in modern culture is the existence of a kind of personal life that is emancipated from premodern forms of cultural belonging and conventional communal worldviews. Instead, political and ethical energy has been invested in fragmented forms of life that cybernetic society has left in its wake. I use the phrase "personal life" in the sense employed by Eli Zaretsky, who argues: "By personal life I mean the experience of having an identity distinct from one's place in the family, in society, and in the social division of labor."[7] Modernity and its social-structural shifts therefore freed the individual from traditional forms of community and communal worldviews. But it also placed the burden of ethical meaning back onto the self. As Zaretsky argues, "Personal identity became a problem and a project for individuals as opposed to something given to them by their place in the family or the community."[8] Although the phenomenon of "defamilization," or "the freeing of individuals from unconscious images of authority originally rooted in the family,"[9] was indeed emancipating, the problem has been

7. Eli Zaretsky, *Political Freud: A History* (New York: Columbia University Press, 2015), 20.

8. Zaretsky, *Political Freud*, 20.

9. Zaretsky, *Political Freud*, 21.

that a genuinely modern system of a ethical life—one where categories of human freedom and common interest can be formulated—has been unable to emerge.

Instead, the cybernetic society has crowded out and made obsolete most objective forms of ethical life, which in turn has placed pressure on individuals to find meaning or collapse into some form of nihilism or, in another sense, merely personalized forms of meaning. An age that celebrates the "market" and the entrepreneur, that sees the symbolic valences of culture as more explanatory of power and freedom than the architectonics of material power, was bound to grind up the frames of political meaning and judgment needed for taking on an era of oligarchic capitalism and the vertiginous forms of inequality and its attendant democratic deficits to which previous movements for social justice had access.[10] This takes various forms from a narrow egoism to a return to conventional forms of meaning and tradition, religion, mysticism, or identity politics and group narcissism. In the end, the decline of critical personhood has also meant the expansion of the cybernetic society and the fragmentation of ethical life. The cybernetic society represses the reality of the interdependent social relations, practices, and structures that produce and sustain it. It is dependent on a false ontology rooted in neo-Hobbesian ideas about human life that posit atomized individuals in search of particular interests and desires. There can be no common good other than the negative freedom ensured by a social contract between persons of differing value spheres. A *modus vivendi* of atomized subjects seeking their own values of the good rather than a common life is to be the lot of modernity.

In terms of contemporary philosophy and political theory in particular, this has led to a paradigm shift toward a "postmetaphysical" conception of practical judgment and reason. According to this

---

10. Daniel T. Rodgers describes this shift as an "age of fracture" and describes it by arguing that: "Concepts of power became more subtle, more intangibly imagined, and harder to pin down. Identity loomed larger than ever before: not as a collective given, now, but as a field of malleability and self-fashioning. The categories of race, class, and gender, after sweeping into academic discourse in the early 1980s, turned less distinct, disaggregated into subcategories and intersections of categories, or slipped into quotation marks. . . . Individualized and privatized, released of its larger burdens, freedom was cut loose from the burdens and responsibilities that had once so closely accompanied it." *Age of Fracture* (Cambridge, MA: Harvard Belknap Press, 2011), 39–40.

conception, our normative propositions should be considered rational and valid only when they can achieve agreement among participants through an exchange of reasons or some other collective procedure. The rationality or validity of ethical propositions must be looked at not in terms of their content but in terms of their pragmatic formulation. The rejection of metaphysics *tout court* is now heralded as the emancipation of thought from any form of heteronomy or foundation. We are no longer to look at what human beings are, what capacities they have as a species, and how actually existing social forms either enhance or degrade those capacities. But concepts such as freedom or power need to be grasped as ontological categories: as concepts that have social-structural and normative and practical dimensions; as constitutive of the symbolic registers of consciousness. Instead, we are now asked to look at how we communicate or intersubjectively come to consensus over norms. Supposedly, the result of this move is the capacity for a fully constructivist form of democratic life, but it can be argued that what has really been achieved is the gutting of critical judgment and any satisfying theory of ethical life. What it lacks is a more complete and comprehensive understanding of human sociality.

Political liberalism, in its various forms, has essentially become the ethical-political paradigm for this phase of modernity. Despite their important differences, theories of ethics and political philosophies from John Rawls to Jürgen Habermas, and their myriad acolytes, have viewed the idea of an intersubjective, pragmatic, and nonmetaphysical view of values as the core way to deal with the decline of premodern expressions of common and organic values and ethical systems. But this has come at a price: the move toward the postmetaphysical inspired by Kant no longer sees society as an object with concrete features and dynamics. Practical reason is now to take the form of a proceduralism that reopens the chasm between the noumenal realm of values and their embodiment in concrete social forms. In place of seeing values such as the good, freedom, justice, and so on in ontological terms—that is, as manifesting certain embodied forms of social relations, processes, and ends—we are to determine them via pragmatic discussions leading toward either an overlapping consensus or universal agreement. Either way, the actual relations we should strive for, the kinds of social ends and purposes that ought to be set for our associational lives together, are now ejected from the horizon of practical reason.

Perhaps more problematic, the postmetaphysical paradigm in ethics and judgment is unable to deal with the problems of reification and relativism—relativism because it cannot secure cultural norms and practices from being immune to critique, and reification because it cannot secure the intersubjective "space of reasons" from itself being colonized by the cognitive and normative patterns of thought shaped by the cybernetic society. There is no way to ensure that the members of any pragmatic exchange are not simply reproducing the very categories that render the status quo legitimate and that reconstitute that social reality. Relativism is another problem because simply relying on reason exchange does not give us criteria for which reasons should count and which should not. There is no way to call a reason into question other than from another perspectival stance. But we cannot rest with such a limited and, to be frank, academicized model of human sociality. Politics is not group therapy, we are not "situated selves." Reason achieves critical valence and power when it can press the given world that we inhabit into new shapes and new modes of being. What is required is that our reasons grip the constitutive powers of the social world and their capacity to shape consciousness and reflection; what is also needed is a kind of practical reason that can articulate an ethical life promoting the ontological social structures, processes, ends, and purposes that are constitutive of a free and rational form of society.

As I see it, the importance of an ontological approach to society and ethical value is that it grants our normative reflections a foundation that is neither external to our social being in the form of some kind of inflated metaphysics (God or some eternal principles deduced from abstract reasoning) nor posited from some immutable source, such as nature. Instead, the thesis is that human beings do have certain essential dynamics or features, such as relational sociality, and that we need to see that any social reality possesses certain common features: relational structures, norms, processes, and ends or purposes that define them. The relevant space for critical judgment is the ensemble of ontological features that any society manifests. The key, indeed, critical idea here is that once we grasp the thesis that our social reality is the objectification of our associative and practical forms of life, we are in a position to inquire into whether these social forms maximize freedom as a concrete, objective condition of our sociality. Once we make this philosophical shift, we begin to see that the ontic manifestations of our reality can be pried open to reveal the forms of dominance, exploitation, oppression, and so on that constitute it.

The ontological approach I advocate here applies critical reason to the objective conditions of our world, revealing how the norms, values, and concepts we employ may sustain or enhance an unjust and freedom-attenuating social reality. Reason itself is seen as having a metaphysical structure: valid reasons, reasons that count, in other words, are those that are not only what we agree on as a result of reasoned agreement; it must also count because its embodiment in the world will objectify forms of free sociality that have developmental ends for the community as a whole and each individual member. Rational social freedom must be seen as embodied in the collective norms, relations, practices, purposes, and ends that serve as the infrastructure to our social reality. At the same time, it brings to consciousness the potentiality inherent within the ontology of our relational and practical lives undermining the defective structures and norms that sustain domination and subordination to elite interests and ends. It may be true that there are no timeless external foundations for human value and knowledge. But it does not follow that there is no internal ensemble of capacities that serve as the infrastructure for our ethical and political lives. The error of this kind of thinking is to posit a dualism between the world of value and the domain of social reality. Breaking down this dichotomy reveals a new ontological framework for judgment and ethics. Value should be seen as having an ontological ground that grants us a synthesis of our critical-cognitive faculties with the normative-evaluative framework for social criticism.

What all of this means for those seeking to understand the question of political judgment is that we must look anew at the question that was passed over long ago: that of the relation between ethics and social existence or, to put it in terms I will use in this book, between value and social ontology. A central thesis I will defend is that without any sense of cognitive comprehension of the ontological shapes of our sociality, our capacity for critical judgment will be increasingly weakened by the cybernetic forces of modernity. Even more, what manifests itself as practical reasoning will continue to fragment and either retreat into the abstractions of irrationalism or simply come to resonate with the "natural" facticity of the prevailing social reality. In either case, what will be lost is a concrete, critical conception of ethics and a rational-critical capacity for critical judgment. The project of antifoundationalism and postmetaphysics has led to an incoherence of critical reason as well as a debasement of a more critical, radical alternative structure of thought rooted in what I describe as a critical social ontological perspective on practical rationality, ethics and judgment. As I see it, critical judgment can only be animated by rational and democratic aims when it can comprehend and resonate with the actual social-relational structures of human life and diagnose how the actually existing forms of life that we inhabit either inhibit or develop our ontological potentialities and potency.

As I see it, the move to pragmatism, Kantianism, and the "linguistic" turn all fail to provide us with a valid critical framework for judgment. Its self-confident emphasis on formal reason, intersubjective praxis, and nonfoundationalism take for granted a rational, normatively critical model of personhood devoid of the pathological effects on the self rooted in cybernetic forms of social power: one not afflicted by reification, alienation, conformity to deontic norms of rational domination, and so on. One of the core reasons for this is that they are unable to immunize reflective thought from the constitutive logics of modern forms of social power. Indeed, the cybernetic dynamics of modern society were something to which thinkers like Arendt, Habermas, and Honneth have sought to react. Their theories of social action were conceived as responses and alternatives to instrumental reason. But in their move to forms of truth rooted in intersubjectivity, they have been unable to secure this kind of rationality from the introjection of social norms and values into the background conditions of consciousness of participants in social action. Put differently, what I call constitutive social power is that capacity for social institutions to shape the internal normative values and collective-intentional norms that grant those institutions their existence and their legitimacy.[11] Constitutive power is thus a crucial problem in the depletion of critical judgment in modern societies and the breakdown of a common ethical framework for the comprehension of social justice.

---

11. See my discussion of "constitutive domination" in Michael J. Thompson, *The Domestication of Critical Theory* (London: Rowman and Littlefield, 2016), and Michael J. Thompson, "A Functionalist Theory of Social Domination." *Journal of Political Power*, vol. 6, no. 2 (2013): 179–99. Also see the development of this thesis by Neal Harris, "Beyond Recognition: A Critique of Contemporary Social Pathology Diagnosis," Ph.D. diss., University of Sussex, 2019.

The postmetaphysical claim, by contrast, asks us to consider thinking about our practical lives—as Hannah Arendt has called it, "thinking
differently without a banister." Tracy Strong speaks for many when he
advocates a conception of political judgment that has no foundation and
rests on no positing of truth claims. Rather, the concept of the "political" becomes a stand-in for ethical life more generally. Strong is correct
when he asserts, "The underlying premise here is that, to the degree that
moral principles are derived not from this world but from something
beyond it (whether this be a Platonic or a theological realm), the events
of the twentieth century have made the belief in or the acceptance of
such principles impossible for any person who faces the world as it has
shown itself."[12] However, this should not entail a move to a vague and
indeterminate form of political and ethical life. The alternative, that of
the "political," must also be rejected as an academic construct emerging
from a phenomenological and existentialist incapacity to deal with modernity. Because "the political rests on nothing other than acknowledging
and being acknowledged,"[13] it simply cannot provide a framework for
the powerful forms of domination exhibited by the cybernetic society,
nor does it provide some kind of normative framework for ontological
validity: that is, for giving us some coherence with respect to what should
count as valid normative reasons and what should not.

For this reason, I want to lay the groundwork for an alternative
conception of ethics and practical reason. Broadly construed, the two
approaches to ethics that have dominated philosophical reflection has
been either a formalist or a substantivist ethics. Formalism in ethics
entails relying on procedures for determining the validity of any ethical proposition or value. This could be purely cognitive, as in Kantian
ethics, where the formula of the categorical imperative is determinative
for rational (and hence valid) ethical postulates, or it can be discursive,
in which case mutual agreement and the procedures for discourse are
determinative of validity. Contrast to this a substantivist conception of
ethics that seeks to root the validity of any ethical premise in the traditions, beliefs, or practices of a given community. My proposition here

---

12. Tracy B. Strong, *Politics without Vision: Thinking without a Banister in the Twentieth Century* (Chicago: University of Chicago Press, 2012), 375.

13. Strong, *Politics without Vision*, 391.

is the construction of an ontological ethics, or an objective ethics, that seeks to root our normative space of reasons in the actual sociopractical reality of human life. According to this ontological account of value, validity cannot be determined arbitrarily via some decision procedure or discourse because we cannot secure that space of reasons from the infiltration of power relations on our evaluative capacities, what I call the reification problem. Even more, substantive ethics simply rest on the content of what a given community does and has no means to gain critical distance from those values and practices and call them into question, or what I call the relativism problem.

In contrast to these approaches, throughout this study I adhere to the Enlightenment concept of the universality of reason and the Hegelian-Marxist conviction that a more concrete system of ethical life can emerge. I think this project can be made meaningful once we see that a modern form of sociality can only be generated by critical subjects. Through a new way of looking at ethics and value, we will be able to reclaim a sense of political and ethical judgment that will not only confront forms of social and political power and domination but also articulate new forms of a meaningful and just life. This can come about, I suggest, once we shift our perspective toward a critical social ontology: that is, a paradigm shift that asks us to take into consideration how our ethical life should be rooted in the ontological capacities of human social being and how social forms of life can be seen to either enhance or stunt those capacities and forms of self-development. As I see it, this was the basic paradigm that united a specific strand in political philosophy stretching from Aristotle to Rousseau to Marx. I seek to revive this paradigm and use it against what I see to be a failed theory of politics and ethics in the form of postmetaphysics.

Briefly put, the alternative I offer is rooted in a different structure of thought, one that I call the social-ontological theory of value and the metaphysical structure of reason. A critical social ontology is able to have in view the phylogenetic capacities of humans, as possessing capacities for relations and the practical realization of ends and purposes in the world. At the same time, it has in view how individuals are ontogenetically shaped by the prevailing forms of social relations, structures, processes, and ends that any given society exhibits. According to this view, judgment asks us to see the social world as a totality, as a whole within which the experiences, practices, and norms that govern our lives are rooted. Critical consciousness can only overcome the powerful pull of the reification of consciousness that is constituted by cybernetic society once it grasps the concept that the purpose of political life should be shaping social relations, processes, and ends that enhance common goods and individual development and enrichment. The instrumental use of humans and nature; the exploitation and expropriation of people, communities, and the natural world; the extension of cultural forms of control, subordination, and exclusion; other forms of subordination and marginalization; or the elaboration of vapid forms of subjectivity—all must be countered with an alternative value system rooted in the concrete purposes of our social membership.

I must emphasize that this is an ontological premise—it derives its categories and concepts from the capacities that humans have and its evaluative concepts from how these capacities are shaped and (mis)directed by any given ontic form of social reality in historical time. An ontological approach to ethics, value, and judgment focuses on how structures of social relations and the norms and practices that instantiate them are organized and sees the shape of these structures as constitutive of individual and common life. It is distinct from formal or substantive approaches to ethics and politics in that it takes our relational lives with others as the basic substance of value, but it also sees these relations as pliable and as the result of practices governed by forms of power that can be transformed and remade once we become self-conscious of our capacity to orient the substantive content of our sociality toward common goods and social freedom. Value is thus to be seen as ontological in nature rather than formal or as an abstract principle—it is circumscribed by the practices and purposes of our social world. Values entail certain ways of living, practices, relations to others and self, and so on. Values are concrete, real. They are functions of practices and the relational structures and processes that the forms of our sociality take. Judgment denotes the ability of individuals to assess and rationally grasp how the objective social processes that surround them either enhance the common forms of sociality and self-development or frustrate or redirect these capacities toward particular ends and purposes. As Andrew Feenberg has pointed out: "Judgment dereifies what were formerly understood as absolutes and reveals them as processes of constitution of self and world. It follows techniques back to their origins, establishing the relation between ends and the life-world from which they emerge. It brings reason and experience into critical contact."[14]

This "critical contact" that Feenberg references is precisely what has been severed in modern culture. Indeed, in 1929, in *The Quest for Certainty*, John Dewey remarked on what he deemed to be the fundamental problem of the modern age, echoing this very thesis. As he put it:

> The problem of restoring integration and cooperation between man's beliefs about the world in which he lives and his beliefs about the values and purposes that should direct his conduct is the deepest problem of modern life. It is the problem of any philosophy that is not isolated from that life.[15]

As I see it, a critical social ontology can provide us with a means to reconnect values with action and ground our values in the concrete nature of our lives together as cooperative, interdependent beings. Judgment is central in this regard because it is the second-order capacity that enables social critique and social transformation. This is too important to leave to the "political" or any other academic abstraction. A new ethical and political philosophy must be rooted in a rational theory of human beings. Once this is achieved, politics can once again speak of having a vision for emancipatory transformation.

Political judgment is therefore entwined with the question of political obligation and of disobedience. The fundamental point toward which any question of political judgment must bring us is not necessarily a question of consensus and agreement, especially within the administrative-capitalist societies racked by inequality and power. Rather, critical judgment will lead us toward dissensus and disobedience to the imperatives, norms, and institutions of the cybernetic society. My argument is that the relation between obligation and disobedience, between consent and dissent are not opposed but dialectically related concepts. A rational stance of disobedience must be rooted in the kinds of social arrangements and norms that would warrant our obedience. John Dunn

---

14. Andrew Feenberg, *Technosystem: The Social Life of Reason* (Cambridge, MA: Harvard University Press, 2017), 131.

15. John Dewey, *The Quest for Certainty: A Study of the Relation of Knowledge and Action* (New York: Capricorn Books, 1929), 255.

has suggested that any theory of political obligation also requires a theory of rationality and a theory of ethics. As he puts it: "The only way in which presumed moral obligations might be conclusively whipped in under the aegis of rational action is by constructing and vindicating a comprehensive theory of what, theoretically, ethically, factually etc., it is rational for men to believe."[16]

As I see it, this is an invitation to a more robust and ontologically grounded form of judgment. Once we see that our ethical lives should be shaped and judged according to how social beings can be morphed by the social and cultural structures that govern self-development can we begin to approach a theory of politics that is once again organized for the purpose of the development and freedom of its members. Domination, exploitation, instrumentality, and other forms of defective sociality can be called into question on objective grounds: that is, based on the foundation that the purposes and rational end of all legitimate sociopolitical associations, norms, institutions, and so on, are the common benefit of all and the development of each person as a social being, an individual who is socially and associationally constituted. But individuality is social and ensconced in social relations and social processes, and judgment must be able to have this as its ground if it is to serve a critical function. I believe this way of thinking can grant us a more critical and more robust way to think about practical reason and political life more generally. It is the burden of the following pages to make this case and show that a new more critically engaged alternative for political and ethical theory remains to be developed.

---

16. John Dunn, *Political Obligation in its Historical Context* (Cambridge: Cambridge University Press, 1980), 247.

Part I

In the Courtyard of Babel

Postmetaphysics and the
Failure of Critical Judgment

Chapter 1

A Critique of the Judgment Paradigm in Contemporary Political Philosophy

Late modernity confronts the Enlightenment project with a distinct problem, one that plagues modern practical philosophy and modern culture more broadly. This problem can be described as the absence of a grounding that can secure normative values that can, in turn, provide coherence for practical judgment. Contemporary philosophy and social theory have embraced an antifoundational and postmetaphysical path to provide a way out of this dilemma. This view advocates a conception of practical reason that emphasizes the reflexive self-creation of norms and values that take as their criterion of legitimacy the intersubjective agreement of participants in discursive activity. Reason is taken to be embodied not only in the practice of reason exchange but also in the noumenal and epistemic powers of agents engaged in discursive practices oriented toward the mutual agreement of norms.

This has been the hallmark of much of what now passes for a "critical theory" of society, and it is largely marked by a turn away from a more radical, more comprehensive, and, I think, more satisfying (albeit more demanding) philosophical project that seeks to provide and clarify value-concepts grounded in ontological properties of human sociality. According to this view, we can elaborate a critical social ontology that is not simply descriptive of social reality and the basic features of human sociality but also provides a critical or evaluative criteria constituting a critical practical rationality.

This shift would seem to be only philosophical in nature, a turn in technical political and moral philosophy that few notice. But it is much more than this. It reflects a broader bankruptcy in how modern societies grasp their internal coherence and the ethical life that informs their lives. The problem of modernity has consistently been found in the contradiction between the moral impulse toward autonomy and human self-determination on one hand and the seemingly cybernetic and impersonal forces and tendencies of social, technological, and economic systems on the other. The crisis of modernity can be brought into view once we see that this disconnect between the individual and the social world is becoming ever wider and ever more destructive of democratic forms of political life. The postmetaphysical turn and the cultivation of phenomenological, intersubjective, pragmatic, and discursive forms of practical reason as the framework for how a modern sense of political judgment should proceed is little more than the philosophical expression of a deeply incoherent and misleading form of self-understanding.

The Dissolution of Political Judgment in Modern Society

The thesis I develop in the pages that follow takes this problem of judgment as the core and indeed the essential pathology of modern society. The erosion of this capacity was starkly and coherently pointed out as the effects of the emergence of mass societies was beginning to be felt during the ninteenth and twentieth centuries. The Enlightenment ideal of the autonomous self, capable of articulating rational moral imperatives that were universalizable was now giving way to the effects of instrumental reason, the administered society, and a culture increasingly bereft of moral content. Max Weber wrote that he was witnessing the dissolution of the capacity of the modern individual to achieve what he called "authentic modernity," or a kind of society peopled by individuals who could express their autonomy amid a community of rational ethical life. The problem Weber pointed to in theory was nothing new. The great novelists of the nineteenth century also had their fingers on the pulse of this problem. Ivan Turgenev's *Fathers and Sons* explored the moral implications of a rising nihilism and the deterioration of any kind of moral compass for expressing judgment even as the novels of Thomas Mann charted the decline of bourgeois and religious forms of meaning and ethical substance in the face of the stony realities of modern society. All of them saw, in some way, that the old moral traditions were fading. A new way had to be found to ground a modern form of ethical life that would serve the ideals of a post-traditional society that lacked constraints on moral reasoning and practice.

After the great tumults of two world wars, the problem of political judgment was again at the center of philosophical concern, and rightly so. The powers of ideology, whether fascist, communist, or capitalist, and the moral implications of the Holocaust in Europe, decolonization struggles, and so on had shown their power to overwhelm and absorb the individual. What began to rise from the ashes of the first half of the twentieth century was a postmetaphysical conception of moral and political philosophy that was rooted not in nature, a philosophical anthropology, a teleological conception of history, or anything of the kind. Rather, it would be through our practices with one another, through the ways we came to solve problems and come to mutual understanding that a new paradigm of political thinking and judging was to emerge. I direct my attention to this paradigm in political theory and I maintain that it is not only ethically bankrupt as an approach to moral philosophy and human ethical life, it is also deeply misleading about its own pretensions to serve democratic and rational social ends.

There is no doubt that the emergence of modernity was strongly associated with a project across the natural sciences and philosophy more generally to overcome the metaphysical baggage that plagued the traditions of thought that carried over from the medieval and early modern periods. The strong influence of scholasticism was premised on a religio-metaphysical system that grounded reason and nature in a transcendental rationality embodied in divine or eternal law, which in turn shaped and influenced natural law. But as pressures from nominalist thought began to grow, an alternative understanding of ontology and epistemology began to take hold. According to this view, what could be known were particular objects, not universals nor essences. Because the essence of things could not be observed, they were deemed "metaphysical" in the sense that they were not properly objects of science or rational cognition. Only particular objects that could be named, as the nominalists initially claimed, or what could be verified via sense perception, as later empiricists and positivists held, were valid objects of knowledge and of being. I can know that the round object in front of me is a ball, but there is no universal category of "ballness" that can be seen to exist in any valid sense of the word. Instead, we have names that serve to delineate particular objects, but no universal concepts exist.

This philosophical impulse also led to empiricism, or the doctrine that valid knowledge about particulars—the only valid knowledge of the objective world—could only be validated by sensual experience.

In this sense, features of human social life that had previously been seen as axiomatic in understanding moral and political life from the classical period through the medieval age—such as Aristotelian ideas about the naturalness of human community—were being undermined and displaced by an analytic, mechanistic, and atomist philosophical view that became central to the projects of liberal and market-based society. No longer could we speak of "social relations" that existed prior to individuals or a common good, let alone any universal features of social life, because they were to be seen as constructed by us rather than inherent to us. For Hobbes, this became one of the central aspects of his political theory: the classical ideas about the social essence of human life or the idea that social relations and relations of social dependency that Aristotle had put at the core of his ontology of human life were now seen to be fictions. Humans were isolated and individual, society was atomistic and aggregated. Any social relations or institutions that existed were constructed by us through consent, not in any way natural to us as a species. Locke and later empiricists, utilitarianism, and Kant's philosophical project shared in this basic line of thinking when it came to any question of an ontology of sociality.

In this sense, the basic fact of a social ontology is not a search for some kind of material substrates for human life, nor is it a search for some rigid categories from which we can derive explanations of the social world. Rather, it is meant to highlight the notion that the categories of human freedom, self-determination, and so on have an irreducibly social basis and this sociality has certain basic features that can be seen to be constitutive of our collective and individual lives.[1] In this sense, as P. F. Strawson correctly notes, "each must see himself in some social relation to others whose purposes interact with his. If our subject is man in his world, it seems necessary to admit that this world is essentially a social world."[2] To make such a claim invites us to think about the nature of the social as a distinct object of inquiry, as something with

---

1. See Michael E. Brown, *The Concept of the Social in Uniting the Humanities and the Social Sciences* (Philadelphia: Temple University Press, 2014).

2. P. F. Strawson, *Analysis and Metaphysics* (New York: Oxford University Press, 1992), 80–81.

ontological weight that must be considered as a crucial element in any critical theory of society. Even more, it invites us to pursue a new way of thinking about practical reason. Whereas traditional forms of ethics were based on a substantive ethics, or one that was attached to a priori accepted truths about how to act and what the "good" consisted of, the modern view was formal and postmetaphysical. Empty of any content, what matters now is the procedure that allows us to arrive at normative truths. But a social-ontological approach differs from both. It maintains that only by understanding the developmental capacities inherent to and determinative of human life (such as social-relationality, praxis, and more) can we grasp how the actually existing social forms of any society deserve our obligation or their transformation.

This is precisely the idea that was under attack by empiricism, nominalism, and utilitarianism at the birth of modern social and political theory. According to these movements, the individual was empirically cognizable, not "society" itself. Relations between individuals were the result of their individual choices and duties, not prior to or formative of those individuals. In the modern philosophical project more broadly, there was a fevered attack on the notion of ontology and metaphysics. Ever since Kant, thinkers within the Western philosophical tradition have labored under a bias against metaphysics and ontology. This should be of little surprise since Kant's critique of metaphysics was constructed in opposition to the early and premodern concerns with transcendental metaphysics and being. There are two important implications of this move in philosophy. First, it entails a separation between facts and values, between knowledge claims that are premised on what exists in any ontological sense on one hand and knowledge claims that deal evaluative-normative claims on the other. Even more, he pointed to "regulative" versus "constitutive" reasons, which further pushed the noumenal from the phenomenal realm. Regulative ideas were those that were capable of constituting objects as objects of cognition rather than as objects in and of themselves. Rational reasons were accountable to themselves, their own rational reasons rather than any kind of substance that inhered in or acted behind what was grasped by consciousness. As such, any ontological speculation was cast out of the realm of rational possibility because it violated the boundary set by Kant between noumena and phenomena. Besides, what we were now to be pursuing was a rationalist project that defended the capacity of the autonomous, reason-giving subject that Kant saw as essential to the Enlightenment project.

A second implication is that reality becomes a construction of cognition. Reality is now dependent on the epistemic subject in the sense that regulative ideas give shape to the chaos of experience. Constitutive reasons would be internal to the object-domain itself, making things what they are in essence. But this is not possible given Kant's insistence on the separation of reason as a capacity of cognition on one hand and the objective world as merely an object of that cognition on the other. The contemporary return to the Kantian doctrine and the nonmetaphysical interpretations of Hegel have therefore sought to construct a postmetaphysical intellectual framework where we are to see practical rationality constituted by reason-giving by concept users who rely on reasons rather than the rational structure of the object-domain to count as what is valid rationally. But this poses important problems, namely, that we are barred from comprehending the actual, essential structure of objects, something that Hegel and Marx saw as essential for a critical grasp of reality. Only once we can comprehend the rational structure of objects in the world can we reconstruct them in cognition and determine the Idea itself, or that unification of the conceptual structure of cognition and the rational structure of the object-domain. This allows us to grasp how descriptive and normative claims dialectically sublate into a higher, more total knowledge of the world with mechanisms, relations, and purposes that are immanent to those objects.[3]

If modernity is defined by the exchange and justification of reasons by intersubjectively interlaced agents, there must be a means by which we can know or judge the extent of the validity of these reasons and justifications. The project of pragmatic justification sees this as circumscribed by the practices and obtaining of mutual agreement by intersubjectively acting participants using only rational reasons as a criterion of objective validity. The more we think about this, the more

---

3. "Immanent metaphysics" is an essential idea that Hegel initiates to save the metaphysical project in the context of a post-Kantian critical philosophy. According to this idea, the function of reason, of philosophy, is to be able to explain the world on its own terms, not according to the precritical metaphysics of theological or transcendent "reasons." As Robert Stern notes, "far from being a form of pre-Kantian metaphysics that tries to claim access to some extramundane absolute, Hegel's idealism is a form of absolute-theory that can be treated as in line with the transcendental turn, of giving us a conception of the world that will show how the need for explanation can be satisfied without going *beyond* it." Robert Stern, *Hegelian Metaphysics* (New York: Oxford University Press, 2009), 61.

question begging it seems to be, for it appears increasingly unable to provide us with a convincing (let alone compelling) form of rational judgment, that is, one that can provide us with judgments about the objective social world and the kinds of goods and ends toward which social life ought to be organized.

Clearly there is an impasse of sorts. On the one hand, we can plainly see that the critical rejection of transcendental metaphysics and the religio-ontological projects of the premodern period was in order. At the same time, it follows from this that the solution offered up by Kant—and absorbed into the basic fabric of modern social science and mainstream philosophy—opens us up to a kind of rationalism that is unable to defend against its own relativist implications. What the critical theory tradition, going back to its origins in Hegel and Marx, posits is that there is some sense in which the Kantian chasm between noumena and phenomena must be overcome for us to possess objectively valid knowledge with ontology as its basic criterion of validity. Indeed, whereas the renewed Kantian-pragmatist project in critical theory is unable to keep in mind is that only ontological claims or those normative claims that have ontological weight can be seen as adequately critical. Only once we are able to grasp the whole, the totality of social reality, and construct normative claims with that social reality in view can we begin to articulate a critical theory of judgment. Critical reason and critical judgment, facts and value, are dialectically sublated into a higher form of critical cognition.

In what follows, I explore this thesis and suggest that a more compelling and more rational path for critical theory to develop seeks to place a critical social ontology at its center and keep in view the notion that normative claims are critical only to the extent that they carry descriptive claims about the essential structures of sociality. According to this view, norms must be evaluated according to an objective criterion that is stronger than the epistemic reason-giving and linguistic-discursive theories can provide. This criterion is rooted in the social-ontological categories that serve as the desideratum for any valid social knowledge and thus any diagnostic or critical account of the social world. This means that the advantage of a critical social ontology is that it can provide us with a means to sublate the division between facts and values, between our cognitive grasp of the social world and our normative-evaluative diagnosis of it. This is a powerful mode of critique because it enables us to bring to critical awareness the perverted and distorted forms of sociation (alienation, reification, etc.) that plague modern forms of life. A critical social ontology therefore grants a more stable ground from which objective ethical postulates can be articulated and defended against the dangers of ethical relativism on one hand and epistemic abstraction on the other.

An Epistemic Hall of Mirrors

What the postmetaphysical account lacks most of all is a robust and compelling criteria for judgment. What I want to suggest is that only by comprehending the social totality as an ontological totality—as a system of relational structures, processes, purposes, norms, and practices—can we begin to articulate rational categories for judging and clarifying the validity of our practical commitments. The error that many contemporary theorists of judgment have made is that they have defined themselves against an inflated conception of the Enlightenment, collapsing reason or objective truth into the categories of natural science of positivism. Instead, they have embraced hermeneutics, intersubjectivity, discourse, and recognition as vehicles for critical judgment and practical reason. What actually enables critical judgment, as I conceive it, is the capacity to understand the particular events, social facts, experiences, pathologies, or whatever as constituted by larger social processes and structures that derive their logics from the nature of the social totality. We are not looking for an inflated metaphysical conception of universality here; we are looking to understand how the structures of relations, the processes, institutions, and ends of the community in which we live is upholding the freedom of individuals to develop full membership in that community. This does not require any kind of transcendental metaphysical commitments, but it must push past what I call the epistemic hall of mirrors problem.

The problem can be described as a form of moral thinking that cannot find any secure footing; to put it another way, is unable to ensure that the normative propositions it articulates or examines are not already infected by the rationalized forms of legitimacy and authority already inherent by agents who have been successfully socialized by institutional authority-norms. Moral ideas and norms are not judged according to objective criteria, because, according to the postmetaphysical thinker, this is impossible, so we look for securing our norms to agreeing with what seems rational to us. Like a hall of mirrors where one cannot be sure of which image is valid and which is a copy, the postmetaphysician has cut all the struts needed to make critical judgment possible and, in the process, lost any semblance of orientation. In other words, we must be able to find an objective standpoint from which to critique, to judge social phenomena and social facts. Since any social totality in this sense is a social ontological account of the dynamics and properties of our social world, a commitment to a social ontology will be a more robust and more critically satisfying path for political judgment.

The postmetaphysical and linguistic turn deprives us of the means to make judgments based on reasons that are relevant to the specific social phenomena under investigation. All norms and social pathologies are emergent properties of the structures and dynamics of the social totality. Critical reflection on political life cannot ignore or overlook these aspects of social reality. Instead, to retrieve any sense of a critical political judgment, we must abandon the postmetaphysical position and embrace a critical social ontology that can allow us cognitive access to the social totality. In this sense, the idea that we can derive rational judgments from the kind of pathological problems facing modern society—alienation, reification, and so on—is simply to split critique from judgment. Indeed, once reification sets in, we can no longer rely on the immanent practices of the community, especially those deliberative practices that serve as the framework for contemporary theories of democracy and judgment, as a ground for rational (i.e., emancipatory) norms. The hall of mirrors problem returns with a different cut: we simply refilter those pathologies back through our sense of what constitutes validity in the first place—first-order pathologies now shape and fuse to second-order forms of reflection. We can view the matter as consisting of first- and second-order pathologies. A first-order pathology is one that affects the social relations we inhabit, whereas second-order pathologies affect our powers of reflection on the first-order pathologies.[4] The second order is the realm of experience and praxis awareness. If we generate norms from that second-order level alone, we will simply refract the first-order pathologies back onto our hermeneutic praxis.

---

4. See the interesting discussion by Titus Stahl, "Verdinglichung als Pathologie zweiter Ordnung," *Deutsche Zeitschrift für Philosophie*, vol. 59, no. 5 (2011): 731–46.

There will be no critique and no valid judgment, no rational grasp of the world and our projects to transform it.

We can say that the dynamics of modern societies create the conditions for alienation and other forms of personal pathology and suffering. We can also see that responses to this kind of modernity are disparate. One can conform to the prevailing order and its norms; another might try to escape it, embrace some conventional form of ethical life, religious identity, or whatever; yet another might seek transgressive outlets for one's pent-up psychic energy and moral frustration and *ressentiment*, and so on. In all cases, we see how the first- and second-order pathologies are related to one another. The response to the pathological structure of social relations and processes (an ontological layer of reality, or first-order problem) precipitates a disturbance and reflex reaction in the cognitive, evaluative, and affective dimensions of the subject (the second-order problem). The "epistemic hall of mirrors" problem emerges when we confine our theoretical inquiries about judgment to the experiential, phenomenological, praxiological, and/or noumenal levels of human consciousness. Once we do this, the capacity for judgment breaks down because we lose a vantage point for critique, or, put another way, we are unable to prevent evaluative concepts and values that have been constituted in our evaluative frameworks by the prevailing social norms from being used in the evaluative activity.

Indeed, it can be said that current ideas about political judgment also rely heavily on the notion that our social practices are the context for understanding our political reality. The thesis here, in contrast to the Kantian-pragmatist view, maintains that our social practices not only mediate the experience of everyday life but also serve as the basic background capacity for political judgment. According to this thesis, social practices are the context for our establishment of valid norms because only by articulating norms via the practices we already share and live within can such norms be valid and authentic. Alessandro Ferrara argues that this allows for a "radically reflexive form of self-grounding," which entails "a situated judgment on our identity."[5] The principle of reflexivity is therefore taken to be a crucial component of valid norms

---

5. Alessandro Ferrara, *Justice and Judgment* (London: Sage, 1999), 12.

based on intersubjective discourse and interaction. But does this confront the hall of mirrors problem as I have laid it out? In other words, even intersubjectively, the reified norms can frame the exchange of reasons. What is required is a means to evaluate the reasons that are being employed; critique demands the examination of the reasons being used. It cannot rest with the procedure or some embedding of formalism in social practices.

What this leads to, however, is not a satisfactory theory of political judgment and critique, but a kind of philosophic hall of mirrors where we become essentially unable to critique and judge the forms of power that sustain modern societies and that essentially constitute the forms of injustice and social pathologies we experience phenomenologically. Attempting to access the source of these forms of injustice and pathology via hermeneutics leads us away from a critical theory of judgment and toward expressivism or, at least, some form of epistemic relativism. These theories essentially root themselves in the experiences of identity politics that has characterized modern liberalism. They place inordinate emphasis on the plurality of conceptions of the good that constitutes modern liberal societies. But the real question is not value pluralism so much as questions of social power seen as the capacity of normative systems to organize relations between people in ways that are unequal and dominating in some basic sense. The intersubjective, communicative ethicist may believe that she can tease out contradictions in the worldview of any participant and thereby open up some aporia in their sense of the world. But this is a deeply mistaken view of the matter. What is needed is a theory of judgment that is immanent to the practices of our world and at the same time achieves an objective vantage point for critical reflection. This may seem like a contradiction in terms, but this is precisely what I maintain can be achieved by engaging in a critical social ontology that replaces the obsession with "reflective judgment" and postmetaphysics.

Critical reflection is not immanent to any practice but must have a point of view, a way of thinking about the world, for there to emerge new insight and expand the moral horizons of judgment. Critique cannot be submerged within the phenomenological experience of a pathology of injustice, it must be able to penetrate appearance into the essential, generative structures and processes that produce them. Ontology, I assert (not pragmatism or postmetaphysics) is the true ground for critical judgment.[6] Indeed, critical judgment begins when we begin to inquire into how values, norms, beliefs, practices, and institutions shape and reconstitute relations of domination. Whether it be in the larger systems of administrative capitalism or in the more communal systems of religion or moral beliefs about the family and so on, what is salient are the ways these social systems constitute power relations and forms of dominance that can become embedded within the cognitive and affective dimensions of those that participate in such systems.[7] Hence, any kind of moral reflexivity has to have an ontological point of view at its core for critical judgment to be enacted.

---

6. One of the more intelligent books on critical judgment to be published in recent years, Albena Azmanova's *The Scandal of Reason* is weakened by its reliance on the postmetaphysical paradigm. Azmanova's flaw, as I see it, is to pursue an anti-essentialist conception of judgment and normative validity. As she argues: "To avoid essentialism in judgments of normative validity (that is, deriving notions of justice from assumptions of a fixed essence of humanity), it is not sufficient to acknowledge that truth is a human product or that it is a collection of the plurality of truth perspectives. We need also to add that, like truth, the just is a relational concept. The relational nature of justice assertions is reflected in . . . a paradigm of articulations and significations, which furnishes the prediscursive conditions enabling and structuring normative debates." *The Scandal of Reason: A Critical Theory of Political Judgment* (New York: Columbia University Press, 2012), 193 and *passim*. The crucial flaw here is to have normative validity merely rely on an "internal point of justification" that provides "a viable internal point of justification" and must "define validity criteria in terms of the notions of shared critical relevance that actors engage when disputing societal norms and rules" (193). But again, this embeds validity in the second-order forms of consciousness and grants us no ground for critique itself. The process of immanent critique is valid once it can derive the source of social pathologies as corruptions of relational structures and processes of our sociality. This moves us beyond hermeneutics and into the realm of social ontology, or the domain of normative validity itself.

7. The thesis that power distorts the deliberative, symbolic, and pragmatic features of discourse is important but still underappreciated. As Robin Celikates has correctly argued: "In the context of existing political systems, political processes of deliberation and decision-making are distorted by almost unavoidable structural democratic deficits—for instance, in the dimensions of representation, participation and deliberation, but also due to the influence of asymmetrical power differences in the public debate, hegemonic discourses and ideological self-conceptions." "Democratizing Civil Disobedience," *Philosophy and Social Criticism*, vol. 42, no. 10 (2016): 982–94, 989. I have also sought to defend this thesis in the light of the weaknesses of contemporary trends in critical theory in Michael J. Thompson, *The Domestication of Critical Theory* (London: Rowman and Littlefield, 2016).

Any sense of critical judgment will therefore require a grasp of the totality, of the social whole within which social facts and phenomena occur. Our language, practices, opinions, and so on are all in some way functionally dependent on the social ontology of this totality. Judgment as critique is the capacity for us to frame and reflectively critique even those practices that the totality itself has made ambient. No totality is "total" in the sense that it forecloses critical reflection; it can always be the object of rational reflection and critique. I argue that this requires a very different understanding of political judgment and critical reflection that contemporary theory has elaborated. What is needed is a means for theorizing the totality and calling into question its dynamics and purposes. What is required is what I call *ontological coherence*, or a grasp of the objective social relations, norms, practices, and purposes that are constitutive of the logics of social power that form and maintain the shapes of our sociality understood as the structures of relations, the processes that these relations instantiate, as well as the ends and purposes toward which these are oriented. Essentialism, in this sense, is not a matter of some fixed form of being or whatever; this is little more than a straw man concept. What it does concern is the generative forms of species-specific dynamics and features that serve as the basis for human beings; it concerns the relational, processual, and praxiological capacities that serve as the substance of our sociality that are shaped and formed into different historical forms of life that are the cause of either our pathologies and injustice or our development and freedom.

As I see it, this constitutes a kind of basic ontological ground for critical political judgment. The central weakness of the judgment paradigm in contemporary philosophy can therefore be described as the hall of mirrors problem. What I mean by this is that in their search for a supposedly postmetaphysical and post-Enlightenment form of practical reason, such thinkers have abandoned any capacity for critical judgment. A norm is taken to be valid to the extent that any discourse community as a whole essentially sanctions it via mutual agreement. But there is no way for me, based on that premise alone, to judge the validity of that norm in any sense other than the fact that it has been mutually agreed on. But this cannot, by itself, make the norm or the ethical proposition right. Indeed, its moral rectitude must be rooted in some structure of meaning that grants us critical perspective. For all the talk of Kant's third *Kritik*, many are quick to forget the Hegelian view that conceptual thought mediates reality and the concepts we employ, if they are rational, are constitutive of the object of knowledge.

This is a serious problem, one that is fatal for any serious theory of judgment. For we are asked to accept the thesis that all valid norms are contingent on their acceptability to any given community, as long as this community reflexively accepts that norm as valid. As one advocate of this approach has put the matter:

> The elements of a postmetaphysical, interactive universalism are: the universal pragmatic reformulation of the basis of the validity of truth claims in terms of a discourse theory of justification; the vision of an embodied and embedded human self whose identity is constituted narratively, and the reformulation of the moral point of view as the contingent achievement of an interactive form of rationality rather than as the timeless standpoint of a legislative reason.[8]

We should take these premises in turn, because they take us far from any sense of a critical theory of judgment. Why should we assume that the validity of any claim can be grounded in discourse theory? The whole thrust of the theory of reification and alienation—classical pathologies of consciousness and reasoning emerging from modern, capitalist societies—was to show that modern forms of social power could colonize consciousness and shape the discursive and cognitive domain of subjects. How, then, can we rely on this alone as the vehicle for judgment?

The epistemic hall of mirrors problem is serious. It points to a serious flaw in the postmetaphysical and pragmatic approach to judgment. The idea that agreement in an intersubjective context alone as a criterion for validity needs to be overcome so that we have critical access to a capacity to judge the content of the norms that are agreed on. The basic problem is that once we abandon the idea of some vantage point for critique and instead use communication or reflexivity alone as a criterion for valid (i.e., universalistic) norms, we cut out

---

8. Seyla Benhabib, *Situating the Self: Gender, Community and Postmodernism in Contemporary Ethics* (New York: Routledge, 1992), 6. Also see the discussion by Calvin O. Schrag, *Communicative Praxis and the Space of Subjectivity* (Bloomington: Indiana University Press, 1986), 94ff.

how social power and social dominance works and affects the capacities for conscious reflection. Once we see power relations as exhibiting what I have called constitutive domination—or the capacity to shape the norms and values through which you navigate and understand the world no less than the basic intentional stances you take when acting as a member of your community—we must abandon the idea of there being no "privileged position" for critique.

Critical judgment is only in play when we can make distinctions about the validity privileged or practice or institution according to the way it shapes the social world of which I am a part. This, in turn, requires that we comprehend the totality from which the phenomena we experience are generated. We need to see that critical judgment has as its referent not epistemic norms but concrete, ontological structures of relations, social processes as well as ends and purposes toward which we as members of any political community are asked to acquiesce and accept. In this sense, a new orientation is required that can encompass the structures of social reality that we inhabit and that constitute our individual and collective lives. Emphasis on the phenomenological structures of consciousness is inadequate for a theory of critical judgment because it cannot ground our concepts about what defective and good forms of sociality should look like and why. Emphasis on experience, trauma, the imaginative, or whatever are simply inadequate and, quite frankly, of no use with respect to actual political judgment.[9] What is needed is a grasp of how social reality is constituted by structures of relations, processes, purposes, norms, and values that sustain and re-create that social reality. The key to understanding trauma and social and personal pathologies lies in its social origins: in how objective social reality patterns forms of self- and other-relations that either promote a free, self-developing individuality or pervert it. We need not a postmetaphysics but a *critical metaphysics* of our sociality.

What is required is a departure from the failed paradigm of postmetaphysics and a revival of a critical social metaphysics—a form of social critique that embeds practical reason in the social world in the sense that we see that social world as made up of much more than our practices but also of an ontology of structures, relations, processes,

---

9. Note the discussion by María Pía Lara, *Narrating Evil: A Postmetaphysical Theory of Reflective Judgment* (New York: Columbia University Press, 2007), 57ff.

and ends that constitute the social totality. We must move beyond the layer of practices and inquire into how these practices are shaped and how these structures and processes—both properties of the ontology of the social totality—help re-create and restructure those practices. This is why we end up in the hall of mirrors problem. Without this, we have no reliable means of critiquing the first- and second-order problems of social reality and consciousness. Without theorizing the social totality—that is, the ontological shape of how our social relations, processes, and purposes are organized—we cannot grasp the norms and practices that are contained within it, constitute it, and are constituted by it. Social ontology is the ground for political judgment because it concerns the very substance of our ethical life. Our sociality is far more than merely intersubjective and phenomenological; it is also, and indeed more important, constituted by relational structures and processes, purposes, and ends, as well as the product of certain basic phylogenetic capacities beyond language. Once committed to a postmetaphysical view of the social, we have sheared off the relevant layers of social reality that grant us insight into a more robust, more rational form of social critique and political judgment. We must, I insist, move beyond the hermeneutic and the linguistic into a deeper conceptual grasp of human social existence itself and the ontic forms that it takes in history.

Intersubjectivity and Discourse

Contemporary critical theory has sought to deal with the problem I have outlined above by moving toward a paradigm that we can broadly describe as one of pragmatic justification. According to this basic view, communication and the justificatory structures inherent in the pragmatics of communication oriented toward mutual understanding will be able to maintain a rational structure and the open-ended inquiry and creativity demanded by a truly democratic, noncoercive society. No ontology is needed here because we are concerned, as Habermas continually maintains, with the problem of discursive justification and the extent to which individuals are able to come to a rational, mutual understanding about the object-domain: "Fundamental to the paradigm of mutual understanding is, rather, the performative attitude of participants in interaction, who coordinate their plans for action by coming to

an understanding about something in the world."[10] Hence, the project
of pragmatic justification holds that the relation between subject and
object, so central to idealist philosophy, is overcome not by monological
reason or through the paradigm of active labor but through the act of
argumentative discourse embedded in an intersubjective life-world premised on rational justification. Hence, Kant's problematic of the chasm
between the noumenal and phenomenal worlds is overcome. Habermas
states the solution: "The unbridgeable gap Kant saw between the intel-
ligible and the empirical becomes, in discourse ethics, a mere tension
manifesting itself in everyday communication as the factual force of
counterfactual presuppositions."[11] This has extended itself into a more
general reinterpretation of many of the core metaphysical attributes of
German idealism.[12]

The project of pragmatic justification takes us back to Kant via
the pragmatist theory of action to pose the thesis that epistemic claims
can be understood not in transcendental form, as Kant had argued, but
in terms immanent to the practice of linguistically mediated communication. Hence, the domain of justification constitutes a kind of realm
of objectivity, moving emphasis away from the object-domain.[13] Where

---

10. Jürgen Habermas, *The Philosophical Discourse of Modernity* (Cambridge, MA:
MIT Press, 1987), 296.

11. Jürgen Habermas, *Moral Consciousness and Communicative Action* (Cambridge,
MA: MIT Press, 1990), 203.

12. Terry Pinkard's reconstruction of Hegel's philosophical project follows a similar
line when he claims that: "the ends of modern life must (1) be reflectively justifiable
yet have a non-reflective subjective hold on the agents, (2) be internal to the history
of modern agency such that they cannot be established outside of the free-standing
social practices of modern life and have their intelligibility depend on how they are
understood to have successfully made up for the insufficiencies of what historically
preceded them, and (3) be such that they can be justified by the 'absolute knowing,'
which is the result of the *Phenomenology of Spirit*." *Hegel's Phenomenology: The Sociality
of Reason* (New York: Cambridge University Press, 1994), 274.

13. Pinkard takes this approach when reinterpreting Hegel by arguing that the ends
of a modern form of life should "combine the *subjectivity of the agent*—his basic
desires, wants and ideals—with the *objectivity of justification*—with what counts as
a justification in the social practice defined by those ends—and that objectivity
should be generated by 'absolute knowing.' That is, the motivations of the agent—
what actually impels him to act—should mesh with the justification for what he

this project suffers is in the important problem that is brought to light
by Hegel's immanent metaphysics, on one hand, and Marx's objectivist
ontology of sociality, on the other. For both, any conception of critical
rationality had to grasp how thought and the objective world related
to one another, not as a construct of a rational subject (as in Kant and
Fichte) but more correctly that cognition should pierce into the rational
structures of the objects of consciousness. This is why Hegel presciently
rejects the approach outlined by contemporary Kantian-pragmatists when
he maintains that any moral truth or conception of the good or right
cannot be based on "the external positive authority of the state or of
the mutual agreement (*Übereinstimmung*) among persons, or through the
authority of inner feeling and the heart or the spirit which immediately
concurs with this."[14] What reason discloses to us is the rational structure
of what actually constitutes those objects. Construed this way, rational
thought has an ontological metric for gauging its own correctness or
incorrectness.[15]

----

is doing, with whatever particular ends he is pursuing, and that justification should
be reflectively available to the agent" (*Hegel's Phenomenology*, 274). Also see Robert
Pippin, *Hegel's Idealism: The Satisfactions of Self-Consciousness* (Cambridge: Cambridge
University Press, 1989), 175ff. Against this approach, Rolf-Peter Horstmann argues
that it is "extremely difficult to see how this approach can avoid the sort of epistemic relativism that Hegel himself clearly repudiated: the view not only that our
knowledge claims can only be justified contextually, but also that the states of affairs
to which those knowledge claims refer, what Hegel calls the 'other' of the concept,
can be dissolved entirely into certain epochally or culturally dependent conceptual
constellations." "Substance, Subject and Infinity: A Case Study of the Role of Logic
in Hegel's System," in Katerina Deligiorgi (ed.), *Hegel: New Directions* (London:
Acumen Press, 2006), 69–84, 70.

14. G. W. F. Hegel, *Grundlinien der Philosophie des Rechts* (Stuttgart: Reclam, 1990),
46.

15. Stephen Houlgate remarks that "A fully self-critical philosophy must thus start
from the twofold idea that (a) thought is the awareness of being and (b) being is
itself simply what thought discloses. This means that the science of logic cannot be
anything other than *ontology*: because the study of thought must be, at the same
time, the study of *being*." "Hegel's Logic," in Frederick Beiser (ed.). *The Cambridge
Companion to Hegel and Nineteenth-Century Philosophy* (New York: Cambridge
University Press, 2008), 111–34, 121. Hegel's basic idea, shared by Marx, is that a
critical conception of reason has an explanatory function in understanding the object,
not a mere exchange of reasons toward agreement about that object. See Stanley
Rosen, *The Idea of Hegel's Science of Logic* (Chicago: University of Chicago Press,

This is why the Kantian-pragmatist thesis elaborated by Habermas and others is insufficient as a valid critical theory of society.[16] Critical rationality must disclose for us the ontology of sociality insofar as the social-relational structures and processes that constitute any given aspect of social reality forms the context for the constitution of its members and determines the extent to which those social forms can promote the kinds of relational, common goods requisite for a robust kind of social freedom. Even more, for Hegel and Marx, the concept of self-determination has to have the basic sociality of the agent in view because a person is only free and self-determined to the extent that they cognize themselves and act within interdependent social-relational contexts that promote their own welfare and the good of the social whole and that these are reciprocally constituted.

The problem with approaching objective moral truths through the process of justification and the exchange of reasons alone is that the "reasons" no longer have the requisite ontological ballast to grant them critical (i.e., properly rational) weight. Indeed, even more, the exchange of reasons and processes of justification that eschew ontological concerns are open to the socialization pressures of the existent reality and its norms and value patterns, thereby distorting the noumenal capacities of agents.[17] When reason is dissolved into the practice of discourse, there is little room left for the importance of speculative (*begreifende*) thought and how certain truth claims should be evaluated based on

---

2014). Hegel's move is to show that analyzing the thought of being is sufficient to grant us an ontology that is rational and critical, whereas Marx reverses this and believes that we must see how structures of being shape and determine structures of thought. Despite this important difference, both see that there are ontological categories of the objective world that must be grasped as rational structures of thought and being, not merely empirical phenomena distinct from noumena.

16. See Dietrich Böhler, "Transcendental Pragmatics and Critical Morality: On the Possibility and Moral Significance of a Self-Enlightenment of Reason," in S. Benhabib and F. Dallmayr (eds.), *The Communicative Ethics Controversy* (Cambridge, MA: MIT Press, 1990), 111–50; Robert Alexy, "A Theory of Practical Discourse," in S. Benhabib and F. Dallmayr (eds.), *The Communicative Ethics Controversy* (Cambridge, MA: MIT Press, 1990), 151–92; Rainer Forst, *The Right to Justification: Toward a Constructivist Theory of Justice* (New York: Columbia University Press, 2011); Rainer Forst, "Noumenal Power," *Journal of Political Philosophy*, vol. 23, no. 2 (2015): 111–27.

17. See Jürgen Habermas, *Between Facts and Norms: Contributions to a Discourse Theory of Law and Democracy* (Cambridge, MA: MIT Press, 1996), 368ff.

ontological considerations. The reason for this was that both men saw—Marx perhaps more strongly than Hegel—that the power of social-institutional forces was too strong for mere pragmatics to overcome. The main issue was that cognition was shaped in intricate ways by the power relations and structural-functional pressures of the existent reality—a reality that was seen to be a distorted form of sociality. Operating in that framework means that we would simply reproduce many of the basic assumptions and value patterns that underwrite the basis of moral cognition and the semantic basis of communication. Epistemic reasons are not sufficient to defend rational agency against the pressures of reification.

We should be clear about what reification means in this context. Since we are the agents of creation of social forms, the key problem of reification is its deformative capacity for agents to be able to hold the norms and practices that guide our lives as expressions of social dominance, particularly norms and practices that uphold social relations, structures, and processes that create an unequal and surplus benefit for others. Reification is the result of a web of norms and practices that orient collective intentionality toward relations of social dominance. Because this entails a corruption of our second-order capacities for reflection, it means that a merely noumenal and praxiological approach to judgment is insufficient.[18] What is necessary is a form of thinking and reflecting that takes into account the broader social ontology within which our practices, norms, and values are embedded and to interrogate how this social totality should be shaped and organized to promote a common life based on social freedom. Once the social ontological domain is hidden from view and we begin to accept the intersubjective, noumenal, and pragmatic turn, we lose any objective basis for critical reflection. We begin to be imprisoned in a relativism of value pluralism without any means to call these values into question.

Hence what we can call a problem of epistemic refraction takes hold once we see that concrete forms of social power have the capacity to shape the presuppositional categories of thought that will serve as the formal foundation for communicative forms of reason—the epistemic hall of mirrors problem returns. As such, discursive forms of

---

18. For a more developed discussion, see Michael J. Thompson, "Collective Intentionality, Social Domination and Reification," *Journal of Social Ontology*, vol. 3, no. 2 (2017): 207–29.

justification are open to epistemic relativism insofar as it is unable to secure universalistic claims outside of mere mutual agreement, something that cannot be secured in any truly rational sense without some degree of appeal to the structure of the object of reference. We cannot rely on reflexivity or some sense of a "situated yet universalistic reflective judgment" to get us out of this problem.[19] An ontology of society can help in securing claims about the valid, rational structure of social life to diagnose pathologies of that sociality and the kinds of defective forms of cognition that accompany them. Second, it reproduces (rather than overcomes) Hegel's charge of the impotence of the mere ought. Since the nature of objectivity is moved from the object-domain, or the ontology of sociality, to that of the "structure of justification" or the internal syntactic structures of language constituting communication, we become unable to address how power relations distort and affect the cognitive powers of subjects as well as how norms and practices come to cement and infiltrate the conceptual powers of agents.

This basic but important philosophical problem is what a return to ontology can help us solve. Indeed, Habermas and his followers have long seen that the overcoming of the subject-object divide is an essential step for critical rationality. What, then, is the role of ontology in critical theory? My answer is that it provides us with the crucial element of a critical theory of judgment that is able to articulate a conception of an objectively determinable interest, one rooted in the kinds of social forms, norms, and practices that might best promote the common interest of a society and its members. This common interest must be construed as promoting and cultivating a structure of interdependent reciprocal relations because that forms the essential ground and objective moment for the capacity of any kind of critical judgment of social reality. Kant's distinction between regulative and constitutive ideas therefore marks a real moment of departure between the epistemic-pragmatic turn in critical theory and the critical-ontological view that I am putting forth here, because the former should be able to ground a critical practical rationality with the potential for us to explode the defective forms of cognition that eventuate from and also perpetuate defective forms of sociality.

---

19. Alessandro Ferrara, *The Force of the Example: Explorations in the Paradigm of Judgment* (New York: Columbia University Press, 2008), 40.

The Revolt against Ontology

The idea of coming to an agreement with others to constitute valid political and moral claims is problematized by its exposure to power relations. Beyond Habermas and thinkers wedded to a more Kantian understanding of moral validity, the theory of judgment has also taken much from the pragmatist thesis of a constructivism that would liberate it from the need to think about reality as a concrete concern for ethical judgments. According to this view, as Richard Rorty has framed it: "Pragmatists—both classical and 'neo'—do not believe that there is a way things really are. So they want to replace the appearance-reality distinction by that between descriptions of the world and of ourselves which are less useful and those which are more useful."[20] Severing our reasoning about the world from the objects in the world was not just an epistemic strategy about things but a normative strategy about the nature of moral reasoning itself. Moral truths can only be understood— not unlike the "truths" about the objective world—as the result of the descriptions that are offered and agreed on by any given community. Language is now the constructivist nexus for all forms of agreement about things—objects as well as morals—and political or moral life "is simply the process of justifying beliefs to audiences."[21]

This move is particularly problematic for any kind of political judgment because it has the opposite effect its defenders claim. Whereas its intention is to emancipate us from a dead metaphysics, it only succeeds in exposing practical reasoning to relativism and arbitrariness and more perniciously exposes our justificatory beliefs and reasons to the prevailing legitimacy and power relations that socialize us. It is frankly shocking to read something as naive as the conclusion Rorty derives from this philosophical turn:

> The fact that most beliefs are justified is, like the fact that most beliefs are true, merely one more consequence of the holistic character of belief-ascription. That, in turn, is a consequence of the fact that beliefs which are expressed as meaningful sentences necessarily have lots of predictable

---

20. Richard Rorty, *Philosophy and Social Hope* (New York: Penguin, 1999), 27.
21. Rorty, *Philosophy and Social Hope*, 36.

> inferential connections with lots of other meaningful sentences. We cannot, no matter how hard we try, continue to hold a belief which we have tried, and conspicuously failed, to weave together without other beliefs into a justificatory web. No matter how much I want to believe an unjustifiable belief, I cannot will myself into doing so.[22]

This is almost certainly false. Rorty proceeds from the presupposition of an unsocialized subject whose reasons and beliefs are "his own." But how can each one of us know, according to this framework, which justifications are valid and which ones are not? What desiderata are we to employ to judge, to critique the beliefs we have, and to know if they are not simply valid because they conform to the reality principle around us? How are we to know if agreeing with others is not simply the expression of dominant, background value patterns? How can we judge a claim's hierarchical validity over any other? Some view this as a mistaken enterprise, but we would have to inquire about the purpose of judgment at that point. Indeed, there would be little need for critical consciousness, or for any real sense of judgment at all, since we would have eroded all of the foundations for critical reflection in the process. Once we accept the thesis that judgment concerns the hermeneutics of difference, that it is circumscribed by rhetoric or some other form of phenomenologically based faculty, then we have stretched the term beyond any useful meaning.

Can we have a theory of judgment that does not work with some sense of an objective form of rationality? One that can account for the relative normative warrant of any given social fact or institution over some other?

The short answer seems to be that we cannot. Kantian pragmatists and communicative ethicists have a similar problem. How can language games, speech acts, and pragmatic agreement on norms provide for us any kind of substantive criteria for judgment? Rorty is insistent and argues that "we shall never be able to step outside of language, never be able to grasp reality unmediated by a linguistic description."[23] This really does not get us far. For one thing, concepts are not the same as language. Indeed, anyone who has studied chemistry and biology knows

---

22. Rorty, *Philosophy and Social Hope*, 37.
23. Rorty, *Philosophy and Social Hope*, 48.

this. The approach to nature and the attempt to understand it rationally is not graspable only by linguistic descriptions. We use sentences to construct concepts—usually clumsily—that are often supplemented by images, charts, diagrams, and so on. Sometimes mathematical models can be used that refer to relations and processes that are meant to represent the essential mechanisms of the process of photosynthesis, for example. But consider a different view of the matter. What can it mean to say that reason, as Hegel, for instance, maintains, is essentially metaphysical in nature, not merely subjective, abstract, or formalist? It means seeing that reason is a property not merely of the faculty of the mind but also of objective reality.

As an example, consider the Pythagorean theorem. It may seem that this is purely an abstract equation, not unlike the logical doctrine of *modus ponens*. It is abstract and formal and requires no concrete substance for it to be a true statement: $x^2 + y^2 = z^2$. But according to the ontological account of reason that I am proposing here, the Pythagorean theorem, the concept formulated by the equation, is valid once it can be seen as embodied in the structure of the objective world. Hence, a tradesman laying tile on a floor will, if he is to lay the tiles out square, be able to ensure this by measuring the length of the vertical tiles (say, three feet) and the horizontal tiles (say, four feet), measure the diagonal from those points, and if that length is equivalent to five feet, the tiles are square. The thesis illustrated here is that the Pythagorean theorem can be understood not only as a formal proportion but as an embodied structure in the world. Viewed in this way, it is not the application of a mathematical principle to a real-world example; it rather demonstrates how reason is embodied in the world, how it is a feature of the objective world and the subjective mind's capacity to grasp it. I think that this can also be understood in practical reason, in political judgment. I want to suggest that this points us toward a more robust paradigm for practical reason and judgment by seeing values as ontologically constituted by our norms, relations, and practices; that we come to see that consciousness and being, thought and action, must be understood in a more unified and richer way.

This is not really comparable to the picture of knowledge laid out by pragmatists such as Rorty, and for good reason: this kind of knowledge makes rational claims about the essence of a real object, whether photosynthesis or the Pythagorean theorem. The concepts are constructed of sentences but are more than the sum of their parts.

The validity of a concept in biology is not agreement among scientists; the criteria for that agreement is the extent to which it can be demonstrated that the proposed hypothesis or concept grasps what it seeks to explain. Photosynthesis is the word we utter, in English, for the mechanism and process of how plants turn light into food. But its validity is not arbitrary in the sense that it is an idea we simply happen to agree on and there exist objective criteria for its validity. What this exercise makes clear is that knowledge does not proceed as Rorty and other anti-essentialist constructivists would have us believe. Instead, knowledge claims about objects require not only the mediation of language but also, as Hegel rightly knew, a conceptual layer that links our subjective ideas about the world and the actual structure of that world.[24] These concepts gain their validity, their rational content, not through our agreement, but according to the extent to which they capture in thought—in concepts—the actual mechanisms and processes in the objective world. We construct the world not through language or through concepts but in thought. The crux of the matter, in this view, is the extent to which these various reconstructions adequately capture the objective mechanisms of the world.

It is not my intention to argue for an empirical or naturalist theory of practical reason here. However, I do mean to argue that language cannot serve as the appropriate nexus for the validity of normative claims. The reason for this is not the same as making an objective, descriptive claim about natural objects—say, rocks, dogs, the electron transport chain, and so on—it means that when we are dealing with political judgment, we have to engage its distinctively ontological character to understand the nature of power and dominance, the real essence of what politics is in the first place. Power and dominance is not simply the capacity of agent A to control agent B. It is, more importantly, embedded in the social structures and processes of our relations with others, and this means that it is also a feature of the cognitive, evaluative, and cathectic ways that pattern the intentional features of consciousness and social action, thereby endowing social domination with constitutive powers over self and society. The way my community is organized, the structures it

---

24. I further disagree with Rorty when he argues: "It would have been better if Hegel had done what Dewey did later: describe intellectual and moral progress simply as the growth of freedom, as leading to democracy rather than to Absolute Knowledge." *Philosophy and Social Hope*, 49.

takes on, the purposes and ends it takes as valid for our collective efforts are all ontological rather than linguistic. They are ontological in the sense that they are congealed forms of practice and value orientations that have causal powers over self and other. Ethical judgment, political judgment, any form of critical reason about the social world therefore requires, *pace* Hilary Putnam, an ontology to grant it validity and efficacy.

We are left with the nagging sense that judgment must be evaluated according to the social-ontological features of human social life. Norms are constitutive of our social world even as they are how we make claims against that world. Norms constitute the ontological domain of social facts and, as such, have to be understood not only as constituting power relations but also rooting themselves in the value patterns and epistemic structures of consciousness. At the same time, this means that we must see the role of critical reason as being able to grasp more than a mere interpretation of the social world: it must seek to have in view the objective features of human sociality that constitute the dynamics of the social world. A critical metaphysics is therefore a means to see the social world as more than an "assemblage of claims to knowledge," as Rorty puts it, and more as an entity with ontological features.

Toward a Critical Social Metaphysics

I believe the postmetaphysical turn—that is, the move toward language, justification, pragmatics, and intersubjectivity—cannot provide a rationally justifiable, politically workable form of political judgment. In the next chapters, I examine these ideas more closely, and each analysis draws from the following basic thesis. Any form of practical reasoning that does not take into account the social-ontological dimensions of our world will fail as a persuasive form of political judgment. What makes this turn toward language, communication, postmetaphysics, and phenomenology problematic is that it has shown itself to be unable to serve actual practical purposes. Indeed, despite its academic success, the capacity of citizens in modern societies to possess critical judgment about their social world has been rapidly eroding, perhaps absorbed into the socialization processes that constitute the modern social order. Can we really proceed with the philosophical fallacy that there can be an "ethics without ontology," let alone an "ethics without principles"? I do not think so. I suggest that there is a repressed way of thinking about judgment—one that can maintain an expanded conception of autonomy and agency, preserve concerns with social reality, and provide us with a more compelling and richer way of thinking about social rationality, social critique, and the possibilities of social transformation and social progress.

For this reason I urge those interested in reviving critical judgment and democratic will-formation to return to metaphysics. Not an inflated, transcendental, or traditional metaphysics that gives us some traditional, nonrational form of ground to base our moral worldviews on, but what I call an immanent metaphysics of our sociality, an ontology of the social world itself as a means of grasping the totality within which social critique can gain coherence. An immanent metaphysics is therefore decidedly against the postmetaphysical turn insofar as it rejects language as the ultimate font of our social reality even as it rejects the mirage of consensus through cognitive of affective agreement through discourse. Conflict will be inherent in all forms of judging. As Benjamin Barber aptly put the matter, "Those political judges whom we call citizens cannot impose cognitive consensus as a solution to the collision of opposing interests."[25] In this sense, adjudicating between different value systems and different norms must reveal not only how they hide certain power interests but how they can be seen as defective forms of social life insofar as they damage members of the community, articulate institutions pervaded by instrumental reason, or truncate common goods for private ends and purposes. This may not appeal to each member of the deliberation, but it can serve as a means to grant us some sense of political clarity that can guide action and practice.

To reiterate, I seek to defend the thesis of ontological coherence, by which I mean the capacity to understand and take into account in our political lives the systemic ways our lives are ordered, shaped, and structured. This will require an immanent metaphysics, a critical social ontology that will ask about the various ways the shape of our social world engenders power relations, articulates interests, and reveals the mechanisms and causes of the various phenomena of social pathology and social injustice that we experience. The norms that we possess and assent to are ontological in a basic sense: they create forms of reality

---

25. Benjamin Barber, *The Conquest of Politics: Liberal Philosophy in Democratic Times* (Princeton, NJ: Princeton University Press, 1988), 208.

that are objective and have causal powers. Norms are not merely utterances, they are linked more essentially to dimensions of a deeper social
reality that has ontological depth and warrant. Thinkers who follow
the postmetaphysical path, as I see it, are deeply mistaken in the view
that sentences are merely descriptive utterances with inferential content.
Rather, norms are much deeper and richer. They form, through mutual
agreement (implicit or otherwise) social structures that generate social
facts. Given their ontological character, they also have causal powers
in the sense that they congeal into forms of life that shape and orient
our behavior, practices, and consciousness. This is what Marx meant by
materialism, after all: not a reduction of spirit to matter but as human
practices congealing into real, objective structures of reality that could
shape social and individual life.

But even more important is the commitment to the thesis that
the whole, the totality is how we can arrive at valid, rational judgments
about our world. Hegel and Marx knew that this was essential. For
them, the totality is not some inflated metaphysical entity but is accessible to consciousness via any rational accounting of our experiences in
the world. Hegel and Marx begin their great works with an account of
how a phenomenology of experience can lead us to a rational account
of the totality. Think of Hegel's master-slave dialectic, where the emergence of recognition leads us to an account of not just the "other," as
too many limited accounts of this thesis have held, but an elaboration
of a cognitive awareness of our relations with others as ontological
properties of our being. This leads to the rational awareness of more
complex structures of these relations constituting ethical life, the family,
civil society, and state. Marx begins *Capital* with the commodity form,
with the object of experience we encounter on an everyday level in
capitalist society. As in Hegel's *Phenomenology*, it then penetrates beyond
the phenomenological layer into the ontological structures of capitalism
as a concrete social process capable of determining and constituting the
entirety of our social reality.

The ontological is therefore an inescapable component of our
practical world and the social reality that constitute it. To deny this, to
reduce things to speech acts or "psychological nominalism" or whatever,
is to commit a deep error in our understanding of practical reasoning.
Practical reason must have ontological ballast. To admit this takes nothing away from the need for reflexivity, for discourse, and so on. What it
does do is force us to ask for a deeper sense of what our social reality

is pressing on us. One reason for this is that we cannot get around the pathologies of reasoning and consciousness if we confine ourselves to the realm of the noumenal and the phenomenological. Once we do this, we are trapped in the confines of that sphere of mind that has been deeply distorted by the colonization of the norms and value orientations of the prevailing reality. We can see that political judgment must move beyond the fetish with intersubjective reasoning, with reason exchange, and with the recognition of others. It must move into what I call here a "critical space of reasons" that seeks to discern the validity of normative statements not based on the arbitrariness of mutual agreement, but via the extent to which the dynamics and shape of social-ontological structures are taken into account as exhibiting power relations that warp our collective lives toward the benefit of a part of the community, rather than the whole.

As a basic entrée into what I argue throughout this book, I want to suggest that we see all forms of our sociality as not just intersubjective in the noumenal or phenomenological sense. We do interact to discuss, exchange reasons, and so on. But this is only one level of what it means to be a member of a social species. Our relations with others are not always cognitive, they are mediated by work, accepted social institutions and forces, and so on. One way this occurs is through the web of norms that we internalize through socialization. This web of norms and values essentially shapes a deep ontological structure that has objective properties and causal powers over the individual. Intersubjective relations with others—in any form—are not autonomous from this deep structure. Indeed, the deep structure shapes and forms many of the noumenal, cognitive, and discursive practices—or surface structures—we have with others. This deep ontological structure must be brought to consciousness and become the focus of political judgment. As modern societies have become increasingly complex, technical, and administrative, the deep ontological structures have become more entrenched and more elaborate.

The relevant question of all forms of political judgment and political critique must concern itself with a metaphysics of sociality that can grant us insight into the ontological shapes and forms that determine our lives. In the end, a rational community can only ground valid judgments once it has penetrated this deep ontological structure. If it does not, it will only reproduce an incoherence with respect to how our social world functions. The essence of political judgment must be found in the capacity of citizens to be able to inquire into and debate the purposes of the social world to which they belong and, along with this, inquire into how the ends and purposes toward which our social world is oriented in turn structures and shapes our relations, our practices, and our norms and values. These purposes are posited as the organizing principle for the institutions and norms they use that socialize them, and they shape and orient the structures of social relations that determine members' individuality and freedom. The essence of a critical theory of judgment is therefore not allied to the tradition of postmetaphysics but openly embraces the idea that only a critical social metaphysics will grant us a true, valid sense of judgment and political awareness. This, it seems to me, was the essence of the tradition of political theory that informed classical authors such as Aristotle and Cicero and modern ones from Rousseau to Hegel and Marx.

The social world is the product of our collective efforts and activities, not just symbolically and linguistically but also in the concrete ways we organize our labor, organize and use our resources (social and natural) and our powers as creative beings.[26] The end of critical judgment must be not simply to steer through value pluralism—more important, it must ask about how our social totality makes certain kinds of values covers for power interests. Power and domination are at the forefront of critical judgment because it is within our capacity to know whether our values, practices, norms, relations, and so on are oriented toward promoting particular ends and goods (as opposed to common goods). This is where critical judgment begins and we leave behind the more incoherent problems contained in the postmetaphysical paradigm. Social domination is not simply the property of individual or collective

---

26. Ronald Beiner is right when he argues: "All political judgments are—implicitly at least—judgments about the form of collective life that it is desirable for us to pursue within a given context of possibilities." *Political Judgment* (Chicago: University of Chicago Press, 1983), 138. Similarly, Linda Zerilli's assertion that "our collective activity as world building: as sustaining, renewing, and expanding the network of tangible and intangible relations, of what counts as an object of shared concern, not just in the sense of our shared view of it but also our awareness of the different perspectives in which the object can be seen and understood," gives us no means to construct any kind of critical judgment because it confines itself to experience and feeling. See her *A Democratic Theory of Judgment* (Chicago: University of Chicago Press, 2016), 274. Indeed, Zerilli's idea of judgment is, not unlike other accounts derivative of Arendt, not a theory of judgment but gestures of where judgment should be taken as a theory and as a practice of politics.

agency, although it is that as well. It is also, and perhaps more saliently, contained in the social-ontological forms that shape our lives and orient our practices and ideas. Social domination is the kind of power that can shape our collective efforts, bend and twist our inherent capacity for reciprocity and cooperation toward the interest of a few. It can also create regimes of justification that embed themselves at the cognitive, evaluative, and affective dimensions of the self. Modern democracies suffer from a malignant form of ontological incoherence in this sense. As David Weissman has insightfully noted: "What do citizens learn in a careless democracy? To love their freedom and abhor interference, but little or nothing about conditions for the reciprocities that create mutual respect among citizens and legislation for the public good."[27]

Immanent critique based on ontological coherence will thus be a central means for citizens to become critical once again and root out the power relations that shape our lives. This kind of critical political judgment takes the ontological as a vantage point for critique. It lays before us a grammar of social critique that is open to all. It does not advocate for a detached perspective from which to view the world, nor does it enmesh us in the discursive, linguistic domain of any given "form of life." Rather, is provides ballast to what has traditionally been called immanent critique: a kind of reasoning that comprehends the object from within rather than from without, from some already accepted transcendental truth—God, tradition, or whatever. In this sense, a critical social ontology can help with the epistemic hall of mirrors problem and the detached privileged position problem. By inquiring critically into the shapes of our sociality, how power is distributed within them, and how our value orientations and cognitive ideas track that reality, we can expose ideological worldviews to scrutiny once we look at the shapes of our interdependence and the ends toward which our society puts those structures and efforts. Indeed, Robin Celikates hints at such an idea when he argues that "critique makes agency possible by criticizing social arrangements, practices, and self-understandings that have an inhibitory rather than an enabling effect."[28]

---

27. David Weissman, *A Social Ontology* (New Haven, CT: Yale University Press, 2000), 139.

28. Robin Celikates, "From Critical Social Theory to a Social Theory of Critique: On the Critique of Ideology after the Pragmatic Turn," *Constellations*, vol. 13, no. 1 (2006): 21–40, 35.

The ontological turn I suggest here implies that we can secure valid claims once we are aware of how social reality is shaped and what ends and purposes its various levels of reality are organized toward. But also, it must begin with an ontology of the species itself; with a sense that humans have essential capacities for relationality and praxis that are shaped and governed by different shapes of social reality. The relevant question of critical judgment must be addressed to these ontological structures. Because the norms, concepts, value orientations, and other cognitive layers of human life are rooted in these ontological social forms, we must be able to get at the root of how these cognitive layers of consciousness and action are shaped and affected by the constitutive causal powers of the ontic realm of social reality. If we remain caught in a noumenal space of reasons, we can never secure the validity of this claim because it will have no objective referent according to which it can be judged.

The pragmatist claim that agreement and utility are to be considered "objective" simply side-steps the issue: intersubjective agreement is still *subjective* in that the objective, ontological structures of the social world have not been addressed or taken fully into account. Add to this that the very concept of reason that pragmatists employ eschews all sense of metaphysical structure in that it is not concerned with how reasons must be considered valid in terms of the systematic and ontological implications that they entail. In this sense, there is no way to ensure whether the prevailing social world and its norms are filtering in, reaffirming, and reconstituting the world as it is back to us. Power and domination can infiltrate the noumenal domain and, in doing so, inoculate the power of intersubjective practices from valid critical insight. Because of this, the kind of second-order reasoning about norms that takes place through intersubjective practices cannot maintain itself in the age of mass society and the pressures on the powers of individual autonomous reflection. Judgment can only be revived and reconstructed, it seems to me, by what I call an ontological turn: a move toward seeing how our lives are shaped and the kinds of objective structures of relations, processes, and purposes toward which the forms of life we inhabit are oriented and structured. This level of reflection will require us to ask about the very essence of the social world and how our sociality has been shaped and determined by forces external to our control and consent. I believe this is the central and determining question for political theory, and working our way back to this as the core of political judgment is the task of the pages that follow.

Chapter 2

Hannah Arendt's Reconstruction of Political Judgment

Few thinkers of the twentieth century have had such a deep and pervasive influence on contemporary political theory as that of Hannah Arendt. Her ideas about human action, thought, and politics have had a persistent influence on political theorists who, after the collapse of Marxism, looked for an intellectual framework to rejuvenate political culture and civic life in an era of bureaucracy and expansive institutional rationality. Scholarship on her ideas has become a veritable academic industry. This is somewhat ironic considering that one of the animating ideas of her work is the notion that activity in the political realm, what she calls "action," the highest expression of the *vita activa*, should be seen as a central and distinct mode of politics. Politics is conceived of as giving and taking opinions, decentering theoretical reason, and embracing communal action. Politics becomes "the political," a term she uses to convey the essential nature of politics not in terms of the control of resources, domination, or other forms of institutionalized power dynamics but as a kind of action where individuals act in concert, sharing opinions, acting freely as equals to constitute a shared understanding of their world. To see politics as a realm with its own practices and ways of thinking and acting, separate from economic or scientific forms of rationality, was a core element of her project. But this would lead her down a path that, I submit, was deeply flawed and that enabled her to reshape the relation between truth, knowledge, and judgment and displace the realist tenets of political theory.

Arendt was motivated to undertake this project by the experience of witnessing the forms of totalitarian domination exemplified by Nazism and Stalinism, which she saw as mutilating the essential core of the political: the capacity to act on one another as equals. Totalitarianism took away the spaces between people that allowed them to interact and communicate. "By pressing men against each other," she writes, "total terror destroys the space between them."[1] The result was the rise of "mass man," not dissimilar to Heidegger's *das Man*, who, because of the loss of this political space and the distinctive form of action there, has become unable to think and judge. Modern man, unable to respond to the events around him and politics, becomes for Arendt the solution to the problem of the modern technical, commercial, bureaucratic world—a world, she felt, was without judgment and thinking. Reaching back to ancient political philosophy and culture, she sought to reinvent a classical form of democratic action and culture in the modern world to grant dignity to man within a world plagued by alienation and anomie—a dignity that could only come with a new, political way of thinking and acting. She blended with this reconstruction of the polis an existential phenomenology of consciousness that was crucial for her approach to the nature of thinking, freedom, and her definition of what the ends of politics should be.

The Flight from the Real

Many currents in contemporary political theory have become dominated by a basic assumption rooted in Arendt's ideas. The assumption can be stated succinctly: that the essential contours of any rational and democratic approach to politics must consist, to a certain degree, in the deliberative actions of citizens, in the intersubjective exchange of opinion about the world. But there is another, perhaps more problematic aspect to Arendt's influence. Her thesis that politics is a kind of action where opinions are shared, where we come to disclose ourselves, is conceived to exist outside of any other kind of social power. She opens up a space for political action that is essentially abstract: bereft of domination, ideology, and reified consciousness, her allegiance to

---

1. Hannah Arendt, *The Origins of Totalitarianism* (New York: Harcourt Brace Jovanovich, 1951), 466.

the existential phenomenology of her teachers, Jaspers and Heidegger, stamps her political philosophy with a curious antipolitics. She allows "the political" to devolve into mere abstraction and relativism. What Arendt really creates is not a political solution to a human problem but a philosophical one: how can we create a world where humans can disclose themselves, where sharing opinions can create a renewed social cohesiveness in an age of atomism and alienation, and where this can somehow lead individuals to "think" and renew judgment in an age devoid of it. But in so doing, she eschews the concrete forms of power that ground domination, the control of man by man; she sidesteps questions of rational authority and its capacity to make certain institutional forms of life legitimate; and she ignores ideological and reified consciousness, believing that each person has the capacity to start and think the world anew, and she is not interested in how interests shape political life and power. Mmy basic thesis here is that this conceptual shift in political theory has paved a way for a defective conception of politics. It has done this by putting undue emphasis on opinion, on the nature of deliberation, and on "civil society" (indeed, not a term Arendt would have approved of) at the expense of realist mechanisms of power, domination, and shaping legitimate authority. It has put whole swaths of contemporary political theorists into a trance around the supposed "power" of friendship, care, and intersubjective dialogue and the power of persuasion.

Her emphasis on a kind of politics that is communal, based on disclosure of the self and opinion to others and on public participation, was conceived as a counterweight to the rise of mass politics, bureaucracy, political parties, and the modern state. There is little wonder why it has enchanted so many political theorists: it conjures the vision of politics that romanticizes public life and friendship. It also had an elective affinity with new social movements and the need to find a theoretical vehicle for a politics of identity and a post-Marxian analysis of how to think politically. But this romanticization simultaneously was a flight from the real, eschewing analysis of the mechanisms that cause and perpetuate social power, and created a sense of the "political" that encourages the rejection of the basic mechanisms of politics. In short, Arendt's ideas deeply distort politics, and their embrace by contemporary political theory has been detrimental for progressive politics. One reason for this, I maintain, is that it turned the emphasis of left politics away from the problems associated with social structure and instead toward

issues of opinion and personal expression. It thereby allowed subsequent
theorists to elevate issues of identity and personhood, something that
has led to the opposite of what Arendt sought: not a greater solidarity
among political subjects, but a fragmentation of identities and group
concerns in the face of real forms of power—of capital, of propertied
interests, of elites more generally. Indeed, it could be said that for all
of its surface philosophical appeal, the political ideas of Hannah Arendt
have bequeathed us a very dim light to steer through the age of oligarchy, mass society, and neoliberalism.

Truth, Power, and Politics

Many of Arendt's central theories about political life are derived from
ideas initially laid out by Karl Jaspers and Martin Heidegger. Jaspers also
put communication at the center of his philosophical approach, which he
cast as the essential structure of truth because there was no meaning, no
genuine sense of self, without others and the meanings we share with
them: "To be genuinely true, truth must be communicable. . . . We are
what we are only through the community of mutually conscious understandings. There can be no man who is a man for himself alone, as a
mere individual."[2] For Jaspers, the act of communication is a mode of
truth, a kind of truth that is distinct from the positivist and empiricist
models of truth to become a process through activity: "truth does not
lie in something already known, or something finally knowable, or in
an absolute, but rather in what arises and comes to pass."[3] So truth is
now conceived as a process of encompassing the meanings of others, of
sharing in the meanings that other selves possess and use to create a
community of meaning. Communication is not simply a means to truth
in some scientific sense, as in pragmatism; it serves to move man from
the sphere of privacy and the Cartesian self: "Communication in the
idea, and in its realization by *Existenz*, will move a man closer to his
fellow man than will the intellect, or a purpose, or primitive community."[4]

---

2. Karl Jaspers, *Reason and Existenz* (1933; New York: Noonday Press, 1955), 77.

3. Jaspers, *Reason and Existenz*, 81.

4. Karl Jaspers, *Philosophy*, vol. 2, trans. E. B. Ashton (1932; Chicago: University
of Chicago Press, 1970, 50.

Arendt was no doubt deeply influenced by this idea, and she builds on this idea of the communicability of selves.[5] But she takes it to a different level, reading it through the historical-philosophical experience of the Greek polis. For Jaspers communication was a means toward a more authentic, more genuine form of truth, whereas for Arendt, it becomes a means to establish opinion in opposition to truth. Arendt subscribes deeply to the neo-Kantian distinction between facts and values. Although she does not pose the problematic in the same terms, she is adamant that there is a deep chasm between knowledge, which aims to achieve truth, and thinking, which seeks to uncover meaning. Meaning, like values for Weber, are not knowable the way scientific truth-claims are. "What science and the quest for knowledge are after is irrefutable truth, that is, propositions human beings are not free to reject—they are compelling."[6] But thinking is different. It does not look for these irrefutable truths but for meanings, those "unanswerable questions" that cannot be reduced to factual or any kind of universalizable criteria. "Behind all the cognitive questions for which men find answers, there lurk the unanswerable ones that seem entirely idle and have always been denounced as such."[7] With this basic division between truth and meaning, we are confronted with the problem in the modern age of the erosion of the latter by the former. Arendt's solution is to reconstruct politics as a distinctive form of action wherein a specific form of thinking takes place. She thereby takes politics out of the realm of rational thought and places it firmly into the sphere of "opinion."

Opinion, "thinking" can only occur within a horizon of interpretive, intersubjective activity where each individual thinks in concert with others. This is why politics is a distinctive realm and kind of activity where the emphasis is shifted from issues of truth to that of opinion. For her, "truth has a despotic character" when brought into the realm of politics. As with Jaspers, who claimed that communication was a "life with others," Arendt sees opinion as a kind of knowledge that is distinct in that it conveys a way of knowing that is multiperspectival. It

---

5. For a further exploration of Arendt's intellectual debts to Jaspers, see Lewis P. Hinchman and Sandra K. Hinchman, "Existentialism Politicized: Arendt's Debt to Jaspers," *Review of Politics*, vol. 53, no. 3 (1991): 435–68.

6. Hannah Arendt, *The Life of the Mind*, vol. 1 (New York: Harcourt, 1971), 59.

7. Arendt, *The Life of the Mind*, vol. 1, 62.

is a kind of understanding not by means of axiomatic truth but of the
world as it is from a highly textured point of view—a way of thinking
that encompasses the views of others into one's thinking and viewing,
giving way to an "enlarged mentality." But rational thinking, the pursuit of truth and claims to truth, is a kind of knowing that she sees,
in line with the ancient idea of speculative philosophy, as the product
of individual thought, of the solitary individual, not the community.
Theoretical reason seeks to establish truths that are axiomatic and defy
alternative interpretation and crush opinion. These truths are based
on facts, whereas politics is based on a different form of knowing, of
opinion, or that kind of thinking Arendt calls "representative thinking."
According to this view, an alternative version of thinking is possible
once we consider that there are certain kinds of things in the affairs
of men that can be viewed from different perspectives and positions.
"The shift from rational truth to opinion implies a shift from man
in the singular to men in the plural, and this means a shift from a
domain where nothing counts except the 'solid reasoning' of one mind
to a realm where 'strength of opinion' is determined by the individual's
reliance upon 'the number which he supposes to have entertained the
same opinions.'"[8]

This basic argument opens Arendt up to the notion that a distinctive sphere of human activity can be understood as political—one
that draws on idiosyncratic ideas about thinking, equality, freedom,
power, and action. Arendt's basic thesis is that because all individuals
come into the world, they initiate a new beginning (she uses the Greek
word ἄρχειν here, which means "to begin" and "to rule"): they see the
world anew and have distinct perspectives on it, which supposedly can
potentially cause "ruptures" in the ways of the world. Only by opening
ourselves up to one another's perspectives can we begin to transform our
consciousness and thinking to embrace the multiperspectival views of
many others. Thinking does not proceed according to abstract concepts,
it is to think along with others, to incorporate their views and opinions
into one's own—to see oneself through the eyes of others. "This kind
of understanding," she writes, "seeing the world (as we rather tritely
say today) from the other fellow's point of view—is the political kind

---

8. Hannah Arendt, "Truth and Politics," in Peter Laslett and W. G. Runciman
(eds.), *Philosophy, Politics and Society* (Oxford: Basil Blackwell, 1969), 104–33, 110.

of insight par excellence."[9] Indeed, this is also the "enlarged mentality" that gives rise to judging. In this way, Arendt takes some of the foundational concepts of political theory and translates them into this new context. Equality is now seen as "isonomy," or that condition where men were considered equal not by nature (φύσει) but by the custom and law (νόμος) extant only in the polis, in the political sphere. Freedom was similarly conceived as a way of life among others, a way of living where one could interact with others as equals without coercion.[10] Power becomes the result of this kind of activity, characterized by isonomy and freedom, where people act in concert and together. This freedom, this space for the political also provides a foundation for "friendship" (φιλία) or a bond between citizens founded on common understanding rather than love. It is "actualized only where word and deed have not parted company, where words are not empty and deeds not brutal, where words are not used to veil intentions but to disclose realities, and deeds are not used to violate and destroy but to establish relations and create new realities."[11]

Arendt's ideas still spring from an existential philosophy of consciousness. She is lured on by the idea that this being-together-with-others will lead to the kind of exchange of opinions and formation of judgment that she sees as the essence of the political. This, too, has Heideggerian traces. For Heidegger, freedom was a mode of being, one that can only occur with others, indeed, only as a "being-with-others" (*Mitsein*). Only when *Dasein* is able to achieve a "disclosedness"

---

9. Hannah Arendt, *The Promise of Politics* (New York: Schocken Books, 2005), 18.

10. Arendt says that freedom is a group phenomenon, constituted by action, and not equivalent with "liberty," which is simply the absence of restraint: "The life of the free man needed the presence of others. Freedom itself needed therefore a place where people could come together—the agora, the market-place, or the polis, the political space proper." *On Revolution* (New York: Penguin Books, 1963), 31. She further equates freedom and action when she argues that "Men are free—as distinguished from their possessing the gift for freedom—as long as they act, neither before nor after; for to be free and to act are the same." Hannah Arendt, *Between Past and Future* (New York: Penguin, 1961), 151. See also her distinction of freedom from liberty with Martin Heidegger, *The Essence of Human Freedom: An Introduction to Philosophy* (New York: Continuum, 2002), §§26–30.

11. Hannah Arendt, *The Human Condition* (Chicago: University of Chicago Press, 1958), 200. Also see Hannah Arendt, *On Violence* (New York: Harcourt Brace, 1970), 43ff.

(*Erschlossenheit*) with others can the "unconcealment" (*Unverborgenheit*) of *Dasein* among and toward others take place. Only then do we find ourselves in the realm of freedom. Heidegger's explicit claim is that "freedom is engagement in the disclosure of beings as such."[12] Freedom is the context that allows this *Erschlossenheit* to take place: "To let an encounter with beings happen and to comport oneself to beings in a mode of openness or disclosedness is possible only on the basis of freedom. Thus freedom is the condition of possibility of the disclosure of the *Dasein* of beings and of the understanding of *Dasein*."[13] In this sense, freedom becomes an act of disclosing the self, quite far removed from the political questions of power, domination, and self-determination that accompany the concept in political philosophy. What is interesting is that Arendt does not modify Heidegger's ideas but simply transposes them into the context of the Greek polis, further removing the concept from real politics.[14]

Intersubjectivity supposedly occurs in the political realm, but absent is any notion of socialization processes, value consensus, and other forces that are highly efficient at closing off the mind—volitionally and in terms of capacity—to the perspectives of others. Because Arendt separates the *vita activa* and the *vita contempliva*, thinking and knowing, she works under the illusion that individuals will be able to come together in solidarity despite the encrusted values and worldviews that socialization has put into place. Reification is not a problem for Arendt, she never questions the basic Heideggerian assumption that selves will be

12. Martin Heidegger, "On the Essence of Truth," in *Martin Heidegger: Basic Writings* (New York: Harper Torchbooks, 1971), 130. Also see the discussion in Martin Heidegger, *Sein und Zeit* (Tübingen: Max Niemeyer, 2001), §§59–60.

13. Heidegger, *The Essence of Human Freedom*, §30.

14. Arendt closely parallels Heidegger when she writes about the nature of speech and action that "This revelatory quality of speech and action comes to the fore where people are *with* others and neither for nor against them—that is, in sheer human togetherness. Although nobody knows whom he reveals when he discloses himself in deed or word, he must be willing to risk the disclosure." *The Human Condition*, 180. See also Arendt, *Between Past and Future*, 146ff. This also has an existential dimension to it for Arendt, because each individual is seen to constitute a novum, and opening oneself to this ability to see the world anew: "freedom . . . is identical with the fact that men are being born and that therefore each of them is a new beginning, begins, in a sense, the world anew." *The Origins of Totalitarianism*, 466.

able to disclose some presocial, authentic self and set of opinions. For her, there is no effect of ideology, of routinized value systems, of false forms of reasoning that lead people toward legitimating norms, values, and practices not to mention institutions and ways of life that may not be in their or the public's interests. Ignoring this, Arendt argues that "I form an opinion by considering a given issue from different viewpoints, by making present to my mind the standpoints of those who are absent, that is, I represent them."[15] Furthermore, "no opinion is self-evident. In matters of opinion, but not in matters of truth, our thinking is truly discursive, running, as it were, from place to place, from one part of the world to the other through all kinds of conflicting views, until it finally ascends from all these particularities to some impartial generality."[16]

The problem here is that she perceives opinions as originating in some existentially distinctive self, rather than from social relations and the ways that ideas and opinions that people come to accept are generally embedded in the institutional functions of the world they inhabit. This is no place for a phenomenological "life-world"; the problem is cognitive: the concepts, opinions, and ideas of people are shaped by the social relations within which they are situated, rather than springing from some existential "beginning." The importance of the ἀρχή in this sense—as rule and as origin or beginning—is that it denotes a self that is somehow presocial and existentially prior to any form of socialization. We are asked to believe that each person does in fact initiate an ἀρχή, that each person is somehow unique and this constitutes a valid basis for forming political knowledge about the world. In contrast to this, the problem of social power must be conceived as a problem of domination. Domination is not simply a process whereby one has legal or some other form of authority over an other; it is a situation wherein social relations are constructed to extract benefit from others, control and subordinate them for some self-interested purpose, and order the field of ideas and opinions to legitimate those structures of extractive power. Opinion thereby becomes victimized by a *sensus communis* colonized by norms and values rooted in the prevailing forms of legitimacy. Opinion effectively becomes reified thought. Without truth, each opinion must

---

15. Arendt, "Truth and Politics," 115.

16. Arendt, "Truth and Politics," 115–16.

be taken and accepted at face value; each is "isonomic" in the political realm, as are their opinions.[17] But if we were to accept this thesis, so crucial for Arendt's thought, we would find ourselves in a condition where ideological consciousness is free to reign, where opinion about things and the world have no objective metric to gauge their relevance. We would find ourselves adrift, with no way to shatter the reified structures of consciousness that allow real political and social power to hold sway. In the modern age, we cannot separate the dimension of surplus extraction from that of the constitution of values, norms, and commonly accepted opinions because they work in tandem to form the social order.

This is one reason that any valid conception of politics cannot remain within the confines of opinion. It is not the case that all knowledge, all search for rational truths, are limited to surface phenomena. The reality is that truth-claims constitute the very substance of political power and authority. Indeed, as Rousseau and Weber knew all too well, the basic problem of political power in the modern world is how it is made legitimate in the minds of its members.[18] Violence and coercion, in contrast to Arendt's thinking, are not the main tools of those who seek domination—rather, it is legitimacy. This legitimacy is constructed by cultivating opinion, by weaving the cognitive and value-orientational

---

17. Arendt's thesis has been used by postmodernists to justify the attack on universalist principles in the formation of any *demos*. As Chantal Mouffe claims, "Hannah Arendt was absolutely right to insist that in the political sphere one finds oneself in the realm of opinion, or 'doxa,' and not in that of truth, and that each sphere has its own criteria of validity and legitimacy. There are those, of course, who will argue that such a position is haunted by the specter of relativism. But such an accusation makes sense only if one remains in the thrall of a traditional problematic, which offers no alternative between objectivism and relativism." "Radical Democracy: Modern or Postmodern?," in Andrew Ross (ed.), *Universal Abandon? The Politics of Postmodernism* (Minneapolis: University of Minnesota Press, 1988), 31–45, 37. But Mouffe fails to show what this could mean: what it would look like to have an alternative category that is not either subjective-relative on one hand or rational-objective on the other.

18. For an excellent comparative study of the ideas of legitimacy in Rousseau and Weber, see J. G. Merquior, *Rousseau and Weber: Two Studies in the Theory of Legitimacy* (London: Routledge and Kegan Paul, 1980), and the discussion in Michael J. Thompson, "The Two Faces of Domination in Republican Political Theory," *European Journal of Political Theory*, vol. 17, no. 1 (2018): 44–64.

prerequisites that in turn legitimate the concrete forms of power that pervade the social world. Domination, the real concern of politics, is therefore functional in nature: institutional power is built from the minds of its participants, not from fiat. Truth is a means by which we shed the ideological valences of thought that are shaped by socialization. It colonizes precisely those capacities and forms of "thinking" that Arendt sees as constituting freedom and "action." Indeed, because Arendt's project is to carve out and define a distinctive sphere of thinking and acting that is nonscientific, she is forced to rely on the phenomenological tools she has ready at hand. The denigration of truth-claims is a major weakness in her approach, and it has encouraged many subsequent theorists to dispense with the importance of truth-claims and their political import.

Deliberation and Its Discontents

It is interesting that Arendt places deliberation at the center of her rejuvenation of politics when the Athenians, who knew well the social problems caused by deliberative politics, questioned it. It is not simply Plato's critique in his *Republic*, *Gorgias*, and *Protagoras* who outlined the problems associated with knowledge built from opinion and persuasion. It is also, perhaps most insightfully, Aristotle in Book X of his *Nicomachean Ethics*, where he identifies a central problem with the kind of "action" that Arendt prizes when he considers how *doxa*, or opinion, becomes stubbornly lodged in the minds of men: "For it is by no means easy, perhaps impossible, to dislodge by argument habits long firmly rooted in their character."[19] Aristotle's thesis is clear: the ideas that people have are not easily changed by argument or deliberation. The reason for this is that he sees an essential and problematic relation between the nature (φύσει) of individuals, their respective character (ἔθος), and the ability to teach them (διδαχῆ). Individuals have their character shaped by habits over time, and teaching different ways of thinking and knowing become difficult. Aristotle is aware, especially in Book IV of the *Politics*, that the structure of social relations can produce different kinds of habits among men. In this sense, the Aristotelian view (as it

---

19. Aristotle, *Nicomachean Ethics* (Oxford: Oxford University Press, 1994), 1180a–20.

was for Rousseau, Hegel, and Marx) was that social conditions shape the character of men. People cannot be conceived of as being able to think and judge on their own terms. They think through the world in the categories their culture has given them.

But Arendt insists that the polis, society and social relations, have no impact on the shaping of consciousness. She explicitly rejects Aristotle's thesis when she writes: "Morality concerns the individual in his singularity. The criterion of right and wrong, the answer to the question, what ought I to do? depends in the last analysis neither on the habits and customs, which I share with those around me, nor on a command of either divine or human origins, but on what I decide with regard to myself."[20] The ability to think on one's own is a remnant of the existentialist philosophy that never left her. It paints a picture of thinking that secures subjective thinking and judging from the pressures of social structure and function. The central problem Arendt sought to overcome was hidden where she refused to look: one cannot change the way one thinks by pressing oneself inward into the realm of conscience. Rather, the key is to change the institutions that produce the individual, shape him, and socialize him and his consciousness. By nature we are not prone to changing our ideas and searching for different opinions. Rather, we generally seek to defend them and secure our worldviews from external threat. Arendt's ideal of deliberation and persuasion is illusory at best. Nevertheless, she continues to place opinions, representative thinking, at the heart of political judgment.

As I have argued above, this view is untenable as a means of understanding political power. Opinions and the reliance on the "enlarged mentality" that supposedly results from taking in the opinions of others is supposed to support the weightier political claims of a deliberative, localized conception of the "political." But truth, not opinion, gets us to the real essence of political power and domination. Any critical form of judgment must advance truth-claims about the prevailing social arrangements and the forms of legitimate authority that are deployed and accepted by the community. Truth-claims are therefore distinctly political in the sense that they shape the cognitive foundations for less cognitive frames of thinking (opinion, worldviews, evaluative judgments, and so on). Truth as a criterion in political thought

---

20. Hannah Arendt, *Responsibility and Judgment* (New York: Schocken Books, 2003), 97.

should not be reduced to the positivistic kind of thinking that Arendt opposed. Hence, if we think about how certain inequalities are justified, how they can be established in law and within the prevailing ideas of political subjects, it is because they rest on the pretension of some kind of truth-claim. Indeed, any enlightened understanding of politics must seek to base legitimate rule and authority on positions that are rationally valid in some basic sense.

When we ground politics in opinion, in the sharing of opinions and subjective perspectives instead of truth-claims, we are not democratizing power; instead, we are allowing illusions to guide the convictions of citizens. The educative function of politics does not come from sharing opinions alone. Opinion can be tamed by facts only through theory; only by the explanation of how the mechanisms of power operate in the world can opinion—the shallowest form of reflection, and the most tainted by ideological consciousness—be forced into the realm of truth. Arendt's philosophical musings take no consideration of the most basic and consistent findings of social psychology: that facts do not persuade, that opinions do not originate in some *arche*, some "natality" of phenomenological perception. They are the result of socialization, of the permeation of social values, and, particularly in mass society, are made of ideas embedded in the macro institutions of economy no less than the provincial worldviews of the suburb.

Arendt never provides us with a mechanism for overcoming these deliberative problems. Instead, we are asked to put our trust in ideas about "disclosure," and the innate capacity to reach judgment from a plethora of opinion. In truth, opinion cannot serve as the substance of political judgment.[21] Arendt's deeply flawed notion about "opinion" is that it is generated spontaneously: "Opinions are formed in a process of open discussion and public debate, and where no opportunity for the forming of opinions exists, there may be moods . . . but no opinion."[22] For it to be critical, and for it to foster progressive ends, it must find

---

21. Jürgen Habermas takes Arendt to task on this point when he argues that "Politics cannot, as with Arendt, be identical with the praxis of those who discourse together in order to act communally. . . . With this outmoded concept of theoretical knowledge that builds upon ultimate evidence, Arendt abstains from conceiving the coming to agreement about political questions as a rational formation of consensus." *Philosophical-Political Profiles* (Cambridge, MA: MIT Press, 1983), 185–86.

22. Arendt, *On Revolution*, 268.

some validity not just in agreement or consensus—for this leads us to
the problem Plato identified where illusory notions about the world are
able to govern the forms of thought of participants, indeed, as opinion,
as doxa—but in an ontological claim that is valid in some objective
sense as a truth-claim. Not in the sense that physical or natural kinds
can be understood, but in the distinctive ways that we, as historically
and socially produced beings, can be understood. By seeing our grasp
on the world as essentially hermeneutic and interpretative, we are left
without any kind of conceptual or rational framework to judge the
validity of the ideas that populate the "space of reasons" or the field
of persuasion. Left to rhetoric rather than rational reflection, how are
we to defend against the articulation of value premises that have not
been saturated by reification and shaped by heteronomous logics and
value orientations from inflecting our capacities for judgment?[23] Because
validity rests on persuasion and on context-dependent worldviews, there
is no way to open up a dimension for rational critique and explode the
powers of reification and relativism.

In the final analysis, I must be able to make a judgment about the
world that in some way is valid for others in the world; not according
to my or their opinions—which are subject to the errors of subjectiv-
ism—but according to how the organization of power and resources, of
how norms orient actions and institutions affect and shape the world we
live in together. These objective truths are always to be seen as historical
and social, not timeless or in some way akin to the truth-claims of the
natural sciences or positivism. Rather, an objective truth-claim must be
social-ontological: it must inquire into how the objective forms of life
that are constitutive of any social scheme are also the generative mechanism of our social pathologies. The key issue here is not hermeneutic,
but one of a critical metaphysics that can penetrate appearance and

---

23. Jonathan Peter Schwartz, for example, intelligently underscores this theme in
Arendt's thought: "Political opinions are functions of our contextual grasp of the
common world, involving our own distinctive perspective on that context. The mode
of validity it appeals to is *persuasive*. One does not seek to compel assent with
this kind of validity; rather, one appeals to another judge's 'enlarged mentality' in
hopes that they will see the common world in a similar way." "Political Judgment
Confronts Ideology: Hannah Arendt's Contribution," *Polity*, vol. 50, no. 3 (2018):
485–511, 503.

grip the essential (i.e., constitutive) logics of our social reality.[24] Again, this in no way entails that any valid political principle must be true in some analytic sense—such as the form "if X then Y"—but it must have some kind of ontological referent in a dialectical sense: where any subject is seen as functionally related to the totality of which it is a part. These are objective judgments—subject to argumentation and debate to be sure—but they are not opinions. They postulate truth-claims about the world, not phenomenologically spontaneous expressions of experience, but claims about the actual structures and mechanisms that operate and shape our reality. The key aim of critique should be not to rely on the *sensus communis* for the simple reason that the constitutive logics of social power and norms have too much power to colonize it, rendering it a mere reflection of the world-as-it-is. Critique should seek to explode the *sensus communis*, not subscribe to its field of meaning; it should seek to find the sources of how our being and consciousness are shaped by social reality.

I cannot simply use opinion to orient judgments about abortion, about race, about the distribution of wealth, and so on. For persuasion to be genuinely political, it would need to be grounded in concepts that achieve this kind of truth-validity because without this, deliberative encounters, "action" in Arendt's sense, would devolve into a plethora of value judgments, none more valid than the other. We would be cast back into the same problem Arendt sought to overcome: the collapse of

---

24. For an attempt to defend Arendt's hermeneutic theory of judgment, see Shmuel Lederman, "The Actor Does Not Judge: Hannah Arendt's Theory of Judgment," *Philosophy and Social Criticism*, vol. 42, no. 7 (2015): 727–41. I think this defense simply side-steps and reproduces the question I continue to raise here about the weakness of any validity claims rooted in hermeneutics rather than in ontology. Indeed, Peter J. Steinberger points to a similar aporia in Arendt's theory of judgment: "We remain without a discussion of just why we should agree that those kinds of endeavor can be a source of knowledge or wisdom or whatever variety; we continue to lack anything approaching a criterion on the basis of which we might reliably distinguish good from bad judgment; we seem to have no very explicit idea of how the faculty of judgment might be cultivated and nurtured; we have no clear reason to believe that such a faculty is, in fact, a feature of human intellectual life; and ultimately, we have no straightforward account of what it might mean to have knowledge in the political, action-relevant, nonrationalist sense." *The Concept of Political Judgment* (Chicago: University of Chicago Press, 1993), 75–76.

meaning and an inertia of political judgment. Perhaps worse, we would
be in a situation of relativism where individuals clump into groups
and subgroups bounded by their subjective opinion structures. What is
needed is a form of critical judgment that can shatter ideological consciousness, and Arendt's philosophical pathway is no way to achieve this
end. Indeed, because her project sought to place friendship at the core
of social solidarity and of a distinctive understanding of "power," she
ends up putting too much weight on what the Greeks called πείθειν,
or "persuasion," as opposed to διαλέγεσθαι, or a more focused form
of conversation, which she falsely refers to as "philosophical speaking,"
thereby misleadingly collapsing it into speculative rationality.[25] Instead,
she urges us to overturn the privileging of philosophical thinking:
"Persuasion appears in Aristotle as the opposite of διαλέγεσθαι, the
philosophical form of speaking, precisely because this type of dialogue
was concerned with knowledge and the finding of truth and therefore
demanded a process of compelling proof."[26] But why should we invest
the act of persuasion, or πείθειν, with any inherent political power? As I

---

25. Given her penchant for Greek, Arendt should have noted that διαλέγεσθαι
is the middle-passive form of the verb διαλέγειν, which means "to pick through,"
connoting the act not of "philosophical conversation," but a more focused kind of
discussion where we seek to come to some kind of understanding through literally
"picking out" those ideas that count and those that do not. This is not related
directly to speculative thought by any means, and she thereby robs the term of its
richer meaning and implications. Of course, this is what she wants to marginalize
and she simplistically codes διαλέγεσθαι as "speculative thought." Nevertheless, her
theory about opinion renders the act of πείθειν problematic since she gives no
method of picking out what matters nor criteria for why one idea should matter
and not another. Schwartz insightfully points to this theme in Arendt: "The category
that political judgment appeals to, in other words, is not that of objectivity, but
neither is it merely arbitrary personal preference. For something to have validity,
it must still be possible to draw distinctions, so that even if no political opinions
are objectively true, some judges' opinions must still remain better than others."
"Political Judgment Confronts Ideology," 502. But it is hard to see how this really
gets us anywhere. What criteria should be used to judge the judgments? Indeed,
the fear here of "objective truth" as conflated with natural science makes this theory
of judgment recede too far into the hermeneutic sphere without any compass for
judging the concrete shapes of sociality that are the substance of political and social
life. See my discussion of Aristotle in chapter 5.

26. Arendt, *Between Past and Future*, 219.

see it, Arendt is effectively blind to how distorted forms of consciousness and defective forms of socialization affect opinions and therefore the hermeneutic attempt to make sense of our world. If this is the case, then persuasion does not occur for rational reasons, but because I find some affinity—emotional, ideological, or whatever—with others.

This, however, has been welcomed by many contemporary political theorists. On one level, with the decline of Marxism, her ideas were well fashioned to provide a theoretical framework for the logic of the new social movements. The crucial move here was toward an understanding of politics and social power that was distinct from the materialist, class-based forms of realism characteristic of Marxism. Arendt's ideas become attractive in a postclass conception of politics because it now is open to all; it allows, in the most superficial sense, for including the other. The problem, as I began arguing above, is that there is a need for some kind of foundational claims to orient the capacity of critical judgment. Arendt equates judgment with the synthesis of a plurality of perspectives, but there is no way to secure a judgment or anchor it in a systematic way of judging what is good from what is bad.[27] By robbing political life of any access to truth, to rationality, to an appeal to rational universals, she thereby destroys, not rejuvenates, critical-political judgment.

Once we collapse knowledge about the world into praxis within the world, we depart from any ground for proper political judgment and, indeed, for rational critique itself. The thesis that we can somehow achieve a form of thinking about the world through praxic activity makes no sense unless there is some means by which we can judge the content of the opinions being articulated. Although Aristotle was correct in his notion that citizenship was an activity and not a status, something Arendt would accept, his idea about phronesis is not detached from the cognition of the social totality—that is, from a cognitive and an ontological claim about humans and how they live together and they live together best. Book III of Aristotle's *Politics* is devoted first to the nature of active citizenship, to πολιτεύεσθαι, and the remainder

---

27. This critique is opened up by Fred Dallmayr, although he does not pursue it to any significant degree. Still, his remarks serve as a starting point for my critique here. See his *Polis and Praxis: Exercises in Contemporary Political Theory* (Cambridge, MA: MIT Press, 1984), 96ff.

of the book is devoted to the analysis of constitutions. Here is where the balance between political activity (subsuming the categories of πολιτεύεσθαι, διαλέγεσθαι, and φρονήσις) and rational thinking about the objective world are brought together through the concept of judgment. Aristotle's thesis is that "correct" (ὄρθαι) as opposed to "perverted" (ἡμαρτείμεναι) forms of constitution are to be judged based on whether they serve the common interest of the polis or only a particular part of it.[28] This judgment is not simply an opinion, a view that is to be accepted through mere persuasion. Rather, it is grounded in the discussion found in Book I, where the nature of humans is found to be social, that all individuals are interdependent and, as a result, the most highly evolved form of social organization, the polis, is judged to be the best because all require the thick relations the polis can provide. Hence, correct from perverted forms of political activity—that is, good and bad citizens—can be judged not on the basis of their action as such but on the basis of whether they further the concerns of the public or common good. Aristotle's basic argument links the concerns of political activity and practical wisdom, phronesis, with the objective postulates about the nature of the good life seen not in mere value terms, but rooted in the material-social conditions of human life.

The connection between the kind of thinking and the actual realities of human social life should be seen as a more promising approach for a theory of political judgment. But Arendt separates what for Aristotle is a necessary connection between an ontological ground or foundation of which human welfare and goods on one hand and the praxis of citizenship on the other. Whereas Arendt subsumes the idealized Athenian polis under an existentialist and phenomenological theory of being and epistemology, Aristotle sees that any kind of valid political judgment must connect the kinds of goods and needs that humans have within an interdependent, relational existence as a pretext for judging what acts, norms, institutions, and so on, should be considered "correct" or valid, in a more modern parlance. Deliberation on its own, as Arendt characterizes it, as the exchange of opinion, cannot be sufficient for the kind of political judgment Aristotle envisions. It is also not sufficient for moderns. Even if we concede that individuals are somehow able to overcome the problems inherent with democratic

---

28. I provide a more robust account of Aristotle's ontological theory of judgment in chapter 5.

will-formation and the epistemic capacities needed for truly democratic deliberation, Arendt simply provides no theory of judgment that can or should be considered political: it side-steps all attempts to deal with building valid propositions about how to judge social arrangements and how to construct new ones.

Democracy Misdirected

Power and realism must be at the heart of the problem of politics. But also, democracy cannot be reduced to the practice of citizens; it is also a feature of institutional action and orientation. As I suggested already, Aristotle's discussion of citizenship is important here because he seeks to show us that there is citizenship as active life that must also be judged based on its ends—the good citizen seeks the common good, and this common good is defined according to certain ontological principles. The practical, epistemic, and the political come together to form a triangle of political judgment that Arendt simply shatters. As a result, we are asked to enter a world where politics can be reduced to practice alone—the very ends of political life fall into abstraction. Now the collective "power" of citizens has freedom not as their end but as their precondition. Rights and institutions play little (if any) real role in her conception of the political, which remains an abstract, existential concern. This is where Arendt's ideas become particularly dangerous. Her philosophical reconstruction of political theory and political action and judgment lead many to believe, without empirical evidence or foundation, that politics can somehow occur external to these most fundamental institutions.

One sees this particularly in her ideas about republicanism, which are decidedly premodern. In her project of investing action over all other forms of politics, she views those institutional arrangements that seem to magnify the phenomenological-intersubjective processes that she puts at the center of politics. Indeed, Arendt's ideas led her to political positions that seem anathema to any real politics today. Her exclusive reduction of politics to a form of life where intersubjective sharing of opinions was matched by a hostility to the modern bureaucratic state. Her understanding of republicanism is one where small communities are able to give rise to the kind of action and freedom that she places at the very center, the very essence of politics. Her praise of Thomas

Jefferson's ward system as well as the *Arbeiterräter* of the worker movements in Europe were exemplars of the kind of political organization
that could give voice to the truly free political form of activity, where
"no one could be called happy without his share in public happiness,
that no one could be called happy without his share in public happiness, that no one could be called free without his experience in public
freedom, and that no one could be called either happy or free without
participating, and having a share, in public power."[29]
   A decentered federalism, firmly rooted in localism as in the
Jeffersonian ideal, as well as the worker-council model, are viewed by
Arendt as the political institutions par excellence. The main reason
for this, again, is that they provide a space for the kind of action she
narrowly sees as political. Her comments on the workers councils are
worth quoting at length:

> The so-called wish of the working class sounds much rather
> like an attempt of the revolutionary party to counteract the
> councils' political aspirations, to drive their members away
> from the political realm and back into the factories. And
> this suspicion is borne out by two facts: the councils have
> always been primarily political, with social and economic
> claims playing a very minor role, and it was precisely this
> lack of interest in social and economic questions which, in
> the view of the revolutionary party, was a sure sign of their
> "lower-middle-class, abstract, liberalistic" mentality. In fact,
> it was a sign of their political maturity, whereas the work-
> ers' wish to run the factories themselves was a sign of the
> understandable, but politically irrelevant desire of individuals
> to rise into positions which up to then had been open only
> to the middle class.[30]

---

29. Arendt, *On Revolution*, 255. Habermas notes on this theme in Arendt's ideas
that "A state relieved of the administrative handling of social affairs, a politics
cleansed of all questions of social politics, an institutionalizing of public liberty that
is independent of the organization of welfare, a radically democratic formation of
consensus that puts a stop to social repression—this is not a conceivable path for
any modern society." *Philosophical-Political Profiles*, 180–81.

30. Arendt, *On Revolution*, 274.

Here Arendt's display for antipolitics masquerading as the "political" is manifest. Not only are we to assume that the worker councils are to be prized based on her idiosyncratic criteria of *constitutio libertatis*, or creating the space where freedom can become realized as action and opinion sharing, we are also told that the economic ends of the radical labor movement were in fact "politically irrelevant." Arendt can come to this view only because she has totally redefined politics as something philosophical, thereby turning political theory on its head. Whereas the aims of the socialist movement should rightly be seen to have been that they wanted to eliminate the social power that sprang from capitalist economic life and the kind of dominance that capital had over the community, the "mature" political view is supposed to be, for Arendt, the ability to share opinions and engage in some abstract and, as I argued already, elusive form of opinion formation. But freedom to participate does nothing to eliminate real power. In fact, it can be said that the less centralization of power any community has at its disposal, the more domination and elite control will be possible.

Her views on the ward system as a political-institutional ideal are therefore also problematic and worthy of comment. Arendt's inflated and romantic view of the Greek polis coupled with her existentialist and Heideggerian ideas about the nature of freedom and human authenticity blinds her to the reality of political power. She sees the state and other modern institutional forms as getting in the way of the "action" she views as central. She looks to Jefferson's advocacy of the ward system as a means to realize these ends:

> Hence, the ward system was not meant to strengthen the power of the many but the power of "every one" within the limits of his competence; and only by breaking up "the many" into assemblies where everyone could count and be counted upon "shall we be as republican as a large society can be." . . . If the ultimate end of revolution was freedom and the constitution of a public space where freedom could appear, the *constitutio libertatis*, then the elementary republics of the wards, the only tangible place where everyone could be free, actually where the end of the great republic whose chief purpose in domestic affairs should have been to provide the people with such places of freedom and to protect them. The basic assumption of the ward system, whether Jefferson knew

it or not, was that no one could be called happy without his
share in public happiness, that no one could be called free
without his experience in public freedom, and that no one
could be called either happy or free without participating,
and having a share, in public power.[31]

But political power construed in this way masks its true nature and
capacity for control and domination—again, concepts foreign to all of
Arendt's musings. There is little point of emphasizing how councils or
the wards could act as "disruptive" spaces—the reality of the matter is
that without establishing some protective covering by the state, there
is no way to guarantee the security and the protection of those within
decentralized locales.[32] Most recently, the Occupy Wall Street movement
strove for just these kinds of local spaces of engagement and isonomic
deliberation, and its failure was largely because no common purpose,
aim, or political goal could be articulated. More especially in the age of
industrial and postindustrial societies, the more we localize politics, the

---

31. Arendt, *On Revolution*, 254–55.

32. This leads to a more contentious question in democratic theory: specifically, does the council and ward system provide a populist-conservative or a
disruptive-progressive force? There seems to be no answer to this question among
her intellectual supporters, who instead seem to simply repeat it uncritically without
noting its obvious difficulties. Patchen Markell, for instance, argues that "From the
point of view of mainstream accounts of democracy as a form of rule, Arendt's
invocation of the ward system and council movement would look like a call—perhaps nostalgic and unrealistic—for a return to direct popular decision-making. For
much radical democratic theory, the wards would seem instead to be mechanisms
of popular unruliness." "The Rule of the People: Arendt, *Archê*, and Democracy,"
American Political Science Review, vol. 100, no. 1 (2006): 1–14, 13. This sounds nice
until we consider that Arendt welds this political-institutional argument with her
thesis about the nature of opinion and judgment. With enhanced "popular unruliness" comes any number of political forces: conservative and radical. The key must
be—and this is something Arendt and her supporters do not face—how to prevent
the kind of localism that can threaten personal interests as well as secure truly
common goods. Without appeal to a common power, the local can all too easily
succumb to particularist interests rather than general interests and ends. Indeed,
the real issue is that the council movement and the ward system were conceived
as alternatives to the state, not simply as counterweights to it. This leads to deeper
problems which I explore later.

less likely it will be to challenge corruption and the power of powerful sociopolitical actors. Arendt's privileging of the Jeffersonian model displays a penchant for unrealism. Indeed, Alexander Hamilton's argument in *Federalist* 70–73 is still salient: that the more local and smaller the unit of political power, the less likely that individual freedoms can be protected. To this should be added James Madison's thesis that decentralized political power leads only to more centralized private power, a view well defended by Grant McConnell in the 1960s:

> The cult of decentralization is based upon a desire to abolish power. Nevertheless, the local elites are readily brought together on a federal basis and their differences are easily reconciled, since these differences are usually only that and not conflicts. Within each sphere of policy, power is not abolished but rather enhanced by decentralization. At the same time, decentralization means weakness of public officers in contests with private organizations and the elites they represent.[33]

Power of the people is therefore not enhanced by Arendt's schemes. Power of elites are, however, and here Arendt's weaknesses as a political thinker have made her influence problematic. For now, political theory, touched by her influential writings, distracts the main, core concern of politics away from view. What kind of world would it be if politics were localized around the so-called political concerns Arendt prizes? In a world of corporate dominance and subdued cultural and racial animosity, lacking a strong state to protect rights and constrain the powerful would create a bleak world indeed. To be sure, concrete power, the capacity for certain members of the community to dominate others, to control them and their life courses and their ability to shape the public good for their own ends—none of this can be captured in any satisfying or sufficient way through Arendt's narrow view of politics. We are led into a new semantic context with words like "natality," "sensus

---

33. Grant McConnell, *Private Power and American Democracy* (New York: Vintage, 1966), 245. Also see the excellent discussion by Philip Green, "In Defense of the State," in *American Democracy: Selected Essays on Theory, Practice and Critique* (New York: Palgrave Macmillan, 2014), 31–60.

communis," "plurality," and so on that conceal the concrete forms of power, the negation of which have always been at the center of radical democratic politics.[34]

The twin pillars of her political theory—the Greek polis and existentialist phenomenology—disable her from dealing with these problems. The Greeks did not deal with this problem explicitly or in any satisfactory sense; their reliance on the institution of slavery dulled their conception of domination. The influence of Jaspers and Heidegger shape a concept of freedom that is overly philosophical and nonrealist. Rights, law, justice—none of these concepts achieve any concrete meaning outside of the power of the state to institute them. Without question, the anarchic and communitarian implications of her thought notwithstanding, the post-Hobbesian concept of the state still has real validity. However, Arendt's dismissal of the modern state places her ideas in an even more precarious relation to the needs of real politics.

She views the state as one of modernity's assaults on the political. The state mitigates the kind of freedom she sees essential to the public, agora-like spaces of the polis. Within those spaces power is created, solidarity formed, and true equality and freedom can have sway. But any realist theory of politics will lead us to the conclusion that democracy requires the state.[35] It requires the state because it is the only

34. Emmanuel Faye is unsparing in his critique of Arendt in this regard, but nevertheless quite accurate when he writes: "Trop souvent, on se satisfait d'utiliser aujourd'hui les mots « natalité », « pluralité », « vivre-ensemble », comme on parlait, dans les années 1920 et 1930, de « destin », de « mission » et de « communauté ». Il s'agit, chaque fois, de termes réunissant les locuteurs d'un même exister authentique ou, dans un langage plus actuel, « spontané ». La signification effective des termes d'Arendt, dont nous avons vu qu'ils renvoient à des conceptions inégalitaires, discriminatoires et dés-humanisantes de la vie sociale et économique, n'est plus aperçue." *Arendt et Heidegger: Extermination nazie et destruction de la pensée* (Paris: Albin Michel, 2016), 429–30. Also see Richard Wolin, *Heidegger's Children: Hannah Arendt, Karl Löwith, Hans Jonas, and Herbert Marcuse* (Princeton, NJ: Princeton University Press, 2001), 30ff.

35. Recently, antistatism has become an ascendant theme in left politics, and Arendt's work is usually cited as one of a series of forerunners. See the discussion by Miguel Abensour, *Democracy against the State: Marx and the Machiavellian Moment* (Cambridge: Polity Press, 2011), 90ff. Abensour and others in this vein see Arendt's idealization of "action" and public space as the core mechanisms of a neo-anarchist vision of politics. See my critique of this conception of radical politics in Michael J.

institution that can be used to counterbalance the kinds of inequalities and injustice that inevitably spring up in societies that have even the slightest degree of inequality in social power, whether based on property, privilege, or whatever. The aim of radical politics must therefore be to democratize the state and to democratize state power, that is, to orient it toward common, public ends. To be sure, justice cannot be fostered by friendship alone; it is doubtful that the kind of friendship that Arendt sees at the core of her conception of the "political" has any real basis historically or sociologically. This does not, of course, minimize the view that social movements are a crucial vehicle for social change, but it does categorically invalidate the view that councils and wards are the proper institutional ends of any kind of modern politics.

Critical Judgment and Radical Politics

Arendt's displacement of truth by opinion seriously affects her concept of judgment. But it is precisely a theory of judgment, a critical theory of judgment, that is needed to reconstitute political practice and political principle. Central to this view, as I see it, is the thesis that political premises, or those normative claims that are postulated for public adoption and that are to take on the power of political force, possess (if they are to be considered rationally valid) an objective element. Arendt's attempt to provide a new theory of political judgment sought to break out of the problematic division between facts and values and to resolve this distinction by returning to what can be called a neo-Athenian conception of politics.[36] The problem with this view is that it seals us off from the Enlightenment project of postulating norms that are to be considered valid not because a group of people have agreed to or consented to them but because they have a deeper foundation in terms of the end or telos or effects that this norm would be able to create. The claim I want to make here is that those norms that are to attain

---

Thompson, "A Theory of Council Republicanism," in James Muldoon (ed.), *Council Democracy: Towards a Democratic Socialist Politics* (London: Routledge, 2018), 108–27.

36. Philip Pettit has made the distinction between "neo-Athenian" and "neo-Roman" conceptions of republicanism. See his "Democracy, Electoral and Contestatory," in Ian Shapiro and Stephen Macedo (eds.), *Designing Democratic Institutions* (New York: New York University Press, 2000), 105–47.

validity in a rational-radical sense can only do so by appealing to how any proposition affects the common interest. Aristotle's argument about the way to judge correct and perverted constitutions retains its validity: we can say that the only kind of criterion of judgment that we can call foundational would be to interrogate whether any norm, practice, institution, and so on has effects on public concern. Critical rationality must be based on not only an epistemic claim but an ontological one: where we articulate reasons based on the ontological referent of social relations and their ability to either enhance, promote, or defend a common interest that does not violate the legitimate rights of individuals. The problem becomes not one of disclosing one's opinions to others but justifying ethical and political concepts, ideas, and values according to the structure of the social world itself. Epistemic claims are dependent on ontological ones; they will remain abstract lest they are able to relate dialectically.

What this means is that if "principle" is the guiding element of action, then we need to be able to judge principle, we need to be able to judge based on reasons that are rational. The reason for this is obvious: opinions grant us little more than perspectival views, nothing that can be used to secure the validity of the ideas that should be taken as principles for political action or concern. This is precisely what Arendt wants to oppose, because what is central is opinion and representative thinking, thereby reducing principle to a postmetaphysical concept: we cannot simply dissolve all foundations and expect principle to be anything less than either ideological, psychological, or perhaps ignorant. Rather, the key issue is to ground the values that support social change in a foundational context that can provide validity to the kinds of norms and institutional arrangements that can enhance social justice and personal development. In this sense, sharing opinions about the world and seeing the world from the point of view of others grant us little insight unless we have some point of reference for judgment.

Arendt's search for a form of thinking that is specifically political, a search for meaning, for opinion, was diametrically opposed to science and rational cognition because she mistakenly saw cognitive rationality as limited to the surfaces of reality. In this sense, science was simply a more elaborate form of common sense because it is simply an "enormously refined prolongation of common-sense reasoning in which sense illusions are constantly dissipated just as errors in science are corrected."[37] More specifically, "Cognition, whose highest criterion is truth, derives that criterion from the world of appearances in which we take our bearings through sense perceptions, whose testimony is self-evident, that is, unshakeable by argument and replaceable only by other evidence."[38] But if everything can essentially be reduced to common sense reasoning, then we are in a position where opinion takes the dominant role. Lacking a rational standpoint, we have no way to make valid ethical judgments. Judgment cannot be reduced to the plurality of opinions because I am given no way, no metric, no criteria for judging a claim's validity. It is one thing to treat others with equal respect in terms of their voiced opinions, it is quite another to give all opinions equal weight. This is precisely a lack of judgment, not judgment itself; Arendt's critique of rationalism puts her in a position where no rational basis for political claims can be made.

Insisting that rational judgments are possible—as opposed to mere opinions or to what John Rawls calls "reasonable" claims—does not mean that some ultimate foundation is being looked for. Rather, it means that any claim must refer to a concrete as well as posit some kind of objective institutional means for its resolution. This is political reasoning par excellence because it has in view the idea that political problems require political solutions. Arendt's denigration of scientific rationalism as relegated to mere surface phenomena is simply an incorrect view of the matter, overly influenced by a phenomenological epistemology. Rational claims are not just claims about surface phenomena, they refer to actual mechanisms in the world. No scientific theory would be considered legitimate unless it could explain the mechanisms of why certain events take place; it is no different in rational forms of ethical life. The forms of life we inhabit are marked by domination, inequality, and forms of practice that are defective in the sense that they serve not common but particular ends of power. To the extent that this is true, we cannot rely on a foundationless form of interaction and mutual acknowledgment to get us out of these kinds of power relations. They are too extensive, too powerful in terms of their capacity to shape consciousness. It is true that no political claim can achieve a rational certainty akin to mathematics

37. Arendt, *The Life of the Mind*, vol. 1, 54.
38. Arendt, *The Life of the Mind*, vol. 1, 57.

or the natural sciences. But this was never the point. The real issue is that we have some kind of ground, some kind of anchor for critical judgment. Political claims are political because they affect others; they have some kind of necessary implication for the lives, powers, capacities, and interests of another in the community. In this sense, we need to ask ourselves about the concrete ways that any law, institutions, practice, or norm has on those effects.

Even more Arendt's conception of judgment is weak because it cannot make distinctions rooted in concrete conceptions of the good.[39] She relies on particularism to create a theory of judgment as "enlarged mentality," but this view cannot connect with rational principle because it cannot find a rational-universal moment for judgment. Her basic thesis is that we can make judgments without reference to any form of universal, instead appealing to the "enlarged mentality" of others that we take into consideration.[40] But this is precisely what judgment cannot be, because it has no capacity to make rational (i.e., useful) distinctions. To be sure, the concept of an "enlarged mentality" is important; but it cannot be achieved without being able to conceptually grasp our essence as associational, relational beings and the ways our agency is dialectically mediated by the relational structures in which we are enmeshed. It is not through the phenomenological experience of others that I can achieve

---

39. Keith Breen remarks on this point that "Arendt's understanding of reflective judgment is unfortunately incomplete. Precisely because discriminating, deciding this is bad, this good, this ugly, this beautiful, judgment and its sense of taste cannot be identified with friendship or human plurality *per se*, since the necessary concomitant of taste, pleasure and approval is distaste, displeasure and disgust. This is so because every evaluative category has positive and negative dimensions, praise making sense only on account of the possibility of censure." "Violence and Power: A Critique of Hannah Arendt on the 'Political,'" *Philosophy and Social Criticism*, vol. 33, no. 3 (2007): 343–72, 362.

40. Arendt seeks to create a philosophical justification for this thesis with a defective reading of Kant, specifically the *Kritik der Urteilskraft*. For a critique of Arendt's reading of Kant in this regard, see Matthew C. Weidenfield, "Visions of Judgment: Arendt, Kant and the Misreading of Judgment," *Political Science Quarterly*, vol. 66, no. 2 (2013): 254–66. Also see the trenchant critique of Arendt's reading of Kant by Ernst Vollrath, "Handeln und Urteilen: Zur Problematik von Hannah Arendts Lektüre von Kants 'Kritik der Urteilskraft' unter einer politischen Perspektive," in Herfried Münkler (ed.), *Bürgerreligion und Bürgertugend. Debatten über die vorpolitischen Grundlagen politischer Ordnung* (Baden-Baden: Nomos, 1998), 228–49.

the enlarged mentality, it can only be achieved by migrating from our phenomenological experience in the world to conceptual grasp of the ontological srtructures of our sociality that we can achieve what I later refer to as "expanded autonomy." To call power relations into question, one must pose counterclaims and must be able to call them into question based on some rational basis, something that this conceptual mediation of our social being can (indeed, must) provide. Lacking this, we simply reproduce the problems that power poses: we can reproduce prevailing relations in another language—as when working people justify capitalist social relations based on the language of individual freedom—or we can create alternative opinions that deflect us from any realist analysis or critique of those power relations.

What is needed from any critical theory of judgment is not just an openness to plurality, but criteria for knowing what counts as good reasons and what does not; to be able to understand value judgments that are beneficial to the community and those that are not; and to be able to ground our value claims and political assertions in some kind of context that can be seen as applying to the needs and goods of all. What Arendt wants is a conception of judgment without foundations, one that no longer needs to appeal to rational universals or the dynamics of the objective world. It is not that the perspectives of participants are unimportant in constructing some kind of social knowledge, but there is no means given to arbitrate between those perspectives. Even more, without an object domain about which truth-claims can be posited, judgment cannot secure itself against the problem of relativism or the problem that the community's discourse and perspectives have already been fused to the legitimate forms of social power that have socialized them. Simply collecting particularist views together cannot be judgment in any useful, critical sense because there is no standard, principle, or category that can be used to evaluate them.[41] The reason for stressing

41. Defenders of Arendt tend to take this view at face value without dealing with the obvious problems it poses. Seyla Benhabib weakly defends Arendt on this point by arguing: "Judgment involves the capacity to represent to oneself the multiplicity of viewpoints, the variety of perspectives, the layers of meaning, etc., which constitute a situation. This representational capacity is crucial for the kind of sensitivity to particulars, which most agree is central for good and perspicacious judgment. The more we can identify the different viewpoints from which a situation can be interpreted and construed, the more we will have sensitivity to the particularities of the perspectives involved. . . . The link then between a universalist model of

this point is not just to call into question the kind of implications of Arendt's views on practical philosophy. It also goes against any kind of rational sense of improvement or progress in social and political life. Hegel was no doubt correct that rational ethical values that emerge in social life—by which he meant those that are grasped as universal and serving rational, universal ends for the community as a whole—must become objectified by political institutions (what he refers to as *objektive Geist*) over time. For Arendt, the ends and the means of politics are the same: to create spaces for interaction and opinion sharing, not the cultivation of critical judgment.

In the end, Arendt's rich philosophical exploration of political theory and her inventive, creative way of reading political texts and political history leaves us with a strikingly antipolitical conception of politics. On many issues, she was correct in her diagnoses. Her critique of the corrosive force of privatism in the modern age, the general collapse of the capacity for critical-political judgment in modern culture, the need for friendship as a form of social solidarity, and her insistence on the power of people against those that would seek to destroy spaces of communication and dissent are all laudable. But these are ultimately overshadowed by the problems in her political philosophy more generally. She refused to look at political history with an eye toward interests; she was blind to the fact that successful political and social movements were focused and brought together not out of a desire for some disclosure of plural selves and opinions but through concrete interests, concerns, and principles. She refused to see how the absence of the state would lead to the abuse of power and corruption; she was equally blind to how human cognition is an essential means to exploding the constraints of ideologi-

---

moral conversation and the exercise of judgment is this capacity for reversing moral perspectives, or what Kant and Arendt name the 'enlarged mentality.'" "Communicative Ethics and Current Controversies in Practical Philosophy," in S. Benhabib and F. Dallmayr (eds.), *The Communicative Ethics Controversy* (Cambridge, MA: MIT Press, 1990), 330–69, 361. But this gets us nowhere. We are still not provided with a means by which we can judge anything—simply saying we are able to see matters from the particular vantage point of others is not judgment, it is its very opposite. We may collect the stories, experiences, and opinions of others, but we have no metric, no rational framework to make sense of them and judge them or their moral rectitude. As a result, we lack the capacity to judge, to critique, to adjudicate between certain views and create some kind of hierarchy of ends that are in some sense rationally valid.

cal consciousness, itself an expression of the admixture of commonsense opinion, provincial attitudes, and values that cement economic hierarchies.

Despite these defects in her political philosophy and their inadequacy for formulating a critical theory of practical reason and judgment, she was correct that the realm of politics had to be understood collectively. Her key insight was to stress the importance of judgment as a central category in the face of a society that was losing the capacity for making judgments. She saw these issues correctly and thus placed political philosophy in a new register. But her deep roots in existentialism and phenomenology distorts her understanding of society, politics, and reason. Indeed, although the idea that making any claim was to make a judgment about the collective form of life we should live has merit. The problem that remains for us, however, is the extent to which the making of such claims can be considered valid and secure itself against the reified structures of modern subjectivity and consciousness. Although Arendt points toward central themes with which contemporary political philosophers must wrestle, it does not seem that she had any way to address these problems.

Chapter 3

The Discursive Fallacy

Language and Power in Practical Reason

In Search of Modern Democracy

The search for a rational democratic society, for a theory of democratic community constituted by the practices of individuals embedded in the "ethical life" of their life-world, has been an obsession of much of what now passes for critical theory. In many ways, this transformation of the tradition of critical theory has been effected by a focus on the pragmatist assertion that a self-reflexive community of equals deliberating on the norms and values of social life offers the potential for a resolution to the problems outlined by Marx, Weber, and the first generation of critical theorists. This association of critical theory with pragmatism has cleaved the tradition into pre- and postpragmatist manifestations. But is this transition justified? Does it in fact qualify as a genuinely critical theory of society? Whereas the first was dominated by the ideas of Hegel, Marx, Freud, and Weber, the pragmatist influence is grounded in an attempt to theorize a form of social action that can account for rational self- and social transformation through social practice and discourse to develop and articulate an intramundane form of social critique. I want to show that this move has been made in error and that as a "paradigm" of critical theory, it is unequal to its task.

What I propose here is that the pragmatist strain of critical theory is, in fact, uncritical in the face of the real manifestations of social power. I want to question the supposedly critical implications of the move toward discourse, communicative action, and justificatory reason exchange. In so doing, I provide an alternative account of language and meaning that takes into account the strong forces of social power and its capacity to shape and distort the cognitive powers of subjects. This occurs through the ways values work to secure compliance to the social order and to irrational worldviews. The basic problem I want to focus on is that these pathologies of consciousness that result from socialization in power-laden social structures cannot be overcome from within the sphere of open, intersubjective discourse and the exchange of justificatory reasons. The model of language and moral cognition that I propose shows the deep constraints on social actors' ability to come to rational, mutual forms of agreement and understanding about norms as well as the alternative problem that pragmatism can lead to the conformism to preexisting social norms and, hence, the existent reality.

The theory of language adopted by Habermas and his followers therefore becomes the key focus of my critique. There seems to be an issue where the meaning context of language is collapsed into the search for valid, objective moral statements. The emergence of pragmatic themes in critical theory presents us with a clear and direct challenge to a fundamental philosophical position that has been at the root of the rationalist, emancipatory critique of modern society. I take this as being the proposition of moral-evaluative statements that have a social-ontological content that seeks to clarify the proper end-states and processes achieved by the forms of social organization and interdependent activity of human practices (labor, communication, or whatever) and the extent to which these end-states and processes are pathological or secure social freedom. This raises an important and largely overlooked aspect of the philosophy of language and meaning with implications for seriousness with which we can take the project of Kantian pragmatism and the theory of justification it seeks to place at the center of the critical project.

This trend should not be seen as a legitimate form of critical theory, in my view. The most salient reason for this is that it reverses what was, for the first generation of critical theorists, the proper order of comprehending the pathologies of modern society. Whereas Habermas and his followers take the capacity of intersubjective and communicative discourse as a means to counteract social power and domination, the original view of critical theorists was that this capacity of modern subjects had been largely coopted by defective forms of socialization and ego formation. The studies in critical social psychology by Adorno, Horkheimer, Fromm, and Marcuse, for instance, showed that the classical, Enlightenment conception of the rational, autonomous subject could no longer be seen as tenable. Now the problems of rationalized domination (Weber and Marcuse), of reification due to the proliferation of the commodity and of exchange value (Marx and Lukács), and the irrational forces of the psyche resulting from defective socialization in the "sick" society (Freud, Adorno, and Fromm), painted a picture of corrupted forms of reflection and self-constitution. How, then, could it be possible for such selves to work their way out of these pathologies through everyday acts of communication and discourse?

In what follows, I question the validity of this discursive move. This cannot be done simply, but must proceed along an immanent critique of linguistic and cognitive processes that the pragmatic and Kantian turn in critical theory has at its core. As I see it, the philosophical appeal of discourse ethics (and the theory of justification to which it has given rise) is unwarranted because it invests agents with too strong a capacity to reason as a process of raising and arguing validity claims. Instead I want to pose an alternative theory of language and the cognitive content of moral reasoning. What I suggest here is that the logics of social power operate in such a way as to disable the critical capacity of language that the Kantian pragmatist thesis entails by fusing basic value systems and belief systems that are embedded in the institutions of the social order to the semantic content of linguistic utterances. In the end, despite its initial philosophical appeal, I aim to show that it is little more than an exercise in abstraction, an academic enterprise sealed off from the realist nature of politics and social power. As such, it cannot count as a critical theory of society and should be seen as a detour in the broader tradition of critique and social transformation that lies at the heart of the critical project.

The Pragmatist Turn in Contemporary Critical Theory

The post–World War II era can be characterized by a philosophical project to establish a system of practical reason that is self-standing and self-justifying. The employment of reason through a system of intersubjective exchanges of justification has meant that the nature of objectivity, so essential as a basic parameter of rationality, has been shifted from the object-domain of reality to the justificatory practices of reason exchange. Habermas was able to formalize this basic approach and translate the problem of objectivity into the structure of language and communication. Rather than construe the subject-object divide as occurring between consciousness and the object domain, now it occurs through an agreement of intersubjectively situated selves oriented toward mutual agreement and understanding. This rational agreement therefore establishes an objective criterion of validity acceptable to all participants and for the uptake of rational, democratic norms. Habermas posits that the central role of discourse ethics is to come to rational understanding not about the object domain but in the realm of values. Justification becomes tied to the effort toward moral validity claims that are only established through a rational agreement about values: "Moral validity claims lack reference to the objective world that is character- istic of claims to truth. This means they are robbed of a justification- transcendent point of reference. The reference to the world is replaced by an orientation toward extending the borders of the social community and its consensus about values."[1]

For others, this foundation has become a new way of defining what the practice of critique actually is. For now, we are to see this Kantian pragmatist approach as re-creating politics as a practice of justification.[2] As Rainer Forst has recently written, "One conceives of the political as a specific practice of justification, as the practice of justification in which persons who are subjected to certain norms or institutions that constitute a 'normative order' examine the reasons for the validity of this order and possibly reject and redefine its norms, and in the process also transform this order."[3] Now the project of justification is further defined as a process of exchanging reasons and examining the validity of the reasons offered for any given claim. This is often viewed as occurring in an "ideal speech community," or some other ideal typical category that can be used to gauge the existing forms of communicative and

---

1. Jürgen Habermas, *Truth and Justification* (Cambridge, MA: MIT Press, 2003), 256–57.

2. For an important discussion of the Kantian pragmatist move, see Richard J. Bernstein, *The Pragmatic Turn* (Cambridge: Polity Press, 2010), 168ff.

3. Rainer Forst, *Justification and Critique: Towards a Critical Theory of Politics* (Cam- bridge: Polity Press, 2014), 2, also see 95ff.

justificatory practices.[4] At the core of this political-theoretic program is a philosophical hypothesis about the nature of language, communication, and cognition and how they relate to practical rationality—a hypothesis that ignores the insights of the basic theses developed by first-generation critical theorists and that I seek to develop here against this Kantian pragmatist turn in contemporary critical and political theory.

The real issue that ought to concern a valid critical theory of society is focused on the problem of reviving critical thought as calling into question the prevailing norms and institutional configurations of the social order. The question that concerns me most is how justification is assumed to have the power to enable participants to come to some kind of critical confrontation with reality, as if the practice of discourse is somehow separate from the reifying and intellectually stultifying world of mass consumer society. The persistent constriction of the public sphere in modern capitalist societies must remain the core focus of any critical social theory. Habermas is not blind to the powerful effects this has on his general project of a discourse ethic for a rational democratic society. As he has noted at length:

> Administrative intrusions and constant supervision corrode the communicative structure of everyday contacts in families and schools, neighborhoods and local municipalities. The destruction of solidary living conditions and the paralysis of initiative and independent engagement in overregulated yet legally uncertain sectors go hand in hand with the crushing of social groups, associations, and networks; with

---

4. Thus, Dietrich Böhler maintains: "The validity claim of a meaningful argument is thus necessarily the claim that all consistent participants in argumentation, under ideal preconditions of understanding, competence and speech, would recognize the argument as valid so that *à la longue a true consensus is to be expected in the unlimited community of argumentation*; i.e., a consensus which, if all the grounds or all relevant grounds that support the argument are understood and considered by all the participants, would arise in the process of argumentation." "Transcendental Pragmatics and Critical Morality: On the Possibility and Moral Significance of a Self-Enlightenment of Reason," in S. Benhabib and F. Dallmayr (eds.), *The Communicative Ethics Controversy* (Cambridge, MA: MIT Press, 1990), 116. Also see the more developed discussion by Ernst Tugendhat, *Self-Consciousness and Self-Determination* (Cambridge, MA: MIT Press, 1986).

indoctrination and the dissolution of cultural identities; with the suffocation of spontaneous public communication. Communicative rationality is thus destroyed simultaneously in both public and private contexts of communication. The more the bonding force of communicative action wanes in private life spheres and the embers of communicative freedom die out, the easier it is for someone who monopolizes the public sphere to align the mutually estranged and isolated actors into a mass that can be directed and mobilized in a plebiscitarian manner.[5]

Here Habermas seems to be channeling the critical orientation of first-generation critical theorists, particularly with the insistence on how the massification of society and the increasing efficiency of soft forms of hegemonic cultural power have been able to destroy the communicative relations that are to constitute a public sphere capable of calling into question and mitigating the forces of power anathema to democratic life. Despite Habermas's more grim and realist outline of the tendencies of contemporary society, I would like to take this problem further and suggest that there is a deeper, more intractable issue with the project of constructing a "critical" theory along the lines of a justificatory liberalism. Indeed, the intricacies of social power should be viewed not only as external to the individual in terms of his isolation from others and the demise of communicative practices. It is perhaps more lethal to the discourse-theoretic paradigm to see how the nature of reified power relations can shape the intentionality of the subject, of cognition, and effectively distort the cognitive content of epistemic and moral knowledge. Indeed, this was what Lukács first uncovered in his theory of reification: that the forms of modern social power exert pressures on consciousness and thought processes in such a way as to shape the cognitive capacities of subjects, to essentially render them constitutive members of the forms of power that rob them of critical consciousness in the first place. Dissecting how social power can achieve this is the my next concern before turning to an alternative approach to the semantics of moral communication.

---

5. Jürgen Habermas, *Between Facts and Norms: Contributions to a Discourse Theory of Law and Democracy* (Cambridge, MA: MIT Press, 1996), 369.

The Nature of Constitutive Social Power

As a basic entrée into my critique of the pragmatist approach in contemporary critical theory, I explore the concept of constitutive domination.[6] According to this view, power works not simply in material terms but constitutes the very cognitive and personality of the individual. It is a kind of power linked to institutionalized forms of power and the kind of legitimating ideas and norms routinized within those institutional contexts. Power plays an active, formative role in ego development, but at a more fundamental level, it plays a strong role in shaping the world of discourse, by which I mean that the shared basic value orientations that individuals attach to the statements generated in the life-world and that form general patterns of belief systems.[7] Unlike concrete forms of power (such as the power of social extraction, exploitation, or coercion), which grant certain agents the ability to divert resources, human capacities, and so on, constitutive power grants agents the capacity to shape norms, codify laws, routinize value patterns, and, as a result, orient consciousness of other agents.

---

6. Elsewhere, I have explored this theme with more depth. See Michael J. Thompson, *The Domestication of Critical Theory* (London: Rowman and Littlefield, 2016), 15–38, and Michael J. Thompson, "The Two Faces of Domination in Republican Political Theory," *European Journal of Political Theory*, vol. 17, no. 1 (2018): 44–64.

7. Basil Bernstein suggests in his sociological analysis of language that "The key is given in terms of the social significance of society's productive system and the power relationships to which the productive system gives rise. Further, access to, control over, orientation of and change in critical symbolic systems, according to the theory, is governed by these power relationships as these are embodied in the class structure. It is not only capital, in the strict economic sense, which is subject to appropriation, manipulation and exploitation, but also cultural capital in the form of the symbolic systems through which man can extend and change the boundaries of his experience." *Class, Codes and Control: Theoretical Studies towards a Philosophy of Language*, vol. 1 (New York: Shocken Books, 1975), 160. Although Bernstein's model is overly mechanistic, we can see it as a basis for moving further into how value orientations and value patterns in the society become embedded in the cognitive frames of meaning of the individual as well as the symbolic forms of meaning that shape communication and language. What is needed is to take this thesis into a more nuanced level where the features of cognition are shaped through the kinds of institutional and cultural norms that are shaped by the dynamics and logics of concrete social power resources.

To have this kind of power means to have the capacity to constitute the subjectivity of subjects, to shape the psychological and cognitive processes and content of others.

What does this mean exactly? For one thing, it means more than simply the manipulation of the symbolic domain of meaning, although it includes this. Constitutive power is a capacity to shape the domain of social facts, indeed, to shape the social reality itself, the domain of what we see as legitimate and valid in any normative sense. This cannot be done by an individual alone, only through the gradual and consistent shaping of social facts through the creation or transformation of norms. These norms govern the very intentional states that give shape to consciousness and cognition. A norm of this kind is what theorists of collective intentionality refer to as "constitutive rules," or those kinds of rules of thinking that orient cognitive patterns and practices such that people come to posit certain normative meanings to things, thereby creating them as social facts.[8] In this sense, the use of money is contingent on the collective acceptance of a constitutive rule, or norm of thought and action, that renders rectangular slips of paper into the social fact of "money" and all of this significance and power that the concept of "money" possesses. This means that there is an inescapable social ontology granting social power its reality as a social fact: it works through the efficient cause of manipulating and erecting these constitutive rules into different configurations and constellations such that a certain kind of social reality is produced and secured.

If this is the case, we can also see that a basic means for this kind of power lies in how social facts can be constructed and re-created through time in the minds of any social group and its members. One way of seeing this is to acknowledge how social relations shape and structure the domain of symbolic meaning used not only in communication but also in self- and other relations more generally. In this sense,

---

8. For a discussion, see John Searle, *The Construction of Social Reality* (New York: Free Press, 1996); John Searle, *Freedom and Neurobiology: Reflections on Free Will, Language, and Political Power* (New York: Columbia University Press, 2007); and John Searle, *Making Sense of the Social World: The Structure of Human Civilization* (New York: Oxford University Press, 2010). Also see Raimo Tuomela, *Social Ontology: Collective Intentionality and Group Agents* (New York: Oxford University Press, 2013).

the primary problem becomes how the socialization process is able to formulate some basic elements of the self and its cognitive capacities. As Basil Bernstein pointed out in the 1970s, "the process of socialization is a complex process of control, whereby a particular moral, cognitive and affective awareness is evoked in the child and given a specific form and content."[9] We can move beyond this basic process into a more intimate mechanism of thought once we see that the mechanisms of evaluative thought and rationality have both a cognitive and a normative basis. This means that the kind of thinking that produces social facts is a distinctive way of thinking about and in the world. According to this view, there is a kind of collective intentionality that can work its way through the rules of thought and action that articulate what we as social actors share as a legitimate reality. Because these social facts are the result of the normative rules that we use to understand empirical and evaluative claims, we can now see that the problem of values is entwined within the nexus of constitutive power. This is because the central locus of power can be seen in how the fabric of norms underpin the cognitive powers of social reasoning.

The individual ego internalizes through processes of routinization and rationalization certain kinds of value orientations that exist to give facticity and legitimacy to certain structures of social relations. As a result, these value concepts and value orientations inhere in the personality and the cognitive processes of the ego. The generative power of these value orientations acts on language and communication just as it acts on the epistemic and evaluative capacities of the self. The key insight I wish to press here is that value orientations are the moral-conceptual variables shaping and underwriting the cognitive and constitutive rules of thought and social action, thereby shaping and creating not only subjective worldviews but also concrete forms of social reality. Hence, values have more than simply a normative function; they also lay the foundation for a basic descriptive account of reality itself. The key issue is the extent to which the normative basis of collective intentionality is able to firm up the existent social reality and weaken the capacity of the subject to call into question, bring to conscious awareness, the deep-rootedness of those norms and their capacity to shape cognition,

---

9. Bernstein, *Class, Codes and Control*, vol. 1, 162.

let alone moral-evaluative consciousness.[10] The decline of the individual as a critical subject remains the stubborn problem—a problem that classical critical theorists knew was the decisive barrier to the modern individual's capacity to grasp, let alone articulate, an objective, emancipatory interest.[11]

---

10. This seems to me to be the most salient weakness of the communicative and justificatory approach to critical theory. Indeed, as Brian Caterino, an advocate of the Habermasian approach to critical inquiry, has recently admitted: "An emancipatory theory also has to recognize that the kind of justifications and ways of making sense are not just embedded in the representations of the world but in the structures of personality and identity of participants along with forms of socialization. These too can limit the communicative freedom of individuals. The formation of personalities that are excessively obedient to authority or on the other hand authoritarian, can have a strong influence on the ability to interpret the world and on one's sense of past injustices and future possibilities. Some of these elements may well be 'unconscious.' A critical theory of ideology following if the not the substance the spirit of the early Frankfurt School researches, have to account for these issues." *The Practical Import of Political Inquiry* (New York: Palgrave Macmillan, 2016), 120–21.

11. This was the powerful result of the theory of reification explored by Lukács, whose central concern was the extent to which the reification of consciousness resulted in a distorted form of cognition that in turn could not grasp the true totality of society. Similarly, Max Horkheimer points to how the decline of the individual can be viewed as a problem of "adaptation," or the gradual and general acceptance of the imperatives and norms of the rational-technical world: "Just as all life today tends increasingly to be subjected to rationalization and planning, so the life of each individual, including his most hidden impulses, which formerly constituted his private domain, must now take the demands of rationalization and planning into account: the individual's self-preservation presupposes his adjustment to the requirements for the preservation of the system. . . . Therefore, adjustment becomes the standard for every conceivable type of subjective behavior." *The Eclipse of Reason* (New York: Continuum, 1974), 95–96. If we take Horkheimer's thesis, we can see that the mechanism is one of power: the subject comes to adapt itself to the prevailing norms of the community. This is perhaps a more pervasive process than Horkheimer lets on. Talcott Parsons is perhaps better at showing how socialization reproduces the functional and normative basis of the social system as a whole, see *The Social System* (New York: Free Press, 1951). For my purposes here, it is sufficient to reference the thesis that individuality becomes more absorbed into the nexus of norms, leaving less and less subjective thought to speculative reasoning and therefore less capacity to critique and call into question the very norms that socialize a person.

The effects of constitutive domination can be one of two broad kinds. First, it can lead to a unification of certain basic value concepts and value orientations that become shared and fundamental to large segments of the population. In this sense, such norms and values have an integrative power in that they become routinized and internalized by agents, thereby granting social institutions legitimacy and stability. These fundamental values and norms become reified in consciousness and secured as background conditions shaping cognitive and evaluative styles of thinking and, as I explore below, the semantic layers of language and communication. Second, there is the problem of the creation of pathological forms of emotive and affectual attitudes brought to bear because of defective forms of socialization. Unequal societies give rise to frustrations and anxieties that pour into the moral cognition of subjects as authoritarian and irrational attitudes that come to shape epistemic notions about how the world is and how it works. Racism, sexism, and other forms of authoritarian attitudes become routinized as responses to certain types of social problems and crises generated by the system.[12] This means that those value and belief systems that contain authoritarian attitudes can have a deep effect on how certain kinds of legitimacy and illegitimacy are conceived and how objective reality is structured for such subjects.[13] Once personalities have internalized these kinds of value patterns and belief systems and worldviews have been constructed, they become difficult to root out, mainly because they actively shape and distort the epistemic/cognitive processing of factual

---

12. Contemporary research on this theme is large. See, for instance, Jim Sidanius and Felicia Pratto, "Racism and Support of Free-Market Capitalism: A Cross-Cultural Analysis," *Political Psychology*, vol. 14, no. 3 (1993): 381–401; Stanley Feldman and Karen Stenner, "Perceived Threat and Authoritarianism," *Political Psychology*, vol. 18, no. 4 (1997): 741–70; Edward J. Rickert, "Authoritarianism and Economic Threat: Implications for Political Behavior," *Political Psychology*, vol. 19, no. 4 (1998): 707–20; J. Duckett and K. Fischer, "The Impact of Social Threat on Worldview and Ideological Attitudes," *Political Psychology*, vol. 24, no. 1 (2003): 199–222.

13. See the discussion by Mark P. Worrell, *Dialectic of Solidarity: Labor, Antisemitism and the Frankfurt School* (Leiden: Brill, 2008), 253ff., and Josef Gabel, *False Consciousness: An Essay on Reification* (New York: Harper and Row, 1975), 145ff. I have elaborated the dynamics of false consciousness as a pathology of social cognition in Michael J. Thompson, "False Consciousness Reconsidered: A Theory of Defective Social Cognition," *Critical Sociology*, vol. 41, no. 3 (2015): 449–61.

information and argument, not the other way around.[14] They also fuse certain affectual and cathectic elements of the personality to those value orientations presenting a further barrier to self-transformation through rational-discursive practices.

What is therefore crucial in the theory of constitutive domination is the mechanism of homogenizing and ingraining norms and values that can secure the acceptance, at the level of the individual, of social forms of power. Attitudes toward power, authority, structures of right/ wrongness, and beliefs about what is good, proper, deviant, threatening, and so on, all become deeply embedded in the psychological complex of the ego and have an active force on the generative principles of language and the epistemic processing that accompanies linguistic communication. The key here is to see that social norms shape cognitive and evaluative capacities within the subject by socializing them into normative schemes and value patterns that they will, in time, accept as legitimate and basic. This becomes the basis of the collective intentionality of the community, of the very kinds of coordinated thinking and acting that creates and re-creates social reality. These value patterns and normative schemes are not simply social abstractions. For them to have any real

---

14. Advocates of discourse ethics seem oddly deaf to the research showing this relationship between values and cognitive thought. For some exemplary studies, see C. Lord, L. Ross, and M. Lepper, "Biased Information and Attitude Polarization: The Effects of Prior Theories on Subsequently Considered Evidence," *Journal of Personality and Social Psychology*, vol. 37, no. 11 (1979): 2098–109; Philip Tetlock, "Cognitive Style and Political Belief Systems in the British House of Commons," *Journal of Personality and Social Psychology*, vol. 46, no. 2 (1984): 365–75; J. Koehler, "The Influence of Prior Beliefs on Scientific Judgments of Evidence Quality," *Organizational Behavior and Human Decision Processes*, vol. 56 (1993): 28–55; D. Larson, "The Role of Belief Systems and Schemas in Foreign Policy Decision-Making," *Political Psychology*, vol. 15, no. 1 (1993): 17–33; C. K. W. De Greu and P. Van Lange, "The Impact of Social Value Orientations on Negotiator Cognition and Behavior," *Personality and Social Psychology Bulletin*, vol. 21, no. 11 (1995): 1178–88; Jonathan Haidt, "The Emotional Dog and Its Rational Tail: A Social Intuitionist Approach to Moral Judgment," *Psychological Review*, vol. 108, no. 4 (2001): 814–34; J. Kuklinski, P. Quirk, J. Jerit, and R. Rich, "The Political Environment and Political Competence," *American Journal of Political Science*, vol. 45, no. 2 (2001): 410–24; George Lakoff, *Moral Politics: How Liberals and Conservatives Think* (Chicago: University of Chicago Press, 2002); B. Gaines, J. Kuklinski, P. Quirk, B. Peyton, and J. Verkuilen, "Same Facts, Different Interpretations: Partisan Motivation and Opinion on Iraq," *Journal of Politics*, vol. 69, no. 4 (2007): 957–74.

power in the world, they also have to shape cognition and, *ex hypothesi*, shape the nature of moral-semantic meaning and descriptive-semantic meaning. Language is unable to escape the force of value patterns and thus cannot be a secure or reliable means out of the refractions of norms and values that secure domination and subjectivist/irrationalist worldviews. In short, it cannot serve as a means of social or moral critique. Language as thought and communication now becomes affected, and this is where the domain of power and the domain of language clash, posing a mortal problem for the project of discursive justification as a critical theory of society.

Two Spheres of Moral Semantics

If constitutive power has any degree of success in shaping the value patterns of a culture and individuals more specifically, then it has the capacity to shape linguistic meaning and communication itself. Herein lies a central weakness to the pragmatist thesis in critical theory, one that has gone largely unchallenged in critical theory circles. What is overlooked are the ways the structure of language can be shaped to reproduce power relations and serve a noncritical or indeed affirmative function in the reproduction of the existent reality rather than a critical engagement with it. Recall that I argued already that constitutive power largely operates by routinizing, rationalizing, and socializing value orientations that are internalized by subjects. Power, rather than open-ended discourse and communication, is the descriptive reality of these institutional logics to the extent that they seek to orient the behaviors and actions of individuals and, more critically, create a sphere of validity around the projects and relations that relate to the interests of those in power as well as system stability more generally. In this sense, the success of any kind of power relation lies in the capacity of those with power to socialize agents into a basic acceptance of the dominant value system that allows for the functional efficiency of the social order. As I suggested, since constitutive power organizes not only symbolic meaning but also the norms and value orientations of individuals, we can see that linguistic meaning can operate on two different levels.

But what if this model of language and communication is misguided? What if we cannot rely on the thick assumptions about the rationality of language and language use that Habermas and his followers assume as basic to their theory? This does not mean embracing an antirationalist position but a position that takes up the sociological theory of power that I have been describing and how this can shape and affect the structure of language and communication in more general ways. Recall that for Habermas the objectivity condition for communicative action is found in the structure of language and the capacity for moral-cognitive statements to lead to a transformation of consciousness and a value-consensus *viz* rational norms. Inherent in the pragmatic use of language is the illocutionary effect where discourse about moral concerns implicitly raises validity claims that need to be validated through rational discourse. But this fuses the syntactic structure of language and the pragmatic action of communication too soon, without any consideration of how latent value orientations and value concepts play a role in shaping the universe of semantic meaning. On this view, any statement uttered must rely on some moral-evaluative infrastructure that grants the descriptive superstructure of manifest meaning its coherence. If this is the case, language is not only embedded in forms practice, it is, more important, supported by normative concepts absorbed in socialization, which form a conceptual-interpretive membrane through which language must move.

One way of thinking about this problem is to see that there exists a problematic distinction between different levels of meaning in linguistic communication. One reason for this is that the external domain of linguistic facts can be differentiated from the internal domain of interpretive meaning that individuals attach to those linguistic facts. What opens up here is a separation between the semantic and hermeneutic dimensions of language, as Hans-Georg Gadamer has argued. Gadamer makes use of this distinction by contrasting the semantic and hermeneutic divide in the experience of language use, arguing:

> Semantics appears to describe the range of linguistic facts externally, as it were, and does so in a way that has made possible the development of a classification of types of behavior with respect to these signs. . . . Hermeneutics, in contrast, focuses upon the internal side of our use of this world of signs, or better said, on the internal process of speaking, which if viewed from the outside, appears as our use of the world of signs. Both semantics and hermeneutics

thematize at some time along their own ways the totality
of our relationship to the world that finds its expression in
language, and both do this by directing their investigations
behind the plurality of natural languages.[15]

Gadamer's thesis here is that the distinction between a world of socially
posited and accepted linguistic "facts" operates within a different sphere
of experience from the interpretive meaning applied to those signs as
we experience them phenomenologically in consciousness. If this is the
case, Gadamer continues, we will be forced to accept a certain limitation
to the attempt to derive a thoroughgoing objective sphere of meaning
in linguistic communication. We must instead accept that:

> Linguistic expressions, when they are what they can be, are
> not simply inexact and in need of refinement, but rather,
> of necessity, they always fall short of what they evoke and
> communicate. For in speaking there is always implied a
> meaning that is imposed on the vehicle of the expression,
> that only functions as a meaning behind the meaning and
> that in fact could be said to lose its meaning when raised
> to the level of what is actually expressed.[16]

The divide between the realm of linguistic facts and that of interpretive meaning grows into a distinct division between different spheres
of meaning in that the semantic field of language entails a system of
objective, socially accepted set of factual meanings that are generally
accepted as true and valid in some basic sense.[17] This does not mean
that the internal, hermeneutic sphere of meaning used by the subject
will be congruous with others, making the nature of moral discourse
and communication particularly problematic and thereby constraining

---

15. Hans-Georg Gadamer, "Semantics and Hermeneutics," in *Philosophical Hermeneutics* (Berkeley: University of California Press, 1976), 82–83.

16. Gadamer, "Semantics and Hermeneutics," 88.

17. Again, Bernstein is insightful on this point, arguing that "Universalistic meanings
are those in which principles and operations are made linguistically explicit whereas
particularistic orders of meaning are meanings in which principles and operation
are relatively linguistically implicit." *Class, Codes and Control*, vol. 1, 163.

the possibility of mutual agreement and the acceptance of justificatory validity claims.[18]

Pushing Gadamer's insight further, we can perhaps pose the problem this way: that the differentiation emerging between factual meaning and hermeneutic meaning can be ascribed to how value orientations can shape consciousness and cognition by shaping the universe of moral semantics. This means that one of the core theses supporting the project of a discourse ethics, taken from Wittgenstein, cannot be maintained when it comes to moral discourse. For Wittgenstein, the very possibility of language was rooted to a prior agreement about judgments. "If language is to be a means of communication," he writes, "there must be not only an agreement in definitions, but (strange as this may sound) an agreement in judgments (*Urteilen*)."[19] I think that value orientations shape these prior normative judgments, and although communiucation will be possible between people with these different value judgments, they will not (necessarily) be able to come to agreements about these value concepts. It is also possible for these prior judgments to be rendered basic and as background conditions, thereby sealing off larger social imperatives from critical awareness and reflection. In the end, I hope to show that this poses real problems for the Kantian, pragmatist, and justificatory turn in critical theory because these approaches are unable to deal with the structural problems that allow for the socialization of values and norms that disable discourse and justification from playing a critical role in modern societies.

---

18. Pierre Bourdieu implies a similar point when he makes sociological sense from the linguistic distinction between "denotation" and "connotation": "If, in contrast to denotation, which represents the 'stable part, common to all speakers,' connotation refers to the singularity of individual experiences, this is because it is constituted in a socially characterized relation to which the recipients bring the diversity of their instruments of symbolic appropriation. The paradox of communication is that it presupposes a common medium, but one which works—as is clearly seen in the limiting case in which, as often in poetry, the aim is to transmit emotions—only by eliciting and reviving singular, and therefore socially marked, experiences." *Language and Symbolic Power* (Cambridge, MA: Harvard University Press, 1991), 39.

19. Ludwig Wittgenstein, *Philosophical Investigations* (Oxford: Blackwell, 1953), §242.

Constitutive Power, Moral Cognition, and Linguistic Communication

I want to argue now that the two spheres of moral semantics consti-tute a distinct structure in moral discourse. We can refer to these two spheres as *descriptive* and *normative* levels of meaning, where the former serves a denotive and the latter a kind of connative function in moral cognition and moral discourse. This distinction leads us to see how the value orientations absorbed through socialization become ingrained in the moral-cognitive frames of understanding that give shape and structure to linguistic forms of communication and the objective-factual levels of meaning in an agent's moral epistemology. In this section, I want to show how this dual structure of semantic meaning works and how it can lead to the problem of moral and epistemic polarization rather than toward mutual consensus around objective forms of moral validity.

My first proposition can therefore be stated:

(α) Normative statements and utterances are tied to value concepts.

Because the core of moral discourse is uttering normative statements, it is important to see that these statements reflect basic value concepts and value orientations that shape the deeper personality structure of the self and the cognitive and evaluative capacities of any agent. Value concepts and orientations therefore play a social function in the sense that they orient the cognitive and evaluative patterns of the self toward certain predefined social norms and values. Language is not simply a syntactic process but a semantic one, the content of which relies on the internalization of certain normative concepts that underwrite the thought processes and normative-evaluative powers of the individual.[20]

---

20. Aaron Cicourel has insightfully noted in reference to this that "the problem of meaning or semantic interpretations of sentences (as bounded by formal gram-matical rules or across open texts) is similar to the idea of inherently meaningful internalized norms and attitudes; there is an implication that a lexicon exists with obvious meanings for all competent users." *Cognitive Sociology: Language and Meaning in Social Interaction* (London: Penguin, 1972), 45. This is in contrast to the standard approach in the philosophy of language where semantic theory is simply seen as

This leads me to my second proposition:

(β) The semantics of any moral-evaluative statement have both descriptive and normative layers of meaning.

This means that any utterance that has some degree of normative force will be linked to a value orientation embedded in the psychological complex of the ego. Speakers and hearers may possess either congruent or asymmetric value systems, which would mean that any given utterance can either be easily processed and agreed to or, in the case of asymmetric systems, lead to fundamental forms of misunderstanding in that attempts to reach objective, factual-descriptive meaning is distorted by the force of the value field shaping the semantics of descriptive and normative valences of meaning. Hence, the last thesis that completes my argument can be stated as:

(γ) The value concepts of speaker and hearer are involved in the utterance and interpretation of value concepts that are internalized through socialization and that underlie the syntactic and generative mechanisms of language use.

This third thesis means that there exists an essential kind of implication in moral utterances and discourse where words and statements relate to a complex semantic field that ties the descriptive and normative layers of meaning together. The illocutionary effect of the utterance therefore misses the deeper problem of the ways that the cognitive content of statements are affected by embedded value-orientations. Hence, we can distinguish between different kinds of utterances, the first exemplified by:

The box is red.
Stones are heavy.
It rains every other Saturday.

These have no significant normative-semantic dimension. The second, those with normative weight and underwritten by value concepts, are exemplified by:

---

referencing a lexicon of meanings but not with any socially relevant, functional purpose. See Jerrold J. Katz, *The Philosophy of Language* (New York: Harper and Row, 1966), 151ff.

The market necessitates we close this factory.
Taxing the wealthy will hurt economic growth.
The poor are the way they are because they lack initiative.
Homosexuals should be permitted to marry.
Human beings are competitive by nature.

In these utterances, there are not only claims to normative validity insofar as they have an illocutionary force. There are also deep structures of moral-semantic meaning being conveyed as well. For the first group of sentences communicate nonnormative forms of information. "Stones," "rain," "boxes," the color "red," and so on have merely descriptive valences of meaning in these contexts in the sense that they communicate empirical or objective-factual meaning to the listener. When we deal with utterances that contain words such as "market," the "poor," "homosexuals," "marry," and so on, we are dealing with the descriptive layer of meaning and a normative level of meaning. By this I mean that not just objective-factual knowledge is being communicated—that is, what poor people are, what a market is, what a homosexual is, and so on—but some normative sense of what those things mean in terms of values or at the level of normative knowledge claims (i.e., homosexuals are deviant, the market is a good thing, poor people are lazy, and so on). This, in turn, reflects deeper structures of evaluative meaning: laziness is deviant, deviance is threatening, and so on.

This means that value orientations need to be seen as more than a matter of opinions at the conscious level, open to dispute and potential transformation.[21] They are more basically embedded in forms of consciousness that shape how an individual cognizes the world in normative terms. These forms of thought can be so basic to the individual's personality that they do not recognize them as values at all but as matters of fact. Consider, then, the hypothesis that moral utterances can be rooted in value orientations to such an extent that communicative action would not be able to lead to mutual understanding, but would instead lead to the oppositional views. Any moral or normative statement can be broken down to show its different semantic or moral-conceptual components. Take the following two sentences as simple examples:

---

21. For a defense of discourse ethics from this presupposition, see Mark E. Warren, "Can Participatory Democracy Produce Better Selves? Psychological Dimensions of Habermas's Discursive Model of Democracy," *Political Psychology*, vol. 14, no. 2 (1993): 209–34.

(1) Homosexuals should not be allowed to marry.
(2) Muslims should not be permitted to build a mosque.

In each sentence, there exist two different kinds of information being communicated simultaneously. First, there are concepts that we can call operators in that they simply direct the normative statement toward a specific end. In the first sentence, it would be contained in the verb "allow," which expresses simply whether one should or should not do something. This lacks a specific value content in that it is just an indicator that is either positive or negative, there are no valences of meaning that can be disputed in "allowing" or "permitting."

But other words have what I call valences of meaning in that they express multiple layers and kinds of meaning at once. Homosexuality is an objective descriptor for a particular sexual orientation and particular sexual practices (we can call this its *descriptive valence*), but it also has a normative layer of meaning as well in that one might see homosexuality referring to more than the mere description of sexual orientation but also a sense of the right/wrongness of that behavior and of that concept (we can call this its *normative valence*). The other elements of the sentence are concepts that are both descriptive and normative. "Homosexual," for instance, is a descriptive noun indicating a type of sexual preference. But it also possesses an intrinsic normative component, a value orientation that the subject attaches to it. I distinguish the different parts of the sentence by using brackets for indicators and parentheses for value concepts. When I am diagramming a sentence to isolate its different normative and descriptive valences, I use parentheses (*) to indicate words that link to value concepts, brackets [*] to isolate operative terms that are parts of the sentence establishing the verbal component of the sentence, and slashes /*/ to distinguish normatively and operationally neutral parts of the sentence. For Habermas, the weight of the illocutionary force of any utterance is put on the operative terms. But my argument here is that the real crux of the problem lies not in the illocutionary but in the semantic levels of language. Hence the statement above can be rewritten:

(1') (Homosexuals) [should not] /be/ [allowed] /to/ (marry).

This indicates that the value concepts making up the statement cannot be circumscribed simply by the syntax of language because each value concept is not merely a descriptor but also a value indicator. Two hearers will therefore cognize different things when they cognitively process the words "homosexual" and "marry" because they are interpreted according to different value orientations. Take the second sentence as an example:

(2') (Muslims) [should not] /be/ [permitted] /to build/ /a/ (mosque).

Here we have another example of how certain words can be seen as having a descriptive and normative valences. We can specify the descriptive and value-laden valences of sentence and rewrite this as:

(2") (Muslims)$\{^d_v$ [should not] /be/ [permitted] /to build/ /a/ (mosque)$\{^d_v$

In this diagram, d represents the descriptive valence of meaning communicated by the word and v the value-concept or normative layer it has. We can call the first the *descriptive level of meaning* for the utterance and the second the *normative level of meaning* of the same utterance. We can see that the linguistic utterance is not rational in itself as a result of its syntactic properties but can be potentially irrational in the sense that the values attached to each concept can be different for different speakers and hearers. This means that the attempt to use language as a means to resolve conflict or come to mutual understanding is more likely to occur between people who have similar or homogeneous values or do not have closed-minded forms of cognition. I discuss this more later in this chapter; for now, it suffices to point to the thesis that descriptors may be shared in common with other speakers and hearers, whereas values come into conflict. But it could also be that the valence for each value concept is linked to others. In the case of "Muslim," it could be, in the case of a racist, that the normative valence is attached to a series of other valences such as "evil," "frightening," or "violent." In this sense, such a hearer or speaker could cognize the word "Muslims" as possessing a descriptive and normative valence simultaneously.

This results from the thesis that the objective-factual dimension of cognition and language is entwined with the value-orientational dimension of moral cognition. The manifest expression of communication may be the same on the descriptive level for two different hearers, but have different normative-evaluative connotation for each of them. Hence, the utterance of "Muslim" or of "mosque," let alone "homosexual" or "marry," may have distinct value-orientational implications for each hearer. These examples are meant to demonstrate how these value orientations can lead to different shapes of meaning and how communication can be stunted and lead not to a paradigm of justification and mutual agreement on norms but to an incapacity for justification and a polarization of groups.[22] This is because the normative valence of meaning attached to the words "homosexual" or "Muslim," and so on, affect the cognitive content of those statements. Indeed, even though they still have an illocutionary force in raising a validity claim, the central problem is that the actual justification inherent within the statements are shaped not by rational reasons but by certain basic value systems that will shape belief systems. Hence, the blockage posed to mutual understanding, let alone mutual agreement, about norms is rooted in the nonrational forms of value concepts that underwrite the epistemic-descriptive levels of knowledge that pollute the reasons used in each person's justificatory "logic." Here the pragmatist move of the illocutionary dimension of the speech act is sidelined by the greater dilemma posed by the very structure of moral cognition and its effect on linguistic meaning and communication.

Similarly, if we take the earlier sentence as an example, we can see that for a hypothetical utterer or hearer:

$$(1") \ (\text{Homosexuals}) \begin{cases} d = \textit{individuals who are attracted to the same sex} \\ v = \textit{abnormal/unnatural/unhealthy/deviant} \end{cases}$$

[should not] /be/ [permitted] /to/

$$(\text{marry.}) \begin{cases} d = \textit{legal union of two individuals to create a family} \\ v = \textit{legal union between members of the opposite sex} \end{cases}$$

At work here is a structure of meaning rooted not in a meta-language that relates to the object language but in a deeper moral-semantic field

---

22. See Cass Sunstein, "The Law of Group Polarization," *Journal of Political Philosophy*, vol. 10, no. 2 (2002): 175–95, and R. Robinson, D. Keltner, A. Ward, and L. Ross, "Actual versus Assumed Differences in Construal: 'Naïve Realism' in Intergroup Perception and Conflict," *Journal of Personality and Social Psychology*, vol. 68, no. 3 (1995): 404–17.

that comes to attach itself to the conscious level of discourse. Although we can distinguish the descriptive from the normative levels of meaning analytically, it is by no means expected that all speakers and hearers will do the same. In fact, it is perhaps more likely to advance the thesis that the descriptive level is fused to the normative, in which case it becomes difficult for individuals to accept alternative moral concepts that underwrite their conscious ideas about the world. The deep structures in which this moral cognition takes place are distinct from everyday speech in the sense that object-language semantics is distinct from moral-cognitive semantics. In this case, we see that values are attached to a matrix of other values that grant them meaning and orient the subject's cognition of those things. Hence we see what I call a *value field* and how it can be used to understand moral semantics. Figure 3.1 shows how certain value concepts are rooted in deeper levels of consciousness such that utterances make use of words that are tied to particular value orientations and meanings.

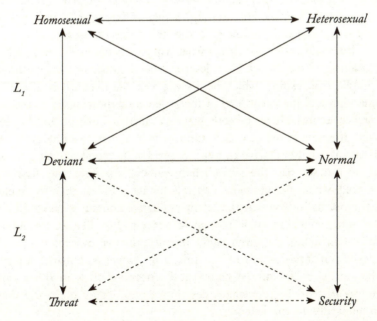

Figure 3.1. Model of Latent and Manifest Semantic Structures in Moral Discourse.

Figure 3.1 shows the hypothesized relation between the object language (L_1) and the value-semantic field that underlies it and gives it shape (L_2). We can also refer to L_1 as the "manifest" meaning of any utterance and to L_2 as the "latent" meaning of that same utterance. Vertical and diagonal lines denote implicative relations and horizontal lines denote oppositional semantic relations. By an "oppositional semantic relation," I mean a semantic relation where the hermeneutic meaning of an utterance, φ, is circumscribed by its evaluative opposite, $\neg\varphi$. Hence, the basic dichotomous structure of values comes into play as an implicature between two opposite poles of that value. Diagonal lines indicate negative implication, by which the meaning of "deviance" signifies some deeper conception of "threat" and is understood to imply that it is the opposite of what is "secure." Any utterance therefore gives rise to a complex of meanings ambient in the utterance and consciousness and is not mediated by language but is experienced as immediate by the speaker/hearer. Hence, the utterance "homosexual," in the example given here, can have a series of descriptive and normative implications that emerge in moral cognition. This can differ in each speaker/hearer to the extent that it distorts the objective-epistemic force of discourse as each participant (or different groups within a deliberative setting) brings different value concepts and hence moral-semantic meaning to the utterances exchanged.

The main reason for this is what happens between the vertical levels of meaning in the model. Each level is related to the one below through an implicative relation, which occurs between the manifest level of communication and the latent level of moral-semantic meaning. Here the same utterance, φ, instantiates a more general evaluative concept that has been linked, through forms of socialization, with the manifest utterance. Now this latent moral-evaluative concept, ψ, gives φ its moral-semantic content, and we can see that the relation between them is essentially functional, $\varphi = \varphi(\psi)$, where the utterance depends for its manifest cognitive content on the normative force of the latent evaluative content generated by the value-scheme within subjective consciousness. Just like at the level of manifest meaning, the given latent moral-evaluative concept has its own opposite semantic relation of $\neg\psi$. This is no longer a connative aspect of φ but forms a part of the hermeneutic meaning of φ; in other words, it forms part of the immediate, descriptive meaning of the world that φ communicates to the listener.

To go further, the latent level of value orientations has its own, deeper structure of implicative relations. For one thing, as described in figure 3.1, we can see that the utterance of "homosexual," a descriptive noun, has not only the implied concept of "deviant" but also a deeper affective-attitudinal implication of "threat." In this case, we can see that the value orienation is related to the more basic, affective concept of "threat," thereby affecting the descrpitive layer of meaning with a normative-evaluative and affective level of meaning in the latent, hermeneutic structure of meaning. Hence, any latent, moral-evaluative concept, ψ, can be seen to instantiate a more basic (in the sense of more basic to the personality and attitudinal structure of the self) affective attitude, Ψ, as part of the basic value system that makes up the subject's particular worldview. Therefore, we can see that any utterance at the descriptive level of meaning is functionally related to deeper, latent values and normative/affective concepts and attitudes or, more simply, as $\varphi = \varphi(\psi[\Psi])$. But here, referring back to Gadamer's distinction between semantic and hermeneutic meaning, we are confronted with the reality that a disconnect exists between the manifest and latent levels of meaning. Once we recognize this, the capacity to come to mutual agreement and consensus on matters of political and practical concern becomes more remote to the extent that a culture is able to shape the moral-evaluative elements of meaning in a society and its socialization processes.

The heart of this thesis can be said to lie in the relation between manifest and latent levels of meaning for any hearer or utterer. This relation entails that an utterance is in a sense polysemantic in that each layer of meaning is related to other through a process of implicature. This means that the relation between the descriptive or objective-factual level of meaning is related to a deeper moral-evaluative conceptual layer of meaning and understanding, via different forms of socialization, that links them. But this is not a simple lexical relation;[23] it is better to see the descriptive level of meaning as implying certain normative

---

23. For instance, Jerrold Katz argues that "the sematic component will have two sub-components: a *dictionary* that provides a representation of the meaning of each of the words in the language, and a system of *projection rules* that provide the combinatorial machinery for projecting the semantic representation for all supraword constituents in a sentence from the representations that are given in the dictionary for the meanings of the words in the sentence." *The Philosophy of Language*, 153. Moral semantics, however, must seek to understand how, in place of a dictionary and projection rules, we deali with value concepts that come to give a normative semantic shape to the descriptive level of meaning. Indeed, Katz's thesis fits better with a more basic model of semantics that deals with value-neutral semantic utterances.

valences of meaning. To say that an utterance implicates a value and that a value implicates an attitude is to say that each resonates with the more basic level of meaning beneath it. Hence "homosexual" can imply either deviance-threat or normal-security depending on the value orientations the subject has. This is a relation characterized by what we can call evaluative implicature, where the value orientations shape the epistemic-descriptive level of utterances.

Therefore, even though a speaker says that-p, and p does not denote q, it can imply q via the semantic shape given to it by ψ. Whereas Paul Grice's theory of "conversational implicature" is meant to describe an aspect of all kinds of utterances,[24] my claim here is that it is both conversational and moral-cognitive. By this I mean that conversational implicature obviously takes place in everyday speech (e.g., where "John ate some of the cookies" = "John did not eat all of the cookies") but that evaluative implicature takes place based on the mechanisms outlined above where certain utterances imply certain deeper moral-evaluative concepts, norms, and so on (e.g., "Homosexuals should not be permitted to marry" = "Since homosexuals engage in deviant behavior, they ought not to be permitted to participate in an institution that is meant for normal people"). What this means is that utterances presuppose a deeper background set of concepts and meaning that the surface or manifest level of language expresses. There exists a more deep-seated structure of meanings that give more particular meanings to specific utterances. This is because, as I have been suggesting, the relation between normative and descriptive layers of meaning imply certain other, more basic and more fundamental psychological value

---

24. Grice urges us to maintain "a distinction between what the speaker has *said* (in a certain favored, and maybe in some degree artificial, sense of 'said'), and what he has *implicated* (e.g., implied, indicated, suggested), taking into account the fact that what he has implicated may be either conventionally implicated (implicated by virtue of the meaning of some word or phrase which he has used) or nonconventionally implicated (in which case the specification of the implicature falls outside the specification of the conventional meaning of the words used)." Paul Grice, *Studies in the Way of Words* (Cambridge, MA: Harvard University Press, 1989), 118. In my concept of evaluative implicature, the speaker/earer who possesses the value orientation ψ will see certain utterances as associated with that value orientation and give certain normative meaning to that utterance. However, this implicature is not simply arbitrary; it is rooted in the moral-cognitive structure of the personality of the self.

orientations and value concepts. Manifest and latent forms of meaning therefore operate on parallel levels and are related through the process of evaluative implicature.

In this sense, any sentence that contains any kind of evaluative statement or contains words that refer to some evaluative concept is related to a series of (perhaps unconscious) value orientations that shape the moral-cognitive understanding of the speaker and listener. Now the descriptive valence of a word, in this case "homosexual," is related to value concepts in ways that nonmoral discourse are not. We would not, for instance (bracketing any mental pathology or eccentricities), associate "house" or "stone" or some other noun with a value field. But words such as "homosexual," "Muslim," and "liberal," not to mention "beautiful," "good," "evil," and so on, undoubtedly do. What makes them important in this regard is that they are open to a pluralism of values that can detract from—indeed, perhaps frustrate and prevent—the capacity of individuals to rationally work toward mutual agreement on norms based on an exchange of argumentative reasons. Rather, what we see emerging is the problem of a deliberative failure where the attempt to establish validity and legitimacy through justificatory reasons alone cannot provide a rational path out of irrationally constructed value patterns and cultural worldviews.

With particularistic value orientations, we can see that the irrationality of the value concepts are transmitted perhaps by the lack of communicative relations with other communities, thereby facilitating a fragmentation of value orientations among different groups (racial, class, and gender groups and so on). Similarly, "mosque" might also link with these same valences and serve to express a cognitive content that is itself objectively biased by values derived from specific socialization pathologies. We could rewrite the sentence again to capture the more complex series of normative valences such a person might express (or hear):

$$(2''') \text{ (Muslims)} \begin{cases} d \\ \psi \\ \Psi \end{cases} \text{[should not] /be/ [permitted] /to build/ /a/ (mosque.)} \begin{cases} d \\ \psi \\ \Psi \end{cases}$$

This means that normative statements all have a complex of valences, both descriptive and normative, and this will affect the cognitive content of the utterance. Hence, although the statement does indeed possess the illocutionary force of raising a validity claim, it nevertheless closes off the possibility of a truly valid validity claim insofar as the more primitive levels of value concepts and value patterns that make up the basic belief system of the speaker/hearer (ψ and Ψ) generate the moral-semantic content of the utterance. It becomes clear that any word expressing a value concept can be seen to have a series of value concepts that in turn shape the moral cognition of the subject. As a result of being braided with the descriptive elements of semantic content, it can even distort epistemic and cognitive claims and powers of reasoning. This entails a problem of reaching mutual consensus as a result of the fragmentation of value spheres in any community. The conception of communicative action as a solvent for irrational beliefs through exposure to counter-factual claims and argument collapses once we realize that the objective dimension of semantic meaning—the descriptive layer of language—is in fact organized by the normative layer of meaning. The project of rooting out bad arguments, correcting incorrect assumptions, and so on are not processes that occur on a merely objective-factual plane of consciousness. Rather, it can be seen that the socialization of norms and values has a real effect on the epistemic domain of the subject, constraining rational thought and instead giving way to rationalizing tendencies or the defense of one's value orientations at the expense of rational justification.[25] Mutual agreement under such circumstances may be impossible and in fact lead to more sociocultural fragmentation as those with similar worldviews clump together against those with different worldviews, and so on.

Reification through the Implicit Validity of Norms

If the deep-rootedness of socialized values and norms in the epistemic and cognitive layers of consciousness are a problem for reaching con-sensus among those who have different value orientations, then an alternate but no less problematic dilemma arises from an opposite, but essentially related problem. In this case, social groups have a consensus

---

25. See the important paper by Dan M. Kahan, "The Cognitively Illiberal State," *Stanford Law Review*, vol. 60 (2007): 101–40. Also see the still relevant discussion by Milton Rokeach, *The Open and Closed Mind* (New York: Basic Books, 1960), 31ff.

about certain norms and rules within the community without having them come to rational scrutiny. This emerges not from the incapacity of individuals to reach mutual consensus based on opposed value orientations, but from how consensus can be fused to the rationalized value patterns of a community with forms of legitimate authority that will impede—perhaps suffocate—the capacity of critique among subjects. What I think is relevant here is not the sense that modern subjects become "oversocialized" as much as they become victimized by a reification of value patterns and value orientations that achieve that reified status as a result of the increasingly efficient means by which rationalized institutions are able to inculcate those values and norms but also have them reflected back through coordinated patterns of mass behavior and practices. These reified norms and values are increasingly entrenched in a culture as the routinization process continues and succeeds in socializing agents into a valid system of norms, thereby cementing attitudes of legitimacy to the prevailing order.

This links to the thesis of reification in the following way: if language can be rooted in specific value orientations, then concepts can be so routinized into consciousness that they become second nature for the subject.[26] A person's value concepts come to underpin the very meaning of those semantic utterances they employ and hear. Hence, value orientations that become cognitively embedded will be processed by the subject—as either hearer or speaker—as different from others. For Habermas and his followers, because consensus takes the place of objective forms of truth, there is no way to ensure that the propositions debated have any kind of correspondence to the real world or to any objective referent. We are unable to secure our normative claims

---

26. The relation between reified value orientations can affect the semantic field by "fixing" certain concepts and signifiers to particular institutional realities. As Rosalind Coward and John Ellis observe: "The production of an ideological *vraisemblable* which is effective precisely for the reason that it appears as 'natural,' 'the way things are,' is the result of a practice of fixing or limiting of the endless productivity of the signifying chain. This fixing is the result of the limiting of certain signifiers to a certain signified or meaning. Limitation does not rely on the imposition of a system of ideas on a natural pre-given sign, but on the construction of a certain subject in relation to a discourse; a subject who then becomes the place of its intelligibility." *Language and Materialism: Developments in Semiology and the Theory of the Subject* (London: Routledge and Kegan Paul, 1977), 67.

against relativism as well as reification.[27] Indeed, there are communities of meaning where groups have an implicit consensus around basic value orientations, a sociological point I explore further later. For now, it is important to understand how linguistic expressions are connected to cognitive content grounded in values that underpin their meaning. The examples given above are perhaps less illustrative of this important point. Indeed, because Lukács was primarily concerned with how rationalization of the systems of production and exchange were becoming embedded in the life-world of individual people, he was more concerned that it was penetrating the structures of consciousness and cognition, leading to forms of implicit consensus on a basic understanding and legitimacy of existent reality. Indeed, it can be seen that the search for consensus constrains the critical activity of subjects, thereby displacing consensus away from critical-rational criteria toward nonconflictual and adaptive criteria of agreement and consensus.[28]

This raises a second but no less pernicious dilemma for the project of Kantian pragmatism and the projects of justificatory critique and discursive self-transformation. This concerns the issue of statements and claims that are essentially impervious in any broad-based requirement for justification. One core pathology of modern society that concerned classical critical theory is the problem of how mass society can integrate

---

27. John Patrick Diggins insightfully notes: "Habermas's hope that consensus can take the place of the older categories of correspondence and coherence as a means of getting around the problem of truth raises the problem of error. His procedure is basically Peirean: a consensus arrived at by investigators whose views have no object of knowing but only ways of discussing and communicating. Can a consensus be freely and constructively arrived at and still be wrong? If the consensus is merely the agreed interpretation, and the interpretation commands assent not because it is closer to the truth of things but rather because it better carries the force of the prevailing argument, how can community participants know that the consensus is not merely another contrived point of view that reconstructs reality rather than represents it?" *The Promise of Pragmatism: Modernism and the Crisis of Knowledge and Authority* (Chicago: University of Chicago Press, 1994), 447–48.

28. See the important paper by Henrik Friberg-Frenros and Johan Karlsson Shaffer, "The Consensus Paradox: Does Deliberative Agreement Impede Rational Discourse?," *Political Studies*, vol. 62, no. 1 (2014): 99–116, and Edward T. Walker, "Legitimating the Corporation through Public Participation," in Caroline W. Lee, Michael McQuarrie, and Edward T. Walker (eds.), *Democratizing Inequalities: Dilemmas of the New Public Participation* (New York: New York University Press, 2015), 66–81.

the ego into a collective framework of thought and feeling to secure social coordination, system legitimacy, and stability. One way this is achieved, when we examine this problem at the level of moral and social cognition, is to have certain value-patterns absorbed through socialization into the normative-evaluative dimensions of the subject. Over time, these values become reified in that they become part of a basic, "second nature" of normative assumptions shared by social actors. This problem we can call implicit validity, where the statements communicate value concepts that are already taken by the community at large to be legitimate and in no need of external validity for them to be accepted as forms of legitimate knowledge about the world. The implicit validity of norms and values is in play whenever a value serves as a basic norm that orients the thought and behavior of a significant amount of the community. Such values have implicit validity insofar as they are taken to be part of a fundamental belief system that constitutes the subject's primary level of social understanding of social facts. The attempt to bring these value concepts and the value orientations to which they give rise is highly difficult and poses perhaps the greatest and most persistently ignored problem for discourse ethics. Ego therefore invests in the values, making a person secure in their respective worldviews.

This gets us to the heart of the pathology of consciousness caused by reification: the problem of restricting the cognition of the subject to the prepatterned value system requisite for the efficiency of social-systemic imperatives.[29] Put another way, reification is not just the imposition of instrumental reason on consciousness, it is the internalization of a system of social norms and value orientations that circumscribe an ever wider frame of social reality. In this sense, the value-semantic field of meaning is unified by forms of rationalized and routinized forms of socialization that grants large segments of any community a basic structure of value concepts (or a basic value pattern) that will

---

29. See Cicourel, who observes: "The acquisition of interpretive procedures provides the actor with a basis for assigning meaning to his environment or a sense of social structure, thus orienting him to the relevance of 'surface rules' or norms." *Cognitive Sociology*, 45 and *passim*. This view holds open the real problem of how social structure and social order gets absorbed not only by consciousness but by the linguistic structures of meaning and communication that permeate the structural-functional forces of modern institutions and their power to shape the epistemic powers of subjects.

shape the legitimacy of the norms and practices of that community.[30] Power to shape these value patterns and have them absorbed by ever larger segments of the community becomes an imperative of constitutive power. The result, at the level of the subject, can be understood as a value or attitudinal congruence between subjects who do not call into question or bring into critical consciousness the basic value pattern they have internalized.[31] What results from this is not a critique of the prevailing norms and institutional reality of the social order but a further cementing of those systems of power. Social critique is displaced by liberal consensus. How could it be otherwise if there is no way for the value concepts to be brought to critical consciousness? How can it serve to critique what is held as basic? The probability of further legitimating forms of domination and authority becomes more likely than the critique of those forms of life.

This further poses a philosophical problem in that the implicit validity of norms means that groups can come to consensus on certain issues of import that deviate from their actual or objective interests. We fall into the problem of epistemic and moral relativism where any community is unable to call into question the foundational values that underpin their institutions and their collective-intentional states of meaning. Hence, the social facts of that community are legitimated and not adequately raised to justificatory consciousness. Even if it were capable of being raised to this level of public awareness, there is no way to secure the public's objective interest as opposed to their relative investment in those values that underpin their consciousness as well as their cognitive capacity to process objective-factual arguments concerning issues of real moral concern.

Language and discourse become the expressions of more deeply seated norms and evaluative concepts in the more primary levels of consciousness and moral cognition where the normative frameworks that guide individual behavior shape the higher conceptual and epistemic categories of meaning and information processing. The central problem becomes the extent to which these values are brought fully to rational awareness in individuals and the community as a whole, something that,

---

30. See Parsons, *The Social System*, 207ff.

31. For more on "attitudinal congruence" and its effects on social cognition, see Thompson, "False Consciousness Reconsidered."

it seems, Habermas saw as an ideal situation for any society. Lacking this overly ambitious idea of reality, we are left with the pathology of the reification of value orientations and its pervasive effects on epistemic capacities. Now language must be seen in the crucible of ideology and therefore from within the frameworks of meaning that value systems and belief systems are able to make ambient within higher levels of consciousness. Communicative action does not have an autonomous way out of this problem because it believes that it can erode power relations through the practice of reason exchange and the search for rational legitimacy and consensus as an essential feature of the validity of values. It seems clear that we are once again thrown back to the classical problem that faced first-generation critical theorists: the problem of reification and ideology and its capacity to constrain critical cognition and progressive, enlightened political activity.

The theoretical supposition that mutual understanding and agreement can follow from the very structure of linguistically mediated communication can now be seen to weaken considerably. If we want to proceed along the Kantian pragmatist path of justificatory agency, the theory of linguistic action and the cognitive content of morality must be able to avoid the kind of pathologies of meaning and understanding that I describe here. Doing this requires, as the thesis of constitutive power suggests, that we can shatter the value fields and patterns that shape consciousness in ways that distort the rational capacity of self-critique and self-awareness. But this assumption of rational autonomy cannot be made in the context of structural-functional logics of inequality, domination, and power relations. Indeed, it rather encourages the problem of epistemic refraction I discussed already, where individuals simply take the normative logics of the existent reality as a background condition and reproduce them in their respective subjective and intersubjective contexts, or it leaves in a condition of epistemic and ethical relativism without any objective criteria for critical judgment. This is the next problem I see as stemming from the alternative theory of language and communication I have sketched here.

A Critique of Justificatory Reason

The model of language and moral semantics that I have been constructing now can be seen to have problematic effects for the project

of justification as a valid branch of critical theory. One thing becomes
clear: the thesis of justification as critique can only succeed if Habermas's
thesis about the essentially rational nature of communication is seen
to hold. Even if we simply see discourse ethics as evincing a kind of
ideal-typical form of action, we are still heading in the wrong direction.
The main reason for this is that we cannot take discourse and language
outside of the power relations that give rise to moral socialization and
distort the moral-semantic structures of communication and cognitive
capacities of agents. Now that I have shown that power relations can
be refracted into the communicative practices and structures of meaning
that operate within the structural-functional systems of social power, it
remains for me to show how this leads the project of justification into
a philosophical, sociological, and ultimately political impasse. Indeed,
it seems clear that any utterance, any statement cannot be described
as rational based purely on the reflexive accountability of statements.
Habermas's postmetaphysical, pragmatist conception of reason therefore
holds that "the rationality of a person is proportionate to his expressing
himself rationally and to his ability to give account for his expressions
in a reflexive stance. A person expresses himself rationally insofar as he
is oriented performatively toward validity claims. . . . We also call this
kind of rationality *accountability* (*Zurechnungsfähigkeit*)."[32]

The pragmatic conception of speech acts Habermas constructs
holds that the illocutionary force of any statement inherently raises a
validity claim that is open to a justificatory exchange between speaker
and hearer. This means that "We understand a speech act when we
know the kinds of reasons that a speaker could provide in order to
convince a hearer that he is entitled in the given circumstances to
claim validity for his utterance—in short, when we know *what makes
it acceptable.* A speaker, with a validity claim, appeals to a reservoir of
potential reasons that he could produce in support of the claim."[33] As
far as I am concerned, this is the crux of the matter. For one thing,
the semantic problem I described above entails that the pragmatic
dimension of language cannot by itself overcome the strong problem
of the cognitive effects that emerge from the shaping of descriptive
valences of language by the normative-evaluative force of background

---

32. Jürgen Habermas, *On the Pragmatics of Communication* (Cambridge, MA: MIT
Press, 1998), 310.

33. Habermas, *On the Pragmatics of Communication*, 232–33.

value orientations. Habermas puts distinctive emphasis on the illocutionary aspects of utterances so he can establish an internal validity claim
to statements oriented toward normative discourse: "The illocutionary
component thereby becomes the locus of a rationality that presents
itself as a structural interconnection between validity conditions, validity
claims that refer to these, and reasons by means of which they may be
vindicated in discourse."[34]

Justification requires that individuals bring reasons to bear on
the matter in question and that this kind of reason-giving capacity
rely on reasons. To call any claim to normative rightness into question
therefore raises the issue of the truth content of the statement being
made.[35] Habermas maintains that one of central dimensions along which
a speech act can be criticized or called into question is its relation to
truth, that is, that the statement being made is truthful or corresponds
to some event or reality in the world.[36] Here is where the problem
of evaluative implicature and its impact on the descriptive aspects of
meaning (and hence on the objective-factual domain of meaning and
knowledge) comes into play. The pragmatic assumption made here is
that the capacity to call speech acts into question as valid or invalid
implies that this capacity is untouched by the distorting effects of value
orientations. The basic value system and belief system of individuals

---

34. Habermas, *On the Pragmatics of Communication*, 232.

35. Habermas claims that any speech act can be called into question as invalid
"from three points of view: as untrue with respect to the statement made (or the
existential presuppositions of its propositional content); as incorrect with respect to
established normative contexts (or the legitimacy of the norms presupposed); or as
lacking in truthfulness with respect to the speaker's intention." Habermas, *On the
Pragmatics*, 231. I concentrate on the first of these three conditions because it gets
us to the core of the pragmatic dimension of moral discourse.

36. This is J. L. Austin's basic definition of truthfulness with respect to any sentence.
Austin says that the descriptive feature of any sentence is true when that statement
"correlates the words (= sentences) with the *types* of situation, thing, event, &c., to
be found in the world." "Truth," in *Philosophical Papers* (Oxford: Oxford University
Press, 1961), 89–90. I take this to be directly related to my understanding of the
"descriptive" level of semantic meaning, discussed already. However, Austin does not
relate this descriptive level to the "normative" level, which can, as I have maintained
in this chapter, affect the capacity to establish valid truth-claims in any objective,
nonrelative sense with respect to a correspondence between an utterance and an
event or thing in the world.

must, as I argued already, be seen to shape and orient the universe of descriptive meaning that grounds a speaker/hearer's capacity to operate in a space of reasons that is in any way amenable to mutual agreement or common understanding. Empirically, we find patterns of this kind emerging: the more controversial, the more morally divisive certain group discussions become, the more polarized groups become.[37] Though we may agree on the descriptive account of some utterance, the normative force of the basic value system can shape that meaning in different ways through evaluative implicature. What results is not a transformation of the self through rational discourse but a prismatic inflection of different value orientations, which can actually cement certain irrational and inenlightened worldviews instead of leading to psychological self-transformation through rational discourse.

This means that the reflexive conception of moral justification cannot serve as an autonomous and foundational concept for social critique. The concept of justification has become so self-confident that it is now seen as capable of serving as a principle of justice. As Rainer Forst has recently written: "Justification of a particular kind are necessary because justice is a matter of being able to *mutually* and *generally* raise and accept claims; and to exclude altruism (with the acceptance of one-sided claims), one should say that justice concerns claims that cannot be reciprocally and generally rejected."[38] How can such an overidealized conception of justification be assumed given the kinds of deliberative, epistemic, and cognitive pathologies that entail from the effects of constitutive power? If, as I have been arguing here, the socialization of norms and values that support certain power relations and/or express authoritarian or intolerant forms of pathological moral cognition can infect the communicative and cognitive structures of thought and language, then we can see that the basic premises necessary for the justificatory project are a philosophical construct at best. Attempts to extend the practice of justification into some kind of basic principle of

---

37. See J. Berdahl and P. Martorana, "Effects of Power on Emotion and Expression during a Controversial Group Discussion," *European Journal of Social Psychology*, vol. 36 (2006): 497–509, and Cass Sunstein, "Deliberative Trouble? Why Groups Go to Extremes," *Yale Law Journal*, vol. 110 (2000): 71–119.

38. Rainer Forst, *The Right to Justification: Elements of a Constructivist Theory of Justice* (New York: Columbia University Press, 2007), 194.

justice therefore misdirect our intellectual efforts.[39] This cannot serve
as a critical theory because it is not possible to secure the capacity
of individuals to call into question the basic values that orient their
worldviews and secure certain forms of coordinated power or social
identities. The assumption of a rational exchange of reciprocal reasons
and validity claims naively sidesteps the problem of the infiltration of
power into the very structures assumed to be the mechanism of critique.

In opposition to this account of rationality, I think there is another,
deeper, and more crucial ground for rationality in that any utterance
has an object to which it refers. On this account, rationality needs to
be construed as the extent to which any utterance can account not only
for itself but for the object it is generated to describe or posit. There
exists, then, an irreducibly ontological dimension to language in that
the object domain to which it refers must have some kind of objective existence. This need not be material, but it need be in some way
objective in that others somehow share in the capacity to judge and
grasp the referent of the utterance. Lacking this, we would not have
real communication at all but a series of idiolects without social sense.
Hence, the object domain is constituted by the collective intentionality
of agents. If this is true, we must also recall that this very capacity and
activity of intentionality is open to the pathology of constitutive power.
Indeed, when constitutive power can be said to infiltrate the intentional
activity of agents, reification can be said to exist in that the very social
reality constituted through their intentional agency is itself shaped and
formed by the power of others. This power of others is what counts
the most: it harks back to the thesis initiated by Rousseau and Marx
concerning the realities of false consciousness and its ability to legitimate forms of social life that are exploitative, unjust, and injurious to
the common interest.

In the end, the deep problem with the project of justification as
type of critical activity is that it falls into the trap of precisely what

---

39. Forst maintains that justification forms the basis for a basic principle of justice: "Within such a framework, therefore, a *highest principle* applies, which prevails
normatively and criterially over all the other values referred to: *the principle of
reciprocal and general justification*, according to which every claim to goods, rights,
or freedoms must be grounded reciprocally and generally, whereby one side may
not project its reasons onto the other, but must discursively justify them." Forst,
The Right to Justification.

first-generation critical theorists saw as so deeply problematic: the problem of how mass societies were capable of molding the personality system of individuals and how these basic personality pathologies shaped the universe of meaning, thereby constraining the capacity to reach objective, rational understanding of the social world. The project of pragmatic justification collapses as a form of practical reason because it is unable to provide a criterion for what kind of content for reason should count as valid and what should not. A critical theory of society must not abandon the concept of discourse and discursive practice but see it as a secondary to the formulation of reasons that has a rational ground in the ontology human sociality. A critical practical reason cannot rely on the exchange of reasons beause there is no valid criterion for how to judge the offered reasons. As Hegel and Marx knew, this requires an ontological component: one that sees reasons as accountable to the object domain and not according to discursive practices. Given the strong force of social pathologies on the formation of selves, the practice of justificatory discourse cannot be relied on to provide a rational-critical set of outcomes.

We should perhaps take this to mean that despite its strong academic and intellectual appeal, the pragmatist turn in critical theory is a kind of surrender in the face of the powerful structural-functional forces that shape social integration, ego development, and moral cognition. Indeed, if the basic hypothesis I have explored here concerning the two spheres of semantic meaning and the resulting inability of language and speech act theory to provide a fulcrum out of the pit of pathological consciousness, then the program of a pragmatic and justificatory critical theory must be abandoned as an adequate paradigm for a critical theory of society. Ideology is not easily evaporated: it roots itself in the conceptual and moral-cognitive structures of thought and intentionality. Advocates of critical theory must not turn their backs on the basic ideas and research program that animated early critical theorists. They rightly saw that social power deforms critical reason; they also saw that only through an account of how social pathologies negated healthy forms of self and sociality could a critical social theory serve some use for political reason.

One last thought. We should not assume from what I have argued here that rationality should be shelved as a criterion of moral judgments or normative concepts. Nor should we assume that communication and discourse are somehow irrelevant. What I maintain, however, is that the notion of politics must be seen once again as essentially conflictual between different groups. We cannot escape this through discourse, nor can we look for the transformation of selves through rational communicative action. Instead, we should begin to accept the view that political struggle must begin with the transformation of the structure of society, that which generated the pathological kinds of personalities and psychological deficits that distort and reify consciousness in the first place. The central reason for this is that critical theory should be able to unmask for us the ideological forms of consciousness that sustain the social order. But ideological forms of consciousness are expressions of forms of socialization, and seeking to dissolve them after they have been ingrained in the value complex of individuals is a not a viable strategy for critique. Perhaps when we see that discourse and justification can play only a small, restricted role, and not serve as a general critical theory of society or a theory of democracy or justice, will we be able to place critical theory in proper relation with the larger project of social transformation and political change.

Chapter 4

Recognition Theory and the
Obfuscation of Critique

As I argued in the previous two chapters, the project of political judgment has been remade by ideas about intersubjectivity, linguistic communication, and other neo-idealist kinds of practice that essentially eject any ontological concerns. These projects have broken with a more robust, more insightful, and more radical project of understanding the mechanisms of social domination, the erosion of character, and the deformations of cognitive and epistemic powers that explain the increasing acceptance of the prevailing social order and the integration and legitimacy of pathological forms of social life.[1] This break was effected with a move toward pragmatist themes on one hand and toward a concern with neo-idealist ideas rooted in Kant and Hegel. This reworking of critical theory was centered on eliminating ideas rooted in Marxism and into a kind of system building that champions the supposed self-transforming powers of intersubjective social action. Whereas Habermas has been highly successful at promoting a Kantian pragmatist paradigm based in discourse, Axel Honneth's work has been premised on a neo-idealist return to Hegelian themes fused to pragmatist ideas about social action and self- and social transformation. I believe this move has been lethal for the actual political relevance of critical theory, that it has drained it of its potency even as it has allowed for

---

1. For a recent expression of these themes in what now passes for critical theory, see Penelope Deutscher and Cristina Lafont (eds.), *Critical Theory in Critical Times: Transforming the Global Political and Economic Order* (New York: Columbia University Press, 2017).

more professionalized success in mainstream intellectual and academic circles. The price paid for winning this acceptance, however, has been dear and it has compromised the very methodological and philosophical commitments of critical theory.

Honneth's project is not exactly nonmetaphysical. He proposes a model of ontogeny based on social relations of recognition that he proposes can serve as a basis for social critique. In this way, he differs from the Kantian strains of Arendt and Habermas. He brings us closer to a social ontological account of sociality. However, what I want to focus on here is the Hegelian pragmatist ideas proposed by Honneth and defend the thesis that it fails the task of fulfilling a critical theory of society. As I see it, the central flaw of recognition theory is that it abstracts its theory of social relations from actual, realist structures of power and domination; it seeks to forge a theory of moral development and social change that is unwarranted given the actual, real nature of modern social life and, as a result, evaporates into a rarefied philosophical system devoid of concrete critical power and potency. Indeed, I will go so far to argue that the turn toward the recognition paradigm in contemporary critical theory constitutes the failure of its aspirations for human emancipation and the confrontation with the nature of modern forms of power and domination. In addition, I maintain that it continues trends in contemporary social theory—trends that began with Habermas's move toward a postmetaphysical turn—to achieve a more nuanced, more sophisticated critique of modern society. Much of this can, I think, be blamed on the embrace of the postmetaphysical turn and on the move away from a more sophisticated reading of Marx and his essential place in any critical theory of society, something I discuss in more detail later. But perhaps most important, it should be seen that the failure of the recognition paradigm is more than an intellectual or academic concern: it also entails diminishing the vibrancy and vitality of the tradition of critical theory more generally.

In this chapter, I present two theses to show how the theory of recognition put forth and developed in Honneth's work fails as a paradigm for critical theory. My main argument is that the theory of recognition cannot achieve the status of a critical theory of society for three reasons. First, it is unable to deal with the dynamics and effects of social power in any meaningful way. Specifically, it is unable to deal with what I see as the core of critical theory as a tradition of thought, what I have called constitutive power. Second, it rests on a flawed theory of the social as intersubjective practices and not as structural and normative based systems of functional integration. This derives from its insistence on the pragmatist ideas that essentially shred society's structural-functional features and reduce society to intersubjective practices. The problem with the pragmatist thesis is that it is insensitive to issues of power and domination and can inculcate conformity to the prevailing reality. By shutting Marx out of his revisionism of critical theory, Honneth ends up defanging it as a system of ideas. The result of these theses is that the theory of recognition fails as a satisfying account of modern social reality and its pathological impulses and trends.

Recognition and Critical Theory

Before I begin to construct my argument against the plausibility of recognition as a viable model for a critical theory of society, I want to point to what I see are its essential, buttressing arguments. Honneth has been consistent in defending the idea of recognition as a critical theory of society because it has what he sees as the defining hallmark of critical theory as an enterprise: the capacity to summon an awareness and transformation on behalf of social agents of the pathological dimensions of their social world via intramundane mechanisms of sociation and self-development. A moral awareness of disrespect and misrecognition are supposed to be rooted in an intrinsic sense of self shaped by the intersubjective-recognitive relations to others in various stages of socialization. The core idea of this approach is that the resources for critical reflection and attitudes are inherent in the very socialization practices that constitute modernity. If we are to take Honneth seriously, then a gradual emancipation of society is happening because of the moral awareness of subjects.

Honneth offers a core argument about the nature of self-formation. The thesis is that recognition carries a symbolic-interactionist dimension that provides subjects with the second-order capacity to see themselves as subjects through interaction with an other: "a subject can only acquire a consciousness of itself to the extent to which it learns to perceive its own action from the symbolically represented second-person perspective."[2] Recognition now can be seen as a process of identity formation and self-formation, one that Honneth sees as developing a

---

2. Axel Honneth, *The Struggle for Recognition: The Grammar of Social Conflicts* (Cambridge, MA: MIT Press, 1995), 75.

practical identity for the subject over time. This core process of identity formation holds much of the descriptive and normative weight for the theory, since Honneth claims that recognition is both a formative and evaluative mechanism. On one hand, it is the means by which we form our sense of self through others and the self-conception of ourselves, our identities. This leads us to have a kind of baseline for how we are respected by others. We seek to have our identities recognized not only by discrete others but through the legal and political system. The "struggle for recognition" is thus the means by which modern subjects seek to change and assert their desire for respect and for their identities to be accepted by the society to which they belong.

Honneth maintains that individuals articulate an identity and a sense of self-worth from the very processes of social relations that constitute them. But these relations are seen as being recognitive relations in that we receive approval and recognition for our actions and for who we are from others. This creates in us a sense of integral identity that constitutes our self-identity as an individual: "human individuation is a process in which the individual can unfold a practical identity to the extent that he is capable of reassuring himself of recognition by a growing circle of communicative partners."[3] Only through the intersubjective pattern of communication that allows for the transfer of emotional ties between subjects is a practical identity able to emerge. This begins in childhood, with relations to parental, specifically "maternal" relations that develop into a search for respect and dignity in the world as adults: "Just as, in the case of love, children acquire, via the continuous experience of 'maternal' care, the basic self-confidence to assert their needs in an unforced manner, adult subjects acquire, via the experience of legal recognition, the possibility of seeing their own actions as the universally respected expression of their own autonomy."[4] To the extent that this happens, we can speak of the existence of an integral sense of self formed through recognition that also comes into tension with the existing social relations that frustrate or deny this recognition in later stages of social development. Hence, the concept of "disrespect" (*Mißachtung*) comes to the fore, which constitutes what Honneth calls a "moral injustice," which, he claims, "is at hand whenever, contrary to

---

3. Honneth, *The Struggle for Recognition*, 249.

4. Honneth, *The Struggle for Recognition*, 118.

their expectations, human subjects are denied the recognition they feel they deserve. I would like to refer to such moral experiences as feelings of social disrespect."[5]

The ideas of "respect" (*Achtung*) and "disrespect" (*Mißachtung*) rest on a prior model of self-development produced by a struggle for one's identity and a need to have one's identity recognized by others. This moves through the initial stage of childhood and then into the secondary stage of an assertion of one's right to be recognized as who one is. The model then culminates with a form of society that has been shaped from these struggles for recognition that grants social integrity and respect to individuals. A new conception of Hegelian "ethical life" (*Sittlichkeit*) now opens up, one that is "now meant to include the entirety of intersubjective conditions that can be shown to serve as necessary preconditions for individual self-realization."[6] Because personal identity is seen to be intersubjectively structured and constituted, according to Honneth the model of recognition provides a convincing paradigm for a critical theory of society. In his view, it meets the theoretical conditions of postmetaphysics, of an intramundane, practical theory of social action, as well as an intersubjective account of social action. All along, the model he espouses, which plays an almost axiomatic role in his social philosophy as a whole, is that the process of recognition is endogenous to human sociation and is also secure from the infiltration of exogenous social forces.

Honneth further maintains that the process of recognition is more deeply rooted in self-formation because it precedes cognition. According to this claim, there exists what he calls an "ontogenetic priority of recognition over cognition."[7] Recognitive processes set up in the structure of consciousness inhere in the subject a second-person perspective, which, through healthy forms of social relations, produces a sense of moral self-worth and a capacity to adopt others' perspective. Fusing the ideas of G. H. Mead with those of the early Hegel, Honneth argues that the developing ego "learns step by step and through the perspective of a second person to perceive objects as entities in an objective world that

---

5. Axel Honneth, *Disrespect: The Normative Foundations of Critical Theory* (Cambridge: Polity Press, 2007), 71.

6. Honneth, *The Struggle for Recognition*, 173.

7. Axel Honneth, *Reification: A New Look at an Old Idea* (New York: Oxford University Press, 2008).

exists independently of our thoughts and feelings about it."[8] What this essentially means for critical theory is that recognitive relations shape a sense of moral awareness about self and other that foster a moral awareness, which in turn cultivates a sense of critical opposition to the forms of misrecognition and disrespect. Honneth believes this achieves a sense of morally motivated struggle that informs a new, modern, and critical process of will formation that creates and sustains a new, democratic ethical life.

I think these conclusions are unfounded. It is not simply enough to focus on issues of respect and recognition for the simple reason that the forms of power and the structural and functional forces of modern social structures shaped by material resources of power disable the socialization processes that Honneth assumes in his model of sociation. To put the matter more bluntly, recognition is rooted not in our critical-rational faculties but in our phenomenological-interpretive capacities. Its embeddedness in the structures of social relations that are ordered and shaped by administrative-capitalist society and imperatives cannot serve as a fulcrum for developing a critical rationality. There is no doubt that recognition as a process is rooted in the progressive aspects of modern society over premodern institutions and norms. But the architectonics of modern society are such that a contradiction emerges between the expansion of the rights proffered by recognitive relations on one hand and the mutilating inequalities of the capitalist order on the other. This contradiction is precisely what critical theory is supposed to call to our attention; it is a contradiction between what appears to us as the progress of relations of respect and the continued vertiginousness of social hierarchies and inequalities of social power and control. The real test of the theory of recognition is therefore whether it can resolve this contradiction and whether it is capable of providing a critical vantage point from within its intramundane and postmetaphysical assumptions.

The Contours of Power and Domination

The problem of the intramundane genesis of critique is an important weakness. Essentially, Honneth claims—after Habermas—that any crit-

---

8. Honneth, *Reification*, 43.

ical theory of society must be generated from the actual practices of social agents and not derived from a transcendental or a priori set of categories or concepts. It must be rooted in our inherent practices and capacities; for Habermas, it is the syntactic structure of language and speech acts, and for Honneth it is the process of recognition. In either case, the intramundane thesis runs up against the problem of power and, more specifically, domination. As the first generation of critical theorists saw the matter, domination was not simply a relation between agents or between classes. It was also, and more important, a systemic and processual phenomenon with the capacity to constitute the self and the cognitive, affective, and evaluative dimensions of the individual.

In contrast to this, Honneth's theory rests on a series of deep assumptions that distort the reality conditions of social relations and self- and cognitive development. Honneth maintains in his writings that the work of many first-generation critical theorists should be seen as resting on an outdated and essentially untenable theory of social action. Whereas they perceived modern society as operating in a structural-functional model, Honneth insists on the intersubjective turn and its model of social relations as forms of practices embedded in intersubjective webs of activity. Although it is true that the early critical theorists did not pursue a theory of social action, they were nevertheless concerned with how the forces of structural and functional imperatives embedded in the historical conditions of administrative capitalism and technical-bureaucratic society shaped and affected ego- and self-formation. Indeed, the price Honneth pays for rejecting this perspective is high—so high, I believe, that it renders his theory of recognition essentially acritical and, perhaps unwittingly, contains the very mechanisms of justification and antipolitical passivity that the Frankfurt School had seen as one of their central concerns to explain.

To defend this thesis, I begin with the issue of social power and domination. The main ideas that inform the tradition of critical theory with respect to the question of power and domination remain perhaps the most salient and crucial contributions to the potency of critical theory. As I see it, the question of a modern form of rational domination—of a form of social power that renders extractive, subor-dinating social relations legitimate in the minds and character structure of individuals—is a core concept for the critical theory tradition. What they saw in their integrated analyses of modern society was that modern subjects were being shaped by the increasingly rationalized and totalizing administrative institutions of modern society. Marx, Weber, and Freud all pointed toward an implicit thesis about the nature of rationalizing institutions not only to administer everyday life but to constitute the consciousness, agency, and personality of the self. What the Frankfurt School saw as an essential pathology of modern capitalist society was a kind of deep-seated reification of consciousness that permeated all spheres of personal, social, and cultural life. The issue of power here is not difficult to discern. Following from Marx and Lukács, they saw that the central problem was of the deformed self-constitution of our agency by social processes that would not only conform our actions and practices to the prevailing reality but also, more importantly, conform our will and cognitive process toward those systemic imperatives.[9]

Central in the thesis of reification they all came to adopt in some form was the idea that—whether because of the impact of instrumental reason, commodification, and so on—the rational faculties of individuals were distorted and shaped to accommodate the systemic imperatives of the social order. This was accomplished through the inculcation of consciousness and the personality structure of the individual—that is, his cathexis and drives—toward the imperatives, goals, and interests of the existing social order. I have called this kind of power *constitutive power*, and I believe we can define it as the capacity of superordinate groups, via their control over material resources, to shape the institutional norms, practices, and collective-intentional rule sets of the community as a whole. The more this superordinate group is able to do this, the more constitutive domination it has over the community. Because the logics of economic and technical rationality generate ever-growing tendencies toward surplus extraction, efficiency, stability, and control, constitutive norms proliferate as more and more institutions are absorbed by their logics.[10]

The mechanisms of this kind of power are important to examine in more detail. The precise way it affects consciousness and attitudes is through its ability to shape the norms and value orientations of subjects. The more entrenched and embedded into economic and instrumental

9. For a more technical discussion of this approach to the theory of domination and reification, see Michael J. Thompson, "Collective Intentionality, Social Domination, and Reification," *Journal of Social Ontology*, vol. 3, no. 2 (2017): 207–29.

10. For a fuller discussion of this thesis, see Michael J. Thompson, *The Domestication of Critical Theory* (London: Rowman and Littlefield, 2016), 91ff.

logics social and cultural institutions become, the more they can routinize certain kinds of norms. The more successful these institutions are, the more these routinized norms become internalized by subjects. The less critical reaction there is to these ambient norms, the more they become internalized; the more they become internalized, the more that they become constitutive rules of consciousness. The more they are shared by the community as a whole, the more they become reified structures of consciousness and as collective-intentional aspects of subjective consciousness as well as intersubjective practices and action. The aspect of power is the capacity of these norms to be organized to legitimate and sustain hierarchical relations of power, whether of the social goals of elites, the property structure of the society, and so on. The point is that our subjective and intersubjective consciousness is in fact rooted in these material forms of power and the kinds of institutionalized norms that become successful and ambient within society. Social power of this kind is therefore constitutive of individuals and the web of intersubjective relations within which they act.

The point of this thesis is that domination must be seen as more than simply an interagent, structural phenomenon. It is also, more importantly, a functional phenomenon constituting the social and the subjective world.[11] Hence, anytime we operate in the confines of a phenomenological and socially embedded approach to an emancipatory theory, we will run up against the boundaries of this problem. Honneth argues that there is a presocial rootedness to the basis of recognition in the mother–child relationship. The problem here is that this relation is not in any sense immune to the pathological impulses of the social world. The relation between mother and child and, in very short time, between the relations of the family are not to be construed as autonomous from the socializing forces of the world external to it. Quite the contrary, in many ways the family is the incubating sphere for the values that promote the status quo as a whole.[12] What Harry Dahms has called the "constitutive logic of modern society" should be seen here as

---

11. For a more developed, technical discussion of this mechanism of domination, see Michael J. Thompson, "A Functionalist Theory of Social Domination," *Journal of Political Power*, vol. 6, no. 2 (2013): 179–99.

12. See the important discussion by Herbert Marcuse, "The Obsolescence of the Freudian Conception of Man," in *Five Lectures* (Boston: Beacon Press, 1970), 44–61.

a central problem in the move toward a recognitive paradigm in critical theory, since there are few places where the self can develop outside of the constitutive powers and logics of these institutions and norms.[13]

Honneth might well respond to this criticism that this simply misses the point. His main claim is that recognition begins with a relation between mother and child and then extends outward over time. As this process unfolds, we develop a sense of self- and other-respect that we seek to have recognized in the world. But there is also a problem here. The phenomenon of a "struggle for recognition" that animated Honneth's early writings on the subject, re-creates the central problem that the early critical theorists were seeking to explain: how the dominated in fact do not experience their world as one of disrespect and as pathological. Rather, they come to internalize its goals and values and accept them as implicitly legitimate, reifying them in their own consciousness and practices. What results is the same problem that motivated Wilhelm Reich's problematic in *The Mass Psychology of Fascism*—namely, why is it that those who have been exploited and disadvantaged by the system do not rebel? The crucial issue with respect to the recognition paradigm is that if we take the thesis of constitutive power seriously, we have no way of securing the assumptions about self-formation that Honneth maintains as the core of his model. Indeed, we are left with the more plausible outcome that individuals are so socialized by the systemic imperatives and norms of the social order that recognition can serve hierarchical psychic needs. Thus, to be "recognized" in the eyes of a domineering parent, lover, or superordinate one might actually reproduce power relations that do not disturb the hierarchical relation and instead play into roles that comfort and secure that hierarchical relation. Recognition is a process that happens in the context of other power relations, not external to them, and therefore it cannot escape the problem of constitutive power and constitutive domination. The thesis that recognition and critical-moral self-development are unified is therefore deeply mistaken.

What this means is that recognition is a process that is itself shaped by power relations; it is vulnerable to the distortions and pathologies it is supposed to combat. The implication is that recognition can then become a process that slows the development of critical attitudes and critical consciousness. This is because power relations shape the

---

13. See Harry Dahms, *Modern Society as Artifice: Critical Theory and the Logic of Capital* (London: Routledge, forthcoming).

recognitive relations between others and the particular attachments and recognitive relations and roles that people come to adopt are shaped by the structural and functional imperatives of the political economic forces of society. This is no reductionist argument—rather, it is a more critical view of the real processes that shape social and psychological content. Indeed, by marginalizing these concerns, Honneth's recognition paradigm lapses into a neo-idealism: an abstraction of recognitive relations from the actual structures and forces that constitute modern society. Even if we cede that recognition is a phylogenetic feature of human development, what we cannot accept is that its ontogenetic manifestation is not constituted by the structures and processes of capitalist economic life and its pathologies. Looking for respect/recognition from others in hierarchical contexts generally leads not to an awareness of a moral wrong but to justificatory attitudes toward those authority relations themselves.[14]

Even more, the thesis of constitutive power entails certain effects on our subjectivity and agency that also disable the critical potentiality of recognition. This is because the culture of capitalist society is such that the alienating effects of everyday life fold the ego back in on itself, and it becomes a refuge from the increasingly dehumanizing world of damaged social relations. This ego is now in less of a place to challenge the social order and more likely to create a protected space of identity that seeks affirmation from others. As Marcuse insightfully notes on this problem: "The ego that has grown without much struggle appears as a pretty weak entity, ill equipped to become a self with and against others, to offer effective resistance to the powers that now enforce the reality principle, and which are so very different from father (and mother)—but also very different from the images purveyed by the mass media."[15] The weakened, withered ego should be seen not only as a consequence of damaged social relations but also as a counterthesis to the idea that recognitive relations, embedded in the "intramundane" fabric of everyday life, are unable to articulate selves with the psychological resources requisite for moral-political resistance.

---

14. See Frederick Solt, "The Social Origins of Authoritarianism," *Political Research Quarterly*, vol. 65, no. 4 (2012): 703–13. This can also be seen in the earlier studies by Robert Lane, "The Fear of Equality," *American Political Science Review*, vol. 53, no. 1 (1959): 35–51; and Jonathan Cobb and Richard Sennett, *The Hidden Injuries of Class* (New York: Norton, 1972).

15. Marcuse, "The Obsolescence," 50.

Recognition without Social Ontology

This leads me to a second flaw in the recognition paradigm. As I have sought to demonstrate, the problem of constitutive power and constitutive domination roots itself in the everyday life contexts—the institutions, practices, norms, and so on—that shape and socialize our agency. If this basic thesis is accepted, it entails a second thesis: namely, that the assumptions of pragmatic social action are also not antecedent to the same processes of power and domination but are in fact constitutive of and constituted by those practices. At its core, the thesis of the postmetaphysical turn is that we can no longer look to any ground for our norms outside of our intersubjective, justificatory practices. For Habermas, this means that valid, binding norms can only be rooted in the consensus of the public. The criterion of universality for any given moral utterance is the consensus around that utterance; it is the procedure of how we achieve consensus that counts. Hence, we no longer need to look for the ontological grounding of any given moral concept but must seek to secure consensus through exchange of reasons via language to obtain moral validity. The pragmatist thesis here is implicit in the capacity to exchange reasons and accept that morality has a cognitive content to the extent that person X is capable of acknowledging the truth potentiality of the utterance from person Y.[16] The cognitive power of moral utterances is then dependent on the extent to which rational agents transform their ideas and normative views and come to consensus around rational, valid norms.

For Honneth, taking off from the work of Habermas and his followers, pragmatism offers us a kind of paradigmatic turn in the theory of social action and self-formation. The reason for this is that he sees recognitive relations as essentially constitutive of one's identity. The basis for this claim is rooted in Mead's thesis that the ego develops a second-person perspective through one's interaction with others, thereby

---

16. As Habermas argues, "The speaker's illocutionary goal is that the hearer not only acknowledge her belief, but that he come to the same opinion, that is, to share that belief. But this is possible only on the basis of the intersubjective recognition of the truth claim raised on behalf of *p*. The speaker can realize her illocutionary goal only if the cognitive function of the speech act is also realized, that is, if the interlocutor accepts her utterance as valid." *Truth and Justification* (Cambridge, MA: MIT Press, 2003), 4. Also see Jürgen Habermas, *Postmetaphysical Thinking: Philosophical Essays* (Cambridge, MA: MIT Press, 1993), 115ff.

internalizing this other perspective and creating the basis for the self as an intersubjective phenomenon. As Mead states the matter: "Any psychological or philosophical treatment of human nature involves the assumption that the human individual belongs to an organized social community, and derives his human nature from his social interactions and relations with that community as a whole and with the other individual members of it."[17] This is because the individual develops a self only in intersubjective conjunction with others: "The self is something which has a development; it is not initially there, at birth, but arises in the process of social experience and activity, that it, develops in the given individual as a result of his relations to that process as a whole and to other individuals within that process."[18]

For Honneth, the core of this process is the recognitive relation between persons. Honneth uses Mead and Dewey to defend this thesis, arguing that "a subject can only acquire a consciousness of itself to the extent to which it learns to perceive its own action from the symbolically represented second-person perspective."[19] Now the crucial move becomes connecting this basic thesis about the development of a social self via recognitive relations and a sense of moral awareness. The postmetaphysical and pragmatist thesis here is that the process is sufficient as a means to generate critical awareness and resistance—no other resources are needed or even rationally acceptable. For Honneth, "The connection between the experience of recognition and one's relation-to-self stems from the intersubjective structure of personal identity. The only way in which individuals are constituted as persons is by learning to refer to themselves, from the perspective of an approving or encouraging other, as beings with certain positive traits and abilities."[20] This is a large leap,

---

17. George Herbert Mead, *Mind, Self and Society* (Chicago: University of Chicago Press, 1934), 229.

18. Mead, *Mind, Self and Society*, 135.

19. Honneth, *The Struggle for Recognition*, 75. Interestingly enough, Mead seems to have anticipated what Honneth elaborates in his recognition theory when he writes about the individual in modern society: "If he could not bring that peculiarity of himself into the common community, if it could not be recognized, if others could not take his attitude in some sense, he could not have appreciation in emotional terms, he could not be the very self he is trying to be." Mead, *Mind, Self and Society*, 324.

20. Honneth, *The Struggle for Recognition*, 173.

for now, Honneth maintains, the socialization process of recognition forms essentially a moral-experiential pattern in the self that is a kind of indicator of social injustice. We come to experience blockages to our recognition as acts of injustice; we begin to see that hampering recognitive relations in mature social life goes against the grain of our socialized experiences of love and respect that has, he believes, constituted us as intersubjective selves.

This runs up against the same issue of constitutive power that I discussed already, but in a more pathological way. I want to now advance the thesis that Honneth does not appreciate the concept or the deep effects of the reification of consciousness that stems from modern forms of power and its capacity to hamper the very practices and reflective capacities that he assumes. Honneth continually rests his theoretical edifice on the brittle assumption that recognitive relations are themselves constitutive of the social. But this sidesteps the ontological dimension of social structure and function. Mead was indeed correct about the formation of the self through social interaction with others. But it is an idealized model of sociation, devoid of the problems of dominance and reification.[21] The pragmatists almost completely sidestepped the issue of social power and domination and its effects on self-formation and cognition.[22] Honneth makes the same error in the core of his model. If we consider that there can be no unsullied recognitive relation, one not tainted and shaped by a power relation in some form, then it becomes difficult to accept the idea of recognition as an intramundane source for critical reflection and critical will formation. But this does not strike me as a plausible hypothesis.

If we take the thesis of reification seriously, it affects the socialization of the self and its cognitive capacities in particular ways. By

---

21. Dewey's problem is a lack of sensitivity to power. John Patrick Diggins's observation also seems to apply to Honneth: "For Dewey not only refused to give much attention to power and its origins, he also had no idea where to look for it other than as some kind of aberration. When Dewey thought at all about power—not as the ability to act and have effect but as control and domination—he usually interpreted it as an example of dislocation and maladjustment, the failure of education and intelligence to catch up with economic development and the rise of big business." *The Promise of Pragmatism: Modernism and the Crisis of Knowledge and Authority* (Chicago: University of Chicago Press, 1994), 288.

22. See the important discussion by Lonnie Athens, *Domination and Subjugation in Everyday Life* (London: Routledge, 2015).

internalizing the constitutive rule sets of the prevailing social institutions via routinizing their norms and practices, they come to be reified in the cognitive and intentional structures of consciousness. This conceals from view much of what is objectively pathological in the society. This is why Marx points to the power of theoretical knowledge to gain access to a critical vantage point. For Honneth critique is immanent within, and an emergent property of, sociation and recognitive intersubjective relations. Against this, Marx sees that alienation and false shapes of consciousness in fact conceal the mechanisms that generate the pathologies that individuals experience. The life-world—no matter how pathologically shaped—is not sufficient to generate a rational critical consciousness. Indeed, the problem is that without a rational critical vantage point, as supplied by theoretical knowledge, there can be pathological responses to pathological conditions—as with far right-wing movements, anti-immigrant sentiments, drug use and abuse, *ressentiment*, and so on. Indeed, although Marx and Mead share a common theoretical view in presuming "the fundamental social nature of man and, indeed, they argue that it is only through their sociality that men can be individuals. . . . [M]an does not exist as man except in terms of social interrelation and interdependence."[23]

For Mead, the limitation exists in his lack of the perception of the constitutive power of pathological relations. Indeed, his view was that domination was essentially a phenomenon of the past, that modern social relations were giving way to freer forms of sociation, something that Honneth makes a central contention of his normative theory. But the problem here, again, is that is simply sidesteps the entire edifice of critical theory itself: the essential question of how false forms of consciousness continually harness the subject to dehumanizing structures and practices of social life. The pragmatist thesis is therefore insufficient to deal with the phenomenon of alienation and reification. Because they radically divorce intersubjective sociation from the causal powers of social structures and their constitutive powers over self- and cognitive development, pragmatists continue to operate in a neo-idealist framework, deluding themselves that they are somehow "postmetaphysical." Critical theory must mitigate this trend, for there is no way to secure the capacity of agents, through recognition, communication, reason exchange,

---

23. Tom W. Goff, *Marx and Mead: Contributions to a Sociology of Knowledge* (London: Routledge and Kegan Paul, 1980), 87.

or whatever, to extirpate the reified structures of consciousness and the defective forms of cognition to which it gives rise. Rather, it seems more likely that these kinds of sociative relations will simply reproduce those acritical views instead of calling them into question.[24] Indeed, the problem is that there is no vantage point for critique. Tom Goff has rightly pointed to the problem in Mead that "while Mead's perspective also suggests the critical orientation, it does not explicitly contain any comprehension of a problematic that would constitute the rationale in terms of which critical analysis wood be necessary and meaningful. Mead stops short of any details consideration of a conceptual equivalent to Marx's ideas of alienation."[25]

My thesis now comes full circle: the recognitive paradigm fails because (a) it ignores (or at least deeply undertheorizes) the nature of modern forms of social power and domination and its causal powers to shape and structure consciousness and the self; and, *ex hypothesi*, (b) that the pragmatist thesis of intersubjective sociation, also lacking a robust theory of domination, alienation, or reification, unwittingly reproduces the pathologies of consciousness that emerge from pathological-domination relations. Honneth's thesis about the immanent, intramundane capacity of recognition to generate critical consciousness is therefore bankrupt, and a return to the ideas of the early critical theorists is in

---

24. Empirically, this seems to be the case. See Henrik Friberg-Frenros and Johan Karlsson Shaffer, "The Consensus Paradox: Does Deliberative Agreement Impede Rational Discourse?," *Political Studies*, vol. 62, no. 1 (2014): 99–116; Edward T. Walker, "Legitimating the Corporation through Public Participation," in Caroline W. Lee, Michael McQuarrie, and Edward T. Walker (eds.), *Democratizing Inequalities: Dilemmas of the New Public Participation* (New York: New York University Press, 2015), 66–81; and Dan M. Kahan, "The Cognitively Illiberal State," *Stanford Law Review*, vol. 60 (2007): 101–40. Also see the still relevant discussion by Milton Rokeach, *The Open and Closed Mind* (New York: Basic Books, 1960); Cass Sunstein, "The Law of Group Polarization," *Journal of Political Philosophy*, vol. 10, no. 2 (2002): 175–95; R. Robinson, D. Keltner, A. Ward, and L. Ross, "Actual versus Assumed Differences in Construal: 'Naïve Realism' in Intergroup Perception and Conflict," *Journal of Personality and Social Psychology*, vol. 68, no. 3 (1995): 404–17; J. Berdahl and P. Martorana, "Effects of Power on Emotion and Expression during a Controversial Group Discussion," *European Journal of Social Psychology*, vol. 36 (2006): 497–509; Cass Sunstein, "Deliberative Trouble? Why Groups Go to Extremes," *Yale Law Journal*, vol. 110 (2000): 71–119.

25. Goff, *Marx and Mead*, 93.

earnest. The postmetaphysical move takes us too far into the realm of the abstract, noumenal realm of subjects and away from the ontological questions that ought to ground our concepts about social reality—in both descriptive and normative senses. Anti-essentialism entails a lack of critique. The reason for this is that unlike the pragmatist understanding of truth-claims, the nature of reality is not dependent on my or our collective concepts of it. A critical grasp of the world is one that is able to grasp its essential features, that is, those things that make it what it is. From a truly Hegelian vantage point, this entails seeing any thing as a metaphysical entity because it must be more than its material or analytically composed parts of the sum thereof. From the Hegelian point of view, valid knowledge—philosophical, critical knowledge—grasps the essentially dynamic nature of objects. Understanding social pathologies therefore must take this strategy, as I demonstrate next.

Recognition and Social Pathology:
Fromm versus Honneth

Now we come to the central and essential concern: to what extent can we see the theory of recognition as a critical theory of society? To explore the limitations of the recognition paradigm, I want to compare Honneth's approach to social pathologies to that of Erich Fromm. What I want to show is that the move away from the ideas about the constitutive power of social structure and damaged relations under capitalism mutes our understanding of social pathologies. Indeed, the Marxian and Freudian elements of early critical theory could diagnose the problem of the desiccation of the self that emerged from the pathologies of alienation and reification that were rooted in the social-structural forces of modern capitalism. And not only the production process but the elaboration of consumerist, technicist, and conformist pressures that it requires for its success. The problem of recognition becomes perhaps more problematic because now we are forced to face the extent to which we actually have a critical criterion for what kinds of identities are worthy of being "recognized." Indeed, Honneth's claim is that the cognitive and the normative layers of the process of recognition are intertwined.

The concept of social pathology is again of interest in social philosophy and the social sciences. For critical theorists, the concept had always denoted a series of different kinds of deviations from a healthy, rational, and self-developing form of subjectivity and social relations. The basic thesis they accepted was that modern social relations—primarily those dominated by commodified, capitalist market forces and instrumental rationality—had the effect of distorting the cognitive and personality structure of individuals, thereby rendering them passive subjects in the context of any system imperative. Pathological social relations therefore gave rise to pathological persons. The key problem the Frankfurt School sought to remedy in its various projects was to expose the mechanisms of this kind of pathology formation to reignite the capacity for critique and social emancipation. Critical theorists therefore rejected the linked concepts of "normal" and "pathological" that Durkheim had laid out, which stated that "the generality of phenomena must be taken as the criterion of their normality."[26] Instead, their idea of social pathology was rooted in the Marxian thesis that saw alienation, commodity fetishism, and reification as the product of a society increasingly organized around the imperatives of surplus production and consumption.

Honneth has taken a decidedly conservative view of the older, Marxian-inspired concept of social pathology that critical theory took as the center of their diagnostic project of social critique. In *Freedom's Right*, Honneth chose to see the concept of social pathology not as the product of a pathological society organized around alienating and reifying relations rooted in capitalist social relations but as a lack on people's part to recognize the norms immanent in modern social institutions, norms that will lead to them pursuing recognitive relations with others and allowing those norms to guide their personal and collective projects. The important point is that in *Freedom's Right* there is a disconnect between the "actual rationality of norms in social practices and the participants' reflexive uptake of these norms (or of their significance)—a disconnect that is itself (purportedly) caused by some internal dynamics of the norms in question (in contrast to misdevelopments, where the disconnect is caused externally)."[27]

26. Emile Durkheim, *The Rules of Sociological Method* (New York: Free Press, 1938), 75.

27. Fabian Freyenhagen, "Honneth on Social Pathologies: A Critique," *Critical Horizons*, vol. 16, no. 2 (2015): 131–52, 144.

According to this view, social pathologies are now to be seen not in Marxian terms, as the by-product of a contradictions in the social order, but as a result of the lack of proper recognitive relations that allow the (supposedly) democratic norms of modernity to seep into the practices and norms of intersubjectively related social agents. A nonpathological society, for Honneth, would not need to change the structure of society but would need to allow the proper uptake of modern norms, which, he maintains, already have the normative content of equality, reflexivity, and self-development. But it must be seen that Honneth's idea of social pathology is in fact deeply flawed and is unable to capture the fuller dimensions of the causes of failed sociality. To provide the groundwork for this critique, I contrast Honneth's conception of social pathology with that of Fromm, who I believe has a richer conception of the dimensions of social pathologies and their manifestation in the self and psyche of individuals and how these pathological states of self and psyche are rooted in the specific historical conditions found in capitalist economic life.

In particular, I want to point to Fromm's alternative account of normal-pathological relations to show how Honneth's contention is unworthy of the aims and goals of critical theory. Fromm holds that capitalist modernity produces flaws in social relations and subjects; that these pathologies are not simply a matter of the recognition of other or of norms but become embedded in the character or personality system of the individual. To go further, I also want to suggest that the pathologies Fromm points to in *The Sane Society* are today considered normal parts of late capitalist society and culture.

Fromm differs from this approach by arguing that failed sociality is the result of how defective social relations are shaped and form the self. In this sense, he works in the shadow of Rousseau's thesis that modern forms of liberal society—premised on atomism, egotism, and interpersonal extraction of benefits (what Rousseau called *amour propre*)—lead to pathologies of the self: that is, to a distended sense of self-interest, and so on. This occurs because social relations give rise to what he refers to as *moeurs*, the norms and customs that exist to protect the powerful and the propertied. Rousseau also points out that only when we abandon this defective form of civil society—one based on inequality and domination—can we glimpse the proper, good community: one appropriate to man's needs within society.[28] This he sees as a community made up of autonomous agents who are cognizant of living in a social context of interdependence. It is not man who is evil or bad or ill by nature (à la Augustine or Kierkegaard) but man's defects, which are the result of a poorly constructed society: institutions, norms, practices, and so on that allow and even legitimate inequality and domination. This kind of society is not yet ours; we cannot take the norms already empirically present in the community as valid but must think dialectically. We must follow the social pathology back to normal or healthy situation of which the pathology is the negation. Inequality and domination shape the practices and norms of individuals, shape the cognitive and evaluative capacities of subjects, and render them over time to the patterns and goals of the social system as a whole. The idea that this is an outdated and overly-mechanistic model of modern society is simply false: it is the growing tendency within industrial and postindustrial society.

I think Fromm works in this same logic of reasoning.[29] Although he takes Marx and Freud as his intellectual fonts, he shares with Rousseau's basic thesis the notion that social pathologies originate in the patterned forms of social life (institutions, practices, value orientations, and so on) that are unique to capitalist society. Fromm, also not unlike Rousseau, sees that there is a central way to understand social pathologies or defects of the self and society more generally by positing that only those social relations that are normal, nonpathological, are those capable of curing the pathologies of the culture and the self. Fromm also posits a theory of social relations that is essentially ontological. For him, relations to others are essential to human existence; they are not merely cognitive or affective but also consist of how we cooperate and form a more substantive form of sociality. Recognition is one layer of this relationality, but it cannot determine it. Rather, Fromm posits that social pathologies result from how ontic social forms shape our phylogenetic capacities. For Fromm, the opposite of any pathological state is one of normalcy, and it would be one where each person's autonomy is

---

28. I think Honneth's conception of social pathology is marred by his misunderstanding of Rousseau's more complete social theory. See Axel Honneth, "Pathologies of the Social: The Past and Present of Social Philosophy," in *Disrespect*, 3–48.

29. Also see the important discussion by Ernst Tugendhat, *Vorlesungen über Ethik* (Frankfurt: Suhrkamp, 1993), 263ff.

shaped and cultivated by creative and solidaristic relations. He points to four crucial continua of normalcy–pathology that cluster these values:

[+]		[–]
Relatedness +	——————————————	— *Narcissism*
Creativeness +	——————————————	— *Destructiveness*
Brotherliness +	——————————————	— *Incest*
Individuality +	——————————————	— *Herd Conformity*

For Fromm, the content of social pathologies is rooted in the deformation of social relations, which lead to shaping the personality of the self. It also shows how the dialectic can serve as a means of critique by revealing how the relative pathology is also the negation of the healthy, normal state of being. The key for the critical theorist is to seek to understand how different social formations, institutional practices, different cultural patterns of life, value orientations, and so on can be seen to routinize either the positive or negative values on each of these continua.

The causes of these pathologies, as Fromm repeatedly points out, are the social conditions rooted in the organization of society itself. We have a means of judgment from the perspective of judging how modern forms of sociality misshape our potentialities for relations and creativity because they are misdirected by forms of dominance and control. Whereas Honneth's new path for critical theory advocates interpersonal recognition and respect as the fundamental ethic of socialization, one that must be seen as the central normative value of modernity, Fromm follows Marx in seeing that this cannot suffice to overcome pathologies of the self. The very thesis Honneth advocates cannot properly emerge in the confines of capitalist society. Fromm's notion of an "analytic social psychology," as he notes in an essay with the same title, posits that "the role of primary formative factors goes to the economic conditions. The family is the essential medium through which the economic situation exerts formative influence on the individual's psyche."[30] In short, the task of a critical social psychology must point to the "influence of economic conditions on libido strivings."[31] This means that the root of social

---

30. Erich Fromm, *The Crisis of Psychoanalysis* (New York: Henry Holt, 1970), 149.

31. Fromm, *The Crisis of Psychoanalysis*, 149.

pathologies is the structural organization of social life which imprints itself on the family and onto the developing ego. Honneth's thesis of an "ethic of recognition" occurs within the pathological conditions Fromm analyzes. As a result, the mechanism of recognition can still take place between pathological forms of self. Although it may overcome some extreme forms of narcissism or acute forms of destructiveness, it does not qualify as an antidote to the kind of automaton conformity Fromm points to, nor does it do anything to prevent the emergence of more general forms of egotism, of self-absorption that follow from atomized, reified, commodified, culturally empty forms of life that characterize modern societies.

At an even larger level of analysis, Fromm's point is that this kind of recognition cannot emerge in a social system that reproduces pathological relations. Honneth's basic idea of social pathology is further called into question because the very antithesis he proposes cannot fully emerge as a social practice, let alone an ethic, of modern social life. We cannot separate out, as Honneth does, the social practice of recognition from the social processes that mitigate it, nor against the social forces that shape and constitute the self and the cognitive and intentional features of the ego's agency. At best, it is a figment of philosophical optimism; at worst, it manifests as a shallow, apolitical means to fortify a inwardly collapsing ego that has withered under the conditions of capitalist modernity.

This calls into question the analytic distinction between first- and second-order pathologies. Fromm's thesis seems to be that the pathologies of society (of structure, social goals and values, relations, and so on) are functionally related to the pathologies of the self: pathological relations form pathological selves who, in turn, re-create pathological relations. But the key for Fromm is that the nucleus of this dynamic is found in a social order that orients and channels the inherent powers and drives of human nature into forms of life that misdirect them and our energies toward contradictory forms of life, thereby necessitating the emergence of personal pathologies as a means to sublimate and even rationalize such irrational forms of life.[32]

---

32. Fromm notes, "For most of them, the culture provides patterns which enable them *to live with a defect without becoming ill.* It is as if each culture provided the remedy against the outbreak of manifest neurotic symptoms which would result from the defect produced by it." *The Sane Society* (New York: Henry Holt, 1955), 16.

Unfortunately for Honneth, there is no phenomenological way out of this circle. We cannot assume, as Honneth does in his earlier writings, that the experience of the pathology will lead to an emancipatory interest in overcoming and eliminating it. Rather, Fromm seems to say that only through a rational grasp of the objective mechanisms that create and re-create defective society and defective selves can we hope to overcome them. Even more, Fromm's ideas retain a radical political content in that they point to the necessity of social transformation (as opposed to some reformist impulse) toward accommodating the norms of what we should see as a deficient form of modernity.[33] As he writes in *The Crisis of Psychoanalysis*, "In present-day society it is *other* impulses [i.e., other than sex] that are repressed; to be fully alive, to be free, and to love. Indeed, if people today were healthy in a human sense, they would be less rather than more capable of fulfilling their social role; they would, however, protest against a sick society, and demand such socio-economic changes as would reduce the dichotomy between health in a social and health in a human sense."[34]

Fromm is particularly against precisely what Honneth's conception of social pathology embraces. Fromm is opposed to any notion of social accommodation, to the idea that health can be equated in any way with an adaptation to the existing reality or its norms. But Honneth claims precisely this: the modern world—the modern form of the family, a regulated market society, modern ideas about rights, and so on—contains norms that can promote the recognitive relations and self-development that is modern social freedom. This is only because Honneth chooses not to see that these sociocultural forces in fact act as modes of sublimation: that the increase in economic consumption, production, exploitation, inequality, and so on requires new cultural modes of interacting to aid

33. Elsewhere I have advanced the thesis of "deficient modernity" as a way to show a Hegelian distinction between a malformed, irrational form of contemporary life and a genuine, rational manifestation of modernity. See Michael J. Thompson, "Capitalism as Deficient Modernity: Hegel against the Modern Economy," in Andrew Buchwalter (ed.), *Hegel and Capitalism* (Albany, NY: SUNY Press, 2015), 117–32. Unlike Honneth, we should not see modern economic institutions as fostering a modern form of ethical life, but in more of a Marxian sense that shows the pathological consequences of atomized market relations and the effects of unequal wealth on the common purposes, relations, and ends of the community as a whole.

34. Fromm, *The Crisis of Psychoanalysis*, 37.

in the adaptation of the self into the dominant values and practices of the community—and these dominant values and practices are only allowed to flourish insofar as they further or at least do not threaten concrete power relations in society. The domination of classes over one another continues, and the vertical slope of inequality increases. In the meantime, people "enjoy" rights to their identities and find the concept of freedom in these narrow confines.

The recognition of another's identity becomes a crucial mechanism of escape from the realities of the social order. The weakened ego now seeks comfort in the nonthreatening embrace of his or her identity-community. The pathological nature of this move is dual. On one hand, the weak ego seeks not resistance but acceptance from particularistic communities. This reinforces the fragmentation of social life insofar as one becomes increasingly embedded in and psychically invested in such particularist communities. What is lost from view is how this search for identity and acceptance are not generally fragments of the totality and instead make room for the particular self rather than a fully developed individuality. These pathologies are not gasped as they are, but are internalized and normalized through different psychological and cultural codes and norms. We cannot get at their essentially pathological nature via recognition, only through critical reflection. At the same time, these newer modes of sublimation cement the dominant social forces and social order and necessitate a passive legitimacy to this system. Whereas Fromm was concerned to point to the dialectical relation between a pathology and its healthy state to draw attention to their respective mechanisms of causation in the dynamism of the social structure, Honneth asks us to reject this and instead to see that there are simply some premodern blockages from the "uptake of modern norms."

The problem of these new modes of sublimation should instead be seen to be proliferating, in fact melding themselves into the very structure of a culture of sublimation in general. The trends of popular culture (music, film, literature, and so on) are ever more evident: what we see is a progressive series of cultural forms that normalize the pathological forms of self to which Fromm points. We can take Fromm and his ideas about the nature of the pathological personality as a starting point for what I am trying to say here. For Fromm, a central consequence of damaged social relations emerging from capitalist society are forms of self that seek out pathological self- and other-relations. But it is equally plausible that they will seek forms of acceptance that protect the weakened self from the forces of social life external to it. In either case, recognition can be seen to function not as a critical mechanism but as a sublimating mechanism: as a means to escape the damaged world rather than confront it and change it.

Resuscitating Critical Judgment:
The Ontological Point of View

The key problem that emerges from the foregoing discussion can be seen as follows. If we reject the postmetaphysical and pragmatist ideas about truth-claims and the validity of norms, how can we rationally discern Fromm's reasons that certain social relations are "pathological" and others "healthy" or "good"? If we turn toward a critical social-ontological perspective, we see that the postmetaphysical view comes up short. As I have tried to show here, this thesis is unable to resist the constitutive effects of power relations, so we can only regain a critical vantage point through an ontological perspective that seeks to interrogate the relational structures, processes, and purposes toward which the society I live within are oriented. Hegel and Marx, no less than Fromm, sought to propose such a view: one that saw the dialectical relation between the pathological social forms with the more rational, more humane forms potential in a reorganization of social relations, processes, and ends. What makes this view ontological is that it seeks to ground the critical perspective not from within actions constituted by the already existing order but from an ontological point that asks about the totality of relations, processes, and purposes of the community as a whole. In place of relying on the moral experience of everyday life, what is required is the juxtaposition of a different way of thinking about what the social is and how it can be conceived. In my view, critical theory must be concerned with precisely this task.

In contrast to the phenomenological, action-theoretic perspective, Fromm shows how the specific structure or shape of our social relations has causal powers over self- and will-formation. There exists an ontology to our social relations, to the kinds of processes those relations articulate, and the kinds of subjects shaped by them. Fromm sees that the social pathologies are negations of correct or healthy relations, but we know this not because one feels "disrespect" or some form of misrecognition. We cannot rely on an internalist and phenomenological reaction because it is far too susceptible to the problem of reification and alienation. The struggle for critical reflection is more difficult than this, and in many ways, the tendencies of modern culture and society show a growing tendency away from the kinds of moral awareness that Honneth proposes dominate modernity.[35]

What is necessary is not simply the act of intersubjective recognition but a broader form of cognition that can recognize our institutions as needing to fulfill the goals of self-development.[36] Not a simple, one-sided form of development, but a manifold, dynamic and progressive conception of the self. Fromm is in line with Marx, Hegel, Rousseau, and even Aristotle on a basic thesis: that humans are social, that they are relational beings, and that their subjective, individual self is a function of how these relations are shaped and structured. Even more, they are of the view that as a result of this basic social ontology, social relations can be arranged to progress the human condition and lead to a kind of perfectionism and self-development that is humane and creative, one that nurtures equal relations and has in critical view the notion that society exists for our collective and individual good. If we go back to Hegel's *Phenomenology* for a moment, we recall that it culminates in "Absolute Spirit," the thesis that all human cognition is truly rational and universal once it can grasp that all our institutions, values, and forms of life are created by us.[37] What is needed is not

---

35. See the important discussion by Pankaj Mishra, *Age of Anger: A History of the Present* (New York: Farrar, Strauss and Giroux, 2017).

36. In contrast with Marx and Mead, Goff rightly argues: "It is precisely Marx's intention to develop a mode of analysis that would enable one to pinpoint and transcend the specific, contingent limitation expressed in the concept of alienation, so that the 'natural problematics,' on the level of praxis, could be handled on a rational, less trial-and-error basis, free of the paradoxical limitations of man's own products." *Marx and Mead*, 93.

37. As Philip Kain has commented on this section of the *Phenomenology*: "The very alienation that leads to estrangement is also the alienation that overcomes the estrangement. When we come to see that it was our own alienation that produced the object as our estranged self in the first place, the consciousness of this fact means we have overcome the estrangement of the object. We no longer see it as other. We see it as our self, our own product, our own essence. We are at home with it." *Hegel and the Other: A Study of the Phenomenology of Spirit* (Albany, NY: SUNY Press, 2005), 222. Jean Hyppolite writes, "The knowledge of being was

simply that these relations be seen as manifesting relations of recognition but that we orient all social forms toward the values of normalcy that Fromm points to and we keep in view that this can only be achieved by rooting out the pathological as a feature of the social institutions we are supposed to call our own.

This is a very different operation of consciousness and thought than that put forward by Honneth and the thesis of recognition. We need to see that the recognitive relations pointed to by Hegel and Mead still have salience. What they entail is not an immanent sense of moral consciousness but the possibility of an expanded subjectivity capable of cognizing the ontological dimensions of human social relatedness and the kinds of processes, relations, and purposes toward which our social lives ought to be organized.[38] Against the postmetaphysical move, we need to see—as Hegel and Marx did—that the core of any radical critical theory of society requires that we rationally grasp the essential nature of human life; this essence consists of the ontological categories of relations, processes, and purposes. This grants us a critical vantage point rather than an immanent-phenomenological sense of moral awareness. The ontological vantage point grants us a means of understanding the essential structures of human social life and asking about the kinds of relations, processes, structures, and purposes our social world commits us to and whether they have validity. The criterion of validity can be seen only if those relations, institutions, norms, practices, and purposes generate realized selves. Of course, this does not mean jettisoning the ideas of recognition no less than the ideas about discourse. It does mean that these theoretical approaches cannot serve, on their own, as a critical social theory.

In their attack on the metaphysical tradition, these approaches have missed the idea that it can offer us a kind of rational-critical grounding for normative claims. The critical ontological perspective does not

shown to be a knowledge of self, and, inversely, self-knowledge has led back to the knowledge of being; finally, reason, the synthesis of consciousness and self-consciousness, did indeed grasp being as thought and thought as being, but it did so in an immediate fashion." *Genesis and Structure of Hegel's Phenomenology of Spirit* (Evanston, IL: Northwestern University Press, 1974), 576.

38. For some preliminary discussions of this, see Joachim Israel, *The Language of Dialectics and the Dialectics of Language* (London: Harvester Press, 1979); David Weissman, *A Social Ontology* (New Haven, CT: Yale University Press, 2000).

embrace a transcendental metaphysics but an immanent metaphysics: one where we keep in view the metaphysics of the social world and the kinds of relations and purposes it contains.[39] There is no final recipe for how any community should be ordered, no Aristotelian point of certainty. But this does not vitiate the ontological perspective. Indeed, when we turn to a social-ontological dimension, we can give form and content to our critical capacities. We cannot deny the essential existence of social relations, of social processes, structures, and purposes. Unlike the postmetaphysical fallacy, we cannot simply create valid social norms through reflexive action. Indeed, what gives critical reflection cognitive ballast is its capacity to think concretely about the social world and how it can provide us a critical and diagnostic point of view. Perhaps this is why we need to rethink the direction that the recognition paradigm has taken critical theory.

I think this is an important question, and one that needs to be sketched here. My criticisms of Honneth's paradigm of recognition as a critical theory of society is not meant in purely negative terms. Rather, as I see it, it takes us away from the foundational concepts and structure of thought that makes critical theory distinctive and compelling. Honneth social theory rests on an implicit and perhaps unacknowledged ontological structure.[40] It accepts the ideas of social development, processual change, the essential nature of social relatedness, and the relation between these relations and subjective development and cognitive formation. But he isolates this ontology to a recognitive, neo-idealist layer without filling out the wider horizon of social reality that is constitutive of the species. As such, he is unable to see that critique cannot come from the experiential phenomena of the life-world but must be seen as a mediated form of social reflection. Honneth therefore gives into a neo-idealist fallacy about sociality, sociation, and social critique.

At the same time, from a dialectical point of view, Honneth represents the fullest articulation of the postmetaphysical paradigm. He sees clearly that there must be a thicker conception of human sociality than

---

39. I argue for an immanent metaphysics in Michael J. Thompson, "The Metaphysical Infrastructure of Hegel's Practical Philosophy," in M. Thompson (ed.), *Hegel's Metaphysics and the Philosophy of Politics* (New York: Routledge, 2018).

40. Honneth does note that social relations are in fact ontological in his *Pathologies of Individual Freedom: Hegel's Social Theory* (Princeton, NJ: Princeton University Press, 2010).

mere linguistic intersubjectivity. At the same time, he sees that social pathologies are rooted in the structures of our (recognitive) relations and that there are phylogenetic capacities (for recognition) that are species-specific and are shaped by the social forms of life that socialize the subject. These insights bring us as close as we can come within the postmetaphysical, neo-idealist framework to a comprehensive account of judgment. But it ultimately fails because, as I have endeavored to show here, it confines itself to the intercognitive dimensions of sociality and, as such, cannot defend against the reification problem—or the refraction of the norms and value orientations rooted in pathological social forms into reflective consciousness and thought itself. What is needed, as the rest of this book argues, is a critical social ontology to ground our capacities for and concept of judgment. In this sense, a critical social metaphysics must grant us comprehension of the social totality, but it must also serve as the ground for a critical practical reason.

Returning to a deeper reading of what Hegel and Marx shared in their ideas about social reality, I will show that an ontological perspective grants their ideas distinctive and critical power. The ontological paradigm is not totally opposed to the recognition and communicative paradigms, but it seeks to privilege the objective structures and processes that constitute human sociality; we cannot work from within the life-world and its immanent practices and derive critique. To attempt this opens us up to the problem of constitutive power and reification. What is needed is a form of judgment, a form of critique that can call into question the social totality, one that can provide valid norms based on criteria immanent to our ontological capacities and how these capacities are misdirected and pathologically shaped by defective forms of sociality marked by domination and power. Such a view does not negate recognitive relations but sees them as one layer among a rich assortment of different relations we share with others. Even more, it grants us access to a critical metaphysics: one that allows us to have an objective-critical vantage point. The pragmatist and neo-idealism of current critical theorists requires a response informed by the desire for a more humane and dignified social world and, from a rational point of view, one that can secure those claims and avoid the pitfalls of alienation, deformed cognition, and relativism. It is the task of a critical social ontology to enable us to generate a theory of ethics and practical rationality that will be up to the challenge of exploding the powers of reification and the pitfalls of relativism.

Part II

Beyond Babel

Social Ontology and the
Reconstruction of Critical Reason

Chapter 5

Recovering the Ontological Infrastructure
of Political Judgment

Up to this point, I have sought to demonstrate that a nonmetaphysical and postmetaphysical project for practical reason fails to provide us with a genuinely critical form of rationality that can stand up to the strong pressures of modern forms of social power and the reification of consciousness. I have also been arguing that there exists a bankruptcy to this postmetaphysical paradigm and that there is a need to consider the content of our social world and the reasons used in democratic deliberation and, further, that only a critical-ontological approach can provide this content for a critical practical reason. My goal moving forward is to chart a path toward a critical social-ontological framework for practical reason that can make a critical theory of political judgment coherent. To do this, I need to show that that there existed a specific kind of social metaphysics shared by a host of thinkers in modern political thought and that this social metaphysics is pregnant with a great deal of meaning and philosophical insight—philosophical insight that has been decidedly sidestepped by the emergence of the postmetaphysical and pragmatic paradigm that gained consensus in moral philosophy.

My critique of the postmetaphysical paradigm should not be construed as a dismissal of the respective insights of the different thinkers I examined here. Honneth's project to construct a theory of recognition that can lead us to a modern form of "ethical life" is a crucial starting point. The insight here is flawed to the extent that critical cognition needs to be perceived as inquiring into the ontological structures of

social reality that pervade our world. A critical theory of political judgment must have in view how the objective, material, and ontological
structures of social reality either promote or pervert the achievement of
those social goods required for individual development and flourishing.

If a theory of judgment is to serve any real political efficacy, it
must deal with the problem of how we can explode the encrusted forms
of legitimation that arrest our critical-reflective capacities. As I see it,
there is a vital structure of thought in Western political philosophy
that grants us a framework to construct a genuinely critical theory of
political judgment. For these thinkers, only a comprehension of the
social totality could grant insight into how we reflect on politics and
the specific norms and institutions that shape our world. The social
totality is both a product of our collective norms and practices and
a causal power in our self- and collective development. The nature of
our relations and the practices and purposes toward which they are
organized manifests the relative "goodness" or "defectiveness" of any
society. The "good" is therefore not some a priori category, nor is it
something that can be adjudicated through intersubjective discourse
alone. It requires an ontological framework for its realization and the
cognitive grasp if its orientation. I see this framework not as a foundation for practical reason and judgment, but rather as an infrastructure
for those projects.

By "ontological," I mean a way of shaping the essentially social-
relational features of human life; these features are viewed not as brute
natural facts but as products of sociality, which in turn is a capacity
natural to the species. The ontology of our sociality then becomes a
distinct realm of freedom: a domain that is not determined by nature
external to our wills and capacities but internally rooted in our distinctive capacities as a species—capacities for relations, purposeful activity
(*praxis*), normativity, and so on. But it also refers to how collective
structures of relations, practices, and purposes become a distinct object
of study, how social reality as a processually organized totality can be
judged and transformed. The ontology of society consists of the ways our
practices, relations, norms, institutions, and purposes constitute a distinct
and systematic reality that has causal powers over us even as they are
products of our practices and norms. In this sense, social critique must
grasp the ontology of our social world as emerging from the various
ways we organize our social-relational structures, the norms and practices that produce them, and the collective ends and purposes they are

organized to realize. The theory of critical judgment I want to defend is rooted in this axis that runs through a robust structure of thought in political philosophy, one that I will seek to trace and tease out here.

My thesis here is that a social-ontological theory of judgment that initially served as the backbone for classical expressions of political and moral thought survived the onslaught of nominalism and empiricism that sought to destroy what early modern philosophers saw as premodern Scholastic and Aristotelian thought. With the emergence of modern science in the late Renaissance, the need to rid modern thought of metaphysics was indeed a worthy goal. But thinkers such as Rousseau, Hegel, and Marx in fact fought against the attack on Aristotelian ideas (implicitly and explicitly) that took root with thinkers like Hobbes and others who argued for the classical liberal paradigm. This tradition—what I call the tradition of modern critical social metaphysics—had at its core the idea that social facts and social reality made an emergent property of the concrete social interdependence of agents. For them, metaphysics represented not an inflated metaphysics associated with God or some other form of intangible "substance." Instead, they saw that social reality was constituted by the norms and practices that interdependent social agents articulated and that concrete forms of life construed as the actual structures of social relations constituted the reality of any community.

At the heart of the theory of judgment is the need to fit our experience of any particular act or phenomenon into a cognitive context allowing us to comprehend it. As I see it, a critical theory of political judgment is only possible once we inquire into how our social relations, processes, and the ends and purposes of those relations and processes are structured and shaped. Only when we ask about how humans are realized from within these concrete social forms can we begin to discuss political judgment in any meaningful sense. The key thesis here that can ground what I defend as a critical theory of judgment is that only when cognition can unite the phenomenological account of reality with a logical account of the totality that produces or conditions reality will subjects be capable of critical judgment. Where the postmetaphysical account fails is in its emphasis on the former at the expense of the latter. The constructivist account of the validity of norms shears off the social-metaphysical account of reality.

Language and norms play a crucial role in this theory of critical ontology. But it is conjoined with a theory about the ontological reality of social forms: that is, of structures of social relations. Just as important is the thesis that humans have certain basic, essential capacities for social relatedness and praxis that are shaped and formed by the ontological structures of social forms. A twofold ontology is thus what thinkers in this structure of thought saw as basic to their conceptions of judgment. On one hand, a first-order ontology of human capacities and a second-order ontology of social structures and forms could either promote and enhance or frustrate and pervert these first-order capacities. They took from classical philosophical anthropology the idea that humans had an essential feature, that of sociation, but denied its essential link to nature or some natural state that would provide the desideratum for justice or the good life. They saw that these social-relational structures had to be judged based on the extent to which they maximized or at least constituted a kind of common good that could provide each member of the political association with the requisite forms of life to promote their self-development.

The significance of this is that judgment had to take account of the organizational shape of our relations with others and how the shapes these relations take either enhance or erode our status as free persons, as fully self-determining agents whose self-determination is a function of one's interdependence with others and the kinds of ends, purposes, and goods these collective forms of life embody and produce. Only in this way would we be able to have a rational and concrete form of judgment that was not prone to the excess of passions or the corrupting influence of self-interest. In this sense, the genealogy I provide here seeks to highlight a different interpretation of modern judgment and the resources that a critical social-ontological approach can provide. Only after this will I be in a position to explore in a more systematic and rigorous way the properties and modes of critical social ontology and its use in the framework for critical judgment.

Aristotle's Social Ontology and the Structure of Political Judgment

Greek and Roman political philosophy have at their core an anthropological model of the human community that is the foundation for thinking about normative and prescriptive ideas about ethics and politics. Theories of politics were unique to the Greek world, and one reason for this was an attempt to understand how to classify and judge the different forms that human association was able to take. The relevant question of this tradition of thought was, to be sure, reliant on what we would consider an outmoded reliance on a theory of nature that we no longer accept. But dismissing the power of this tradition on this basis would be a mistake. It holds out a fruitful way of framing political judgment and securing forms of political judgment. What I want to suggest here is that we can carry over into contemporary critical practical reason the structure of thought they outlined and defended. For them, the diagnosis of social ills was to be comprehended with an ontological grasp of the social totality.

Aristotle's thesis about the nature of humans is well known. The basic model that he outlines in Book I of his *Politics* remains a central framework for understanding how a theory of judgment can be built from his ideas. Aristotle wants to provide an empirical classification of political forms in the *Politics*, and more importantly he provides an implicit theory of judgment: how we can think through these forms and evaluate them on a rational and concrete basis. Indeed, the unification of description and prescription is bound together in the first sentence of the work: "We can see that every *polis* (political community) is a kind of association (κοινωνίαν) and every association is formed with a view to some good."[1] The relation of the individual to this social-ontological entity of the polis is what concerns the problem of political judgment. In this sense, the properties of our associations with others and the mechanisms of development that inhere in these relations constitute the social metaphysical basis for Aristotle's conception of the good and social justice. Indeed, Aristotle's thought gives us the first detailed look at what a social metaphysics can achieve when tied to an evaluative project of judgment for the sake of political life.

Aristotle is clear that there is a metaphysical structure to his conception of human life understood as a social and political form of life.[2] Although it is clear that humans are biologically distinct from one another, that no material links them to one another, this nevertheless does not entail (a) that there is no metaphysical relatedness between human beings and (b) that our essence (οὐσία) can be reduced to what is biological. In both cases, there are metaphysical categories that

---

1. Aristotle, *Politics* (Oxford: Oxford University Press, 1975), 1252a-1.

2. On Aristotle's anthropology as an ontology, see the valuable discussion by Rüdiger Bubner, *Polis und Staat. Grundlinien der Politischen Philosophie* (Frankfurt: Suhrkamp, 2002).

apply for a coherent grasp of the object of human being—metaphysical in the sense that they are features of being that are nonreducible to matter (ὕλη) alone but have modes of existence that move beyond the material structure of being. Aristotle's metaphysical categories embrace not only this feature of reality but also a dynamic or processual aspect of reality. He maintains that we need to look at the composition of reality as consisting of four "causes" or, better, four features that are constitutive of the complete emergence of any object: a "material" cause of the material substance that composes anything; a "formal" cause, or the shape or structure that an object takes; an "efficient" cause that captures the activity that brings that object into existence; and last, a "final" cause capturing an object's purpose or end.[3]

Aristotle's analysis of politics begins with an ontology of the human being. Human life is grasped as a product of the relations that shape and form us. There is a twofold argument here, and both are metaphysical in a basic sense. First, there is the thesis that the individual must be construed as a relational being. Human life can only achieve its end (τελός) when it is able to achieve "self-sufficiency" (αὐτάρκεια), which is a state of being where the individual can develop its rational and practical capacities. "Self-sufficiency," for Aristotle, is itself a relational category in the sense that it is only achieved when the individual no longer has needs that cannot be met. The denser and more complex the structure of relations to which any individual belongs, the more "self-sufficiency" that person has. The polis is now seen as a complex of relations that provides the thick context for development of the individual. The thesis here is that an essential feature of human life is the property of relatedness with others, that an essential feature of humans as a species is this property of associational life.

The nature of these relations are, in the most basic sense, social-ontological features of our existence. They begin in the most basic form as a "coupling" (συνδυάζεσθαι) between male and female and ends in the polis. Individuals require increasingly dense and complex forms of association to achieve self-sufficiency. With each expansion of the sphere of these associations—from individuals to family, to village and then to the polis—the associations that ensconce each member of the association

---

3. See the discussion by T. H. Irwin, "The Metaphysical and Psychological Basis of Aristotle's Ethics," in Amélie Oksenberg Rorty (ed.), *Essays on Aristotle's Ethics* (Berkeley: University of California Press, 1980), 35–53.

help them achieve a state of self-sufficiency. Hence, the polis comes to be seen as the realization of the essence of associational life; it is the "best end" (τέλος βέλτιστον) toward which human association strives.[4]

Second is the thesis that humans are developmental or processual beings. Aristotle sees the process of becoming as an essential feature of humans. The relation between these two ideas is that relations are the context within which one's being unfolds and develops. For Aristotle, our relations with others constitute an essential feature of the nature of the species. It is not a product of the will that we associate with others but a function of our natural desires. The development of our capacities is also a function of the kinds of relations we inhabit. Any polis can be constructed in different ways. Each is constituted by different structures of relations that exert causal powers on the development of the individual. An association may not have natural or physical existence, but it has objective and causal powers. It has formative powers on the individual and on the association as a whole. This is a basic key for understanding how Aristotle constructs an objective, social-ontological account of political reality and the concept of the correct forms of association.

The polis therefore constitutes the highest form of sociality we can inhabit. It constitutes a social totality (σύνθετον) composed of lesser subsystems and substructures of relations (such as the family), all of which have as their proper, rational role the achievement of the good. This category is not, in this sense, a value claim in the modern, Kantian sense. It should more richly be understood as an ontological claim about the quality of the totality and the structures and processes of the associations that constitute it. Aristotle's theory of social justice requires certain ways that social relations are structured and enacted. This is not derived from a pirori categories but internally from the dynamics and features of human association itself. Justice (δίκαιος) is itself not an a priori principle regulating our norms and actions. Rather, it is a grasped

---

4. Martha Nussbaum states Aristotle's ethical-political project nicely when she writes: "That task, as he saw it, is to make available to each and every citizen the material, institutional, and educational circumstances in which good human functioning may be chosen; to move each and every one of them across a threshold of capability into circumstances in which they may choose to live and functional well." "Aristotelian Social Democracy," in Aristide Tessitore (ed.), *Aristotle and Modern Politics* (Notre Dame, IN: University of Notre Dame Press, 2002), 47.

as a feature of the totality of the association—characteristic of how the
social-relational structures of the community are shaped to promote
the full development of its members' capacities. Only by grasping how
particular acts, relations, norms, and institutions function according to
their respective ends, that is, as oriented toward the common good of
the community as a totality, can they be assessed. As Aristotle says in
the *Nicomachean Ethics*:

> It is necessary that we do not forget that what we are
> searching for are both justice and political justice. Political
> justice means justice between free and equal (whether actually
> equal or proportionally equal) persons, living a common life
> for the purpose of satisfying their needs. The result is that
> political justice cannot exist between people who are not
> equal and not free, in which case only a dim resemblance
> of justice exist.[5]

Equality and freedom are rich categories for Aristotle in that they
denote the features of our activities-with-others; they constitute the
actual reality of our relations with others.[6]

The totality (σύνθετον) of our relations with others can be characterized by the structure of its constituent substructures and subsystems.
Indeed, the σύνθετον is not simply a whole (ὅλον) but a special kind
of structure. It is a higher form of being than the aggregation of its
parts; it is a *totum* not a *compositum*. Its constitutive parts play not a
mechanical but a functional role in its operation in that the subsystems
in the totality are interdependent and participate in the process and
telos of the totality. The individual is therefore enhanced by his relations
with others. Mere biological life (τὸ ζῆν) is at an ontological level lower
than our lives with others, or our sociality (τὸ συζῆν), which alone can

---

5. Aristotle, *Nicomachean Ethics* (Oxford: Oxford University Press, 1994), 1134a-25.

6. As George E. McCarthy has argued, "Reciprocity is not an end in itself but
a necessary prerequisite in a moral economy designed to ensure self-sufficiency in
the household and the polis for a life of civic virtue, public deliberation, and policy judgment in daily government and the affairs of state. It is only this form of
activity which will realize the moral and political function of man as an 'activity of
soul in accordance with virtue.'" *Dreams in Exile: Rediscovering Science and Ethics in
Nineteenth-Century Social Theory* (Albany, NY: SUNY Press, 2009), 41.

provide for the good life or common good (τὸ εὖ ζῆν). The key idea here becomes that the shape of the totality, the specific ways it is constructed by its constitutive parts, determines whether the actual purpose of the community is ever realized in any concrete sense. The purpose of our associations with others and therefore the general purpose or telos of the political community as a whole is a kind of good in which each person shares: "People are brought together by common advantage (τὸ κοινῇ συμφερόν) as long as each person has a share accorded to them of the good life. The best end of society is therefore the good life, both for the collectivity and for each individual."[7]

This in turn can be judged by the extent to which those relations and the ends toward which those relations are oriented can realize the highest good possible for the community as a whole. The reason for this is that, as Aristotle continually emphasizes, the good of any individual is a function of the good of the social whole. The relation between particular and universal is symbiotic rather than analytically separate.[8] The individual is not a separate entity from the polis, from society as a whole. Rather, the polis can be said to exist in how the individual acts, the relations he has with others, the logic of those relations, and the kind of ends and purposes toward which those actions, habits, norms, and relations are organized. The polis exists not as a concrete entity but in the social ontology of these features of shared life, norms, and activities. In this sense, the individual participates in the structure of the social totality.[9] Defective forms of relations, defective ends of the community, and so on are those that fail to realize the proper end immanent within them. Aristotle does not see these as natural in the same sense as nonrational nature. Clearly, he sees that humans are an aspect of nature, but their nature differs from the rest of nature because humans

---

7. Aristotle, *Politics*, 1278b-20.

8. As Ernest Barker notes: "Particular could not for him be separated from universal: the particular only existed so far as it 'imitated' or 'participated' in the universal. To study it separately was to study nothing." *The Political Thought of Plato and Aristotle* (New York: Dover, 1959), 248.

9. Barker again notes that "To Aristotle the relation between particular and universal appeared in a different light: the individual had emphatically a real existence, and the universal was no divine 'Abstraction' separate from the individual, but a concrete being immanent in the thing which it informed." *The Political Thought of Plato and Aristotle*, 248.

have reason and speech (λόγος) and thus choice (προαίρεισις). To the extent that this is the case, we have to be able to make judgments for our proper end to be realized. Unlike nonrational nature, where ends are realized by nonrational and mechanical processes, humans must intentionally choose to realize their end.

The ontology of our sociality must be read in accordance with the metaphysic of the person that Aristotle outlines in the *Nicomachean Ethics*. There we see that the essence of each person is his "function" (ἔργον). The layered ontology of the person is one where "mere act of living" (τὸ ζῆν) common to plants and other animals is followed by "sentient" life (αἰσθητική) shared by animals and humans, and finally to what is distinctive to human life—that of the "practical life of the rational part of man" (πρακτική τις τοῦ λόγον ἔχοντος). As such, the link is made between the individual and the community; it is one of dialectical-developmental process where the self-reflecting practical lives of the members of the community organize and orient their practices, relations, norms, and institutions toward the common good because the common good is the proper context for the development of each member's functioning and attainment of the good life.[10]

How does this help us grasp Aristotle as a theorist of judgment? Broadly construed, Aristotle has no single word to denote "judgment." Instead, he uses several words in different contexts referring to capacities or activities of the practical mind. The most widely discussed in contemporary literature is that of phronesis (φρονήσις), which denotes an experienced form of "practical wisdom" achieved after the accumulation of much practical experience in politics. Next is *gnome* (γνώμη) which denotes the kind of judgment about fairness and equity (ἐπιεικές) and can be employed with others together (συγγνώμη). Last is *kritikos* (κριτικός) or a judgment that is essentially cognitive and pertains to the capacity to make distinctions between different objects, states, or phenomena in general. In these cases, in the practical realm judgment shares a hermeneutic dimension where our perception of particular social facts or particular circumstances are related to the universal to

---

10. See the discussion by Kathleen V. Wilkes, "The Good Man and the Good for Man in Aristotle's Ethics," in Amélie Oksenberg Rorty (ed.), *Essays on Aristotle's Ethics* (Berkeley: University of California Press, 1980), 341–57.

give them meaning.[11] For Aristotle, judgment is not a constructivist or phenomenological concern. Instead, it seeks to comprehend the particular as either ontologically good or defective, as "correct" (ὄρθος) or as "perverted" (ἡμαρτήμεναι) based on its capacity to bring about the common good or thwart it—the common good being the ultimate telos of the political community, the full realization of the capacities of its members. The rationale undergirding this is recursive to the social ontology that Aristotle sees as the basis for political life. This means that there are in effect good and defective ways to organize our social relations and the goods we produce.

It seems clear now that Aristotle's theory of judgment is more layered and complex than initially assumed. But it does have a discernible structure that is more than any phenomenological account can offer. Indeed, the metaphysical structure of judgment is in view whenever we make decisions about how to proceed in our activities and what kinds of praxis are to be considered good. Since he views associational life as a basic feature of the species, he also posits that the proper telos of such a species is the orientation of these associations toward the maximal common goods requisite for individual development and not the instrumental use of others for narrow particular benefit. (Of course, the defense of slavery negates this principle in Aristotle's political theory, but it does not do damage the validity of the thesis as a whole.) Judgment is necessary because our social reality is not a mechanical aspect of nature but is something shaped and created by us. Judgment is the capacity that provides a rational means for us to make cognitive distinctions between things (κριτικός); when employed among and toward others, it is a means to distinguish what is truly fair from what is not (γνώμη).

Finally, when employed in a properly political context it is a capacity to make distinctions about principles for action and normative judgments that should and must be acted on (φρονήσις). It is clear that when read in this way, Aristotle's theory of political judgment is thicker and more complex than some form of Arendtian "reflective judgment."

---

11. As McCarthy rightly says: "Without the application of the particular to the universal in hermeneutics and politics, there is no practical wisdom, no purpose to human life, and no natural limitations to the application of technical knowledge, the art of commercial trade, or the acquisition of property." *Dreams in Exile*, 57.

The phronetic capacity is one whereby we are able to understand the particular and its relation to the whole. It is different from epistemic or theoretical knowledge in the sense that it does not seek to classify or work in abstract first principles. On the contrary, the capacity of judgment is a hermeneutic activity where the particular is linked to the whole—in the case of politics, it is a matter of inquiring into the extent to which any given action, norm, law, practice, institution, or whatever, promotes or realizes the good. Indeed, this is what Aristotle emphasizes in his discussion of phronesis, that even though it requires "knowledge of particular facts more than knowledge of general principles," it requires it be subject to "some overall general and directing structural framework (τις καὶ ἐνταῦθα ἀρχιτεκτονική)."[12] This is to be provided, he tells us, by his *Politics*—and this would indicate that we are not dealing with a detached form of hermeneutics à la Arendt but a critical social ontology insofar as the point of judgment becomes seeing whether a given social form promotes its telos: the common good, to serve as the supportive context for individual development. Philosophy must be the guide for practical politics; justice cannot be derived from experience alone.[13]

This latter point is an important and often overlooked one. Aristotle's thesis is that that any form of judgment—in particular phronetic activity—must be "directed" by the science of politics. It is transcultural in the sense that it asks about the features of the species and what forms of relational association and ends are best fits for a just form of life. This is a critical hermeneutic that links the experience of particularity with the knowledge of the social whole—but it does this by linking the ontic with the ontological, that is, the prevailing reality with the "correct" forms of sociality that would produce common goods and ends.

---

12. Aristotle, *Nicomachean Ethics*, 1141b-20.

13. Richard S. Ruderman shares this interpretation: "Aristotle repeatedly tries to show, however, that political life devoid of philosophy either becomes an amoral power struggle or mistakenly submits to the 'charms of civic republicanism,' the view that participation alone guarantees wise or at least legitimate policy." "Aristotle and the Recovery of Political Judgment," *American Political Science Review*, vol. 91, no. 2 (1997): 409–20, 411. This view should be contrasted with interpretations of Aristotelian judgment rooted in "persuasion" rather than the ontological presuppositions of political life. See Bryan Garsten, *Saving Persuasion: A Defense of Rhetoric and Judgment* (Cambridge, MA: Harvard University Press, 2006), 115ff.

In modern philosophical parlance, the phenomenological is linked to the metaphysical in that it is necessary to inquire into how social relations are shaped and structured and how they have causal powers over their members. Indeed, we can only make critical judgments about our social and political world once we inquire into how our particular world of ontic structures of relations are able or unable to realize the common good of the whole. Because this common good is also a particular good for each individual insofar as it enables each member of the association to achieve self-sufficiency.

As such, the ontic dimension of the reality we inhabit can be defined by certain habits, relations, or associations that are in turn given shape by particular constitutions. But these particular ontic structures and social facts cannot be construed as relatively equal to any other. They can only be judged in a normatively useful and political sense when they are interrogated as either promoting the good or thwarting it. Only by considering the social-metaphysical features of human life are we able to discern, to judge in the critical sense of the term, these forms against what lies *in potentia* in alternative forms of social structure and social norms. This is why, in the *Politics*, Aristotle discusses how certain practices and relations are inherently defective and others are not. The criterion for judgment seems to be the extent to which actual relations and practices can realize mutual forms of the good. For instance, Aristotle lays down a theoretical distinction between "household management" (οἰκονομική) oriented toward self-sufficiency and "wealth-acquisition" (χρηματιστική). What makes the latter a defective form of activity is discerned from how it treats and structures the relations and ends between members of the same association. In increasing property and wealth beyond what is necessary for self-sufficiency, one must take from another.[14] Judgment is indeed involved here, as *kritikos*—the cognitive distinction between one form of activity and another. This critical form of judgment in the *Politics* entails that we use these theoretical ideas in our practical lives, in the gnomic and phronetic activities we employ as citizens.

Indeed, if the *Politics* provides us with a theory of social forms and an explicit social ontology, then the *Nicomachean Ethics* provides the model for ethical judgment and activity. The two projects are

---

14. See Aristotle, *Politics*, 1258b.

dimensions of a higher, more complex theory of how thinking subjects can achieve the good in their context as social beings. I actually think that his theory of judgment is more fruitfully seen by grasping how we evaluate political forms in relation to the substantial forms that the polis takes. Put another way, Aristotle's social ontology is fused to his evaluative schema of social forms (constitutions, *politeiai*) in that any factual knowledge claim about social reality is also an evaluative claim. The reason for this is also a feature of the ontological theory of judgment: the values of any community are emergent properties of the social arrangements they engender. There is no pure sphere of value, it is inherent in and concretized by the social practices we enact. These, in turn, are shaped by habits that are the product of the formal structures of the social arrangements of the community. These, in turn, are organized by and for certain ends or purposes. This is fundamentally ontological in the sense that being is determinative of and determined by our social practices.[15]

The relation between particular and universal that lies at the heart of the theory of political judgment is, in Aristotle, resolved in an interesting way—a way that, as I see it, can serve as the interpretive pivot for a critical theory of judgment. Although he sees that practical wisdom or phronesis is distinct from scientific knowledge (ἐπιστήμη), this does not mean that there is no objective or rational way to discern the what is "correct" and what is "defective." Indeed, Aristotle sees theory not as opposed to practice but as the highest expression of human activity. Hence, judgment is not a separate, detached form of *vita contempliva*, as Arendt would have it, but is constituted by practice itself, a *hexis* of expressing truth.[16] What it means is that theoretical knowledge cannot be used to derive the means to the end. The key idea is that phronesis or rational judgment more generally needs to be understood as linked to our rational development. Indeed, even though

---

15. See the interesting discussion by Ernst Vollrath, *Die These der Metaphysik. Zur Gestalt der Metaphysik bei Aristoteles, Kant und Hegel* (Wuppertal: Alois Henn, 1969), 56ff., as well as by Joachim Ritter, *Metaphysik und Politik. Studien zu Aristoteles und Hegel* (Frankfurt: Suhrkamp, 1969), 106ff.

16. See the excellent discussion by Hans-Georg Gadamer, "On the Possibility of a Philosophical Ethics," in Ronald Beiner and William James Booth (eds.), *Kant and Political Philosophy: The Contemporary Legacy* (New Haven, CT: Yale University Press, 1993), 361–73.

his *Rhetoric* places emphasis on the forms of argument requisite for persuasion, there is nevertheless a connection between rhetorical persuasion and the underlying rational structures of reason that grasp at universality. In contrast to thinkers like Arendt and Beiner, we are not moving from the particular to construct a universal based on agreement, but using particular forms of persuasion (examples and less formal modes of syllogism) to persuade.[17] Indeed, rhetoric and persuasion are distinct from philosophical modes of reasoning but are interdependent, not autonomous from them. Political rhetoric, public reason, still needs to have a conceptual and ontological core.

From a broader context, for Aristotle, a life well lived (happiness) is one where any individual is governed by a kind of practical rationality that promotes self- and other-relations conducive to the development of one's functional potencies. Such a practical rationality would have in view the thesis that human sociality is a basic and essential component of one's individuality and that they can only reach their optimal state as individuals when the social whole is "properly" ordered. This is why Aristotle says that "phronesis is a virtue of reason that grants the capacity to deliberate well concerning the good and bad."[18] As he says in the *Nicomachean Ethics*:

> It is apparent that phronesis is not scientific knowledge. . . .
> Phronesis deals with the ultimate particular thing which cannot be apprehended by scientific knowledge, but through perception; not the perception specific to any one of the sense, but a perception akin to that by which we perceive a triangle in mathematics.[19]

This passage is telling in that it makes a subtle connection between a theoretical and practical science. Aristotle argues that the good life, that of living well, is to be understood not as the cultivation of some abstract capacity for reason. Rather, the thesis is that the development

---

17. See Aristotle, *Rhetoric*, 1356b1ff., and the discussion by Russell Bentley, "Rhetorical Democracy," in Benedetto Fontana, Cary J. Nederman, and Gary Remer (eds.), *Talking Democracy: Historical Perspectives on Rhetoric and Democracy* (University Park: Pennsylvania State University Press, 2004), 115–34.

18. Aristotle, *Rhetoric*, 1366b-13.

19. Aristotle, *Nicomachean Ethics*, 1142a-25.

of the rational faculties in accordance with excellence is what is sought after.[20] Political judgment becomes the capacity to judge what practical forms of life are best for a community that seeks to achieve the highest good: that is, the good that will provide for the enrichment, development, and perfectibility (εὐδαιμονία) of each member of the association. What Aristotle seems to be saying here is that judgment, even phronesis, cannot be without some kind of rootedness in theoretical truth. Critical judgment emerges as the synthesis of these faculties, and it is only when we see that the social-ontological account of the polis laid out in the *Politics* is the grounding for our normative and practical activities that a comprehensive theory of judgment begins to emerge.

The connection between any social ontology and our practical forms of activity becomes more intimate when we consider that the latter is the efficient cause of the former even as the former is the ground or final cause of the latter. For Aristotle, there are "natural" forms or expressions of justice and social facts and "conventional" ones. The difference lies in that "natural" forms of justice resonate with what is universal and "conventional" to what has been arbitrarily accepted as valid.[21] We need a means for making the distinction between the two, and here the ontological ground of the polis reveals its critical role. Once we have considered the concrete and objective ways our social reality has been constructed, we can have a sense of judgment about the relative goodness of those social arrangements. Hence, what is ontological differs here from what is ontic in the sense that the latter refers to what merely exists, whereas the former refers to a richer form of existence that still lies *in potentia*, yet to be realized.

Phronesis reveals itself to be not simply a matter of experience or wisdom, and certainly not restricted to rhetorical and persuasion, but a distinct capacity to deliberate rationally about the proper ends and purposes the community should seek.[22] There is, then, a fundamental

---

20. This excellence is the totality of excellences that any individual can achieve over the course of a whole life. It is to be construed not as instrumental but as an end in itself.

21. "Political justice is either natural or it is conventional, natural when it has the same validity everywhere and does not depend on our acceptance of it; it is conventional when from the beginning it may be settled one way or another indifferently." Aristotle, *Nicomachean Ethics*, 1134b-20.

22. See David Wiggins, "Deliberation and Practical Reason," in Amélie Oksenberg Rorty (ed.), *Essays on Aristotle's Ethics* (Berkeley: University of California Press,

metaphysical ground to our correct deliberations about public affairs. Not a recipe or manual, to be sure, but a guiding framework that grants insight into the criteria for making and delineating good and bad judgments about the good. The key issue of judgment is a kind of thinking about the ends of our associations with others and which ends qualify as just, as best for the common benefit of that association.

The procedure is to inquire into the ends and purposes for our association with others—which Aristotle emphasizes over and over again is our common good life (τὸ εὖ ζῆν) as opposed to merely living (τὸ ζῆν)—and to see how those ends shape and structure our relations with others (τὸ συζῆν). The difference between what is conventionally accepted (νομικόν) and what is "natural" (φυσικόν) is of great critical importance because for Aristotle, our "nature" is not something mechanistic and externally defined but something immanent to us as a species. It is not an inflated metaphysical concept that defines Aristotle's concept of human nature; it is more akin to the idea that there are certain forms of activity that will be possible in certain social arrangements and not possible in others. The form (μορφή) that our social reality takes can either be arranged for the full range of those activities, or it can be arranged to limit what is potentially active.[23] Each constitutional form is itself constituted by the kinds of economic, civic, and social-relational practices and structures that shape them. When we are unable to deliberate as free persons, when inequality creates relations of domina-

---

1980), 221–40. Ruderman further notes that "Since, in practical life, there are always multiple ends to pursue (e.g., security and freedom, inclusiveness and excellence, etc.), *phronesis* should determine, at any given time, which end to pursue (in light of the resources, not least the moral resources, required to pursue it)." "Aristotle and the Recovery of Political Judgment," 416.

23. For a more technical discussion of the internal metaphysics of this thesis, see Aryeh Kosman, *The Activity of Being: An Essay on Aristotle's Ontology* (Cambridge, MA: Harvard University Press, 2013), 75ff. More specifically, Kosman argues that for Aristotle: "I can exercise an ability, and the ability and its exercise are one thing: a capacity in operation. So it is with substance. Matter and form are not linked together by possibilities of becoming. They are present together in the being that is nothing other than the active essence—that is, the essential activity—of the one being that both are. It is in this sense that matter is the locus of ability and capacity—*dunamis*—and form, as the principle of that ability's exercise, is the principle of its active being—its *energeia*. Form, we might say, is the principle of matter in operation; in instances of substantial being, it is the operation of being that is substance." *Activity of Being*, 81 and *passim*.

tion rather than reciprocity, when property determines the end of the state—all of these are defective, perverted forms of life not because of an inflated social metaphysics. Rather, it is the result of the imposition of a kind of social structure and social form that disables our capacities to act as fully developed agents.

The theme of the "form" or "formal cause" is a crucial step in Aristotle's metaphysical account of justice and the judgment of just and unjust regimes. He is aware that social relations and the various shapes they can take have causal powers on the rational and habitual features of the individual. The full development of each person therefore requires the social whole to be organized for the good of all because each member's self-sufficiency (the prerequisite for self-development) is determined by the self-sufficiency of others. Aristotle's critique of wealth acquisition is not, in this sense, a value separate from the facts of human life. Instead, it is rooted in how wealth is derived from having more than what one needs, which, he reasons, takes away from others. This constitutes an abuse of the social bond, and it is not the (natural) purpose of our relations with others. Natural in this sense means that category of social being that allows for the self-development and flourishing (εὐδαιμονία or τὸ εὖ ζῆν) of each member of the political association: "a *polis* is a well-living association of households and clans, and its purpose is a full and self-sufficient life."[24]

Conventional laws and institutions, however, may be rationalized and accepted by members of a political community, but this does not mean they are the correct forms. Natural justice is meant to contrast with these ontic forms of life. Natural justice allows us to see that the existing reality need not be taken as the best or proper forms of life we can inhabit. Defective forms of life, after all, can still allow us to live together, but not to reach the "good life." We can see this in his discussion of two different kinds of political association: one that has wealth acquisition as its purpose and the other, the good life of its members: "If men associated and assembled together for the sake of wealth their share in the political community is proportionate to their share in property with the result that the rationale of those that support oligarchy would seem to be valid."[25] On the other hand, if the association was formed not for the sake of mere life (τὸ ζῆν) but for

24. Aristotle, *Politics*, 1280b-34.
25. Aristotle, *Politics*, 1280a-31.

the good life (τὸ εὖ ζῆν), it would not be organized in this way, because it creates forms of dependency and forms of inequality that mitigate social relations that provide for mutual self-sufficiency and reciprocity. With the emergence of unequal wealth, social relations begin to warp, and the habits and norms of the community begin to transform. An ontological change begins to affect the polis where relations that were once reciprocal become dependent and exploitative. The norms of the community also begin to change and very character of the polis with it.

It should be clearer now that Aristotle's conception of judgment embraces much more than his concept of phronesis and is instead a feature of his more comprehensive discussion of politics and practical philosophy. The political community as an association of individuals oriented toward the common good because the common good is the good of each, which is a part of this basic idea. He is also clear that the features of our relations with others are constitutive of this further goal, that a whole pattern of practices, forms of reflection, and institutional structures need to be cultivated for this kind of comprehensive good to be realized. All of this nevertheless serves a basically critical function as we can judge the extent to which the ontological structures we inhabit either diverge from or actualize the common good and virtues requisite for the good life.[26]

Aristotle lays out a critical theory of judgment insofar as he is able to connect the hermeneutic apprehension of particular states and affairs with the logic of the whole; he can provide a social-ontological account of how our sociality is shaped and organized.[27] The good is therefore an ontological reality rather than a value proposition: it emerges as real, is itself realized and constituted by the very ways our associations are organized and shaped. In the end, Aristotle constructs a model of

---

26. Hans-Georg Gadamer rightly notes on this aspect of Aristotle's hermeneutics that: "In truth, as his distinction shows, the idea of natural right for Aristotle has only a critical function. One cannot make any dogmatic use of it, in other words, one cannot award the content of particular laws with the honor and universality of natural right." *Warheit und Methode* (Tübingen: J.C.B. Mohr [Paul Siebeck], 1975), 303.

27. McCarthy notes: "Without the application of the particular to the universal in hermeneutics and politics, there is no understanding or judgment; without the application of moral knowledge to the world, there is no practical wisdom, no purpose to human life, and no natural limitations to the application of technical knowledge, the art of commercial trade, or the acquisition of property." *Dreams in Exile*, 57.

political theory that informs a broader theory of judgment as one that
guides our ideas toward the social-ontological structures requisite for the
common good and common interests. He does this in a way that sets
out a kind of structure of thought that will be expanded and reworked
by subsequent theorists who sought a more radical, rational inquiry into
the capacity of political judgment. Implicit in Aristotle's theory about
judgment is a complex fusion of descriptive and normative categories.

Inequality and Rousseau's Ontological Account of Social Pathology

If Aristotle's framework for political judgment is rooted in his metaphysics of sociality and human personhood, Rousseau approaches this
problem via his theory of inequality. For Rousseau, we are also relational
beings. We have certain natural traits toward sympathy and relationality
that are developed in our interaction with others. We are not naturally
social, but we build a more complex and more sophisticated form of
reality through cooperative relations with others. In his *Discourse on the
Origins of Inequality among Men*, Rousseau outlines a social theory with
deep social-ontological implications. Although he provides nothing like
a systematic treatment, he constructs an argument about how our individuality is either promoted or deformed by the kinds of social relations
we inhabit. His critical social theory is also, I contend, rooted in a
fundamentally ontological theory of value and society. What I mean is
that unlike the neo-Kantian approach of the separation of social facts
and values, Rousseau sees that values are both constituted by the social
arrangements we inhabit and reconstituted by us. Humans are perfectible;
they can thrive and achieve self-development and freedom only in a
community that is arranged by them self-consciously for their common
good and common purposes. What Rousseau sees is that judgment is
a crucial feature of a kind of free agency that will have in view the
free community.

From Rousseau, I think we can derive an important insight into
how a social-ontological approach to human sociality can be shaped
into a distinctly modern thesis about critical judgment. Rousseau centers his ideas not on a "natural" theory of human sociality but on the
articulation of normative and political concepts that emerge from our
responsiveness to others and what kind of relations can best fit a free

self and vice versa. Our sociality is an essential part of who we are and serves as the fundamental context for critical judgment.[28] An emphasis on the self, on the individual, means that judgment plays a heightened role in his thought: for all social arrangements either are sustained or collapse based on how each person either conforms or dissents from the norms that hold them together. Here, as with Aristotle, the structure of thought I am trying to make clear becomes even more defined. Each member of the political association must be able to think in terms of the cooperative, social interdependence that allows for the context for individual good and development. Each member must achieve that form of "we-thinking" that will enable the group to function for the common benefit of its members. The common good and the individual good are thus two dimensions of the same social reality.

Rousseau's path to this thesis is important to trace. In the *Second Discourse*, he seeks to provide a genealogy of the phenomenon of social inequality. As he does this, he traces for us the initial emergence of human sociality and then its corruption and demise. He maintains that the move from the solitary, "natural" state of human beings to an artificial, social one is not a natural state but nevertheless creates a new kind of self: one that develops new powers and new forms of moral reflection.[29] We are not naturally social—on this point, Rousseau is emphatic. But we have natural capacities that will enhance and encourage our sociality with others. We choose association with others to enhance our capacity to solve certain problems. Our shared sociality is a product of our will, and in time comes to take on a life of its own.

What is central is a basic thesis that Rousseau seeks to defend time and again: that the forms of life we inhabit are reproduced by our own norms and habits (*moeurs*) and that to judge the rational

28. For an extended discussion, see Michael E. Brown, *The Concept of the Social in Uniting the Humanities and Social Sciences* (Philadelphia: Temple University Press, 2014), 23ff.

29. Peter Alexander Meyers writes, "Indeed, it was Rousseau who first, and with vertiginous acumen, construed this moral field as social, and no as bodily habit, psychological attachment, or stalwart façade of sacred or civic devotion. . . . Society is shown to be the site of the moral, and the ongoing articulation of the moral constitution of society. This step is specifically modern. It is a modernity that begins with Rousseau. It is a view of human life that gears things toward politics in a new way." *Abandoned to Ourselves* (New Haven, CT: Yale University Press, 2013), 14–15.

validity of these norms, we need access to a we-consciousness or at least a "we-perspective" that calls into question the purposes and ends of our interaction and cooperative activities with others. His infamous and often maligned and misunderstood category of the "general will" is meant to solve this problem. This is a form of cognition that accounts for the proper social substrates that would produce a common good for all members of the political association without being subject to the irrational pressures of the already existing categories of thought and practices ambient in the world. Rousseau constitutes a crucial further step along the pathway to constructing a critical theory of judgment.

In the initial stages of social development, men form cooperative relations with each other to satisfy needs. That "happiest epoch," as he describes it, is characterized by sufficiency: each has what he needs for himself by his own means. The beginning of it emerges not from fear of insecurity but from the limits imposed on our independence. Natural man is independent—he does not require the assistance of others. But there comes a time when this independence is not sufficient for the kind of problems that confront us. We need to construct social relations of cooperation to expand our powers and solve problems that we could not otherwise solve as independent selves. As he says in the *Social Contract*:

> I take it that men have reached the point at which the obstacles to their survival in the state of nature overpower each individual's resources for maintaining himself in that state. So this primitive condition can't go on; the human race will perish unless it changes its manner of existence.[30]

But there exist limits to our natural independence:

> men cannot create new forces; they can only bring together ones that already exist, and steer them. So their only way to preserve themselves is to unite a number of forces so that they are jointly powerful enough to deal with the obstacles. They have to bring these forces into play in such a way that they act together in a single thrust.[31]

30. Jean-Jacques Rousseau, *Du contrat social*, in *Oeuvres Complètes*, vol. 3 (Paris: Éditions Gallimard, 1964), 360.

31. Rousseau, *Du contrat social*, 360.

Cooperation is an expression of collective power, a new, distinctly social form of reality. It articulates a change in the members of the cooperative activity. In their emergence as interdependent persons, each begins to think differently about self and other. Consciousness and social reality are therefore dialectically shaped.

Cooperation, however, is also the entry point for the fall of man—not because it is intrinsically problematic but because it is open to becoming abused and usurped by the passions of those that seek to exploit others for gain and for benefit. *Amour propre*, the emotion driving us to seek particular benefit at the expense of others, leads to restructuring these early cooperative and interdependent relations. In the *Discourse on Inequality*, Rousseau finds that the association with others is immediately transformed by the drive for *amour propre*:

> from the moment one man began to stand in need of the help of another; from the moment it appeared advantageous to any one man to have enough provisions for two, equality disappeared, property was introduced, work became indispensable, and vast forests became smiling fields, which man had to water with the sweat of his brow, and where slavery and misery were soon seen to germinate and grow up with the crops.[32]

Inequality emerges not from some natural difference in abilities between us but from the drive of those who seek extractive gain at the expense of others. *Amour propre* must be controlled and channeled lest it become a logic of domination and servitude. This is the key project of the *Emile*—to chart the proper formation of the self toward moral relations with others. The genesis of civilization is the genesis of inequality among men, but it need not be the final stage of our development.

The thesis thus far, if we compare the arguments of the *Second Discourse* and the *Social Contract*, seems to be that there is a movement from natural independence to an artificial dependence on others. The cooperation that characterizes the first happy phase of the golden age of early human settlements is manipulated by those who seek their own interests in surplus and the benefits it bestows at the

---

32. Jean-Jacques Rousseau, *Discours sur l'origine et les fondemens de l'inégalité parmi les hommes*, in *Oeuvres Complètes*, vol. 3 (Paris: Éditions Gallimard, 1964), 166.

expense of others. This takes the explicit form of extractive dominance, where, as Rousseau puts it, "one man realized that it was useful for a single individual to have provisions for two." Here is born the roots of defective social relations, of the inequality among men that is so destructive of his potential for self-development and happiness. For now, man's independence is surrendered to others, and the few can come to control and to dominate the many. What results is a pathology of society. Rousseau's project is to show that this pathological sociality as social dependence under conditions of inequality requires not a return to natural independence but a transformation of the ontology of our sociality and relational-life toward interdependence: a cooperative form of sociality where each member is cognizant of the common benefits bestowed by their cooperative activities and life together, that is, where each member is governed by the general will.

It could be hypothesized that if cooperation were, at this point, governed by a general will, human society likely would have developed toward that condition of perfective freedom and happiness that Rousseau has in mind. Instead, it opened up the domain for economic self-interest, for a kind of self-interest where one sought one's advantage over others and, more important, at the expense of others. This need to have more than what makes one sufficient is made possible by the social configuration beginning to emerge with cooperation. This ontology is not predetermined by nature but is the product of a developmental anthropology formed by human choice and will. The key insight here is that Rousseau attributes a metaphysical transformation to the species by this shift from solitary independence to cooperative dependence. We become ensconced in relations-with-others, which in turn has fundamentally transformative effects on consciousness, conscience, and cognition. The key problem that he will have to work out is how we judge which forms of social life are worthy of our rational obligations and which are not. The key to his political theory will rest on the concept of judgment.

The initial stages of social development begin to flesh out the psychology of the individual. Compassion, a natural impulse, is activated by our relations with others and leads to deeper, more enduring social bonds, more than merely the search for material self-sufficiency, but new psychological needs. When socialized properly, that is, when our psychology and morality are educated to internalize our interdependence, then we can think in a new, expanded form: we can begin to think in terms of the general will.[33] Indeed, although exaggerated *amour propre* is the first cause of the social or what he calls "metaphysical" differences between men, Rousseau is consistent in seeing the nature of inequality as essentially revolving around economic power.[34] The reason for this is that, as Rousseau notes in many other writings, his concern is that bourgeois-liberal society places an atomic form of self-interest over what he sees to be the correct form of self-interest: one characterized by an interest in the common interest. The interests of the few, those with the ends of capturing social surplus created by cooperation, truly dominate our age. They express the need to legitimate this arrangement by any means necessary: "For two men whose interests agree, a hundred thousand can be opposed to them, and there is in this case no other means to succeed than to deceive or ruin all these people."[35]

Through cooperation, some men find that they can have more for themselves than if they were to labor alone. The desire for surplus has

---

33. Much needs to be left out here to justify this thesis with more firmness. I have done this elsewhere. See Michael J. Thompson, "Autonomy and Common Good: Interpreting Rousseau's General Will." *International Journal of Philosophical Studies*, vol. 25, no. 2 (2017): 266–85.

34. Frederick Neuhouser places exclusive emphasis on *amour propre* as an origin for inequality. As he argues:, "the concern for relative standing, and as soon as one takes the view that an affirmation of one's own worth requires being esteemed not merely as good but as better than others, *amour propre* requires inequality in order to be satisfied." *Rousseau's Critique of Inequality: Reconstructing the Second Discourse* (New York: Cambridge University Press, 2014), 78 and *passim*. Neuhouser's reading sees material self-interest as a function of *amour propre* when Rousseau's text suggests that there is an elective affinity between the kinds of pride and status satisfied by unequal gain and the interest in acquiring surplus for purposes of particular self-interest (an interest in leisure, comfort, luxury, etc.). However, this reading goes out of its way to avoid the material argument that is essential for Rousseau's fuller account of the problem with bourgeois-liberal society and the promises inherent in a society governed by a republican ethos and institutions oriented toward the common interest. Indeed, this interpretation rips Rousseau's concern about the social effects of unequal property out of context of those discussions in the *Discourse on Political Economy* and the *Social Contract* and seems to be an attempt to make Rousseau into a theorist of recognition rather than a critic of the emerging bourgeois social relations that he saw as causing defective social relations.

35. Jean-Jacques Rousseau, "Preface" to "Narcisse," in *Oeuvres Complètes*, vol. 2 (Paris: Éditions Gallimard, 1961), 966.

the effect of satisfying an exaggerated *amour propre* and has an intrinsic logic in the division of labor. This finds an elective affinity with an already existing *amour propre*, opening up a new, expanded space for a deformed, mutilated subjectivity. This new subjectivity is shaped by this social inequality: mastery and slavery now corrupt man's capacity to recognize freedom as his once natural state: "although man had previously been free and independent, we find him, so to speak, subject by virtue of a multitude of fresh needs, to all of nature and particularly his fellow men, whose slave in a sense he becomes even in becoming their master; rich he needs their services; poor he needs their help."[36] Economic inequality is not constitutive of a form of consciousness and subjectivity unable and unwilling to distinguish its particular interests from the interests of the community as a whole. Defective social relations can be seen to shape a defective subjectivity. For Rousseau, value is to be seen as rooted in the features of our social reality: the good is not an abstract, formal, or a priori procedure; it is a property of the kinds of relations we inhabit—relations that will activate and depend on how they structure our relations with others. Rousseau has a first- and second-order social ontology: humans can either unfold and develop their capacities or be debased and malformed based on the structure of relations that they inhabit.

Defective sociality is therefore what marks inequality as problematic. Rousseau sees this not because of some sense of fairness or whatever but because of an abuse of the social bond; it is not the purpose of our lives to be the instrument of others. Of course, *amour propre* exists prior to the emergence of these extractive relations; they enable it to expand and inflate, pushing aside the feelings of compassion and sufficiency that exist in the "golden age" preceding it.[37] The emergence

---

36. Rousseau, *Discourse sur l'origine de l'inégalité*, 174–75.

37. I think Neuhouser is wrong when he argues, "Despite the prominent role Rousseau's genealogy gives to the advent of private property . . . he also makes clear that it is *amour propre*, not a straightforward desire for the necessities or comforts of life, that ultimately explains the rapid growth—perhaps even the origin—of private property. The drive to possess acquires the importance for human that it does only because the extent and value of a person's property is so readily perceived by others as an external sign of her worth as an individual." *Rousseau's Theodicy of Self-Love: Evil, Rationality, and the Drive for Recognition* (New York: Oxford University Press, 2008), 122–23. The problem here is that Rousseau's text indicates, as I quoted above, that "as soon as one man realized that it was useful for a single individual to have

of inequality transforms the drives of man, making him enemies with those on whom he depends for his livelihood. He becomes an enemy with himself: suppressing and denying more authentic drives for the honor and narcissistic need for social standing. Man becomes constituted so as to exist "for others" rather that being shaped by relations of domination and servitude.[38]

Considering this argument, one thing is certain and more important to emphasize: Rousseau is offering up not simply a genealogy of inequality but, more importantly, a theory about the nature of social power and domination and a negative exploration of the true, "correct" purposes of social cooperation concealed in the pathological culture of defective social relations. If we reduce his argument to one that is primarily psychologistic, we get him wrong. The key problematic that Rousseau is after is that of power, of domination, and this has its roots in the development of social relations and the search for surplus extraction. This provides *amour propre* with its more expanded manifestation, not the other way around. To go even further, *amour propre* becomes the basic substance of the legitimating power of these new extractive relations of dependence and control. Now man will be under the yoke of these unequal relations—indeed, both master and servant will—and actively search them out. The basic idea here is that Rousseau would like to show how defective social relations compel us to perceive and look for a remedy, for a means of solving the dilemmas of unequal society. As Kant saw the matter, "Rousseau's purpose did not involve inviting man to go back to the state of nature, but rather to

provisions for two, equality disappeared, property was introduced," and nowhere does he claim that the search for confirmation of their worth makes this new social system of relations come about. The emphasis is important because it would seem to indicate (as would make sense given Rousseau's other arguments) that the social relations that man inhabits comes to shape and mold his being and his psychology, not the other way around. Only by changing the social structure, how humans are governed, can we change the inner world of man.

38. As Nicholas Dent remarks, "Since it is so widely held that if *any* of our self-constitution has come to be constituted as it is 'for others' then by that fact alone we are self-dispossessed or have lost our own proper integrity, it is desirable to spend a moment showing that this is not so. It is when, and only when, our self-constituted is determined in *particular* ways by (what we feel to be) the requirements that others lay upon us that we become self-estranged." *Rousseau: An Introduction to His Psychological, Social and Political Theory* (Oxford: Basil Blackwell, 1988), 57.

look back to it in order to become aware of the errors and weaknesses of conventional society."[39]

The key idea here is not only psychological, as with the analysis of *amour propre*. More essentially, there is the effect that this has on the nature of "right" and the norms of culture and politics more broadly. Rousseau is grasping a complex notion about the nature of power: that the sustenance of these defective social relations are dependent on forms of legitimacy that take hold in the minds of men. He describes how this new inequality between rich and poor leads to an instability in the cooperative relations based on extraction: "there began to arise, according to the diverse characters of rich and poor, domination and servitude, violence and threats."[40] A series of "new needs" come to be seen as necessary, replacing the natural freedom that once gave man his dignity and independence. A new social reality is constituted by these defective social relations and the roles and practices that are loaded onto them.

This is a central theme in Rousseau's critique of defective civil society: that economic inequality corrupts the capacity of people to judge the good in contrast to false needs; that because of the new forms of culture and the habits and practices of mind that accompany it, they become unable to discern an alternative form of social reality than what already pervades their world. The key is to break out of this defective social reality and break with it. By the end of the *Second Discourse*, we are left with the view that modernity has a tragic end: it will result only in our mutual debasement and unfreedom.

The essential, defining characteristic of inequality and its debasing power over human life is that is mutilates the true nature of social bonds. Social relations have the potential to increase man's mutual benefit; however, they are perpetuated in defective civil society by the presence and activity of atomic self-interest, where each person seeks their own particular gain and interest—and satisfy the feelings for honor and status—at the expense of others. This is not simply an argument about the nature of material welfare; more essentially, it is an argument about how man is shaped and cultivated. It's Rousseau's fundamental proposition that the inequality between men produces corruption at the

---

39. Ernst Cassirer, *Rousseau, Kant and Goethe* (New York: Harper, 1963), 25.

40. Rousseau, *Discourse sur l'origine de l'inégalité*, 176.

moral and psychological level by inhibiting the innate capacities for a deeper, more developed subjectivity and moral-political life. The institutions of society, the creative *techne* of human individual and collective life, the forms of authority to which we submit, and the kind of lives we live—all are deeply corrupted by defective social relations. Instead of freeing man, deepening his subjectivity and happiness, it has led to his subjection and a pathological form of life.

But pathological in what sense? The common way of thinking about this is that there is some metaphysically prior or ideal state from which one can judge the pathological condition. This is an overly simplistic and incorrect interpretation. Rousseau argues that—and in this he is not unlike Aristotle—we have inherent qualities that could be developed and made concrete via our practices and social arrangements, or we can suffer the consequences of this frustrated maldevelopment and experience the pathological state of distended *amour propre*. This can never lead to happiness or freedom. This will become evident over time. As long we are conscious of the origins of our pathologies, there will always be room for critique; where there is room for critique, there will be space for social and self-transformation. What is required is the proper etiology of our pathologies. But even this requires a new way of thinking, and Rousseau seems to have known this. It springs not from some philosophical process of deduction nor from some social-scientific procedure. Rather, it begins with the simplest question of all: what is the purpose of my association with others? Following from Rousseau's discussion about the expansion of human powers resulting from our cooperative association with others and how this has changed and transformed the species, it is a fundamentally ontological question about that is at stake here. The reason for this is that when we ask about the purpose of our association with one another, we are actually asking about how our relations with others are structured and their purpose.

The *Social Contract* therefore proposes a theory of judgment in the concept of the general will. This concept, which has been consistently misunderstood as a group-based preference, is actually a property of each person's reflective powers. The general will is a property not of the group but of the self. It is a cognitive structure of reasoning that is shaped by our associational life. Each member of the association must, according to Rousseau, think not in terms of his own particularity or his interests as an atomistic, independent being, nor as a dependent being.

Rather, the general will asks us to think in terms of our cooperative interdependence; it asks us to think in terms of the we-intentionality that is requisite for cooperative forms of life. It is an attempt to produce a kind of normative space of reasons structured by and reflecting our associational reality. The idea now is that the natural liberty of the "noble savage" will be replaced with a conception of social freedom. This new form of freedom will require that we, as autonomous selves, think in an expanded form: that is, according to the common good rather than the particular interest. Now the question becomes how can we transform this debased reality? Once again, the question concerns how we organize our relations with others and the purposes of those relations. Inequality disseminates *amour propre* as a debased form of self, warping our reflective capacities. Once *amour propre* has infected the self, it will seek only vapid self-satisfaction and dominance or tolerate dominance by others for the sake of achieving that self-satisfaction.

The way out of this approach is a new sensibility—one that allows for an awareness of the essence of our sociality. This is the psychological journey of *Emile*, whose psychological and moral development prepare him for republican citizenship. At the heart of this approach is the thesis that our activities, practices, and norms constitute the social reality we inhabit. At the same time, the shape of our social relations generates certain practices and norms to sustain them. The connection is between the objective social structure and the cognitive and evaluative features of the self.[41] The ontology of our social reality is constituted by our practices and the norms that orient them, but these norms are themselves rooted in the structures of social relations (i.e., the institutions) which in turn are organized toward certain ends and purposes. This is how the *Second Discourse* unfolds: once our associations with others are oriented not toward mutual benefit but toward the surplus benefit of a particular member of the association, our self- and other-relations begin to shift—our social reality itself begins to transform. Lest we forget that this is always dependent on the maintenance of the generative power of norms and ideas, Rousseau reminds us of the connection between them and our material social structure:

---

41. I have developed this concept of power in Rousseau as the concept of "constitutive power" and "constitutive domination." See Michael J. Thompson, *The Domestication of Critical Theory* (London: Rowman and Littlefield, 2016).

The first man who, having enclosed a piece of ground, bethought himself of saying This is mine, and found people simple enough to believe him, was the real founder of civil society. From how many crimes, wars and murders, from how many horrors and misfortunes might not any one have saved mankind, by pulling up the stakes, or filling up the ditch, and crying to his fellows, "Beware of listening to this impostor; you are undone if you once forget that the fruits of the earth belong to us all, and the earth itself to nobody."[42]

Rousseau's thesis is deeply ontological in the sense that there is an objectivity and causal efficacy to our social relations. Individuals develop as a function of the ensemble of social relations that shape and form them. More important, these relations are themselves pliable and not "natural" and predetermined. We can shape and form them to enhance and perfect the individual. Like Aristotle, the common good now becomes not only a precondition of the individual good but a dimension of the individual good as well. What is required is a shift in consciousness and cognition that will allow the reflective agent to have this social-ontological reality in view. Only then will each be able to think and act in accordance with the general will—that form of consciousness and reason that operates under conditions of the social-relational features of the good.

Rousseau's theory of judgment becomes critical in the sense that it is framed by an attempt to link the particular with the universal in a new way: now each person is to think and reflect in a particularly political way, that is, as a way distinct for a life with and among others. The general will is a critical concept that has reflexivity in the sense that it can shape public discourse, but it is also the product of a new kind of self, a new kind of individual, one that has been transformed by a self-consciousness of his relational interdependence. Now we can discern a more comprehensive normative structure to Rousseau's social theory. He sees that each phase of human self- and social-relatedness is tied with a kind of ontological quality of life. I outline this in table 5.1.

---

42. Rousseau, *Discours sur l'origine de l'inégalité*, 164.

Table 5.1. Rousseau's Categories of Self- and Social Relatedness

Feature / Relational Structure	Social State	Social Relations	Structure of Self	Ontology	Political	Purpose of Association
Independence	Nature	—	Personal dignity (*amour de soi*)	Atomistic	—	—
Dependence	Liberal-market civil society	Unequal	Heteronomous (*distended amour propre*)	Relational-extractive	Domination	Particular good for acquisition
Interdependence	Republic	Equal	Expanded autonomy (*amour de soi parmi les autres*)	Relational-Reciprocal	Freedom	Common good for self-development

Rousseau's normative theory is therefore rooted in an ontological concern with a new kind of self and a new kind of political association. The structure of thought of the classical view is retained but also extended: for now, Rousseau is suggesting that the good of the whole, the common good, be seen as a dimension of our individual good. He also insists that we, as rational reflective agents, have this serve as the core of our wills, as the guiding structure of our normative and practical consciousness and lives. The individual is ontologically transformed by thinking and acting in this way, and as a result, a new form of society is maintained. Rousseau's social ontology therefore heralds a new and expanded dimension for political judgment.

Hegel and the Metaphysics of Modern Ethical Life

Hegel's *Phenomenology* has the root thesis that a true form of rational knowledge will be grounded in the cognitive grasp of our sociality and the products of that sociality. At the center of the famous "master-slave dialectic" is the thesis that mutual recognition is not just the recognition of one by an other but, more important, the recognition of both as mutually constituting the other. Through the process of mutual recognition, each particular consciousness becomes aware of the ontological relationality that constitutes each other's subjectivity. Self-consciousness migrates to the status of reason once this mutual dependence of ego upon the other is grasped and then seen to constitute a more complex system of relations that lays the cognitive foundation for a universal self-consciousness. A migration from a narrow form of particular "I-consciousness" toward a "we-consciousness" therefore becomes a central theme in *Phenomenology*, but it also forms the seed for a richer argument in the *Philosophy of Right* where self-determination can only occur within the institutional and collective nexus of individuals who self-consciously grasp that the concrete ontology of their status as free beings is itself dependent on the nexus of relational structures that produce that good. This was only a step in Hegel's project to develop a system of "ethical life," or a form of ethics rooted in the ontology of our relations with others and how each member's personhood is developed via these relational structures toward a kind of social freedom. Hegel is therefore a direct heir to the social-ontological structure of thought that also was the basis of Aristotle's and Rousseau's social and political theories.

There is no natural givenness to our self-understanding, and there is no way for us to reason about ourselves from outside the sphere of spirit itself. Rather, the basic project is to construct a system of shared ethical concepts, an "ethical life," rooted in the ontology of our mutual relatedness and interdependence. Hegel's insight is that this ontology not fixed nor given by nature, but is a product of the constellations of our ideas and practices. A such, our practical lives are generative of more complex structures of norms, practices and institutions, but they develop diachronically through history as rational forms emerge from the contradictions of previous shapes of collective self-understanding. What emerges from this is not the strong holism of Aristotle or classical ontology, but a more nuanced thesis about the ways our sociality is originary (*ursprünglich*) of the norms, practices and institutions that are constitutive of our social reality.[43]

This project is also crucial for any theory of judgment since, as with Rousseau before him, Hegel insists on the capacity of individuals to have critical reflective powers over the world they inhabit.[44] Judgment, once again, is a matter of connecting the phenomenological experience of particularity with the concrete determinations of the concept, of that which is rational because of its universality; it is a matter of contrasting what conforms to reason to what does not, to what is defective. The difference between the two is grounded in how our ethical life is structured. Irrational forms of life do not maximize the conditions of social freedom. They manifest as practices of domination and subordination where members of the community act not in reciprocal, mutually enhancing ways but through coercion or power. Again, we see that the ontology of our sociality and the ways individuals constitute it is at the heart of political judgment.

Hegel continues this powerful idea of critical judgment to a new level and, in the process, relies on an ontology of our social relatedness with others as a basis for his categories of practical reason. Reason is

---

43. See the interesting discussion by Luigi Ruggiu, "Reason and Social Ontology," in Italo Testa and Luigi Ruggiu (eds.), *"I That Is We, We That Is I": Perspectives on Contemporary Hegel* (Leiden: Brill, 2016), 86–105.

44. For a fuller defense of this thesis, see Michael J. Thompson, "Critical Agency in Hegelian Ethics: Social Metaphysics versus Moral Constructivism," in James Gledhill and Sebastian Stein (eds.), *Beyond Kantian Constructivism: Post-Kantian Idealism and Contemporary Practical Philosophy* (London: Routledge, 2020).

social not just in terms of how cognition is generated and validated but also in the sense that our own self-understanding can only proceed from a grasp of how our norms and ideas are interwoven with the ontological structures of life that define the perimeter of any culture. Hegel therefore subscribes to the view that humans are processual beings; we have distinctive capacities that can only be developed in certain social contexts. The good is an ontological category—it denotes the extent to which practices, norms, relations, institutions, and so on maximize the development and articulation of these distinctive human capacities. Hence we can judge ethical life, the constellation of our social world, according to these parameters. As Dudley Knowles has pointed out:

> It is important that Hegel believes he is describing the uniquely rational form of social life, that which best permits humans to express distinctive elements of their nature. The rules of ethical life do not operate as constraints, they liberate persons who would otherwise be unable to develop, in the case of family life, their capacities for loving, long-term commitment to other persons.[45]

The nucleus of this theory of ethical life is contained in the thesis of recognition that begins in the *Phenomenology*, but it is developed and expanded in Hegel's subsequent writings. Mutual recognition means that subjects come to realize in the ethical culmination in their "struggle for recognition" that they are relational beings, that their own sense of meaning and self is essentially dependent on the other. Although this is "discovered" phenomenologically, it reveals to human reason a deeper ontological thesis about the foundations for ethical life and the ethical "substance" that will be worked up into institutions and more complex forms of life. Much has been made in recent literature of Hegel's theory of recognition, as my discussion of Honneth's philosophy in chapter 4 demonstrated. But it is important to read Hegel's thesis differently. Instead of seeing that the recognitive relations overcome the subject-object problem by a theory of intersubjectivity, it should perhaps be seen that what really occurs is that, by the process of recognition, our intersubjective nexus also transforms the subject's cognitive powers

45. Dudley Knowles, *Political Obligation: A Critical Introduction* (New York: Routledge, 2010), 173.

by mediating it socially. In this sense, the subject-object problem is not overcome but transposed: each individual must be able to think in terms of the objective social-relational nexus that is the context for our being. In other words, the subject can reflect on the ontology of the social relations that objectively mediate and shape him. We are intersubjective, to be sure, but these relations-with-others take on onto-logical (i.e., objective and mediating) powers.[46] As such, they become the object of our critical-reflective powers even as they are the subject of our developmental and social being.

This thesis is developed and enhanced in the *Philosophy of Right* into an ontological theory about the nature of rational, free sociality. It leaves the confines of phenomenology and becomes a constitutive logic of our objective being. Indeed, as the *Phenomenology* develops, our social reality is revealed to be a collective product. *Geist*, "spirit," is this collective and socially active web of concepts and collective intention-ality generating the social forms that we inhabit, articulate, and that recursively come to shape us. Freedom therefore is a unity of that self-consciousness of this collective self-generating capacity with the objective social forms that constitute our world. They achieve knowledge of the other and of the other as a precondition for their own self-knowledge. They also come to realize that this relation is not unique to them only; these relations constitute their social reality as a whole. Overcoming our diremption from a world of our own making is the central struggle of true, rational cognition—it is the core axis around which Hegel sees the trajectory of history taking place.

This does not mean that reason is somehow external to us, a sub-stance or force that is "metaphysical" in the precritical sense of the term. Rather, the thesis is that reason is an internal evolutionary tendency as it reflects on itself and the shapes of sociality within which it emerges. The idea that our social relations are natural to us does not quite capture what Hegel is after. *Geist* is a decisive break with raw nature; it is the sphere in which reason can act in a self-determined way. The emergence of a self-determining agent is itself an articulation of a kind of sociality where I see myself, via the constitutive relation of recognition, as more than mere ego, but as an I constituted by the relations in which I am ensconced. Once a rational agent is cognizant of his or her relationality

46. See the discussion by Philip J. Kain, *Hegel and the Other: A Study of the* Phe-nomenology of Spirit (Albany, NY: SUNY Press, 2005), 131ff.

with others, that this relationality is not natural and unchangeable but a product of our intentions and practices, then the stage for modern freedom as socially embodied (i.e., as ontological) has been set.[47]

This ontology of our sociality can be seen in the ways that *Geist* is objectivized in institutional forms. Objective spirit is therefore an instantiation of the metaphysical structures of reason that Hegel explores in his *Logic*. For Hegel, modern metaphysics marks a break with all previous forms of metaphysics by showing that philosophy, reason, is itself ontological: it is always something realized in the world, an "onto-logic."[48] Hegel insightfully pushes the thesis that ideas can be either mere "representations" of one's subjective mind, or they can be actual ideas that are embodied in the ways that we act, relate and essentially which define our social being.[49] The question is not about a neat mapping of the metaphysical categories onto the empirical social forms. Rather, the key is to see that the metaphysical categories of the *Logic* emerge as social-ontological structures that can then be understood and judged based on the deep

---

47. Luigi Ruggiu argues insightfully on this point: "The leap of evolution is constituted by the complex interweaving of individuals who can exist only in a social dimension, which comes to light gradually with the construction of selves. But I can become I only if I become conscious of myself as a subject in a social dimension in which a plurality of subjects take part. Self-consciousness is not a natural given—on the contrary it is the result of the sociality produced by human interaction." "Reason and Social Ontology," 97.

48. Jean-François Kervégan insightfully argues that the purpose of Hegel's logic "is to show—in accordance with a strong understanding of what *logos* is—that rational discourse is the very discourse of being, that logic is an onto-logic. According to its explicit ambition, Hegelian logic, setting itself apart from all that is said or thought by means of this word, including from the point of view of transcendental philosophy, claims to be not a discourse on being but rather the discourse *of* being." *The Actual and the Rational: Hegel and Objective Spirit* (Chicago: University of Chicago Press, 2018), iii. Also see the discussion of actuality and rationality in Hegel's treatment of modern ethical life by Ido Geiger, *The Founding Act of Ethical Life: Hegel's Critique of Kant's Moral and Political Philosophy* (Stanford, CA: Stanford University Press, 2007), 73ff.

49. Kervégan notes elsewhere that "Hegel . . . makes a distinction between ideas that people 'have' (and which are often 'mere ideas,' in Hegelian terms, 'representations') and ideas that people 'are'; that is to say, ideas that are incorporated in their collective mode of being, speaking and acting." "Towards an Institutional Theory of Rights," in Italo Testa and Luigi Ruggiu (eds.), *"I That Is We, We That Is I": Perspectives on Contemporary Hegel* (Leiden: Brill, 2016), 68–85, 71.

grammar of those categories. Hegel's proposition is that the collective practices and institutions of objective spirit can be understood as moving toward free, self-determining forms of life once we see them as evolving toward the rational structures of the concept. On one level, the *Philosophy of Right* is an attempt to demonstrate how the structures of modernity can bring us closer to the essential, substantial core of what it means to be self-determining, that is, toward realizing in our self-consciousness our status as interdependent beings that cooperate for some good, some end. The directive ideas that animate our social institutions must also be grasped by each member of the modern community as advancing and determining their freedom—it is this that gives modernity its self-determining and rational character. The metaphysical structures explored above therefore constitute the kinds of social being that any given society might instantiate. At the center of the concept is the movement of the process from mechanism to chemism and on to its telos.[50] At the core of this is the structural transformation (*Übergehen*) of the object from mechanistic to reciprocal relations. In human social existence, the essential substance of human life is shown to be our interdependence.

The more that this is brought to consciousness, the more this interdependence becomes the object of our individual will and the more rational (i.e., more universal) our social and ethical world becomes. The more this is brought to consciousness, the more we will be able to question the prevailing norms, practices, and institutions that shape our relations-with-others; we will be able to use reason to bring about better, more ethically robust ideas about how we can organize the social-relational substance of our social world.[51] Freedom and progress can be

---

50. See the important discussion of this aspect of Hegel's Logic and its implications for social and political thought by Nathan Ross, *On Mechanism in Hegel's Social and Political Philosophy* (New York: Routledge, 2008).

51. Stephen Houlgate observes this aspect of the idea of freedom and the power of negation when he argues, "my very identity as a practical being lies in knowing myself to be the source of possible changes in the world that follow from as yet unrealized possibilities conceived and 'posited by me.' Such a consciousness of oneself as essentially the source of new possibilities involves what Hegel refers to as a 'negative determination,' that is, an awareness that what is now the case need *not* be, that one's activity is not simply restricted to sustaining what at present exists, and that one is able to bring about through one's own activity what is not yet the case." "The Unity of Theoretical and Practical Spirit in Hegel's Concept of Freedom," *Review of Metaphysics*, vol. 48, no. 4 (1995): 859–81, 864–65.

seen to have a concrete, objective dimension of existence and actuality. Critical reason (judgment, as I am construing it) now becomes the activity of inquiring into the rational validity of the objective institutional forms that shape our social world. The criteria are not pragmatically given, but can only be grasped via the metaphysics of sociality that Hegel sees at the core of modern, rational, self-determining forms of life.

The concept of freedom is entwined with the capacity of an ethical agent to relate the current forms of life to those mediated by universality, to constantly remake the world in light of the structure of universality. Hegel states this in the *Philosophy of Right* in a passage that is worth quoting in full:

> But concrete freedom consists in this: that the personal individuality (*persönliche Einzelnheit*) and its particular interests not only achieve their complete development and gain explicit recognition for their right—as they do in the sphere of the family and civil society—but, for one thing, they also pass over of their own accord into the interest of the Universal, and, for another thing, they know and will the universal. They even recognize it as their own substantive mind; they take it as their end and aim and are active in its pursuit. The result is that the Universal does not prevail or achieve completion except along with particular interests and through the cooperation of particular knowing and willing. And individuals likewise do not live as private persons for their own ends alone but in the very act of willing these they will the Universal in the light of the universal and their activity is consciously aimed at none but the universal end.[52]

This passage is important because it essentially lays out the conceptual, that is, syllogistic, formula for the kind of freedom Hegel thinks constitutes the relation between individual and society. But is also highlights the thesis that the rational, free, ethical agent seeks to act according to a space of reasons that are structurally higher than mere interpersonal relations. The universal refers to those reasons that grasp the whole of the social totality, the common good, the *res publica* that can now be

---

52. G. W. F. Hegel, *Grundlinien der Philosophie des Rechts* (Stuttgart: Reclam, 1970), §260.

seen as the ends toward which our essentially interdependent selves
are oriented. We move beyond the mere interaction of agents and the
pragmatic dimension of intersubjectivity and enter a space of reasons
constitutive of the whole social reality. The free person acts according to
a will that wills a universal end, and this means overcoming immediate
particularity and instead pursuing ends that have in mind the substance
of the universal.

The universal is therefore a property not of the self but of the
individual's relation to the society as a whole; society has an ontological
existence because it has features beyond the mere aggregation of its
members. Against thinkers like Hobbes, Locke, and utilitarians, society is not a creation of the agreement of its members; it has features
and logics of its own, an order that gives shape and meaning to the
moments that constitute it.[53] Our interdependence is therefore one of
the key logical dynamics that Hegel traces through the various structures
of ethical life. He sees them as forms within which the substance of
our essentially interdependence is shaped and organized, and these are
forms that we, as free beings, can reshape and restructure according to
universal interests and ends. The more the individuals making up these
forms of life are able to cognize this essential substance, the more it
becomes the end of their activities and wills, the more it shapes the
purposeful activities of each rational subject. We therefore realize in our

---

53. Dieter Henrich has called this the project of a "monistic ontology," which
he describes as a program that "attempts explicitly to defend and to explicate in
proper conceptual form the claim that the sheer multiplicity of singular moments
need not and should not constitute the ultimately irreducible point of departure
for any attempted comprehension of the structural character of the world. The
coexistence and order of singularities is not simply an ultimate fact that cannot be
further comprehended, one that merely corresponds to the factual multiplicity of
those singularities. For we are here confronted with 'order' in a quite different sense
altogether, and one in which the very concept of order allows us to *understand* the
existence of the singularities in question. The concept of order here is derived not
from the presupposition of the existence of many singularities, and in relation to
which it thus would function only in secondary or at least dependent fashion, in
the way in which irreducibly dependent elements may depend on one another. The
unitary significance of order here is itself a autarchic, and the singularity of the finite
dependent moments is radically dependent on and reducible to that order." "Logical
Form and Real Totality: The Authentic Conceptual Form of Hegel's Concept of
the State," in Robert Pippin and Otfried Höffe (eds.), *Hegel on Ethics and Politics*
(Cambridge: Cambridge University Press, 2004), 241–67, 249.

activities and ends the universal, and it thereby achieves objective reality in the world. It is no longer a regulative ideal; it becomes constitutive of our individuality and the social world we inhabit.

Hence, the *Philosophy of Right* seeks to outline how this implicit substance of our relations and the processes and ends of those relations can come to be the substance of concrete freedom. In the family, we see this substantial content and it begins to express our "absolute essence": "The family has as its *immediate substantiality* of spirit its *feeling* of its own unity, *love* as its determination such that one has in view the self-consciousness of one's individuality within this unity as the absolute essence (*an und für sich seiender Wesentlichkeit*) of oneself and that one is in it not as an independent person but as a member."[54] The family only exists as a system of relations that form a totality.[55] Members of the family experience sensuous love for one another but only as an "external embodiment of the ethical bond which can only subsist exclusively in mutual (*gegenseitge*) love and support."[56] The mutual and reciprocal relations of family members are brought to ethical consciousness in modernity because previous iterations of the institution did not have the same reciprocal structure among individuals—say, as *pater familias* or patriarchal family forms—and were not aware that the purpose of the family was to serve the aims of the whole family and those of the individuals conscious of this collective aim: "The ethical aspect of marriage consists in the parties' consciousness of this unity as their substantive aim, and so in their love, trust and common sharing of their entire existence as individuals."[57] The modern family combines two principles of modern ethical life: the good of the relational structure of the members of the community and the good of the individual.[58]

---

54. Hegel, *Philosophie des Rechts*, §158.

55. "Since marriage is a substantial relation, the life involved in it is life in its totality." Hegel, *Philosophie des Rechts*, §161.

56. Hegel, *Philosophie des Rechts*, §164.

57. Hegel, *Philosophie des Rechts*, §163.

58. Hegel contrasts the initial drive to create a family with its deeper, rational, and ethical purpose in the modern world: "The ethical principle which is conjoined with the natural generation of children and which was assumed to have primary importance in first forming the marriage union, is actually realized in the second or spiritual birth of the children: in educating them to be independent persons (*selbständigen Personen*)." *Enzyklopädie*, §521.

In civil society this substance begins to lose its ethical character because individuals lapse into their particularity, delinking their activities from the universal. "Substance, as spirit, abstracts itself in many *persons* (the family is only *one* person), in families or individuals (*Einzelne besondernd*), who exist independent and free, as private persons, loses its ethical character: for these persons as such have in their consciousness and as their end (*Zweck*) not the absolute unity, but their own particularity (*Besonderheit*) and narrow self-regard (*Fürsichsein*)."[59] As a result, the "system becomes atomistic,"[60] and the relations between people become characteristic of mechanism rather than chemism, as was intimately achieved in the family. These relations lose their reciprocal character; they become atomistic when driven by particular needs. But this leads to a contradiction, for if this mechanistic logic were to play itself out, society would disintegrate: "Particularity by itself given free rein in every direction to satisfy its needs, accidental caprices, and subjective desires, destroys itself and its substantive concept in this process of gratification."[61] Relations cease to be reciprocal and oriented toward a higher, more developed end, and society becomes a concatenation of particular selves.[62] These atomistic selves act on one another not unlike parts of a mechanism in that they react in the search for their particular interests and needs.

This leads to a contradiction that is overcome in civil society. Because each can only obtain what he needs through work, and each different need and skill creates a division of labor in the society, this mechanistic particularity begins to give way to the chemistic reciprocity of economic life: "In the particularity of needs the universal begins to shine through in the way that understanding creates differences in them and thus causes an indefinite multiplication both of wants and of means for their different wants."[63] In this way, a new structure of

59. Hegel, *Enzyklopädie*, §523.

60. Hegel, *Enzyklopädie*, §523.

61. Hegel, *Philosophie des Rechts*, §185.

62. In the atomism of civil society "the substance is reduced to a general system of adjustments to connect independent (*selbständigen*) extremes and their particular interests. The developed totality of this complex of connections is the state as bourgeois association (*bürgerliche Gesellschaft*) or *external state*." *Enzyklopädie*, §523.

63. Hegel, *Enzyklopädie*, §525.

relations begins to evolve wherein interdependence becomes the mode of relations: "In the course of the actual attainment of selfish ends, an attainment determined by universality, there is formed a system of total interdependence (*ein System allseitiger Abhängigkeit*) wherein the subsistence, welfare, and legal status of one man is interwoven with the subsistence, welfare and rights of all."[64] In this way, the narrow particularity of each member of society passes over into the universal on its own because for each to realize his welfare or need he must use the means that are the cooperative interdependent relations connecting his particular good with the good of the community: "This [particular] end is mediated through the universal which thus appears as a means to its realization so individuals can attain their ends only insofar as they themselves determine their intention, wants and activity in a universal way and make themselves members of this chain of social connections (*Gliede der Kette dieses Zusammenhangs machen*)."[65]

The emergence of the division of labor is not a structure of recognition between people, it is an social-ontological structure that evinces the metaphysical structures of relations and process that Hegel examined in his *Logic*. The importance Hegel finds in the interdependent and reciprocity of economic life leads to a richer, more intense interlocking of people: "this abstraction of one man's skill and means of production from another's completes and makes necessary everywhere the dependence of men on one another and their reciprocal relation (*Wechselbeziehung*) in the satisfaction of their other needs."[66] Since the universal is the rational criteria needed to balance out the syllogism embedded in civil society, the increasing pressures from the force of particularity—that is, for the satisfaction of particular interests—threaten the interdependent structures of civil society. But the universal becomes particularized in the individual once the rational self can grasp these complex interdependencies as the substance of our social essence. The subject-object relation now enlarges, and a new framework for judgment becomes possible. What is crucial is that although in civil society this becomes the case ontologically, it remains to be taken up conceptually by the subjects participating in

---

64. Hegel, *Philosophie des Rechts*, §183.

65. Hegel, *Philosophie des Rechts*, §187.

66. Hegel, *Philosophie des Rechts*, §198.

them.[67] As such, there is an increasing need for the universal to mediate this particularity and give structure to individuality.

The liberal economy, which starts out with the arbitrary choices and desires of particular persons, therefore has to be mediated by the universal to make the particular beneficial for the public end:

> This interest invokes freedom of trade and commerce against control from above; but the more blindly it sinks into self-seeking aims, the more it requires such control to bring it back to the universal. Control is also necessary to diminish the danger of upheavals arising from clashing interests and to abbreviate the period in which their tension should be eased through the working of a necessity of which they know nothing.[68]

Particularity, cultivated by anomic market forces and the division of labor, cannot hold together a cooperative working life on its own. This impulse in civil society can lead to defective social relations—for example, relations of dependence instead of interdependence—that entail diminishing its members rather than their cultivation as free persons: "This results in the dependence and distress of the class tied to work of that sort and these again entail inability to feel and enjoy the broader freedoms and especially the cultural benefits of civil society."[69] This occurs in civil society because the members of the association are not cognizant of the social structures in which they participate and on which they are dependent, nor are they aware of the purposes of these structures of interdependence.

---

67. David Kolb remarks that: "In the categories involving reciprocal interaction under law, the attempt to make one category basic is abandoned, and all the aspects are posited as mediated by their mutual interaction. This explicitly posits the lack of a first immediate foundation and replaces the demand for such a basic starting point with the movement of the whole constituted by mutual reciprocity (*Wechselwirkung*). At this stage each member is thought of as constituted by interaction with the others, but there is not yet any thought of the system as a whole distinguished from its members, and the whole remains indeterminate." *The Critique of Pure Modernity: Hegel, Heidegger and After* (Chicago: University of Chicago Press, 1986), 58.

68. Hegel, *Philosophie des Rechts*, §236z.

69. Hegel, *Philosophie des Rechts*, §243.

As such, they become objects rather than subjects of these structures and processes. Freedom can become concrete only when the members of these interdependent structures become conceptually aware of the logic of said structures and expand their agency and transform their practices. They come to see themselves not as mere objects of these social structures and processes, nor as constructivist subjects of them, but as participating in a reciprocal subject-object structure where they actively constitute and are constituted by these structures and processes. The key ethical moment is the rational awareness that this subject-object structure is to be the organized toward ends and a form of the good that in enhancing that structure, those common relations, and ends, their own individuality is activated and realized. This, it seems to me, is the radical kernel inside of the moderate, social-democratic shell that is Hegel's political philosophy.

Now the contradiction of civil society leads us to the need for the universal to posit itself as the end of our association with one another. The relations of interdependence that Hegel sees as the essential substance of human life is only raised to consciousness once it is realized that the contradictions of civil society, of the needs of the external state, defeat the higher end of the political community.[70] To say this is the higher end of the community means that each of us finally comes to realize (through rational reflection via recognitive relations) that our interdependence requires the maintenance of the whole because the whole fortifies and develops its parts and vice versa. The interdependent chemism instantiated in the family and in civil society, which was merely in itself in those spheres of ethical life, now becomes in and for itself: "The state is absolutely *rational (an und für sich Vernünftige)* as the actuality of the substantial will which it possesses in the particular self-consciousness once that consciousness has been raised to consciousness of its universality."[71] This ceases to be chemism and now becomes self-conscious teleological activity. Each member of a rational social order knows the rational reasons for the ends they seek to achieve, ends endowed with freedom. The relations, processes, norms, and institutions of such a community would not be alien to each member but

---

70. For a more developed discussion of this aspect of Hegel's theory of the state, see Michael J. Thompson, "Hegel's Anti-Capitalist State," *Discusiones Filosoficas* 14, no. 22 (2013): 43–72.

71. Hegel, *Philosophie des Rechts*, §258.

are genuine expressions of their free will. The key issue is that these structures of ethical life, of objective spirit, can only attain rational form once the reciprocal interdependence constituting each sphere is cognized by each agent as constitutive of their freedom. Once this is grasped, a metaphysical core can be seen to reside in the sphere of practical reason: for now, the ethical life of the community—its norms and practices—have an objective content that shapes its self-understanding.

The key moment for judgment, however, becomes clear once we seek to understand what validates a rational, free form of life and what does not. Ultimately, Hegel's idealism comes down to the individual's rational capacity to cognize this sociality and ratify it in some sense as valid because he or she sees the ends or "directive ideas" of its institutions and norms as rational (i.e., as enhancing a self-determination rooted in sociality).[72] It is according to the end (*Zweck*) that the relations and processes that produce it are to be judged because the end, in effect, causes the relations and processes that produce it. The metaphysical account Hegel gives of teleological causality is crucial because it asks the practical question, when applied to ethical and political affairs: what are the ends of the social structures, institutions, and practices in which I participate and which constitute my world? The Good and the end of this association is a common good—but is richer and more complex than precritical philosophy would have articulated it. Now the common good and common interest of modern society is made concrete in the world through our objectification of common ends that track our deep structure (essence) as beings constituted by sociality. But it can only be achieved by agents endowed with universal self-consciousness or that capacity to hold in view a non-alienated grasp that the social world is our product and is most rational when it serves the requisite ends for us as a community of individuals seeking socially mediated self-determination.

Hegel's social ontology embraces the thesis that only a rational comprehension of the social totality and its rational ends can supply rational agents with the requisite capacity to live in a context of social freedom. Because the institutions of the family, civil society, and the

---

72. For a discussion of the concept of a "directive idea," see Maurice Hariou, "La théorie de l'institution et de la fondation," in *Aux sources du droit: le pouvoir, l'ordre, la liberté* (Caen: Presses Universitaires de Caen, 1986), 98–100. Also see the rich discussion of institutions in relation to Hegel's social ontology by Kervégan, "Towards an Institutional Theory of Rights."

state are increasingly rich shells of a more complete account of social reality, each is also rational, that is, constitutive of freedom, to the extent that they are defined by reciprocal forms of interdependence rather than forms of dependence or nonreciprocal forms of social relations. A critical theory of judgment now achieves a richer and more compelling structure. The social forms we inhabit are supported by our subjective intentions and practices. But these subjective intentions and practices are organized according to objective and universal ends. In this view, it would be fundamentally irrational for me to accede to any social arrangement, any norm or value practice that would violate such social arrangements. Critique is always implicit in this ontological perspective. Perhaps more than anyone else, Hegel's rebellious heir would take this to its next, more radical stage of development.

Marx, Labor, and the Ontology of Social Forms

Marx's thought gives us a more concrete account of a social ontology in that he explicitly states the social-relational "essence" of human life, which serves as the critical-evaluative framework for his social theory. Marx develops the ideas in the classical and modern social-ontological structure of thought by emphasizing the practical essence of social reality. Labor is a practice of distinctive depth that consists of the process of realizing some abstract idea in material form. Our social reality is therefore constituted by the nested forms of social-relational structures that are coordinated to realize more complex material realizations. These structures of relations and processes are ontological in the sense that they are objective but nevertheless dependent on all of our collective practices. These ontological forms have causal powers over our development as individuals and are the result not of natural forces but of social decisions in previously maintained structural forms. Materialism is a perspective that shows how our practices and consciousness are rooted in regimes of power that shape the contexts of action, consciousness, and practices responsible for our self-realization. The task of critique, of critical judgment, is therefore of central importance for Marx's political theory.

What I would like to do first is frame Marx's ideas about human sociality and show that they conform to a critical social-ontological project. For Marx, any critical science of society would have to begin with the proper establishment of its object of study. Ideology or other forms of false consciousness take root in the fertile soil of corrupt conceptions about humans and their actual existence. Marx saw theoretical justifications in Hobbes and Locke for the kind of market society that would mature into capitalism. Indeed, thinkers at the root of the liberal tradition invested in overturning the older ontology of individual and community that had its roots in Aristotle and Scholasticism and grounded a new theory of rights, social action, and a justification for property and personal acquisition on new metaphysical commitments. But Marx also saw that Hegelian idealism pushed a conception of human life that was one-sided and lacking in fuller richness. Thus, Marx's social ontology contains several features, all of which need to be taken together to fill out his systemic understanding of human sociality and the ontological features of human social life.

Briefly stated, we can see the framework of Marx's critical social ontology as rooted in a complex series of theses:

i.   human activity as praxis, or a special kind of activity that has teleological force;

ii. human individuals are social-relational and form an interdependent nexus of structures that organize praxis and orient it toward certain collective ends and purposes;

iii. these social relational structures of practical activities constitute society as an objective entity with processual properties; and

iv. all social process have ends and purposes toward which previous features are oriented.

We can see that the implication is that Marx's social ontology is a theory of nested or layered dimensions of social reality that are not natural or objective in any physical sense. They are ontological in the sense that they are rooted in human practices and constitute a reality that is not natural but distinctly social in nature.[73] This latter point is of particular importance because for Marx practices constitute the basic nucleus of an ontology of sociality. Marx takes after Aristotle's thesis

---

73. See Vardaman R. Smith, "Marx's Social Ontology, His Critical Method and Contemporary Social Economics," *Review of Social Economy*, vol. 42, no. 2 (1984): 143–69.

that thought requires activity in the world for it to be an effective reality. As Aristotle argues the matter: "Thought (διάνοια) by itself however moves nothing, only *thought directed toward an end* and concerning action (πρακτική) does. For this is indeed the moving cause of productive activity (του ποιεῖ) also since he who makes something always has some further end (τέλος) in view."[74] Praxis is not simply activity, it is activity that is directed toward an end and is therefore the basis of "productive activity," or of making and doing things in the world (τῆς ποιητικῆς).

For Marx, this basic idea is taken over from Aristotle to obtain a more comprehensive grasp of human activity. For Marx also sees that human praxis (πρακτική) and human labor (ποιητική) are to be understood as a more complex way of understanding the ways that thought and world are united. But this thesis is also dependent on a prior one elaborated by Hegel and explored above that holds that the essence of any thing is not some abstraction or some a priori formalism but is inherent within the dynamics of any object. For Marx, the essence (*Wesen*) of humans is their practico-relational feature: it is a constitutive attribute of the species that marks it as distinct and causal of secondary and tertiary attributes that emerge in the ontogenetic development of the species. Essence therefore inheres within the species just as it inheres within each member of the species.[75] It is not in itself determinative, but is the basic capacity that determines other higher features of human social reality. Unlike Hegel, who saw thought working itself out via cognition and norms, Marx pushes this idea further to show that the world must be actively shaped by reason and activity in the world. More to the point, social relations are not only constituted by norms, they are also constituted by relations of practice with one another and the natural and material world. Marx's revolt against Hegel, in this sense, pivots on a more radical understanding of how reason interacts with the world. For Marx, praxis is clearly the very means by which humans can transform and thereby make rational the environment in which they live. It is not a matter of an instrumental treatment of nature but a means of understanding how capitalist society misshapes and distorts the onto-

---

74. Aristotle, *Nicomachean Ethics*, 1139b-1, emphasis added.

75. See the discussion by Étienne Balibar, "From Philosophical Anthropology to Social Ontology and Back: What to Do with Marx's Sixth Thesis on Feuerbach?," *Postmodern Culture*, vol. 22, no. 3 (2012): 1–35. Also see the discussion by Richard Lichtman, *The Production of Desire: The Integration of Psychoanalysis into Marxist Theory* (New York: Free Press, 1982), 225ff.

logical reality of human life at issue here. According to Marx, we need insight into the essential metaphysical structure inherent within human sociality if we are to achieve this kind of radical transformative power.

Marx makes many of these ideas explicit in the *Theses on Feuerbach*. In the first thesis, he posits a new kind of relation between subject and object: "The chief defect of all previous materialism . . . is that the object, actuality, sensuousness is conceived only in the form of the *object of perception* (*Anschauung*), but not as *sensuous human activity, Praxis*, not subjectively."[76] He complains that "Feuerbach wants sensuous objects actually different from thought objects: but he does not comprehend human activity itself as objective."[77] Furthermore, Marx claims that "in practice (*Praxis*) man must prove the truth, that is, actuality and power, this-sidedness of his thinking."[78] Putting these ideas together gives us a first step in Marx's ontological conception of man. Thinking and being are united in the concept of praxis just as in the Aristotelian thesis that cognition cannot be complete without activity. For Marx, too, this is a critique of idealism in that only the dialectic of subject and object can be made complete through praxis, that is, through externalizing thought into the world. This makes the objective world actual (*Wirklich*), or "active," in that things realize their active completion via this dialectic.[79]

This thesis is distinctly *ontological* as opposed to material and idealist. It is obvious that a book is not merely paper, that paper is not merely a tree. Only via the idea of "bookness" synthesized with the practical working of natural substrates into a specific form is the telos (or aim of practice) an actual book, possible and achieves any kind of reality in social, that is, human, terms.[80] In contrast to mechanical

---

76. Karl Marx, *Theses on Feuerbach*, in Lloyd Easton and Kurt Guddat (eds.), *Writings of the Young Marx on Philosophy and Society* (New York: Doubleday, 1967), 400.

77. Marx, *Theses on Feuerbach*, 400.

78. Marx, *Theses on Feuerbach*, 401.

79. For a more textured discussion of the Aristotelian concept of "activity," on which Marx draws, see Kosman, *The Activity of Being*, specifically 87ff.

80. Norman D. Livergood argues on this point: "Reality, according to Marx, must be viewed as the result of the redirective activity of human beings in relation to changing conditions in external reality. Both the object and the subject are continually active; human history may be seen as a process in which changes in material reality create new needs which in turn bring about human transformations of material reality." *Activity in Marx's Philosophy* (The Hague: Martinus Nijhoff, 1967), 20.

forms of materialism, Marx argues that human praxis conceived as the externalization of human thought into the world can be understood as proper human activity.[81] Hence, Marx argues: "The coincidence of the change of circumstances and of human activity or self-change can be comprehended and rationally understood only as *revolutionary practice*."[82] This means that the very capacity to understand and grasp what we are as human requires that we understand our world as created by us. But there is more. In a next step, Marx wants us to see that practice is not simply a feature of us *qua* individuals. Rather, praxis is social just as society itself is practical: "All social life is essentially practical. All mysteries which lead theory to mysticism find their rational solution in human practice and the comprehension of this practice."[83]

Now we can see that classical materialism and the mechanistic-empiricist materialism of the Enlightenment are overcome and a new materialism is grasped, one that is rooted in a new conception of human essence as social-relational and practical.[84] Marx's new materialism is essentially a social ontology, one that comprehends human essence not in terms of any given, individual person but as an essentially social capacity: "the essence of man is no abstraction inhering in each single individual. In its actuality it is the ensemble of social relationships."[85] Now we see that practical activity is not merely a property of the self, a given individual, but

81. See the important discussion by William James Booth, "The Limits of Autonomy: Karl Marx's Kant Critique," in Ronald Beiner and William James Booth (eds.), *Kant and Political Philosophy: The Contemporary Legacy* (New Haven, CT: Yale University Press, 1993), 245–75.

82. Marx, *Theses on Feuerbach*, 401.

83. Marx, *Theses on Feuerbach*, 402.

84. Balibar insightfully notes on this moment in Marx's development in the *Theses on Feuerbach*: "The full argument then becomes explicit: 'ancient Materialism' (to which Feuerbach still belongs) will not be able to overcome the alienation that it loudly denounces, because it is still a 'bourgeois' philosophy assuming an individual 'naturally' separated from others (or *separately* referred to the essence of the 'human'), whereas a 'new Materialism'—whose key categories are 'social relations' constituting the human and *praxis*, or a practical transformation already at work in every form of society—is able to explain how *humanity* returns to its essence (or its authentic being) by *acknowledging* (not denying, repressing, or contradicting) its own 'social' determination." "From Philosophical Anthropology," 9–10.

85. Marx, *Theses on Feuerbach*, 402.

is itself activated by our interactions with others.[86] Human essence is not a posited abstract concept or substance, it is the very social-relationality that shapes and articulates our developmental capacities and functionings. Social relations are the product of a capacity for sociality, not a pregiven natural objectivity: "it is an insipid notion to conceive of this merely *objective bond* as a spontaneous, natural attribute inherent in individuals and inseparable form their nature (in antithesis to their conscious knowing and willing). This bond is their product. It is a historic product."[87] In our relations with others, our practices are shaped and oriented toward ends and purposes. Things are what they are because of how we act on them; we act not alone but in concert with others. Hence brute natural facts are transformed into human, social facts. Trees and grass exist as brute facts of nature; parks and lawns do not. Parks and lawns only have meaning because we have externalized the ideas of parks and lawns into a transformed physical organization of matter corresponding with the idea of a park or lawn—it achieves an ontological reality as a result of the synthesis of the two. No one does this alone; it is always essentially social. Hence Marx writes in the *Economic and Philosophical Manuscripts*:

> Even when I carry out *scientific* work, etc. an activity which I can seldom conduct in direct association with other men, I perform a *social*, because *human*, act. It is not only the material of my activity—such as the language itself which the thinker uses—which is given to me as a social product. *My own existence* is a social activity. For this reason, what I myself produce I produce for society, and with the consciousness of acting as a social being.[88]

Marx's radical thesis now comes more clearly into view. If we see humans as essentially social, our sociality is constituted by the

---

86. It is important to emphasize that Marx has a philosophical anthropology not just of the individual human but also of our essential sociality and relatedness with others. Autonomy, in this sense, has to be seen in Marxian terms as more than simply the individual as tool user. It must also encompass the idea, first formalized by Rousseau, that each is a member of a social-relational nexus and our individuality is dialectically related to that nexus and the particular form it takes and the processes it instantiates.

87. Karl Marx, *Grundrisse* (New York: Penguin, 1973), 162.

88. Karl Marx, *The Economic and Philosophical Manuscripts*, in Erich Fromm (ed.) *Marx's Concept of Man* (New York: Frederick Ungar, 1964), 130.

interdependent practices that engage us and in which we participate. If we see humans as possessing an essential structure or a first-order ontology, we can see that the species has certain phylogenetic features or *capacities* such that we are:

(1) First-order or phylogenetic level =
(α) social-relational
(β) processual-developmental; and
(γ) practical-teleological

We can also discern a second-order social ontology describing properties of the social forms taken by our collective praxis. These are objective in the sense that they are collectively instantiated and independent of any single individual. In this sense, the social world we inhabit has the features of:

(2) Second-order or socio-ontogenetic level =
(a) relational structures;
(b) social processes; and
(c) social ends/purposes

These are ontological features of the objective social world we inhabit that have causal powers on our first-order ontological features and capacities. What we are dealing with here, then, is what I call a "generative social ontology," by which I mean an account of our social being that rests on certain capacities that make up our essential structure. This essential structure, this ensemble of capacities, defines us as a species and yet it can be shaped and formed in different ways via the structures or "shapes" of the social reality historically produced and instantiated at any given time. Indeed, this follows from Marx for whom first-order phylogenetic capacities are mediated by the second-order ontological features of our social world. Second-order properties of society have causal powers over the first-order phylogenetic features and therefore mediate in a concrete way the developmental shape or ontogenetic features of our historical being. Here critique becomes important, for we can see that there are defective expressions of these ontological dimensions to social reality. Our social relations can be dependent instead of interdependent; the social processes exploitative or extractive instead of cooperative; and social ends or purposes can serve either particular interests and oligarchic wealth or they can produce common goods and social wealth, and so on (see table 5.2).

Table 5.2. Social Ontological Properties and Their Expressions

Feature \ Expression	Defective	Good
Relational structures	Dependent	Interdependent
Social processes	Extractive/expropriative	Cooperative
Ends and purposes	Particular	Common

The different shapes or forms that the ontology of our sociality takes have causal powers on the development of the members of that society. Freedom is concrete to the extent that these defective relations are overcome forming what Marx refers to as the "fully constituted society":

> The fully constituted society produces man in all the plenitude of his being, the wealthy man endowed with all the sense, as an enduring reality. It is only in a social context that subjectivism and objectivism, spiritualism and materialism, activity and passivity, cease to be antinomies and thus cease to exist as antinomies.[89]

Marx reaches back to Aristotle and his thesis about the essence of human life being social and constituted by a series of relations with others forming a coherent whole. As Marx notes in the *Grundrisse*: "The human being is in the most literal sense a ζῷον πολιτικόν, not merely a gregarious animal, but an animal which can individuate itself only in the midst of society."[90] Individuation is the process whereby the second-order socio-ontogenetic level interpenetrates the first-order phylogenetic capacities of the subject. The nexus of social relations and individuality are therefore not distinct spheres of reality. They are dialectically fused. The illusion of the ideology of market society is precisely to split this unity, to see individuals as producing their relations as products of their will. Marx's alternative ontology holds that these two spheres are ideological, that both categories are interdependent on one

89. Marx, *Economic and Philosophical Manuscripts*, 135.

90. Karl Marx, *Grundrisse*, 84.

another in a systematic rather than directly causal way.[91] A Marxian ethics is therefore not an application of a priori categories to empirical reality; rather, it is a matter of assessing how the various shapes of our social reality either promote free development of the members of the community or frustrate or pervert them.

For now, it is enough to argue that what is crucial here is the insight that free individuality is a function of free sociality.[92] Interdependence is not mere relations between individuals, it constitutes a higher structure of being where individuals are interdependent with the relational structure of the community as a whole and, if society is rationally conceived, is interdependent in terms of consciousness.[93] The critical key, as Marx sees it, is that critique must be historically situated because it is only in the modern, capitalist world that social relations have been developed to such an extent that they can prop up a more enriched and developed form of society and individuality. The key is that we dealienate these relations, see them as ontological and not merely objective—in other words, that we see them as products of our praxis and not as given and "natural." As Marx puts it about this phase of our sociorelational development: "It belongs to a specific phase of their development. The alien and independent character in which it presently exists vis-à-vis individuals proves only that the latter are still engaged in the creation of the conditions of their social life, and that

---

91. Richard Lichtman observes on this point: "Ontologically, neither the individual nor the ensemble of social relations can take priority. The question of which category is fundamental already signifies an alienated consciousness, and arises compellingly under capitalism only because capitalism splits these aspects of existence and sets them against each other as antagonistic spheres. The developing universal powers of human beings come to stand over against these human beings as a set of forces determining their activity and consciousness." *The Production of Desire*, 221–22.

92. For important discussions of Marx's theory of individuality, see Adam Schaff, *Marxism and the Human Individual* (New York: McGraw-Hill, 1970); Lucien Sève, *Marxism and the Theory of Personality* (London: Harvester Press, 1975); and Ian Forbes, *Marx and the New Individual* (London: Unwin Hyman, 1990), 165ff.

93. Michael Brown notes on this aspect of Marx: "Marx's reference to 'manifold relations' avoid characterizing interdependence as the dependence of each person on specific others: both are distinct from a mere assembly and have properties of their own that cannot be reduced to properties, dispositions, or accomplishments of their incorporated individuals." *The Concept of the Social in Uniting the Humanities and Social Sciences*, 187 and *passim*.

they have not yet begun, on the basis of these conditions, to live it."[94]
Class power is not merely an economic power, it is socio-economic: it
indicates the capacity of a certain subset of the community to shape
social relations, structures, practices, norms and so on according to their
interests and will. The ontological is therefore, in some sense, the basic
terrain of all social power.

In turn, free sociality is one where the relations, processes, ends
and purposes of our social world are oriented toward the development
of such a free individuality.[95] It is not simply a mastery over nature that
is of concern, but a comprehension of the social-ontological structures
requisite for the articulation of a free sociality. There does not exist
some metaphysical recipe of principles that can be determined *a priori*
to achieve this free sociality, but they can be determined by grasping the
premise that our sociality and each member's individuality are functions
of the other. That my development and freedom is dependent on the
structures and processes of the social world around me. I come to grasp
contradictions in my social reality what I judge them as either promoting
common goods or as existing to promote hierarchical ends and purposes.
Of course, such comprehension is only concretely free if it instantiates
itself practically in the world: only once our lived lives unfold in relations
of practices oriented toward common ends and purposes that cultivate a
common, social form of wealth that has its purpose and end, its telos,
the full development of each individual. Since Marx's social ontology
dialectically sublates the concepts of individual and community insofar
as it sees individuality as functionally related to the particular shape of
interdependencies within which it is embedded, the concept of freedom
must become a social category, not just an individual one.

Freedom is therefore to be understood in a new way—in terms
of the concrete, the ontological. Human life that can comprehend and
actively shape these ontological properties constitutes a new kind of

---

94. Marx, *Grundrisse*, 162.

95. Carol Gould insightfully remarks: "for Marx freedom arises through interaction
with these empirical conditions, that is, by a transformative process in which a
subject who is originally heteronomous becomes autonomous by achieving mastery
over nature, and freedom from social domination." *Marx's Social Ontology: Individuality and Community in Marx's Theory of Social Reality* (Cambridge, MA: MIT
Press, 1978), 107.

freedom that is not simply abstract in an idealist sense but will be made concrete via the actual social facts constituting our social reality. Again, what is crucial here is the insight that free individuality is a function of free sociality. In turn, free sociality is one where the relations, processes, ends and purposes of our social world are oriented toward the development of such a free individuality. It is not simply a mastery over nature that is of concern, but a comprehension of the social-ontological structures requisite for the articulation of a free sociality. A central aspect of Marx's theory of social relations is that they are not merely idealist, consisting of norms and recognition, but also take on a more objective (the word Marx uses is *sachlicher*) form. When discussing the historical progression of social forms, Marx notes that: "Personal independence founded on *objective* (*sachlicher*) dependence is the second great form in which a system of general social metabolism, of universal relations, of all-round needs and universal capacities is formed for the first time."[96]

Marx's concept of social relations now takes on a more concrete character. Relations are *sachlicher* when they are not merely normative relations but relations of interdependence that take on a more systematic social metabolism. Societies with modern systems of plumbing and electrification are not simply normative relations of recognition and so on, they are objective in a more concrete sense. A television, for example, is not merely a product of productive relations between workers in a factory producing screens, plastics, and so on. A television also requires systems of communication, antennae, cable lines, production studios, writers, actors, and so on that constitute it as an ontological entity and not merely a material object. This gives us a stronger sense of what Marx's social ontology is after and how it differs from the Hegelian account. Indeed, not unlike Aristotle's concept of *autarky*, it denotes the relations of praxis that provide an enhancement of the metabolism between humans and nature. Labor as the process of externalizing a telos in the world, of realizing a plan via the transformation of raw nature, is not a monological process but requires relations of activity and coordination that include and move beyond merely cognitive relations of recognition and status attribution. They point to the concrete forms of activity and products of that activity that form the basis for new and more developed forms of individuality.

---

96. Marx, *Grundrisse*, 158.

Marx sees that only through the conscious direction of these kinds of relations can a more emancipated society emerge. This requires an overcoming of the fetish character of the ontic world generated by capitalist social relations—it requires the capacity to comprehend these relations as rooted in cooperative forms of praxis. Of course, such comprehension is only concretely free if it instantiates itself practically in the world: only once our actual lived lives unfold within relations of practices oriented toward common ends and purposes that cultivate a common, social form of wealth that has its purpose and end, its *telos*, the full development of each individual. Since Marx's social ontology dialectically sublates the concepts of individual and community insofar as it sees our individuality as functionally related to the particular shape of interdependencies within which it is embedded, then the concept of freedom must become a social category, not merely an individual one.

Labor and social relations are therefore natural capacities given form or shape in different historical periods. Labor and relations also achieve a concreteness in the world because they are directed toward some purpose, end, or *telos*. Aristotle's basic metaphysical categories come back in a fresher way in that they are put together to articulate new theory of materialism. Marx's "materialism" is critical in that it sees concrete social forms and their ends (or social goals) as constituted by the concrete and objective forms labor takes in any given social complex. History is therefore the transformation of these shapes or forms of organization of labor and, with it, the structures of consciousness, intentionality, norms, and practices that are the subsystems granting them their social reality. In this sense capital is a highly complex phenomenon because of its power to constitute and shape the antecedent subsystems producing our social reality. It is morphogenetic in the sense that it imposes form on (i) our social relations, (ii) our intentions, (iii) our norms and practices, and (iv) on the ends toward which these are oriented. Alienation becomes a more concrete category in that one's powers become appropriated by the directive powers of capital.

Marx's critical social ontology therefore has within it a conflation between descriptive and normative claims: by comprehending the essential structure of human life as interdependent and practical, we see that those ends and purposes that such descriptive categories are put toward can also be seen as having evaluative categories embedded in it. The key idea seems to me that any proper, rational cognition of an object also provides us with the evaluative categories for that object.

The reason for this lies in the structure of teleological reasoning Marx elaborates. This is not a premodern, transcendental form of teleological reasoning. Rather, it is confined to the activity of labor—but labor itself is an expression of praxis, of the capacity of an idea in an individual's mind to orient actual human actions and activities and the production of some kind of end. In this sense, it need not be confined to physical labor but can be seen as a basic capacity in the human species that enables the projection and the realization of some conscious end, some idea, some telos. Marx's philosophical innovation is to buttress his philosophical anthropology with a new conception of teleology: one based solely on human intentionality and the capacities inherent in human action (praxis) to realize those intentions in the world. This also means a modification of the kind of reasoning that modern forms of reason sought to undermine. Primary among these was that of teleological reasoning. Marx's reworking of this idea entails the thesis that telos is not a structure of nature or of history; it has no transcendental metaphysical warrant at all. At the same time, various forms of rationalism and idealism that seek to eviscerate teleology also miss the mark because they cannot account for the structure of practice; they are unable to comprehend the true, that is, concrete structure of human activity and of human life and sociality more generally.

What Marx is after here is an account of human praxis that can inform a new framework for social critique. Once we posit the thesis of human praxis as a concrete activity of projecting ends and social relations as more complex evolutions of praxis, we can inquire in a critical sense about the purposes and ends for which those practices are instantiated. Far from being a mere descriptive exercise, then, Marx's thesis about human praxis (i.e., labor) entails the inquiry into the kinds of ends, what *telē*, a community orients its various levels of praxis to. For Marx, the question of human emancipation becomes tied to the structure of human practices and the kinds of social reality that create them and are created by them. The essential point seems to be that the structure of praxis contains the nucleus for a kind of social critique that can question the objective social structures, relations, and processes that any community manifests. The reason for this can be found in the kind of reasoning distinctive of a critical ontology that takes ends or purposes as decisive for critical judgment. Marx sees the theory of value—value taken to mean the various social objects that result from nature transformed by the practice of labor—as the conceptual space of judging the ends or purposes of labor (individual or collective). His distinction between "use value" and "exchange value," taken from Aristotle, is an example of how Marx's social ontological categories are both descriptive and evaluative.[97] The importance of the theory of value is therefore ontological rather than material because it can only be comprehended as a social form and not a form of nature or matter.

To say that value is a social form is to say that it is a particular outcome of our practices. The question of value is therefore an ontological question because any object can only have value once it is endowed with and transformed by labor. Labor is the mechanism for the elevation of raw nature into human use. Since labor is a distinctively human form of activity, value is the result of some intentional, some teleological activity. Then again, the more complex the levels of praxis (say, of labor) that produce the object, the more density of value it has. At last, we can evaluate the value of the object based on the role it plays in society as a whole. To say that many humans organize themselves into productive forms of activity to produce shoes, to sell the shoes, to produce surplus profit means that we can judge how such a community organizes its layers of praxis—of sewing, shipping, distributing such shoes—according to the ends that are produced. Capitalism constitutes a system of power that is thoroughly ontological in that its way of organizing the practical activities of society is a regime of power.[98] The power consists in the capacity of capitalists to orient the community toward their ends and purposes rather than democratic or common ends and purposes. The relevant question for critical consciousness therefore becomes: do such ends serve common, social goals or particular, private goals? Capitalism's logic of producing for surplus value now becomes a social ontological question: is society organized according its common ends, judged according to some conception of human progress in an emancipatory sense, or is it organized according to the domination logics of inequality and surplus extraction?

---

97. Elsewhere I have tackled the issue of the sublation of descriptive and evaluative forms of knowledge in Marx's thought. See Michael J. Thompson, "Philosophical Foundations for a Marxian Ethics," in M. Thompson (ed.), *Constructing Marxist Ethics: Critique, Normativity, Praxis* (Leiden: Brill, 2015), 235–65.

98. On the idea of capitalism as manifesting an ontology of power, see the important discussion by Giulio Palermo, "The Ontology of Economic Power in Capitalism: Mainstream Economics and Marx," *Cambridge Journal of Economics*, vol. 31 (2007): 539–61.

Freedom as a form of self-determination takes on a very different form: it is now only possible in a kind of social totality that places the comprehensive development and good of that totality as the premise of the development and fulfillment of the individual members of that association. In opposition to liberal or individualist conceptions of self-determination, the self is embedded in a context of sociality and must live in a world where the relations, processes, and ends of that reality reinforce and enrich one's personhood. Indeed, as Nicolai Hartmann observed: "What is hidden ontologically in the so-called freedom of the will is nothing less than a new, unique, and obviously higher form of determination."[99]

In the end, Marx brings to culmination many of the ideas that previous thinkers—such as Aristotle, Rousseau, and Hegel—develop with different degrees of emphasis. Critical consciousness can only emerge when it has a cognitive grasp of how structures of sociality are causal over self-development. It also brings into view the thesis that we cannot detach moral concepts from the structure of the social totality; that there needs to be a way that we see norms and practices as rooted in wider ontological systems of reality. Here the defects of the postmetaphysical paradigm become most apparent. What the social-ontological structure of thought makes evident is that a more critical theory of society is possible only once we grasp the concrete structures of social reality—and that means the relations, processes, and ends or purposes—and whether they cultivate contexts, practices, and goods that enhance our cooperative interdependence or foster forms of dependence and extraction. Formalizing this structure of thought into a more systemic form of critical-practical reason is the focus of the following chapters.

---

99. Nicolai Hartmann, *The New Ways of Ontology* (Boston: Henry Regnery, 1949), 72.

Chapter 6

The Properties and Modes
of Critical Social Ontology

The structure of thought I have sketched in the previous chapter makes it clear that an alternative way of thinking about the concept of political judgment rests on the structures of sociality each individual inhabits. The capacity to make useful, critical judgments about our world rests on how we are able conceptualize the social totality. It also puts emphasis on judgment as a mode of reasoning that seeks to enhance the structures of sociality shaping us as individuals and providing some access to goods that can expand and cultivate our development as members of an association. The divergence between the classical and modern paradigms on this issue are significant, insofar as the latter makes evident the need for each member of the political community to expand his or her subjectivity beyond narrow self-interest and into a broader space of reasons that are informed by the fact that our membership in this association provides us with the prerequisites for our freedom as social beings. Hence we are asked not to choose between a liberal conception of the individual and a communal conception of membership, but to sublate the two into what I call an expanded subjectivity: or that kind of power of reflection that takes into account the social basis of our practices and goods and considers how these fit into a broader form of social reality based on our power to legitimate and re-create them.

What I think is powerful in this way of thinking is an implicit social ontology that can be teased out from the ideas I outlined in the previous chapter. What I want to do here is explore what this social ontology could look like and delineate the logic that gives it coherence and critical-diagnostic power. I also consider how this social ontology can provide critical reflection with a more powerful means to critique and cognize the social forms that are pathological and that promote the social goods needed for a more robust kind of individual development and freedom. I proceed to show how this critical social ontology can be used to form a new kind of theory of political judgment, a new mode of political reflection, and a way of formulating and adjudicating between different normative views of the social and political world.

My goal here is explore a basic outline of what a critical social ontology would look like and show how a critical theory of political judgment can be derived from it. What I think is important is the thesis that social-ontological categories are crucial for any adequate grasp of the social world and, at the same time, any sense of coherence with respect to critical judgments about that social world and what kind of change and social transformation might be desired. As I showed in chapter 5, this was the implicit foundation for the critical ideas of classical and modern thinkers and their model of a comprehensive social theory that could hold the totality in view. A critical social ontology can help reconstruct this project by delineating how social forms shape consciousness and human capacities. The aim of this chapter is be to serve as a framework or grounds for a critical practical reason that will be developed in the next chapter.

The Concept of Social Ontology

To speak of a social ontology is not to speak of something transcendent or transcendental; nor is it to speak of something externally foundational or a priori to our knowledge of the social world. Instead, it entails looking at sociality as something with distinct properties and features. Human sociality is not merely a recognitive or normative capacity for human interaction, it is also an objective, systematic, structural, and processual domain with causal properties on our development and capacities. To speak of a critical social ontology is not only to locate how we as subjects articulate social reality, it is also an approach to social reality that seeks to understand how our social reality is the accretion of norms and practices and how these pattern our forms of life and the ways we organize our reality, both social and subjective. It is ready-made as we enter the world and changeable and sustained by us as we live through it. The ontological is therefore, as I see it, the object of critical reflection; it is also the context within which we must articulate and find validity for norms and values. The ways that our concrete lives are shaped must be the subject of judgment and normative reflection. The deep question for any theory of crital judgment must be the extent to which we can articulate rational norms that generate self-determining forms of life, of social freedom itself. The social is the very substance (consisting of relational, practical, processual, teleological features) that constitutes both the object of social critique and the infrastructure for valid normative claims. Since any norm constitutes a relational practice, and ensembles of relational practices constitute institutions, and institutions have directive ideas or purposes, it seems the reciprocal relation between our construction of it and its causal power over us is precisely the nexus that critical social ontology seeks to explore and take the domain of critical thouhght itself.

To say that society has an ontological status entails that it is trans-individual insofar as it is not contained in or circumscribed by an empirical agent or subject; it is also objective (i.e., not simply mental states or representational ideas), and it has some kind of causal power in the sense that it produces effects in the world that are not just the product of a single agent or individual actor. Ontology is not a reification of the social, nor is it a static concept. It has different levels of development and change and can be seen to be shaped and reshaped in different ways. But these different forms and levels of development and change can be judged based on the kinds of ends it achieves. In this sense, a social ontology has as its object sociality itself as a distinct and centrally defining characteristic of human phenomena. More specifically, it seeks to lay out conceptual categories that determine social reality. This does not entail reifying the social against the creative, reason-giving capacities and practices of social agents but instead seeks to use the ontology of the social as a criterion of the validity of values, norms, and practices. This gives us a ground for judging what kinds of reasons, practices, institutions, norms, and so on should count as better than others. This kind of thinking is aware that there exist rational structures in the world that can be reconstructed in and through cognition.

This means that philosophy's role is to be able to grasp the structures that constitute both the real world and conceptual thought, and this process leads us toward a comprehension of reason itself. In this sense, Hegel and Marx saw—in somewhat different ways—that critical knowledge about the world would have to be accountable to the structures in the world or those structures and processes that constitute the objective world. We cannot simply hold reasons accountable to their own internal validity or some social, intersubjective norm or agreement because this would bypass the object about which those reasons are accountable. The main reason for this was that it was an insufficient means to counter the problem of relativism, and therefore such an approach would be open to the subrational conditions of contradiction and arbitrariness in our practical rationality.[1] In contrast, an ontological approach anchors our reasons and forms of justification within an objective realm and looks for universal reasons that inhere within that object-domain. A critical theory of society must make an assessment of the objective structures of the social world on one hand. But it must also seek to understand these structures, relations and processes, institutions, norms, and so on and grasp how they can be seen as either promoting or negating the kind of relational, common goods needed for robust forms of sociality and individuality.

All of this implies that sociality is more than an epistemic or purely phenomenological concern—it must also be an ontological concern to the extent that we can understand how different shapes of social forms and relational structures articulate different kinds of goods and ends. This means that a critical theory of judgment is characterized not by the intersubjective exchange of reasons grounded in rational communication, but in the content of claims and the extent to which the institutional ends and purposes of society can satisfy the unique ontological needs of a collective, common social good. Critical judgment is a kind of critical thinking that poses the ontological frame

---

1. Rolf-Peter Horstmann has argued in defense of an ontological approach to Hegel's philosophical project that: "He is essentially concerned, in a radical departure from the entire philosophical tradition of the modern period at least, with establishing a new paradigm for the proper philosophical comprehension of reality. The attempt to establish this new paradigm depends entirely for Hegel on successfully communicating a basic insight: that we require an entirely new way of conceptualizing reality, one that is grounded not in the contingent epistemic apparatus of cognitive subjects but in the very constitution of reality itself." "Substance, Subject and Infinity: A Case Study of the Role of Logic in Hegel's System," in Katerina Deligiorgi (ed.), *Hegel: New Directions* (London: Acumen Press, 2006), 69–84, 73.

as an essential component of any kind of rational political discourse, thinking, or institutional logic. The central question a social-ontological investigation therefore seeks to keep in mind is the extent to which an objective interest exists that any rational society should seek to track and any critical sense of judgment must put at the center of its self-critical awareness. The general object of a critical social ontology and its role as shaping a critical theory of judgment can be seen to consist in the capacity to discern an objective interest immanent in the social-relational structure of social life and the extent this can be used to shape and articulate a critical-practical reason.

One of the core theses here is that the ontological perspective can provide the means of uniting the efforts of so-called idealists and materialists or realists that have worked at cross-purposes. As I argued in earlier chapters, the problem with the intersubjective turn is that it casts social relations as far too thin to capture the actual contours of our sociality and the dynamics of social power. The noumenal and phenomenal framework of intersubjectivity requires a thicker understanding of our relations with others and the realization that the social has ontological properties that must be raised to conscious, rational awareness if critical judgment is to be possible. One reason for this is that the social-ontological framework provides certain kinds of questions and a need for answers that are different from the intersubjective-noumenal framework. Ontological questions ask us to consider the deeper reasons for how our lives are organized and to break out of certain reified and ideological ways of thinking—something the intersubjective paradigm cannot do. We have to move from seeing our social world as constituted by language and experience to seeing it as a structure of reality that shapes and forms the language, norms, and experiences we have within it.

One way of seeing this is to consider how the noumenal and communicative relations between people are contained in a broader ontological context. Wittgenstein's famous example in §2 of *Philosophical Investigations* is illustrative of this problem. Wittgenstein wants to show that language is more than a system of signs naming things, it also constitutes a "form of life" (*Lebensform*) where language games are an activity in the world. Wittgenstein claims that the language game constitutes the whole within which language and actions are contained: "I shall also call the whole, consisting of language and the actions into which it is woven, the 'language game.'"[2] I think this led the theory of political judgment down a very confused path, for it has shrunk the social whole down to the level of language games. The problem is that it brackets out the broader social-ontological reality that requires rational cognition and reflection for judgment to be effective. Consider the example Wittgensein uses in §2 to illustrate the language game:

> The language is meant to serve for communication between a builder A and an assistant B. A is building with building-stones: there are blocks, pillars, slabs and beams. B has to pass the stones, and that in the order in which A needs them. For this purpose they use a language consisting of the words "block," "pillar," "slab," "beam." A calls them out;—B brings the stone which he has learnt to bring at such-and-such a call.—Conceive this as a complete primitive language.[3]

Consider this example from a different perspective. The very existence of the relation between A and B, between builder and assistant and how that relation constitutes a structure, how this structure contains and is constituted by a system of norms and value orientations, and how it interacts with the material world and orders and reorders that world, as well as the purposes and ends of the labors of those actors, and so on. All of this points to a much thicker and richer social ontology within which language games are embedded and which orients and structures those language games and the phenomenological experiences the participants have.

This social-ontological view means that we should move from seeing this as a "form of life" (*Lebensform*)—an idea that has been given far too much weightless attention in recent writings—and instead see it as a social form that has a specific kind of "ontological shape." This latter view contains the idea that we live in a world constituted by objective structures and relations with one another and nature, even as it includes the idea that these relations are given shape and continuity by a web of norms and values that shape our practices and language games. The social ontological shape of any community can be discerned not

---

2. Ludwig Wittgenstein, *Philosophical Investigations* (Oxford: Blackwell, 1953), §7.

3. Wittgenstein, *Philosophical Investigations*, §2.

phenomenologically but through the practice of social critique. Judging that ontological shape also asks about the purposes of our social forms; these social forms are constituted by nested structures of relations, and these relations are maintained by some basic way of legitimating those relations, which in turn gives shape to our cooperative efforts. In this sense, social power, ideology, legitimation, language, norms, and values are all incorporated into a broader framework that forms the basic grammar for an ontology of society.

The Two Dimensions of Social Ontology

One of the unifying theses of the social ontological account of political life from Aristotle through Marx was that individuals have an onto-logical structure, one circumscribed by the features of the species. In this sense, an ontology of social being places emphasis on certain core features of what it means to be human. This is understood not as a list or some kind of menu of characteristics but as a view that sees humans as essentially relational, processual, and practical beings. This means that these features constitute what it means to be human in a basic sense, something Aristotle seeks to formulate in his philosoph-ical anthropology in Book I of the *Politics* and Marx's attempt to do the same in the early *Manuscripts* as well as the *Theses on Feuerbach*. This first dimension of social ontology holds that there are specific features that constitute being a member of the species. These features or capacities can be realized or truncated; they can be fully expressed or partly or even wholly repressed. This depends on how the objective social order is organized. These phylogenetic capacities are for coopera-tive relatedness with others, processual development over time, and our practical-teleological capacities to realize conceptual ends in the world by manipulating the object domain (labor, language, etc.).

This leads to the second dimension, which refers to the objective social-ontological domain of institutions, norms, and established practices that shape and form these essential features of the individual. Objective social structures and processes have causal powers on the development of each member of the society—they form the basis for the ontogenetic features of individuals relative to the ontological shape of social relations, processes, and purposes of the social forms that shape him. They are causally responsible for the relative development or debasement of the individual's capacities and powers. Individuals therefore have phylogenetic capacities that are either manifested or suppressed in the ontogenetic form one takes. This is a result of the central dialectic between the individual and society. The basis of critical judgment is therefore in the ways that the ontic—or actually existing—forms of social and personal being diverge from what we can call higher ontological expressions of self and society. Critique and judgment must operate in this structure: it must seek to understand how the relations, structures, processes, norms, practices, and ends that make up our objective social forms shape and develop (or misshape and maldevelop) the individual.

Of course, there can be other core substantial features that we can use to understand human life. John Searle's social ontology posits "intentionality" as a central feature that we can add to this list given above by Aristotle and Marx, among others. Searle's social-ontological account of social reality can be incorporated into a broader critical social ontology once we see that the kinds of constitutive rules and forms of collective intentionality he describes are not only mechanisms for ascribing power relations and legitimating them but also shaped and formed by the prevailing structure of social relations that govern the various developmental and reproductive processes of the community. The power of this approach is that it shows how social phenomena are generated by social actors and the forms of collective intentionality they use to create social facts. The weakness of this approach is that it is essentially abstract: it does not integrate the material component of social reality—that is, how control over resources shapes norms, ideas, social relations, and so on. It also does not consider the objective features of sociality that make up a more comprehensive social ontology. What is needed for a fuller, more critical account of sociality is to bring together the theory of social ontology as a critical space for political judgment.

The collective intentionality approach to social ontology opens up the critical capacity immanent in the ontological project. Since there exists a collective-intentional element to social facts, the moment of critique opens up once the fabric of norms and constitutive rules that govern our collective intentionality are interrogated for the kinds of objective social relations, structures, and processes they promote and help re-create. This brings us to what I believe is one (if not *the*) fundamental insight of the critical theory tradition: namely, its inquiry into the forms of consciousness in society that help reconstitute patho-logical and inhumane forms of social life. We can gain insight into the pathologies of social life via a social ontology because this enables us to examine how shapes of sociality (in terms of institutionalized social formations and consciousness) promote ends that may not be for the good and self-determined interests of all. We cannot begin from the narrow ontology of human life given by postmetaphysics. Intersubjectivity, phenomenological, linguistic, communicative, recognitive, or whatever—none are up to the task because they provide no basis from which to judge the concrete ways that social forms shape our social reality. There needs to be a means for critique that grounds our grasp of social reality, one that exposes the dialectic between thought and being, between self and society, and between agency and structure. To not do this is to open consciousness up to the problem of reification: to the reassertion of the prevailing norms and ideas in our "rational" conception of the world. Once we consider the problem from this angle, we can see that a critical social ontology can be understood as bringing together a critical theory of norms with the principles immanent in the objective features of sociality, thereby granting us a kind of desideratum for a critical theory of judgment.

Properties of an Ontology of Sociality and Social Forms

A basic premise of any social-ontological approach to judgment must begin with the ways that our inherent sociality is given different shapes and forms. I use the phrase "inherent sociality" to describe the fact that humans are essentially cooperative and social creatures. Language, for instance, would not be possible without our inherent relationality with others. Our inherent sociality can be put into different shapes or forms, any of which constitute the social ontology granting our social reality. In addition, this inherent sociality can be modified, expanded, or constricted at different levels. Conversing with one another or moving a piano together are small-scale forms of sociality that are organized for particular purposes. These emerge out of a broader shared background of sociality that makes pianos, language, and so on possible in the first place. The forms that our sociality take are what I am most interested in. In this we can find the dynamics of social and political power that ought to be the primary objects of any form of political judgment. Political judgment must be about judging power; judging power must be concerned with interrogating how we legitimate and organize our inherent sociality.

Social ontology does not look for the content of all forms of social life, but for the basic underlying categories that undergird different forms of social reality. What conceptual structures are essential for the explanation of social reality and, perhaps to go further, what conceptual structures and mechanisms can we detect that will allow us to comprehend that reality and judge it according to critical-rational principles? We can see that the first forces our cognition to deal with objective structures of reality and the second with the dynamics of potentiality and actuality of those objective structures. From an analytic perspective, the ontology of social reality must be broken down into four distinct branches or dimensions. In much of the literature on social ontology, these dimensions are generally taken on its own and more often taken to be incompatible with the others. However, to construct a critical social ontology, we will clearly need to dialectically unify these four branches of social ontology and the distinctive areas of reality they seek to theorize. This is achieved once we see that each dimension dialectically leads us to the next and ultimately to a comprehensive theoretical structure that is a conceptual scheme and is immanent in the concept of society and therefore of social reality itself.

Our sociality is constituted by much more than noumenal and epistemic layers of relations. Sociality is more than intersubjectivity in the sense that it is constituted by structures, relations, processes, and ends that have causal powers and objectivity. This need not be material in nature. We cannot see social facts the way we can empirically experience, but this merely robs them of their materiality, not their ontology. We can see how this works in even the simplest interaction. You and I agree to meet for dinner at a restaurant in a particular part of town. Once this intersubjective exchange has been completed, we have articulated an agreement with certain expectations that are objective, binding each of us. We will see this date as having objective and causal features. But the norms that make us uphold the promise of meeting are more than an imperative of obeying this duty. It has deeper effects: it nurtures our friendship, renews social bonds, and so on. It is the same as we enlarge these structures of sociality.

We can see how this can extend into more complex layers of ontological reality. Whole structures of relations are articulated, along with the processes and ends to those structures. Add to this the roles, values, value orientations, and so on we need to internalize to maintain and grant those social forms their ontological reality. We should therefore distinguish between the properties, levels, and modes of a critical social ontology. The *properties* of a social ontology describe the features of what counts as social ontological; the *levels* describe the qualitative different phases of being that social reality takes; and the *modes* of the social ontology are the constitutive categories of society. Taken together, these aspects of social ontology provide a common structure to allow cognitive grasp of the social totality.

OBJECTIVITY AND MEDIATION

The basic properties of what allow us to account for a social ontology must be the following. First, it must be objective in the sense that it is a shared reality among members of the community. The objectivity of any social-ontological fact is one whose meaning or existence is a function of human cooperative practices. In this sense, it encompasses symbolic forms of cooperative practice—language and other communicative codes—as well as labor and physical transformation of nature. A law has objective existence without any natural substrate even as a house is what it is not because of its natural substrates (i.e., wood, concrete) but because of how these natural objects have been shaped and reformed for a nonnatural (i.e., human) social purpose. This should be sharply contrasted to what is material in the traditional sense. A legal code, money, rules, and the kind of rule-following that allows for a game of baseball or checkers—all are objective social facts that constitute objects with social facticity rather than material (or natural) facticity. Hence, Searle's conception of "constitutive rules" means the normative rule-following that creates certain objective social facts. The game of baseball is not a material fact, it is a social fact constituted by certain rules and rule-following behavior accepted by all who participate in it. But we can also say, after Marx and Lukács, that there are objective social facts that are material: hence, the human interaction with nature and the resulting transformation of nature into human products is itself an expression of the objective sociality.

We have to distinguish between those aspects of social ontology that are active and those that are congealed in the material world. Both are significant. We can say that an active aspect of social ontology would have objectivity but not materiality. Whenever I follow a rule or norm in tandem with others, I create an objective social fact, as when students and teacher behave in different ways according to different statuses and norms. This creates the category of teacher and student as an objective but not a material social fact, and they are only real when enacted in practices. Of course, this objective reality also shapes our cognition since the categories of teacher and student are embedded in larger institutions, in this case a school, that has other rules shaping and structuring the relations among people within it.

Practices that manipulate the natural world into socially meaningful objects have an objective social reality and a social-material reality. A violin or a baseball bat are essentially, in a brute material sense, pieces of wood, plastic, and other materials from nature. But these have been shaped and formed according to a purpose, end, or use that opens up new horizons of possibility for those forms of brute nature. At the same time, both are the product of an ensemble of social relations and practices that have manipulated the natural world—trees into wood, plastic into tuning keys, and so on—that have brought those elements from the sphere of nature into the sphere of the social. The material world of cities, electric power stations, paintings, paint, parks, and so on are all the result of sociohuman praxis in a congealed, material form. Hence, the first property of social ontology embraces what is objective and material, but not necessarily both at the same time.[4] In this sense, the ontology of social facts are not only objective in that they are shared norms of behavior, they also refer to the objectivity of the relations, structures, and processes these norms instantiate. They are able to propagate into complex forms of social reality that, in turn, mediate our consciousness and behavior. This leads to the feature of causal powers.

Causal Powers and Social Power

A second property of social ontology is that it has causal powers over social agents. A social fact must have causal powers in some basic sense for it to be social ontological. Searle says, for instance, that social facts have "deontic power," which means the norms we accept as constitutive

---

4. In this sense, unicorns, for instance, are not possible by an ontological scheme because it makes claims about material reality, whereas merely objective social facts are forms of reality that have objectivity because we accept their reality (say, interest rates on a loan) but make no claims about the organization of matter.

of social facts make demands on us and our commitments, behavior, and conscience. This entails the capacity of any social fact to be able to cause us to perform, think, or feel in some way. Social reality would not be real in any efficacious sense if it did not have some causal power. This can come in a myriad forms. On the one hand, they can be embedded in norms of behavior in that the roles, functions, and statuses of individuals in a given social context will entail certain expectations, behaviors, and additional norms. Social power is therefore intricately entwined with these causal powers, for the capacity to shape and develop efficacious forms of deontic power carry the capacity to control and shape others. In this sense, capital, for instance, is not a material reality but a social-ontological one: it is a structural and processual set of congealed norms that force certain kinds of behaviors and expectations. It only has power to the extent that it is embedded in the basic background worldview and institutional logics of society as a whole. But herein lies its essentially ontological constitution: it is constituted by the kinds of rule-following (coercive or tacit) that the institutions shaped and affected by capital absorbed and then enacted by agents.

As a result of the complex activities of objective forms of social reality that shape and orient our behavior, as these kinds of activities congeal into more complex social forms we can see that they further develop their ontological sophistication and reality. We can see a third property of social ontology: that social reality is systemic, meaning they are not static things of reality but operate within a context of other social facts (relations, structures, processes, and so on). Given the interrelatedness of social facts, their constitution as a system brings us to higher levels of complexity and toward the totality. As David Weissman has argued, "Systems take causality one step further: mutual activation and inhibition—causal reciprocities—stabilize interactions that have created a system."[5] Systems are not aggregates of the smaller elements that constitute them, they are composed of elements related via mutual forms of determination. In this sense, higher, more complex forms of reality can be articulated by enlarging the web of mutually related elements. This gives rise to what I call regressive causation, or the capacity of higher structures of social reality to be not just the product of lower or prior structures but also the very cause for those prior structures.

5. David Weissman, *A Social Ontology* (New Haven, CT: Yale University Press, 2000), 64.

In this sense, systems are nonlinear, but interactive as a totality. Each substructure in the totality interacts with the other to produce itself.

But social power itself is also a property of social ontology. Any time we cooperate with others, whether that cooperation is done out of volition or necessity, it leads to what Talcott Parsons called "collective power," or the amplification of human capacities through cooperative activity. Power of this kind is an ontological rather than purely natural reality; it is generated through the coordination of individual activities into a higher, more complex systemic totality. The act of moving a sofa or building a nuclear power plant require coordinated forms of activity that can achieve some more difficult purposes than one person could accomplish on their own. Marx makes this point about capital when he says that it is "not a private but a social power (*eine gesellschaftliche Macht*)." One core problem for critical social ontology is to understand how forms of social power are articulated. The relevant evaluative questions emerge when we begin to ask how the social powers that our associational lives contribute to are used, what ends they serve, and how they instantiate certain kinds of social relations and norms.

THE ONTOLOGICAL STATUS OF NORMS AND VALUES

An essential property of social ontology is the role played by norms and values. Social reality can only be maintained and come into existence by the coordination of rules of behavior that shape and orient our subjective inclinations toward certain forms of activity. Norms in this sense have an ontological character because they are objective and have causal powers. Norms and values shape and orient the cognitive, evaluative, and cathectic structures of subjectivity. They absorb aspects of subjectivity into a collectively governed realm of the social. Norms are the very stuff that prop up our relations with others, the institutions that pervade our world, and the regimes of labor that pattern our cooperative powers with others as well as our relation with nature. Norms therefore constitute our social world in that they collectively shape the structure of roles and practices that emerge from them. A norm is not an abstract "ought"; it is embedded in an objective nexus of practices and social structures that shape and diffuse them even as they are constituted by them.

The relevant question for any critical social ontology is not simply to describe the mechanisms and properties that make sociality possible, but to inquire into how power is constituted by the forms of life any society instantiates. Norms are crucial, in this regard, because they are the seat of this link between the individual agency and the self on one hand and the social totality on the other. As Searle notes, norms have a deontic power in that they can command my actions. Deontic forms of power occur when a norm has the capacity to form in me a sense of duty to that practice. The key problem of deontic norms, something that Searle does not explore, is how they can be fused to broader objective social structures to internalize domination within the subject.

These norms are not the source of all social reality. Rather, they are the substance that can be formed and shaped to realize higher order forms of social reality. A given regime of norms generates certain kinds of social reality in that they can shape the structures of social relations and the practices that enact social reality. The key here is that norms cannot be torn from totality in some analytic fashion. They are part of the systematic constitutive process of social reality; they constitute forms of social power because they shape the practices and social structures that govern our coordinated activities. Norms are a crucial property of how power is expressed, and they are therefore part of a larger social scheme. Norms are part of the larger systemic dynamics of social reality and unite individual consciousness with larger social-ontological processes and structures.

In this sense, values should be seen as having ontological ballast insofar as they can arrange our relations, norms, and practices and articulate forms of social reality. Hence, the value of friendship fashions a particular kind of relationship between two people. Values have constitutive power over our social reality and should not be seen as arbitrary or subjective. Rather, they link the subjective and objective spheres of social reality in particular ways. Values are generally seen in Kantian or neo-Kantian fashion as abstract, formal principles that transcend reality. But this is not really correct. Values are in fact ontological to the extent that they orient and shape our practices and relations with others. Values are abstract only when they fail to have that grip in the world; when they are unable to shape and orient practices and become constitutive of forms of social reality. In this sense, our values and norms are ontological in that they emerge as real in the world. The transformation of values therefore entails, if such transformation is truly successful, a transformation of our social forms.

The Ontological and the Ontic

This raises another crucial property of the ontological point of view: that of the distinction between what is and what is potentially possible in the structural-conceptual parameters of what exists. Put another way, we can see the distinction between the ontology of any thing and its ontic status as consisting of the mere empirical-descriptive traits of any given social fact and the constitutive substrates that make it what it is and what it could otherwise be. In this sense, an institution or some other social phenomenon may indeed exist and have certain descriptive, ontic properties. But critique must be able to unveil and lay bare to consciousness the defective attributes of that ontic state and seek to transform it via immanent critique, that is, by rethinking how the social relations, practices, norms, and purposes of that institution can be rearticulated to express interdependent relations and common benefits and ends.

Hence, any given family, to take a concrete example, may indeed exist, say, as a patriarchal family, each member taking the ontic role of father, mother, son, daughter, sibling, and so on. But this mere ontic expression of an empirical family has an ontological dimension as well. Each family member may have internalized their roles and the attendant practices of the patriarchal family. But the ontological dimension allows critique to come more substantively to the fore: each may question if the hierarchical-patriarchal relations are worthy of their obligations; they may ask whether the purpose of the family is to serve the men of the household; and they may come to see that the norms and practices they engage in constitute this hierarchical structure and the particular benefits it bestows on certain family members in place of others. The ontological therefore immanently opens up a field of judgment and critique in that these relations, norms, practices, and ends can be altered (or seek to be altered) to manifest a more rational, more interdependent form of association for the equal benefit of each family member. But if this transformation is successful, it will no longer be the same family: it will have transformed itself.

In this example we can see that the ontic is static and the merely descriptive status of the object, as opposed to the ontological, which grasps the deep constitutive structures of that object. I think the same can be said for almost any social phenomenon: the state, economy, schools, friendships, and so on. This distinction has its most fertile roots in Hegel's metaphysics and its conception of being as process rather than static existence. The emergence of freedom as an ontological and objective property of a society depends on the extent to which we organize our interdependent relations where each community member constitutes a self-conscious agent and the institutional schemes we participate in fulfill common ends and purposes or are brought into line with common ends and purposes.

But Marx also sees an implicit distinction between these two aspects of being. Take the following as an example: "A Negro is a Negro. He only becomes a *slave* in certain relations. A cotton-spinning jenny is a machine for spinning cotton. It becomes capital only in certain relations. Torn from these relationships it is no more capital than gold in itself is money or sugar the price of sugar."[6] Capitalist social relations constitute the individual (say, the "Negro" or the cotton-spinning jenny) as what they are. The extent to which a slave exists is the ontic expression of that person, constituted by social-ontological structures, relations, norms, and processes. But the "Negro," in Marx's example, can also be more than a slave; he or she possesses an ontological potential to become more than that historically specified status. The transformation of the "material" relations of society (in truth, these are ontological relations made concrete by practices relating to others and to nature) is thus transformative of the very being of the "Negro," say, into a full equal member of the community, a man, a citizen, and so on. The shift effects a change—say, the abolition of slavery, the technical transformation of work, or whatever—in the person from slave to free person. The ontic is therefore transitory although it appears static and permanent. It is captured empirically by consciousness, but a consciousness that is unable to cognize the deeper ontological potentiality of that thing; its status as what it is, its ontic status, is in fact dependent on the social-ontological field that constitutes it.

What this all means is that the status of the ontic in social ontology can be judged according to alternative constitutive relational structures, processes, norms, and practices. Social critique must seek to comprehend the social totality as a constitutive ontological context for the rational cognition of social phenomena. Even more, restricting ourselves to the intersubjective or intercognitive realm of the "space of

---

6. Karl Marx, "Wage Labor and Capital," in *Collected Works*, vol. 9 (London: Lawrence and Wishart, 2010), 211.

reasons" does not allow us to penetrate the essential-constitutive dimensions of social reality. A critical social ontology allows us to grasp how social reality has constitutive effects on the objects of consciousness. In this sense, it leads into the very mode of thinking that will enable and ground critical judgment. But to do this, the modes of social ontology will have to be delineated and explored.

Modes of Social Ontology

These three basic properties of social ontology therefore describe what counts as social-ontological as opposed to natural. They are descriptive of the qualities that inhere to any social-ontological phenomenon. We can turn to the basic categories that are constitutive of social reality itself, that is, those categories that essentially account for social-ontological phenomena. As I see it, these will have to expand beyond the basic ideas described by Marx and Lukács. First we must keep in mind that we can understand these categories by breaking them down analytically, but in reality they operate dialectically, as will be shown.

The first fundamental analytic division must be made between what we can call subjective and objective modes of social ontology. I take these respective terms to indicate not a separately delineated sphere of reality but that subjective and objective things interpenetrate dialectically, that is, mutually cause each other. A subjective facet of social ontology is therefore nevertheless rooted in social forms and reality. But it can manifest itself without external agents. Hence, Robinson Crusoe could utter a language and perform other practices that he absorbed through socialization without having others around him. However, objective facets of social ontology cannot exist without others: relations, structures, processes, and ends all have an ontological objectivity that transcend any given individual and require multiple agents for their emergence.

What is crucial here is to see that any practice, even if performed by an individual, is a socially mediated activity. The capacity for language is innate, but language, communication, and so on are socially mediated developments. These become social-ontological realities, social facts that have objectivity, causal powers, and the status of a system. But because practices are socially mediated forms of activity, more developed forms of praxis are essentially social and, as such, require cooperation with others. In this sense, social facts are constituted by relations between individuals performing collective praxis. A conversation has ontological status as a social fact constituted by a cooperative interplay of the practice of speaking. Going further, these relations can become structured in that they are patterned by rules, norms, status functions, and so on. Producing a commodity in a factory therefore entails a structural relationship in that each productive members depends in an interdependent way on the activities of others.

Intentions and Practices

One of the most basic phylogenetic capacities of the species is the ability to form an intention, or the capacity for our mental states to be about something or be pointed toward something. Intentionality achieves social-ontological significance when multiple people come to agree that a certain sign or utterance should be accepted as a common signifier for a given thing. This grants that object a social-ontological quality in that it has meaning for us collectively because we collectively attribute a meaning, significance, or status to it. Intentions are essentially our capacity to project meaning onto objects and make them the basis for an activity or collective forms of meaning and activity. Hence, practices are related to intentions in that they are activities we perform that in many ways rely on the existence of others. The practice of laboring, for Marx, is social when it is done for someone else. When I labor to produce something for another—when I prepare a meal, utter a sentence, and so on—I move in a social space in that my intentions and practices are oriented toward others and take account of others.

We can have intentions that are purely personal and nonsocial, but there are not many. Even when I am alone, I use collective forms of meaning and intentionality. Reading and thinking use social concepts, socially accepted structures of patterned significance (i.e., language), or other conceptual schemes that are shared structures of meaning. Intentions and practices are therefore part of the basic substantial modes of social reality in that they are the phylogenetic capacities that are shaped and formed in certain ways to generate higher, richer, more complex forms of life and social reality. The existence of complex social forms are the product of the various ways organize and pattern the intentional and practical capacities of individuals. Collective intentionality therefore comes into play as a central means by which social reality is constituted. What makes us distinctively human is our capacity to think and act from a "we-perspective" rather than a narrow "I-perspective."[7] Social relations and social structures are part of how these intentions achieve this more ontologically rich form and become more complex forms of social reality.

RELATIONS AND STRUCTURES

Another feature of substance is our relationality with others. Social relations are the product of an inherent, phylogenetic capacity to associate with others. Their existence is not empirical, but ontological: they have an objective, causal power over us. They can be shaped and formed in different ways, from simple forms of connectivity to complex forms of interdependence. They can also achieve a richer ontological content, as when we pattern our norms and practices in accordance with them and to sustain and reproduce them, in which case they become structures. We begin to see that part of what makes human sociality what it is, an essential part of its basic structure, is that it is relational: individuals require others and relations with them to exercise biological and cultural forms of life, and so on. The nature of these relations constitute the essential structure of any sociality. Hence, the substantialist view quickly forces us to the next dimension of social ontology, that of the existence of relations.

We can say the basic substance of social ontology is what I have been calling our inherent sociality. Once we think in these terms, we can see the essential substance of human life as consisting in our sociality, in the basic forms of cooperations that humans (and higher primates) use to solve problems and enhance the powers of the species as a whole. The relevant question now becomes the extent to which this substance is put into different shapes and the consequences of these shapes of sociality. Sociality is not spontaneously generated but is structured by forms of power that stabailize them and grant them causal powers over the socialization of subjects. When I talk about shapes of social substance, I have in mind the ways that any community or association of persons forms and objectifies the phylogenetic capacities of intentions, practices, and relationality. These are substantive modes in that they are the very substance that is taken up and put into specific

---

7. See the important discussion by Michael Tomasello, *Becoming Human: A Theory of Ontogeny* (Cambridge, MA: Harvard University Press, 2019).

forms or shapes that produce the ontological forms of life we inhabit. Hence, a school is an institution that makes use of our capacities for intentions, practices, and relations but puts them in a specific shape: teachers, students, custodians, administrators, and so on, take on different roles due to the collective intentionality shared by members of the association; practices are shaped according to the purposes of the institution (studying, lecturing, and so on); and how individuals relate to one another are defined by how social relations and structures of the institution are enacted by norms and practices defined by the structure. We are inquiring into the totality of society and the mechanisms and processes that constitute it.

Back to relations. Things can also be understood as a function of their relations with other things, they can be produced by *relatum* and they are themselves *relata*. The social relations that constitute the essential structure of human social life have distinctive ontological characteristics. According to this view, the relations between entities is more central that the entities themselves. This view is in dialectical tension with the substantialist view, which would seek to understand society as an entity, whereas the social-relational ontology seeks to make the structure of relations the essential substance of society. The substantialist view does not ignore the existence of relations; it places them in a subordinate position to the entities that are nodes in the relations. A relational ontology, by contrast, sees that the modes are predicated on the relational field within which they are ensconced. Hence, the relational and substantialist views are at odds concerning what is primary: the entities being related or the relations linking the entities.

Relational ontologies see that relations predicate the substantial entities related by them. A rook or a bishop in the game of chess only have substantive meaning in relation to each other, to their relation to the chessboard, and to the rules governing their motion during play. Changing the relations between these things changes what those objects are. Similarly, a key only has substantive meaning in relation to a lock: the nature of one thing is dependent on another, hence the *relatum* are given primacy to the *relata*. Of course, human beings have relations: to each other, to the world as a whole, to nature, and to themselves as subjects. But in this case, human relations with others constitute not only an arbitrary feature, but a necessary feature of human life because it can be shown that relational structures between social members give rise to the kinds of properties and powers that are uniquely human (language, cognition, etc.). Subjects are therefore conceived as "relational subjects" insofar as they give rise to relational goods and properties.[8] The nature of the division between the individual and society is sublated. The question is whether these relations are constitutive of who they are or the other way around. For Marx, the question is settled dialectically in that he sees that human agents create social relations, which then have reflexive powers over them. Social relations and social reality or being are dialectically related and one is not subordinate to the other.[9]

It is important that we do not view the kinds of relations that I have just described as mechanical insofar as each element of their relation acts on the other in some unidirectional, causal sense. The relations that serve as the substantive, structural essence of sociality must be comprehended as reciprocal in the sense that Hegel discusses it in his *Logic*. For Hegel, the nature of reciprocal relations are different from causal relations in that the "first cause, which first acts and receives its effect back into itself as reaction, thus reappears as cause, whereby the action, which in finite causality runs on into the spuriously infinite progress, is bent around and becomes an action that returns into itself, an infinite reciprocal action."[10] What this means is

---

8. As Donati and Archer insightfully note: "The term *'Relational Subject'* refers to individual and collective social subjects in that they are *'relationally constituted,'* that is, *in as much as they generate emergent properties and powers through their social relations.* These relational goods and evils have internal effects upon the subjects themselves and external effects upon their social environments." Pierpaolo Donati and Margaret Archer, *The Relational Subject* (Cambridge: Cambridge University Press, 2015), 31.

9. Carol Gould is therefore incorrect when she argues that Marx privileges substance over relations. In her view, "for Marx, although such individuals do not exist apart from their relations, and in fact develop and change themselves through these relations, yet the existence and mode of activity of these individuals is the ontological presupposition of the relations into which they enter. These individuals, who are agents, according to Marx, may be regarded as constituting these relations by their activity and therefore cannot be seen as products of these relations. Thus these individuals have fundamental ontological status and are not to be understood as mere nodes of relations or as wholly constituted by their relations." *Karl Marx's Social Ontology* (Cambridge, MA: MIT Press, 1978), 38. The more correct view is to see that there is no privileging of one over the other, but a dialectical relation between them as well as the processual ontology I describe below.

10. G. W. F. Hegel, *Wissenschaft der Logik*, vol. 1 (Frankfurt: Suhrkamp, 1959), 237.

that reciprocal actions (*Wechselwirken*) are to be understood as a kind of structure of relations that also have a dynamism or processual logic as a totality and unity.[11] Each *relata* in any given structure of *relatum* is to be understood as having taken part in self-determination in the sense that the element is interdependently related to a reciprocal structure that constitutes a structure of necessity for the development of each *relata* and the whole they collectively make up. Relations may be the essential substance of social life, but these relations are to be seen as dynamic, as working toward some purposes or ends. They can also be seen as processes, as systems of reciprocal action that possess a telos and actualize the members of that social-relational nexus. Individuals are ensconced in a structure of intrinsically reciprocal relations that have an ontological determinateness. This relational structure is the framework of sociality, something that possesses causal powers or the capacity to shape ends and goals that members of any social act participate toward. At the same time, this relational structure acts on each individual member and helps in constituting that individual's individuality.[12] Therefore, we can see that any ontology of social relations that possesses causal powers also has the capacity to produce certain ends and can be considered a process.

---

11. Dieter Henrich notes on this aspect of Hegel's logical system that "This unity permits the independent existence of its determinations but still holds these independent moments within the unity of its own organized form, not merely with respect to the movements of these moments but in every aspect of their actual existence as well." "Logical Form and Real Totality: The Authentic Conceptual Form of Hegel's Concept of the State," in Robert Pippin and Otfried Höffe (eds.), *Hegel on Ethics and Politics* (Cambridge: Cambridge University Press, 2004), 241–67, 253.

12. Hence Richard Dien Winfield argues, "In the ethical community, the good at which conduct aims contains the activity of its realization insofar as membership involves knowing and willing goals whose achievement reproduces the whole, thereby securing the unity of each member's volition with the performance of the rest." "Ethical Community without Communitarianism," *Philosophy Today*, vol. 40, no. 2 (1996): 310–20, 318. Christopher Yeomans also argues that this structure of reciprocal relations can be considered a "structure of freedom." See Christopher Yeomans, *Freedom and Reflection: Hegel and the Logic of Agency* (New York: Oxford University Press, 2012), 216ff., for a discussion of reciprocal relations and their implication for rational agency, as well as Donati and Archer, *The Relational Subject*, 33ff. for a discussion of reflexivity from a sociological perspective.

Relations are only discernible analytically, they do not exist in reality in that form. Any relation can be understood to exist ontologically, but it is a process in that each relation is also an activity. A marriage is not simply a relation, it is a process constituted by relations of activity.[13] A family is a larger structure of relations than a marriage, but it, too, is a structure of relations of activity, and its ontological status can be found in the activities that happen within that structure. An individual, in this sense, is also an ontological status supported by specific forms of relational structures and practices.[14] For all intents and purposes, one's status as an individual or the existence of a marriage are processes. In this sense, emphasizing a relational sociology is necessary but insufficient to account for the reality of social facts. As an example of this thesis, Margaret Archer and Pierpaolo Donati contend:

> The term "Relational Subject" refers to individual and collective social subjects in that they are "relationally constituted," that is, in as much as they generate emergent properties and powers through their social relations. These relational goods and evils have internal effects upon the subjects themselves and external effects upon their social environments.[15]

Although it is clear that relations are constitutive of social facts, they alone cannot account for a social ontology in any comprehensive sense. Archer and Donati are right to see relations as constitutive of social facts and (in Donati's case in particular) quite right to see the goods

---

13. See the important discussion by Richard T. De George, "Social Reality and Social Relations," *Review of Metaphysics*, vol. 37, no. 1 (1983): 3–20.

14. Michael E. Brown insightfully argues on this point: "Individuality must therefore be held to express irreducible social facts. The individual cannot be coneived of alone, 'in isolation,' but only as an abiding possibility among people caught up in their relations, and, given the dependence of each on all, conceived of in such a way that individuality is an extrusion, or moment, and not a logically prior concept or basic fact. It follows that *agency, which has to do with the nature of activity, cannot be understood in individualistic terms or by reference to pre-social individuality.*" *The Concept of the Social in Uniting the Humanities and Social Sciences* (Philadelphia: Temple University Press, 2014), 103.

15. Donati and Archer, *The Relational Subject*, 31. Also see Dave Elder-Vass, "Social Structure and Social Relations," *Journal for the Theory of Social Behaviour*, vol. 37, no. 4 (2007): 463–77.

produced and shared by society as "relational goods."[16] The limitation here is in the constricted social metaphysics that this perspective confines us. Relations are constitutive of higher social-ontological forms, and in parsing these various modes, we can grasp a more total conception of social reality. More to the point, once we see that relations constitute structures, that structures constitute processes, and that processes constitute ends and purposes, we are on our way to a more comprehensive and critical grasp of social reality or social reality as a totality.[17]

Processes

Social structure can be understood not as static forms of relations but as a process: that is, as collective, interactive activities oriented toward an end or purpose. Processes are a higher ontological form than relational structures insofar as they are defined by reciprocal causes among the component parts of the structure. Relations are dynamic and achieve processual features because these dynamic relations constitute a degree of change in the substance of the object or in its relation to other objects.[18] In this sense, structures evolve into processes once the component parts of the structure act on one another to form a coherent system with ontological properties—ontological properties that are irreducible to the component parts or elements of the structure that constitute them.[19]

---

16. See Pierpaolo Donati's excellent paper, "The Common Good as a Relational Good," *Nova et Vetera*, vol. 7, no. 3 (2009): 603–24, and his "Social Capital and Associative Democracy: A Relational Perspective," *Journal for the Theory of Social Behaviour*, vol. 44, no. 1 (2013): 24–45, as well as his discussion in Donati and Archer, *The Relational Subject*, 198ff.

17. I have outlined the Hegelian foundations for this approach in Michael J. Thompson, "The Metaphysical Infrastructure of Hegel's Practical Philosophy," in M. Thompson (ed.), *Hegel's Metaphysics and the Philosophy of Politics* (New York: Routledge, 2018), 101–41.

18. See the important discussion of processual ontology by Emmanuel Renault, "Critical Theory and Processual Social Ontology," *Journal of Social Ontology*, vol. 2, no. 1 (2016): 17–32.

19. David Weissman notes on this aspect of social ontology: "High-order systems are formed when reciprocal causal relations are established between lower-order systems (starting with elementary particles). Causal reciprocity is the relation of agents whose characters or behaviors are mutually determining, hence mutually controlling, over a cycle of back-and-forth interactions." *A Social Ontology*, 46.

Social facts can be seen as constituted by processes once we see that they are the result of a complex of practices.[20] Processes are dialectically related to ends or purposes. Indeed, just as relations are dialectically related to structures and structures to processes, so are processes defined in some basic sense as essentially related to the ends or purposes they are organized to produce.

Families are an example of this. Although they do not necessarily produce some concrete commodity or good, they can be seen as relational structures where each component member acts in particular ways toward others in some reciprocal fashion, thereby constituting a system or process that produces an end or set of ends—mutual emotional or economic support, the raising of children, and so on. Clearly the more we expand the horizon of what counts as social facts, the more we see that we are increasingly ensconced in overlapping systems of relational structures that generally have some kind of purpose or end that gives them their coherence and defines their activities in some basic sense. The end or purpose can also be seen to shape and organize the other modes that lead up to it: the nature of relational structures and processes. Hence, the imperative to increase productive efficiency in an economic activity may entail transforming the relational structures of the factory, which in turn changes the processes that constitute it. Indeed, the more general point I want to make here in discussing the objective aspects of social-ontological modes is that when the totality of these modes is taken into account, we can approach a comprehensive grasp of the social totality.

Objects are dynamic to the extent that they exist in process, which means that the reciprocal relations within any structure possess the power to generate outcomes and particular kinds of ends or goods. They are not static entities. Process ontology is the view that the nature of existence must be grasped as dynamic and in motion rather than static, analytically comprehensible entities. According to the processual dimension of ontology, we must see that being is something that unfolds along a time horizon and therefore has a developmental character. In this sense, it is important to point out that different stages of the time horizon posit

---

20. As Georg Lukács notes: "Thus the knowledge that social facts are not objects but relations between men is intensified to the point where facts are wholly dissolved into processes." *History and Class Consciousness* (Cambridge, MA: MIT Press, 1971), 180.

distinct and qualitative changes in the structure of being.[21] Processes have both mechanistic and organic features constituting a dynamic structure where particular moments of that structure constitute and are constituted by the reciprocal-relational activity of the whole entity. In social terms, processes are essential for understanding human agency and culture as an achieved status: as a kind space of collective, developmental change that can also be an object of rational reflection. In this way, Hegel sees that the process of history is teleological in the self-unserstanding of human freedom, not because of a transcendent ontological plan but because the development of social-ontological properties of human interdependence and the reflection of that reality in cognition through recognition leads toward a self-understanding of freedom as social freedom. Indeed, even once we posit that process is an essential aspect of the human biological and psychological life, it is also true of the sphere of culture. Processes are shaped and affected by the kinds of structured relations within which they are enacted, and these processes in turn result in the actualization of ends. Process is therefore dialectically related to substance and relations in that the structure of relations that exist determine the shaping of the very substance of the object.

Although Aristotle privileges a substantivist conception of ontology, he also sees that part of the substance of any thing is that it exists in motion—that is, it is constituted by an organic process of development and change that reaches an end state.[22] Process is an element of ontology

---

21. Lukács therefore points out that: "A careful and correct approach to ontological problems always requires one to keep constantly in mind that every leap signifies a qualitative and structural change in being, in the course of which, though the transition stage may contain certain preconditions and possibilities of the later, higher stages, the latter cannot be developed from the former in a simple straight-line continuity." Georg Lukács, *The Ontology of Social Being*, vol. 3, *Labor* (London: Merlin Press, 1977), 2.

22. Aryeh Kosman has recently commented on this idea in Aristotle that the "realization that he defines motion to be is in fact an activity—an *energeia*. It is the activity of a subject's being able to be something than it now is, prior to its having realized that ability by actually having become other than it now is. This activity is the thing's most fully exercising its *ability*, its most actively being *able to be* something qua being able to be it, while not actually *being* it. This is what Aristotle means by saying that a motion is the realization of what is able to be, as he puts it, *qua* able to be; it is the *activity* of being able to be." *The Activity of Being: An Essay on Aristotle's Ontology* (Cambridge, MA: Harvard University Press, 2013), 68.

once we grasp that things, objects, are never simply what they are as things in themselves (substantivist ontology) or merely the result of the relations with other things. Rather, things exist within a dynamic context of reciprocal relations and processes that constitute them and that in turn constitute through their particular actions. They can only be understood outside the function they play in a system. Hence, our understanding of hearts require not only a substantivist view that they are made of muscles, electrical impulses, arteries, and so on; we must also see that the heart is related to other organs to which it supplies blood. Hence we must grasp that it is not just a static object ensconced in relations to other things but that it works in process through those relations, it has a function, a telos.[23] Its end, its purpose, is to perform a specific function that can only occur in a context of relations.

The nature of process opens up the critical question of potentiality and actuality, which I explore in more detail in the next section. We now have the basic vocabulary for an evaluative language by which we can think about the difference between the proper achievement of any end state and the defective end state that may pervade the emipirical manifestation of an object.[24] If one seeks to make wine and it instead becomes vinegar, it has failed to become wine—perhaps because the structural conditions of the wine shaped the processes of the chemical reactions in such a way that they failed to become what could have become wine under different circumstances. We can diagnose hearts that are defective by noting how they fail to achieve an end state. The

---

23. Hegel's metaphysics has this concept of process and change at its core. As Frederick Beiser has noted: "To state that a natural object serves a purpose is not to hold that there is some intention behind its creation, still less that there is some concealed intention within the object itself. Rather, all that it means is that the object serves a function, that it plays an essential role in the structure of the organism." *Hegel* (London: Routledge, 2005), 101. Also see this discussion in Songsuk Susan Hahn, *Contradiction in Motion: Hegel's Organic Concept of Life and Value* (Ithaca, NY: Cornell University Press, 2007), 9–53.

24. Hegel, in particular, after Aristotle, saw that the nature of the given reality, of *Dasein*, needs to be contrasted with the fuller reality, *Wirklichkeit*, that any thing can achieve. As Charles Taylor rightly notes, "what exists is not to be seen as simply there, as merely contingent, but rather as the manifestation of a thoroughgoing systematic web of necessary relations." *Hegel* (Cambridge: Cambridge University Press, 1975), 258. This further emphasizes the necessary, dialectical relation between relational and processual dimensions of ontology.

distinction between potentiality, actuality, and empirical existence is crucial: the three are in dialectical tension and are ontological categories insofar as they are categories about states of being. In this sense, Aristotle's distinction between the end (τέλος) and its nonrealized or deficiently realized, "pathological" state (ἀτελής) can be grasped from an objective-factual and a normative-evaluative sense. This is because any given social reality can be scrutinized with respect to the question of how much the potentialities of its deeper purposes or ends have been brought forth and realized.

The processual features of relational dynamics are not open-ended or without purpose. Rather, they are oriented toward some end or some purpose. In social ontology, this means that structures of relations are organized to effect certain processes that have some end or purpose. Associations are not static, and they are not without a purpose or end. Friendship is not just a relation between two (or more) persons, it also consists of certain practices and activities that make the individuals in that structure change to some degree. The purpose of friendship can be multifarious, but they could be to offer emotional support, psychological comfort, and so on. These purposes need not be utilitarian, but they are ends for which the relational structure and processes of activity are to be oriented. In this sense, relations, processes, and ends are not to be seen as separate from one another but dialectically related ino a coherent totality that is constitutive of the object itself.[25]

ENDS AND PURPOSES

This brings me to the final basic category of a critical social ontology: ends and purposes. We can say that any social process has an end or purpose in the sense that it is done to achieve some goal or realize some end. The basic concept is that the end or purpose of any given form of sociality can often determine the structure of relations and processes that realize them. Ends or purposes have a retrogressive causal relation to the other modes. It may appear that a light switch is the cause of the light being turned on. In truth, we can say that the light is the

---

25. I think Renault is wrong in his otherwise insightful paper in arguing that a processual ontology is distinct from and superior to relational and substantial ontologies. My thesis here is that they are dialectically related. See his discussion in "Critical Theory and Processual Social Ontology."

cause of the switch itself: the end of turning the light on can only be enacted via the existence of the switch. From the conceptual view of a critical metaphysics that wants to comprehend systemic totalities, the end, the telos of any system, is the retrogressive cause of the modes organized to realize it.

Once we inquire into the function of society—the end, its telos, so to speak—is such that it exists for the good of all of its members. But this can only be achieved by the rational unity of free individuals who act in a self-determined fashion but toward collective ends. The reason for this is that a kind of social freedom picks up on the ontological premise of sociality and must reflect the notion that particulars and universals are related into a more unified relational whole. In social terms, each member of society comes to grasp and recognize that his own welfare is dependent on the relational goods that the community as a whole are able to achieve and that the means for these kinds of goods are irreducibly social in nature in that they require joint forms of action and interdependence, without which they either could not be achieved or are achieved deficiently.[26]

This is the primary context, Hegel and Marx believed, that would make clear for us the self-determining content of modern life insofar as true, modern forms of freedom were only possible in a context of social relations and processes that had as their proper ends the enhancement its members and, at the same time, the conscious awareness of those members as rational individuals, that they would need to endorse those practices, norms, and institutions that had precisely those ends as their proper telos. Hence, there is a necessary cognitive dimension to this social ontological reality insofar as these relations, processes, and the essential substance they produce as the structure of any community are reproduced by the intentional acts of individuals. There is, in our final dimension of social ontology, a constructivist aspect to sociality because a crucial component of it concerns the norms of collective intentionality that organize and shape social facts.

The objective modes of social ontology are dialectically related to the subjective modes. As I point out in figure 6.1, the subjective modes are made up of individual practices, and norms make up the basic

---

26. I cannot develop this thesis here in any substantive way. Interested readers should see the discussion on the idea of relational goods by Donati, "The Common Good as a Relational Good."

structure of the subjective dimension of social reality. For the objective modes to achieve ontological activity, they must be enacted by agents. At the same time, already existing ontological social forms are acting on agents, integrating them into the norms and practices requisite for the reproduction of those institutions and structures. At the level of the subject, we need to see that the cognitive, evaluative, and cathectic levels of the subject need to be shaped and brought into compliance, to some basic degree, with the norms and rules institutions deploy. When an institution is unable to achieve this level of social conformity, it begins to disintegrate. Once agents no longer think in terms of the dominant institutions, judge the world according to the norms it emanates, and feel no personal investment in them, they will begin to fall apart. Hence, the ontological forms a kind of system involving the objective and subjective in a higher totality. When whole societies are affected by the disintegration of this social system, they will collapse, as in the fall of Soviet communism in the late twentieth century.

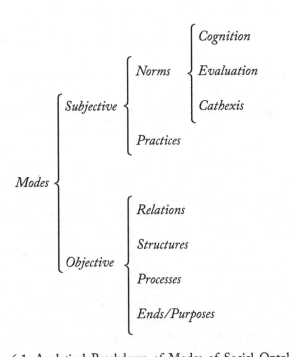

Figure 6.1. Analytical Breakdown of Modes of Social Ontology.

SUBJECTIVE MODES AND THE FORMATION OF SYSTEMS

It is important to stress that the self has ontological features. The objective modes described above are not to be taken as independent from one another but as forming the basis for an integration into a system. For this to be the case, we must consider how the subjective modes mesh with the objective modes. In dialectical fashion, they relate in a functional form: the norms are shaped to constitute forms of practice that in turn articulate institutions. Norms are constitutive of and constituted by institutions. Hence, the process of socialization is crucial as a means by which norms are inculcated and institutions achieve stability and permanence. Once norms begin to erode, the social structures, processes, and ends they support will also begin to erode. The individual's cognitive and evaluative capacities are shaped by the value orientations and normative structure of society. This occurs by the process of the internalization of norms and values that shape not only practices but the second-order reflective and evaluative capacities on those practices. As the social totality becomes more systematized and patterned by logics of domination and control, the socialization of the individual becomes more and more defined by the internalization of rationalized heteronomous value systems and norms that originate in hierarchical social forms.

This is why the problem of power and domination are so central to a critical social ontology. As I argued in the introduction, the powerful centripetal forces of the cybernetic society are such that reifying the consciousness of the modern individual is tied to how socialization and internalization processes are shaped. Domination requires that norms are successfully internalized. Only when they serve the interests of others and are heteronomous do we have a domination relation in play. To internalize collective intentional norms is not, of course, an expression of domination. But when these collective intentional norms are shaped to buttress and sustain hierarchical relations of power, we can see how the ontology of social relations and the norms that instantiate them are caught within (and can come to be constituted by) the nexus of power relations. The key to a critical social ontology is therefore the capacity to evaluate the relations, norms, practices, institutions, and so on in any society and discern when they are defective (i.e., serve particular, hierarchical, or oligarchic interests) or "good," that is, when they serve the cooperative interests of interdependent beings and the individual development of its constituent members. Hence, the concept of a social scheme can be introduced to tie these layers of social ontology together.

The Concept of a Social Scheme

We can call a social scheme any shape taken by these various modes of social ontology. Social schemes refer to the specific ways that social relations, structures, norms, practices, and ends are organized into a totality. Families are an example of social scheme, as are schools, workplaces, and so on. The scheme is bounded by the reach of its various modes. The scheme of a school is bounded by school session, membership in the school, and so on. They key importance of a social scheme is to see it as a specific shape of social-ontological modes. It is ontological shape that our cooperative activities take to realize some collective goal or purpose. It is bounded by the structure of roles and practices and the norms that constitute them. In all cases, social schemes are organized for some specific or concrete end or purpose—schools to educate, corporations to maximize surplus value, and so on. We can see the social contract tradition as an example. Although Hobbes argues against any kind of metaphysic of human sociality, the concept of a social contract can be seen as a self-imposed social scheme. Unlike Hobbes who saw this as essentially creating society, we should instead see it as the creation of a particular kind of social reality, a social scheme with attendant norms, practices, relations, and powers created by the scheme.

Social schemes are not just objective social facts, they have causal powers on agency and consciousness as well. Because the requisite coordination of activity requires the deployment of stable norms that will regulate and reconstitute the scheme, it is crucial that the roles and practical courses of action of individuals be shaped to create the scheme. Hence, schools as an institution will fall apart if the roles of teacher and student no longer have norms and practices attached to them. The relevant roles give structure to the group activity. Structures of relations create roles, which in turn are created and sustained by norms and practices. Judgment of any social scheme becomes critical once we ask about the purpose of these schemes. It is the task of critique to evaluate how the complexes of social reality fit together and what ends they serve. These ends can be evaluated according to whether they enhance or stunt the phylogenetic capacities of their members. Once social schemes are colonized by logics of domination, they can be difficult to dislodge. The key importance of critique is to break down the ontological layers of social being and transform social schemes toward those that fit with the cooperative interdependence that is the substance of social freedom.

Of course, not every hierarchical social scheme is to be transformed. Families and schools are examples where some degree of hierarchy is required. These schemes only become defective when domination is in play. That is, when the purpose of the scheme, in this case the hierarchy between teacher and student or parent and child, are extractive and some surplus gain is garnered as a result of the hierarchy. Defective social relations do not hold the members of the social scheme to a common purpose benefitting all members of the scheme; they are instantiated for the particular benefit of one or some subset of its members and not for the members as a whole. Hence, the instrumental use of others in any social scheme must be considered a defective form of sociality because it cannot (or most likely cannot) properly develop the capacities and benefits of its members. We can gain a more sensitive grasp of this problem by breaking social reality into a series of structural levels.

Structural Levels of Social Ontology

The ontological modes remain abstract in that they are unable to account for how social reality manifests itself. To move from these abstract categories to the concrete structure of ontology, there needs to be a series of levels that compose any social-ontological entity. These levels constitute what I call an ontological field in that they define the structural levels that constitute social reality. As I see it, when taken with the ontological modes described above, this gives us access to a critical conceptual vocabulary that will account for how social facts manifest themselves and their systemic properties. In this sense, these different structural levels are not to be understood as existing independently of one another but as nested in each other, each interdependent features of the other expanding the richness of our account of the social world.

These structures are levels of reality or, more precisely, levels of the genesis of certain kinds of social reality. As such, each structural level discussed below are components of what I call the *ontological field*, or that conceptual manifold where our natural capacities become worked up into richer and more complex forms of social reality. As such, the ontological field enables us to construct a critical social ontology by seeing how any given social reality, R, is really the product of a range of structural sublevels of reality (r_1, r_2, r_3, r_4) that produce and regulate it. The key question this will lead to is how we ethically evaluate this ontological field and the ways it gives reality to our social forms. By grasping the conceptual structure of the ontological field along with the modes and properties of social ontology explored above, I believe we can have a firm means by which to comprehend the social totality and express diagnostic and normative knowledge about the social schemes shaping our world. Judgment of our social world and the normative assessment of the space of norms we move within must be rooted in how these norms are shaped by the social-ontological structures that give it shape. Judgment must be rooted in social criticism because our values, norms, and practices are themselves rooted in the objective, ontological forms of life that constitute our accepted reality. Criticism of this reality, the capacity to resist and indeed explode reification, rests on our ability to deconstruct this totality, to decode the prevailing social reality and discern how power and domination can hide from phenomenological view.

PHYLOGENETIC LEVEL

Every thing embodies some basic natural property of propensity. Rocks cannot be rocks without the property of hardness or solidity, liquid without the property of viscosity, and so on. Humans also have these properties and propensities. Language is certainly not natural to the species, but the potential for language is. Phylogenetic properties alone are mere capacities for higher-order forms of reality. The capacity to make an utterance is not yet language, which requires more complex levels of action and interaction. The key property of the phylogenetic level of social reality is its openness to different kinds of development based on the kinds the higher-order structures of social ontology that are in place. The idea is that there is a developmental dimension to ontology, that there exist higher forms of being what is naturally given to us. Our development as a social species is rooted in certain basic phylogenetic capacities that we have by nature, but this does not determine the social forms we articulate.

In this sense, the phylogenetic level denotes those basic properties or potentialities that individuals have as members of the species.

Because it remains incomplete to stop there, it is crucial to see how the phylogenetic level is expanded and becomes something new via the successive structural levels in the ontological field. In this sense, social relations, for example, are the result of a basic property of our species to be able to live and work with others. Our capacity for sociality is therefore natural, but the forms of society we live in are not. The different levels of the social-ontological manifold are responsible for how the phylogenetic capacities of the species will be articulated.

MORPHOGENETIC LEVEL

The phylogenetic level only becomes concrete as it is placed into some form. We may have the capacity to form social relations, but this is a mere abstraction until we actually form those relations. These relations, as described above, become structures once they are placed into some form that shapes the structuring of relations with each individual. The morphogenetic level is therefore that level of ontology that exerts form on the phylogenetic level. These forms have generative powers in that they can give structure to those phylogenetic properties and capacities inherent in the species. Similarly, utterances only become language when patterned by the form-giving structure of some sort of grammar. Social relations form structures only when they are placed in some formal, institutional shape, and so on. This is the distinctiveness of the morphogenetic level: it grants form to the phylogenetic substance and simultaneously develops that substance into a more enhanced and more efficacious expression of reality. Social reality takes on a more complex, richer level of existence as the phylogenetic capacities of people are put into formal structures and relations.

The morphogenetic level is therefore responsible for how our phylogenetic capacities are shaped and formed for further development (or suppression). In this sense, my use of the term differs from others who employ it to define a core feature of the relation between structure and agency.[27] As I see it, a wider field of meaning needs to be attached to this concept because social forms have a deeply constitutive power over individuals. The extent to which the efficacy of these forms can exert itself is also an index of the power of any social form over the

27. See Margaret Gilbert, *Living Together: Rationality, Sociality and Obligation* (Lanham, MD: Rowman and Littlefield, 1996).

individual because the process of morphogenesis shapes the subjective aspects of the self insofar as it requires certain relational structures between us and certain norms and practices for that form to be enacted. The morphogenetic level is dialectically related to the praxiogenetic level. Only by proceeding through the remaining levels of the ontological field will we be able to account for the full richness of any social fact and the systematic ways it is produced and reproduced.

PRAXIOGENETIC LEVEL

These forms that take shape in the morphogenetic level are not static but are enacted by and through social practices. At the same time, these practices are shaped by the form in which they occur. The praxiogenetic level refers to how social practices exert causal pressure on social facts. The kinds of practices that are larded onto the structural forms of relations we inhabit have a retrogressive relation to those structural forms in that they are shaped by and shape the forms. The relation between a teacher and student has a particular formal structure. But this makes little sense without understanding how the formal structure shapes the practices of those in the roles of teacher and student. The practices are prescribed by the formal roles of the structure, and the enactment of those practices articulates the structure itself.

Practices and structural forms therefore have an interactive and mutually nested relation to one another. The interaction between the two levels means that there is a patterned relation in that they begin to constitute a system. The relation between teacher and student is not simply a role inscribed in conceptual terms; it is also, and indeed more importantly, the result of practices shaped by the formal requirements of that structural relation. The norms that govern the relation also constitute the practices that each individual enacts in their respective roles. It makes no sense to speak of norms without the existence of social relations, especially stable forms of social relations. Norms are therefore constitutive of our practices and connect the phylogenetic, morphogenetic, and praxiogenetic levels into a concrete social form. This becomes institutional and therefore systemic in that the roles and the practices move through time and shape our activities as well as our cognitive, affective, and cathectic layers of agency. We see now that the modes of intention, relation, structure, and process are fusing into a distinct form of social reality—a reality that is more than the sum of its parts and whose parts become defined by the systemic whole that they articulate.

TELEOGENETIC LEVEL

Any system has to have some purpose or end. As we saw in the modes, the end or purpose of any social process retrogressively shapes the relations, structures, and processes designed to achieve it. We can now see how the teleogenetic level comes to take on a causal rather than merely passive status. The purpose of the relations, the norms, the practices that orient and shape our phylogenetic capacities is therefore the crucial keystone to the vault of critical social ontology. Form is not simply done for its own sake. Recall that a crucial mode of social ontology is that of *process*: relations are not static forms, but are enacted diachronically and toward some end or purpose. But ends and purposes have a retrogressive effect on the prior levels that are ordered to instantiate it. Hence, if a group of people cooperate to build a house, there will be a set of relational structures to organize that activity, certain practices that will be used, and so on. These will themselves be defined by the end or purpose of that activity. Similarly with any social-ontological fact: the ends and purposes toward which the activities are oriented has a causal effect on the other levels of the ontological manifold.

Indeed, taking the teacher and student example cited above, we can say that the teleogenetic force of education of the student is the retrogressive cause for the structure and practices that constitute it. Without considering the ends or purposes for the given relation and practice (in this example, a school), the practices and forms either lose their coherence and fall away or simply become reified and are enacted by agents without a consciousness of the ends and purposes toward which they are oriented. Another problem can be misleading those in a social institution about the true ends of the institution, thereby creating legitimacy for the structures of relations, norms, and practices that may be unwarranted.

ONTOGENETIC LEVEL

Last, the ontogenetic level describes the level of social reality and its dynamics. Specifically, it describes the ontic states of reality and their dynamics and features. In this sense, the specific articulation of each individual in the community and his or her capacities and pathologies are ontogenetic, but they are the effect of how the previous levels in the manifold have been shaped and organized. In this sense, the ontogenetic level is the result or the constituted reality articulated by the prior levels. We can diagnose pathologies such as reification, alienation, and so on by inquiring into how the structural levels of the manifold are organized, just as we can assess the development or suppression of certain capacities that individuals possess as a result of how they are a function of the dynamics of the social forms they inhabit. In this sense, there is a deeply functional relation between social being and the social-ontological forms of life that manifest it in that the structures of relations, practices, norms, and purposes toward which any society organizes itself will have causal powers to shape and socialize the individuals making up that association.

The ontogenetic level is not separate from the previous levels, as I have been emphasizing, but is related to them in a dialectical way. This is important to keep in mind because it brings to bear the extent to which any critical theory of judgment needs to be tied to a project of social critique. We cannot shear off practices at the ontogenetic level—such as language, discourse, recognition—without seeing how these have been formed by the ontological manifold. The subjective and agentic features exhibited at the ontogenetic level are those capacities that have been either developed or maldeveloped; the level of social being is the result of the social totality. Since social ontology shows that the social totality is systematic and processual, its causal powers over the individual is expressed in the various ways the self has been shaped and formed by the norms, practices, and social-relational structures of that totality. Critical inquiry and critical judgment must proceed by deconstructing the manifold and seeing how a given social order or institution is ontologically generated. The ontogenetic level is that entrée point for our critical inquiry into social reality.

GENERATIVE SOCIAL ONTOLOGY AND THE ONTOLOGICAL MANIFOLD

If this way of approaching social reality has any validity, we can see that the different levels of social ontology together constitute what we can call a *social-ontological manifold*, by which I mean the systematic integration of the structural levels and how they shape and put into particular forms the ontological modes explored earlier. The key idea of the manifold is that it is the field through which our natural, species-specific capacities are made into higher-order social forms. The project of social critique should be focused on how our awareness of the social-ontological manifold can aid in the transformation of our social reality. The essence of the Hegelian-Marxist conception of freedom as the "insight into necessity" takes on a concrete meaning: it is the insight into how our social forms and processes have been ordered to generate a specific kind of social existence. Our sociality also ties us to a concrete, objective conception of human life that is lived relationally and continually raises the question of who and what forces give shape to our social reality. Lacking this, we fall back into a prerational or nonrational mode of reflection. Either we come to take for granted the conventions and norms that pervade the given reality, or we come to see them as rooted in certain "natural" and "infinite" ways of being.

We can refer to a generative social ontology in the sense that the structural levels of the manifold are not static but only achieve existence by their generative activities. The ontological manifold can also be described as how any systematic form of social reality is established. It refers to the deep structures that give shape to the social world and the specific ways it is formed and articulates itself via shaping and orienting the subjective structures of the individual self. The crucial idea here is that we must see that the forms of reality we inhabit are not only the emergent property of our relations, practices, and so on. It is, most importantly, the result of the efficient cause that members of the community can express in terms of their ability to shape the morphogenetic and teleogenetic levels of the manifold. A critical social ontology has in mind the descriptive aspects of our social reality and how they are shaped and sustained. A critical theory of society must also be a critical social ontology: it must inquire into how human organization is put into place, how it takes the specific forms it does, and how the ontological manifold produces pathologies and contradictions or are in some ways nonrationally shaped and formed.

I should emphasize that this approach to social ontology does not fall into the traps generally presupposed by nonmetaphysical thinkers. What many fear in any kind of ontological approach is that it posits an ahistorical perspective or essence about human sociality with little room for innovation and change. I think a generative critical social ontology does not suffer from this pitfall. Instead, it has the features of being able to make objective judgments based on how the ontic social-ontological manifold maximizes interdependence, self-development, and common ends and purposes, but it also has the feature of immanence in that it is able dialectically to become critically conscious of the social manifold by grasping the features that negate the ontological potential of the ontic. This is done immanently once we inquire into how our social-relational forms, the processes and purposes of our social world, either maximize our interdependent common interest or frustrate it. There is no external perspective needed—the ontological is an immanent form of critique. This means that critique and transformative agency are united as well. It entails seeing that the given structure of reality can be reshaped and re-created in different ways, but this structure is real, not merely a discourse over norms that concerns us, but over relations, institutions, purposes, ends, and the values, norms, and practices that sustain them. Critical social ontology therefore satisfies the needs posited by post- and nonmetaphysical thinkers who make a crude and, to be sure, incorrect conflation between social ontology and precritical forms of metaphysics. Immanence, historicity, and transformative social constructivism all are basic features of critical social ontology.

Critical reason in general and critical practical reason in particular are both dependent on the capacity to see the shape of the social totality or, put another way, the ontological structure of the social schemes that make up our lives. The central reason for this is that any kind of practical reason conceived as separate from the social-ontological properties and mechanisms of the totality cannot have in view a valid critical account of that reality. Only by seeing how the values we hold, the principles that guide our actions, are rooted in the ontological structure of social forms can we begin to see how a critical practical reason can emerge. Indeed, any value proposition is itself a proposition about how the ensemble of any social scheme are to be organized. The way to judge a value is the same: does it protect forms of dominance and control, or does it seek to transform social forms into more democratic, more robust forms of common good? This, it seems to me, is at the heart of critical social ontology as a basis for ethics and the critical social sciences.

The Basic Model of Critical Social Ontology

We have some of the necessary conceptual pieces to construct a critical social ontology, one that will ground a critical theory of ethics and a critical theory of judgment. My thesis here is that a critical social ontology is possible only once we can put the concepts of teleology and totality as the final conceptual elements of our comprehension of social reality. The reason for this is that, as Lukács pointed out in his attempt to understand reification, the only adequate means to explode reification was to embed our experience of particular social facts into the social totality as a whole. As he puts it in *History and Class Consciousness*: "Every contemplative, purely cognitive stance leads ultimately to a divided relationship to its object. . . . For every purely cognitive stance bears the stigma of immediacy. That is to say, it never ceases to be confronted by a whole series of ready-made objects that cannot be dissolved into processes."[28]

Lukács's thesis is that any valid, true knowledge of an object (a social fact) will understand it as the product of praxis, and as praxis, as *processual*, as encompassing the structures of relations and ends toward which those structures have been activated to achieve. This capacity to see each social fact as linked to larger objective ontological modes of practices, relations, structures, processes, and ends entails a capacity to explode reification, or the state of cognition that remains fixed in the ready-made instituted norms and concepts generated by the prevailing social reality. In contrast to the "purely contemplative stance," Lukács asks us to consider a stance informed by praxis.[29] I suggest that we see this as an implicit argument to adopt a critical social ontology. Once we take the stance of praxis, we move in a categorical scheme very different from pure cognition. The reason is, as we saw above, the concept of praxis is a structure that combines activity and thought in the form of a telos or teleological positing. For Lukács this means that reification is the negation of this form of comprehension; it means seeing the world as disarticulated particulars or even chunks of static reality rather than as a totality. It is to be caught in the grip of the ontic instead of the ontological. Any social fact is the product of practice: it is therefore underwritten by human activity, human relational structures and processes. Once we see this, we can assess the validity of these practices and the ends toward which they are organized.

Herein lies a crucial split between what I call *descriptive* and *critical* social ontologies. In the case of the former, we are asked to understand

---

28. Lukács, *History and Class Consciousness*, 205.

29. See the important discussion by Konstantinos Kavoulakos, *Georg Lukács's Philosophy of Praxis* (New York: Bloomsbury, 2018), 177ff.

features of sociality that lack any sense of power shaping the totality of social forms. They are descriptive because they offer us no sense of the social whole and how we can evaluate it critically. A critical social ontology, in contrast, seeks to understand how power relations in the society also shape and organize the social totality. It seeks to comprehend how social relations, structures, processes, and purposes are shaped to grasp the dynamic and systemic features that articulate the scheme of social power. The core idea here is the concept of an end or purpose—the telos of our social activities. Critique becomes possible and judgment finds its ultimate ground in the activity of immanently deciphering how these schemes are also constitutive of consciousness.

Critical social ontology wants to see how the different modes and levels described already open up our reified social reality to deeper understanding. More specifically, it uncovers how the shapes and processes that pervade our social reality can be opened up to a power-centric form of inquiry—to a kind of social knowledge that will reveal the structures of dominance and how they undergird the phenomenological experiences of our everyday life. In descriptive social ontologies, emphasis is not on the ends in any systematic sense but on the means. Take the following from Michael E. Bratman as an illustration of my thesis:

> Think of the coordinated activities of the thousands of employees around the world involved in making iPhones. Here the source of the organization is not likely to be an intention shared by the participants. Instead, the complex social coordination is externally orchestrated by a managerial group.[30]

Bratman's brief description is an example of the descriptive, noncritical social ontology I am describing. For him, the features of acting together, of cooperative and planning collective actions is what is crucial. What is missed here is, for instance, the teleogenetic level of this reality: the purpose of this mass organization of labor to produce commodities for the expansion of capital; or perhaps the ways this kind of labor practice takes shape due to the morphogenetic level required by this kind of

---

30. Michael E. Bratman, *Shared Agency: A Planning Theory of Acting Together* (New York: Oxford University Press, 2014), 10.

production. Or consider how these formal structures of the organization of work affect the practices of labor and so on.

Consider Marx's discussion in the first volume of *Capital*. For him, humans have the phylogenetic capacity to labor; laboring is itself an ontological activity insofar as it is a capacity to transform nature into another phase of being via the activity of giving new form to matter. As he puts it when discussing the nature of labor embodied in the commodity:

> The use-values, coat, linen, etc., i.e., the bodies of commodities, are combinations of two elements—matter and labor. If we take away the useful labor expended upon them, a material substratum is always left, which is furnished by nature without the help of man. The latter can work only as nature does, that is by changing the form of matter. Nay more, in this work in changing the form he is constantly helped by natural forces. We see, then, that labor is not the only source of material wealth, of use-values produced by labor.[31]

Here we can see Marx make use of the scheme of the ontology of labor in the sense that labor is the praxiogenetic level of social being that creates a social object, a commodity, which has use-value because of the form-giving capacity that is labor. Labor as praxis is the process of giving form to matter. What is raw matter, brute fact, now becomes endowed with social meaning and significance. It is no longer a piece of nature but has been transformed into a social product—something that can be of use to others. Marx further argues that this process of labor also has a teleogenetic property:

> At the end of every labor process, a result emerges which had already been conceived by the worker at the beginning, hence already existed ideally. Man not only effects a change of form in the materials of nature; he also realizes (*verwirklicht*) his own purpose in those materials. And this is a purpose he is conscious of, it determines the mode of his activity with the rigidity of law, and he must subordinate his will to it.[32]

---

31. Karl Marx, *Capital*, vol. 1 (New York: Vintage, 1977), 133; translation modified.
32. Marx, *Capital*, vol. 1, 284.

But this ontological manifold can itself be changed by capital. It can be reshaped and reorganized by the capitalist; in the process, the levels of the manifold can be altered according to the ends and purposes set by the capitalist and the laws of capital agglomeration itself:

> The cooperation of wage-laborers is entirely brought about by the capital that employs them. Their unification into one single productive body, and the establishment of a connection between their individual functions, lies outside their competence. These things are not their own act, but the act of the capital that brings them together and maintains them in that situation. Hence the interconnection between their various labors confronts them, in the realm of ideas, as a plan drawn up by the capitalist, and, in practice, as his authority, as the powerful will of a being outside them, who subjects their activity to his purpose.[33]

Under capitalism, then, the ontological manifold has been transformed by capital, and the levels of praxis, form, and the teleological have been shifted by its constitutive power and logics. This transformed social reality also entails a transformation of the subjects involved. Alienation, reification, and other social, personal, and cognitive pathologies come to be rooted in the social forms of life that have been generated by the transformation of the ontological manifold.

A critical social ontology can be seen to possess a powerful framework for explanation and critique. From the point of view of critical social ontology, it is not a matter of mere description but a fuller account of the process as a totality—a process of totality that comes to be naturalized by subjects, thereby short-circuiting the capacity of reflective critical consciousness. The problem with the account given by Bratman is that there is no sense that the ultimate aim of the total organization of this kind is the capacity of some agents to direct and organize the intentional agency of others, to create the structures of organization and production and the social-relational structures and processes that go along with them, that are ultimately oriented toward the extraction of surplus from the participants. There is a lack of any kind of teleological structure that penetrates into the essence of the

---

33. Marx, *Capital*, vol. 1, 449–50.

production of commodities such as iPhones (or any other commodity). Think of the interlocking layers of norms, practices, structures, and so on that are put into motion. Think of how this kind of work and working life comes to shape and structure the people involved in these processes. The critical-ontological moment gets us to consider the normative dimensions of these kinds of reality.

This will require us to consider a more robust form of practical reason, a form of judgment that will see the norms and practices of social life as embedded in structural forms of power that are often reified in the consciousness of its participants. The postmetaphysical turn that was critiqued in the first part of this study reveals itself to be specious and a deeply noncritical approach to the social world.

Chapter 7

An Ontological Framework
for Critical Practical Reason

Hilary Putnam was one of the more persistent thinkers in contemporary philosophy to press the thesis that our normative ideas and practical reason require no reliance on ontology or metaphysics. His thesis has been similar to postmetaphysical thinkers throughout the late twentieth and early twentieth centuries: that we must restrict our practical reasoning to language and the discursive practices of a pluralistic community. As Putnam argues:

> In place of Ontology (note the capital "O"), I shall be defending what one might call pragmatic pluralism, the recognition that it is no accident that in everyday language we employ many different kinds of discourses, discourses subject to different standards and possessing different sorts of applications, with different logical and grammatical features—different "language games" in Wittgenstein's sense—no accident because it is an illusion that there could be just one sort of language game which could be sufficient for the description of all reality![1]

The premise that our normative and practical judgments must be devoid of ontological commitments is, I argue in this chapter, deeply mistaken

---

1. Hilary Putnam, *Ethics without Ontology* (Cambridge, MA: Harvard University Press, 2004), 21–22.

and can only lead practical reason into the central problem of modern ethical life, which can be understood as the abstraction of value and the decomposition of critical judgment. This has occurred as modern societies have become increasingly technologically complex and cybernetic. In other words, it has been the result of the loss of practical autonomy on the part of individuals as their social world becomes increasingly dominated by self-regulating social and technical systems and as social power and inequality becomes increasingly impersonal and constitutive of the deep cognitive and evaluative structures of the self.

There has also been a failure, in my estimation, of practical philosophy to respond to this reality with any kind of critical efficacy. Indeed, at a philosophical level, as I have been trying to show, this sociological reality has only been compounded by the detachment of practical reason from the socio-ontological features of our social being, from a retreat from the effort to absorb the actual structures of sociality into the validity of our normative values and judgments and consider core purpose of practical reason to be the capacity to judge the essential legitimacy of our social institutions, norms, and practices. I have also been suggesting that the postmetaphysical turn has eschewed the core intellectual equipment necessary for this kind of critical practical reason. Only by a return to the unity of our normative judgments and the actual structures and forms of life we inhabit can we again speak of a critical form of judgment. The reasons we use in discourse must be accountable to the ontological features of our world and how it can be shaped and reshaped to realize concepts such as justice or freedom. The role of a critical social ontology becomes central to the articulation of a critical kind of practical reason that can explode the problems that plague modern ethical life: of the twin problems of reification and relativism. These problems plague practical reason and the critical capacity of modern subjects because as the systemic logics of techno-administrative societies becomes more pervasive, so do the functional logics of power that support and animate them. The role of the individual's reflective capacities is weakened because they are required less and less as the social system becomes more and more autonomous from their decision-making powers.

The twin problems of reification and relativism come into play because of these features of modernity. The critical force of subjective reflection weakens as the social system becomes imbued with cybernetic features replacing norms and capacities for autonomy with heteronomous logics and value patterns taken up from patterns of socialization. But it is also the case that the more encompassing the administrative logics become, the less space there is for nonadministrative logics of sociation to take place. Traditional spheres of life, such as the family, religious communities, secular associational life, and so on, all begin to dry up and become increasingly absorbed into the technical and commodified rationality of cybernetic society. These more traditional spheres of association were circumscribed by particular normative traditions and logics that gave rise to a more organic pluralism of worldviews. Their traditional forms of authority were also crucibles for critical ego development as individuals strove for liberation from these traditionally rigid mentalities and role expectations. As a result, critical subjectivity was poised to seek the construction of a more rational, democratic form of life for society as a whole. The Enlightenment vision of the rational society was concerned with this form of autonomy. As the logics of technical and administrative capitalism began to crowd out these spheres of life and displace them with a more pervasive instrumental and functional form of social domination, ego development was also weakened.

The bankruptcy of postmetaphysical practical philosophy can therefore be glimpsed against this backdrop. Reification occurs, in the way I construe it, as the normative and collective-intentional structures of consciousness are shaped by the imperatives of the social systems that socialize the subject. As such, we cannot rely on intersubjective agreement and discourse to achieve critical reflection and critical rational validity of norms. As I argued in earlier chapters, this is because the normative structures of hierarchical systems of power become introjected into the self and, as a result, cycle back through consciousness as reflectively valid norms and values. Arendt and Habermas give us no way to guard against the infiltration of objective, functional norms into the subjective structures of evaluative reason and cognition. They also hold to the Kantian view that substantive values are essentially heteronomous: that is, that any nonformal ethics curtails autonomy because it tethers us to a foundation.

I think this view is deeply mistaken and has not resulted in an enhanced form of emancipatory practical reason but has robbed us of critical coherence in an age when the reification of ethical life has only increased. My thesis here is that critical practical reason will have to absorb the insights of critical social ontology explored in the last chapter. The basic idea is that critical judgments about human affairs will have to have a structure that can get at the ontological structures of our social reality and how we should organize our lives, evaluate the norms and practices that substantiate our social reality, to inquire into the validity of those social forms. Since critical social ontology reveals how we can mediate our relation to our social world, it also grants us a certain logic to examine the objective structures and shapes our existent sociality takes, as well as the norms and value orientations that are constitutive of them and our consciousness. The key to proposing a form of critical-practical reason grounded in a social-ontological framework is that it can put us at the center of the systems of power that shape our sociality and, at the same time, hold out a criterion for judgment. In this way, we can view the potentiality of an alternative form of social reality in dialectical tension with the prevailing forms of social reality.

John Dunn has insightfully posed the problem of political obligation as consisting of "how we see the relations between three types of consideration: the nature of rationality, the character and epistemic status of human values and the causal possibilities of human social existence."[2] This chapter seeks to provide a coherent answer to this problem by treating these three elements of political judgment. I believe a coherent theory exists that will enable us to tie these together, but the answer is rooted in the social-ontological framework I outlined in the previous chapter. Briefly stated, rationality about practical affairs requires that we use reasons that encompass the ontological structure of social reality. Reasons only count, in this sense, when they are rooted in the relational, processual, and teleological dimensions that constitute social schemes. Second, once we accept this account of valid practical reasons, we can also see the nature of values as consisting of objective forms of life. Value has ontological standing because they entail certain ways of acting and certain role- and relational expectations of others that constitute a social scheme. In this sense, our values are not transcendent principles but are rooted in our objective, practical lives. Last, we can consider the potentiality of human social existence only by considering the shapes our social schemes take. The purposes and ends that we put our cooperative activities toward, the relational structures that organize and enact those practical interdependent activities, and how these purposes and relations constitute our being as individuals

2. John Dunn, *Political Obligation in its Historical Contexts* (Cambridge: Cambridge University Press, 1980), 257.

all factor in to whether a social scheme or social reality warrant our obligation or, perhaps, our disobedience.

If we bring this back to Putnam's premise that our practical reason should be concerned only with different kinds of discourse, there is no criterion for knowing when a discourse is valid, which discourse has been able to resist the pressures of reification, and which discourses grant us access to the actual, objective features of human life. As I see it, the social-ontological approach is superior to this pragmatist perspective because it asks us consider how the features of our sociality can be reworked and reformed to realize genuinely free and just forms of life. Practical reasons, as Hegel and Marx knew all too well, cannot be sealed off from the objective social-relational features of our life as a species. To posit a cleavage between our principles and the ontology of our sociality is to lapse into either relativism or reification.

At a different level, my premise is that our practical discourse, given that it is about human affairs, must describe and have as its referent human affairs. In the last chapter, I argued that human affairs can be understood and cognized via a social ontology that seeks to thematize the structure and process any social totality takes. Put another way, our practical discourse can be judged by how it tracks the real processes and dynamics of the ontological manifold. Normative statements achieve validity, in this view, not by the universal acceptance on the part of those involved in a communicative community, for this does nothing to prevent reification and relativism from acting in practical affairs. Our reasons become rational only when they are can have in view the thick ontological structure of human sociality and how this sociality is mediated by the social totality. Rather, a critical conception of judgment operates with a different structure of reason: one that accounts for the kind of ontological structures that constitute social forms. To say that practical reason is rational, as I see it, entails ways of reasoning about normative affairs that account for the objective structural and functional dynamics of our social being.

My burden is to show that judgment requires what I call *objective critical forms of judgment*, where the basis of the validity of any norm is the extent to which it satisfies such a criterion of rationality. Indeed, because the bias against social ontology has largely been based in the idea that it lapses into a kind of conventionalism, my burden is to show that a critical social ontology as I have developed it here not only avoids this problem but offers us a critical means of resisting con-

ventionalism, reification, and relativism. The key thesis is that a theory
of critical judgment, of critical practical reason more generally, rests on
how it can inquire into the social-ontological features of our sociality
are shaped in any ontic sense and try to grasp alternative shapes of
sociality that can more fully realize our status as interdependent, free
beings. The mistake of the postmetaphysician is that he believes the
principles contained in any practical discourse are simply that: abstract
principles, and the only concern should be the mode of validity. But
this cannot be correct. We must see that the normative categories of
our practical reasoning are themselves ontological categories in that
they entail forms of social reality—that is, relations, processes, norms,
structures, and purposes—that will follow from them. Our normative
categories, in this sense, are not regulative of our reality, they are constitutive of it. In this respect, when we talk about practical reason, we
must abandon a unitary focus on the mode of reaching validity (say,
through intersubjective agreement, a social contract, or whatever) and
instead shift our horizon of meaning to reveal our normative categories
as constituted by ontological modes of sociality.

The social ontological basis for judgment resides in the capacity to
posit forms of cooperative, interdependent relations that are organized
for common purposes, as opposed to those social forms that consist of
dependent, instrumental, and extractive forms of relations and purposes
that are particularistic as opposed to universalistic. This judgment itself
rests on the ontological thesis that humans have an essential structure
of features that were discussed in the last two chapters, specifically those
of social-relatedness, processual development, and practical-teleological
activity. The relevant question for critical practical reason is what kinds of
social-ontological structures and schemes can best realize these features
and the kind of collective powers to which they give rise? A critical-
ontological theory of judgment therefore is not based in arbitrary or a
priori categories. The key thesis is that pragmatic and postmetaphysical
theories of practical reason must fail because they cannot secure the
requisite ontological field to grant normative claims validity.

The Metaphysical Structure of Reason and the Ontology of Value

What does it mean to say that practical judgments have an ontological
basis or metaphysical structure? For one thing, it means attributing to

practical reason a particular kind of cognitive content: that ethical discourse is not merely about expressivism or subjective beliefs but about actual knowledge claims. It also means that if normative claims express claims to knowledge, if they have cognitive content, then the question becomes what kind of knowledge do they express to make claims to? Recall that the postmetaphysical structure of practical reason that eschews ontological concerns believes that validity for our norms can only be achieved via "a reflexive application of the universalization test calls for a form of deliberation in which each participant is compelled to adopt the perspective of all others in order to examine whether a norm could be willed by all *from the perspective of each person.*"[3] Here Habermas moves the question of the cognitive content of morality from one of the content of any moral proposition to that of the form of agreement based on public reasons on which its adoption rests. Rationality is construed in a Kantian (rather than a Hegelian sense): as consisting of the formal conditions of possible agreement instead of according to the objective or metaphysical substance of the proposition itself. The right now defines the perimeter of the good.[4]

Consider moral discourse from a different point of view, reversing Habermas's thesis. Suppose that we consider the validity of any normative proposition to be judged not on the basis of it being accepted by the relevant group or decision body but in terms of its *content*. To do this, we would have to think of our ethical categories in a different way. Rather than take an ethical category or principle as a discursive utterance alone and judge its rationality based on the extent to which all affected are in agreement with it, suppose we inquired into the substantive (i.e., ontological) dimensions of that proposition. This would mean something very different, for it would mean inquiring into the social-ontological structure of the value itself. Saying a value has a social-ontological structure means that it is a particular judgment about what the excellence of a social practice, structural relation, purpose, or end actually is. No moral proposition can lack a social-ontological content: all will entail

---

3. Jürgen Habermas, *The Inclusion of the Other: Studies in Political Theory* (Cambridge, MA: MIT Press, 1998), 33.

4. For an incisive critique of this move toward proceduralism and the subsumption of the good under the right, see Charles Taylor, "The Motivation behind a Procedural Ethics," in Ronald Beiner and William James Booth (eds.), *Kant and Political Philosophy: The Contemporary Legacy* (New Haven, CT: Yale University Press, 1993), 337–60.

certain ways of acting, structural shapes of relations, and purposes toward which we organize those practices and relations. For reasons to count, for our reasons to be valid and taken to express true moral content, we need to be able to examine how a moral proposition has implicit social-ontological content. To do this, we must adopt a richer conception of reason than that put forth by Kantians and pragmatists—we must see our reasons as possessing metaphysical content. The metaphysical structure of reason would demand us to think in richer terms than one of formal agreement. We would be asked to consider the conceptual structure of that underlies the principle and the proposition itself. In nonnormative knowledge claims, we can see this in operation. Take the following statement:

(1) Green plants use sunlight to synthesize food from carbon dioxide and water.

The validity of this claim rests not on whether others accept it but on the actual structure toward which the proposition is oriented. To say that reason has a "metaphysical structure" is to say that, in an example like this, the cognitive claim is resonant with or shares the same conceptual structure as the object itself. Hence, photosynthesis as a concept that does not merely describe how green plants synthesize food; it is more correctly understood as an explanatory statement in that the conceptual form of the statement is resonant with, or shares the same basic structure, as the objective mechanism being explained. Photosynthesis is not simply a conceptual device regulating our knowledge about what happens chemically inside green plants. Rather, it is constitutive of that process: photosynthesis as a concept is objective and informs the concept we have about green plants and the chemical process itself.

If we take a similar approach to our evaluative reasons about normative claims, we can see something similar but distinct. The thesis that values or normative claims have a social-ontological content means that they express values and norms that require some kind of ordering of the social-ontological manifold. In other words, by supporting, believing in, or possessing a value that orders my thinking, I am also adopting a worldview that sanctions certain social relations, legitimates certain norms, underpins and supports specific social practices, and, consciously or not, supports certain ends and purposes of those relations, norms, and practices. Rather, the claim here is that normative concepts have some kind of ontological structure as well—ontological in the sense that they entail certain kinds of relations, norms, structures, and processes that are not merely regulated by the principle but are enactments of it. To say that reasons have a metaphysical structure means that the cognitive content of the claim can be assessed based on the objective modes of that enact that claim. If I maintain that:

(2) homosexuals should not have the right to marry,

I am not making a normative claim based on an abstract value. I am making a claim—indeed, it is an utterance—but its validity can only be assessed based on how such a claim would be enacted in social-ontological terms. Utterance 2 therefore implies 2':

(2') Homosexuals should be excluded from rights I enjoy,

which, if we drill down even further, implies:

(2") Homosexuals should not be permitted to enjoy inter-subjective family life as I do,

and so on. The value, the normative utterance, is not merely an utterance but carries with it an implicit social-ontological content: practices, relations, and so on that shape the social reality of which I am a part.

The thesis that values have an ontology may seem odd if not dangerous to some. On one hand, if they do, then are they rooted in nature? Perhaps some posited realm of values rooted in God or some other metaphysical aberration? I think it is clear after my discussion of critical social ontology in the last chapter that we should dispel such worries and instead see that the thesis merely entails that our values not only are mental concepts but also indicate certain objective social forms of reality. The key critical moment, however, is that if this is the case, the criteria for a critical practical reason needs to be grasped as the extent to which the values we prize, the norms that secure our social relations and constitute our practices, are in fact oriented toward a conception of human freedom and social justice. The twin values of freedom and justice are not abstract categories but achieve validity as social-ontological categories: they are to be understood as the concrete ways we express and objectify our social relatedness and the ends and

purposes of that social relatedness. They are not abstract principles regulating conduct (as in liberalism), nor are they situated concepts relative
to a given community (as in communitarian schemes). Rather, they are
informed by social-ontological considerations as to how we shape and
organize our relatedness with others and the purposes toward which
those structures and practices of relatedness are oriented. Indeed, as I
will discuss, they constitute the ontological ground for critical practical
reasoning.

Before getting to this, we need to dig deeper into the relation
between values and social ontology. I think it is essential to point to the
thesis that values are themselves ontological, that is, that their nature
is essentially social and can be grasped by the conceptual apparatus I
explored in the previous chapter. Knowledge of value, in this view, is
knowledge of the social-ontological basis of human life. This bears some
similarity with the approach to value elaborated by Joseph Raz, but
with some important differences. For Raz, the concept of value needs
to be understood as being dependent on social practices, what he calls
the "social dependence thesis." As he explains it:

> The dependence of value on practice that the thesis affirms
> is not simultaneous and continuous. The thesis is that the
> existence of values depends on the existence of sustaining
> practices at some point, not that these practices must persist
> as long as the value does. The usual pattern is for the emer-
> gence, out of previous social forms, of a new set of practices,
> bringing into life a new form: monogamous marriage between
> partners chosen by each other, the opera and so on, with
> their attendant excellences.[5]

This gets us somewhat closer to the idea that values have an ontological
character or, as I have been suggesting, that values have social-ontological
ballast. Indeed, practices do sustain values, but the questions as to the
validity of those practices and, mutatis mutandis, the validity of the
values, require more than this: they require reasons that are resonant
with those ends and purposes that are rational, that is, that express and
constitute social forms that enhance the realization of human capacities

---

5. Joseph Raz, *The Practice of Value* (New York: Oxford University Press, 2008),
21–22.

and development. The idea that values are sustained by social practices is only useful to us to the extent that we then inquire into the rational validity of the practice itself and, following the modes of social ontology, the ends and purposes they realize.

For Raz, the idea that our values have a dependence on social practices is an ontological thesis, as he readily admits. But it is difficult to see how this can be made into a critical conception of judgment rather than one that is merely descriptive.[6] He maintains that specific values, such as the value I place on my friendship with someone at work or school, is dependent on general concepts of friendship writ large. As he explains:

> For example, we can explain the value of friendship—which is a fairly general value standing for whatever is of value in one-on-one human relationships of one kind or another, which are relatively stable, and at least not totally instrumental in character—by reference to the more specific, to the value of various specific types of relationships. Thus, the value of friendship in general is explained by reference to the relatively distinct values of intimate friendships, or work friendships, of friendships based on common interests, and so on.[7]

Is this really a sufficient account? As I have been arguing, a critical theory of practical reason would have to inquire into the dependence of our values on social practices, but it would also have to consider the extent to which any social practice is of value. Hence, friendships have an ontological structure in the sense that, Raz explains, they are (should be) forms of one-on-one relations that are noninstrumental, are stable over time, and provide mutual benefits for members in the

---

6. Raz does argue that his project is not critical but explanatory: "My aim is explanation, explanation of concepts that are central to our practical thought, to our understanding of ourselves as persons, capable of intentional action—namely, an explanation of the closely related concepts of value, of being a value, and of having value or being of value. In explaining a concept we explain aspects of that of which it is a concept. An explanation of the concept of value is a (partial) explanation of the nature (that is, essential properties) of value." *The Practice of Value*, 121.

7. Raz, *The Practice of Value*, 37.

friendship. But consider: why is friendship of value in the first place? More to the point, what criteria would a person use to judge whether a particular friendship warrants his or her obligation and the attendant obligations of friendship?

To answer a question like this, it seems to me that we need to grasp the social ontology of the value in question and do so from the critical social-ontological framework I outlined in the last chapter. When we use reasons with metaphysical structure, we can open these kinds of questions up to critical scrutiny. For one, we can say that the reasons that underpin a friendship should be judged against the extent to which mutual benefit is bestowed on each member. If a hierarchy exists between the two, if one benefits at the expense of another, then we can say this violates the purpose of the friendship since a friendship is a structural relation between two people for mutual, reciprocal benefit. Instrumentality erodes the concept of friendship and more essentially erodes the practices of friendship and, by logical extension, the relation of friendship. Indeed, if a friendship is ontologically organized around that purpose—that is, of mutual, reciprocal, nontransactional benefit— then the attendant norms and practices of friendship will also be shaped and organized toward that purpose. I will give gifts, be patient, give help and aid, and so on to enrich and stabilize the friendship relation.

I possess critical judgment only when I am able to see that the ontological features of my friendship with another has these modes as part of the ensemble of social reality that is friendship. Friendship is therefore more than an abstract principle, it is a value with ontological ballast in that it entails certain structural-relational features, norms, practices, and purposes that make it friendship. In this sense, judgment requires a metaphysical kind of reasoning that can grasp these ontological features. When practicing judgment, the reasons I use must carry this metaphysical structure—it must be able to grasp the totality of the ontological modes that are constitutive of friendship. To not do so would be to collapse into convention and fail to have a rational grasp of what sustains the practices one does with that other person.

We can now see that value is an ontological category in an immanent sense: it does not express abstract content or some naturalistic, unchanging content. Instead, its substance consists of the ways that the concrete social-ontological structures of reality are shaped, and these shapes are constitutive of the social reality we inhabit. Values, in this sense, are fused to the ways we judge and reason about these forms of life, about how we either justify or rationalize them. Values are not merely dependent on social practices, they constitute the ensemble of the ontology of our social reality. To say that our reasons should have a metaphysical structure means simply that reasons that count in practical affairs should contain substantive ontological content about the shapes and features of social reality. It is an immanent metaphysics in the sense that it does not rely on any inflated sense of value concepts, nor does it collapse into nature or any abstract formalism. The metaphysical structure of reason is accountable to the ontological structures that shape our reality. This means that a critical social metaphysics relies on a critical social ontology: it is the means by which we can comprehend the systemic nature of social facts and allow the different layers of social reality to cohere.[8]

But clearly this cannot be enough. This is merely description and not judgment, unless we are able to express a concept of the good or some other means by which we can distinguish what is truly rational from what is defective. What comes to the fore now is a need for historically situated reasoning. We cannot analytically drop down into any given social reality and seek to grasp it critically. This was Hegel's and Marx's point of insistence in their attempt to bring forth a critical form of evaluative reason. What both could see, despite their relative differences, was that a substantive conception of reason—that is, one that did not move within the confines of a priori abstraction—had to be one that grasped the transformation of social forms over time. What was distinct about modernity was that freedom could be seen not as an abstract value but as an ontological category, one that was emergent in the actual, concrete social forms and practices that pervaded our lives. Hence, for both objective idealism and critical materialism, freedom was not a value separated from facts, it was a matter of the actual, ontological structures of reality. Hence, critical practical reason's dependence on a metaphysical conception of reason needs to grasp the social-ontological dimensions of reality and the critical perspective of seeing that certain kinds of features characterize freedom or any other evaluative category.

---

8. Gilbert Ryle once insightfully pointed out that: "What is commonly expected of a metaphysician is that he should assert the existence or occurrence of things unseen and give for these assertions purely philosophical or conceptual reasons. If he is not an ontologist, he is not a metaphysician." "Final Discussion," in D. F. Pears (ed.), *The Nature of Metaphysics* (London: Macmillan, 1965), 144.

The Ontological Ground of Critique and Judgment

In his defense of democracy, Spinoza notes, "In a democracy, irrational commands are still less to be feared: for it is almost impossible that the majority of a people especially if it be a large one, should agree in an irrational design."[9] By now it should be obvious that this is a mistaken judgment. Spinoza believed, as do many who insist on a more proceduralist conception of democracy, that the "space of reasons" will be sufficient to weed out irrational desires and beliefs. It would be sufficient to provide the needed ground for valid norms and laws because all would be able to participate in their formulation and articulation. But the limitations of this approach are not difficult to discern. What is required for a critical form of evaluative reason and judgment is a conception of value that has ontological warrant. Indeed, Spinoza's argument for the justification of democracy was social-ontological: he believed that the mechanism would secure a kind of state that would have the development of each member of the community as its aim: "No, the object of government is not to change men from rational beings into beasts or puppets, but to enable them to develop their minds and bodies in security, and to employ their reason unshackled; neither showing hatred, anger or deceit nor watched with the eyes of jealousy and injustice. In fact, the true aim of government is liberty."[10]

Precisely this Enlightenment view directed the labors of Hegel and Marx as well.[11] But their answer to this question was to show that freedom was both ontologically and historically determined. Against the thesis of liberal, "negative" freedom, Hegel and Marx put forth a new paradigm for the concept. Now human freedom was not merely a legal state, it was instead to be understood as an ontological state: a mode of being that was socially structured and mediated. This conception of freedom was based on the metaphysical conception of reason: only by

---

9. Benedict Spinoza, *A Theological-Political Treatise*, trans. R. H. M. Elwes (New York: Dover, 1951), 206.

10. Spinoza, *Theological-Political Treatise*, 259.

11. For a discussion of the important differences between them on the metaphysics of freedom, see Iring Fetcher, "Marx's Concretization of the Concept of Freedom," in Erich Fromm (ed.), *Socialist Humanism: An International Symposium* (New York: Doubleday, 1965), 238–49; Manfred Baum, "Freedom in Marx," *Radical Philosophy Review*, vol. 10, no. 2 (2007): 117–31.

grasping human praxis and the essential substrates of the species—for instance, relationality, cooperative-poietic praxis—was it possible to construct a substantive, ontological conception of freedom. In this sense, freedom was to be constructed via the shapes our sociality take. Freedom was not a state one can achieve alone; it requires a variety of social-relational structures, processes, and purposes that enact development and expand one's capacities as a person. The essential point here is that freedom becomes a grounding concept for any rational form evaluative reflection.

To say that freedom as a concept constitutes a ground for critical judgment and for critical practical reason more broadly is to argue about the ontological content of value. Up to this point, the claim has been that only a thicker, metaphysical conception of reason will be up to the task of revealing the full account of social reality. But this ontology is merely descriptive unless we begin to ask about the reasons the shapes of our social ontology take the forms they do. What Spinoza, Rousseau, Hegel, and Marx all seem to share is a thesis that the only legitimate purpose of our association with one another is the mutual benefit produced by that association. Whether it is the state, the family, economic activity, or friendship, the only rational, legitimate purpose of these forms of sociation is that they produce mutual benefits for the members of the association. This political thesis relies on a social-ontological thesis: that our species is relational, developmental, and practical—that is, that we realize our potentials and capacities over time via social relations and practices. Freedom is not merely a state one enjoys but a reality that one helps construct and reconstitute over time. It cannot be separate from a conception of the good, nor can it be separated from that of necessity. It does not take us long to begin to see that the ground of critical practical reason is an ontological conception of the value of freedom and the attendant goods that support and cultivate it.

What we now have is a series of basic features of what an ontological conception of freedom would look like. Freedom is not a negative "freedom from," but a social conception that enables self-development and the enhancement of functions. At a higher social level, it implies that our associative nature, a basic ontological feature of the species, is organized in certain ways to maximize the kinds of common goods needed for individual development. To say that freedom has an ontological structure is to say that it is a matter of what ends or purposes we choose and what ends and purposes come to pattern our associative structures and processes. Freedom consists of the capacity to choose the ends that best enhance the mutual benefits of associational members of the community, it is not to be construed as a freedom from necessity but a matter of organizing our associative, cooperative practical lives toward ends that maximize the goods and benefits for the members of the community.

This needs more clarification to get us to the fundamental ontological ground for norms and practical reasoning. As I have been insisting, the associative feature of human beings as a species is most fundamental to higher phylogenetic functions and capacities, such as language, culture, and cooperation. If we accept this basic thesis, we must be able to judge in some sense the different shapes that our associational life can take. The modes of our social ontology can be organized into different kinds of social schemes. The argument that thinkers like Aristotle, Rousseau, Hegel, and Marx, among others, articulated was that there were certain good or rational features of sociality and social reality that we were capable of achieving. These could only be grasped by understanding that the fundamental purpose of human association was a distinctive kind of social freedom constituted by our interdependent relations acting in social processes that were cooperative and for ends, purposes, or goods that were for common needs and that nurtured the social-relational nexus that individuated us. Members of any social association should not be exploited, treated instrumentally, or seek their own particular interests or ends to the extent that they negate common purposes and goods in any way. The fundamental ontological ground therefore leads us to this basic normative principle, what we can call the basic principle of ontological ethics. The good is distinguished from the defective, in this sense, to the extent that our sociality and its products either maximize this principle or deviate from it.

The ends and purposes of any social scheme are some of the most determinative dimensions for our critical consciousness's grip on the ontic and its capacity to open it up to critique because it is the end or purpose of any social scheme that shapes the relations and processes organized to produce or constitute it. We should not see the emphasis on teleological judgments as negating freedom. In fact, judgment must grasp the teleological structure of our social practices and relations because the end of any social practice comes to organize and shape the means toward its realization. Humans are not teleologically organized as an unfolding blueprint, but insofar as we realize that we are free to consciously, rationally choose the ends toward which our practical lives are oriented. Nicolai Hartmann's insight here is worth exploring:

> Were the world ordered teleologically from below upwards, man would be unable to develop any kind of activity. His purposes would be in no position to insert themselves into the course of events. But if the world is determined causally only, and if teleological determination is the prerogative of man, he is free to deflect processes within the limits of his understanding of causality. For the causal chains admit as new components the purposes set by him, and they are given a sequence of causal effects in the same way as the indigenous components.[12]

We are always determined and determining. We are always caught in the web of relations that constitute us and that we in turn reconstitute. The question is therefore not one of "freedom from," but what it means to be self-determining in an intrinsically social world. The answer seems to be that of how we order and shape this social world—the kinds of relations we construct, the norms and practices we adopt, and the purposes and ends to which we commit ourselves. Given the basic ontology of our sociality, the social ontological ground for judgment must consist of these immanent questions.

Now we have some of the necessary conceptual pieces to construct a critical theory of practical reason and judgment. Every framework must have a ground of some kind—some sort of basic commitment to an ontological conception of human life that underpins the rationale for that framework. As I argued in the last chapter, there exists an essential mode of human sociality. The question is no longer whether the species is solitary or social, as it was for seventeenth- and eighteenth-century social contract theorists; the relevant question is, what shapes and forms will the modes of our sociality take? If we restrict the concept of sociality to cognitive, recognitive, or practical alone, we miss far too much of what constitutes human sociality. The last chapter showed that what I called the social-ontological manifold is in fact the framework for understanding the contours of social reality, in other words, how our

---

12. Nicolai Hartmann, *The New Ways of Ontology* (Chicago: Henry Regnery, 1953), 131.

social relations are shaped and form processes according to particular ends and purposes.

Hartmann's claim about teleology and freedom becomes apposite here. The thesis is that teleology works, in a sense, backward, not forward. We do not have a natural teleology imprinted in us that seeks to be realized. Rather, the ends that we set for ourselves have retrogressive effects on the relations and processes put in place to realize them. We enter social relations without generally being aware of the posited ends of those relations. However, all relational structures and the processes they instantiate realize some end or purpose. The relevant question of critical judgment is to grasp what those ends are and how they ground the relations and processes (as well as the attendant norms and practices that support and constitute them) in which I am embedded. The ontological order of causality is different from the temporal order of causality; it is systematic and holistic rather than linear. It forces us out of the false and dichotomous mode of reflection that sees social structure as external to subjective consciousness or socioeconomic structures as separate from social-psychological structures, and so on. It is dialectical in that it emphasizes process and system over lineal causality. Each feature is a moment in a larger process, a totality. Hence, we see something akin to figure 7.1.

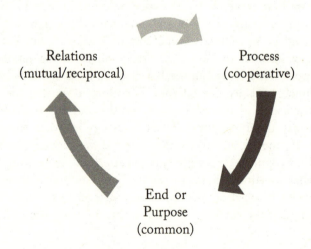

Relations
(mutual/reciprocal)

Process
(cooperative)

End or
Purpose
(common)

Figure 7.1. Ontological Causality.

If we view this argument in tandem with the claim that the cognitive content of our ethical claims must have a metaphysical structure, then I can defend the thesis that there is an ontological ground for moral and political judgment. Simply stated, this ontological ground claims that there are certain basic ontological features of human life that are organized and combined in different ways to articulate different kinds of social reality. Primary among these is the purpose of our sociality. From Aristotle through Rousseau, Hegel, and Marx, one common thesis was variously defined and elaborated: that the species is relational; that our powers and capacities as individuals are enhanced only by our cooperation with others. These forms of cooperation can be organized in a multitude of ways, but they are organized with the benefit of the particular or of the association as a whole in mind. This means that judgment concerns the shapes that our forms of life take. Aristotle's scheme of constitutions is organized around the concept of which shapes of social organization were organized for the common good, seen as the essential purpose of living our lives together. Rousseau similarly saw inequality as a defective form of sociality because it benefited some at the expense of others; Marx saw the organization of cooperative labor and the employment of technology for surplus value as contradictory because it was being used not for the enhancement of all, but for the few. As I suggested in chapter 5, this structure of thought elaborates a fundamental social-ontological thesis. The validity of certain norms, institutions, practices, intentional ends, and so on is grounded in the social-ontological thesis: those acts that harm the association—and by extension the individuals within it—are defective and do not promote the "good."

Formalizing this, we can see that any objective conception of the good needs to be understood as satisfying some basic social-ontological criteria, and these should guide how critical reflection proceeds. The ontological ground provides evaluative criteria for ethical life insofar as they guide our practical reasoning and push it toward a kind of validity that moves into the actual, concrete nature of life rather than the merely pragmatic, interepistemic dimensions of formal reasoning. Social relations that are structured according to mutual, reciprocal needs and benefit; processes that are essentially nonextractive (i.e., nonexploitative and nonexpropriative); and ends or purposes that serve common needs and goods constitute a kind of social-ontological context for self-developing individuality. These principles of mutuality/reciprocity, nonextractiveness, and common good serve not as regulative but as constitutive judgments insofar as they shape the actual forms of life that we inhabit and that become active in the world. The cooperative networks of interaction and practices are therefore shaped according to *universal* purposes. This applies to economic and legal, political relations and to private and personal relations. Good economies would be those that maximize these social-ontological principles just as good friendships and good families would be the same. Judgment is the capacity to understand and decide when these kinds of relations and institutions instantiate these principles and when they do not.

The idea that our practical reasoning must have a ground at all will strike many as suspect. The entire weight of the antifoundational and postmetaphysical philosophical apparatus bears down against such a proposition. But since I have been arguing that this philosophical move is essentially wrong-headed, I will defend the thesis that we must posit a grounding for our practical reasoning, that without this there can be no genuine critical judgment. The ground is therefore to be understood as the systemic, functional nature of sociality. Once we posit the principle that society should be organized for the freedom of the individual, we are forced to consider how individuality is related to sociality, how our relations with others either promotes or hampers the development of the self, how the power of particular interests can corrupt the structures of our associations, and so on. The impotence of the postmetaphysical mode of reasoning lies not in its attempt to engage public reason; it is that it is unable to give any substantive guidance to the actual reality of human sociality and thereby grant us some ontological ballast for our conceptions of the good and the defective.

Recall that postmetaphysical thinkers from Arendt, Rorty, Putnam, and Habermas despite their relative differences, have supported the view that any modern conception of practical reason needs to be understood as basically proceduralist. In contrast to this, thinkers that have led to what I am calling the critical social-ontological approach to practical reason and judgment maintain that there exists a basic ontological "substance" to the species that can be shaped and formed in different ways, but the optimal organization of our social lives should produce a flourishing of our potentialities as members of an interdependent, cooperative community. The various properties and modes of critical social ontology provide a distinctive mode of practical reasoning in the sense that we have a more nuanced way to comprehend the object of moral and political reality. The core thesis of the last chapter was that we must be able to comprehend social facts as different shapes and forms of human social relations. These social relations are also to be understood in processual and teleological terms, that is, as possessing a dynamic and purposive character. Because social facts are also rooted in human practices, it is also crucial to see that all forms of sociopolitical judgment must be able to discern the irreducibly social essence of all practical phenomena. Political judgment, in this sense, is always tied to the ontological structure of what is because what is, in the social-ontological sense, is always rooted in the norms that shape the practices of others and the ensemble of these practices that form and re-form the structures and institutions that make up our social reality.

What these basic categories of a social ontology are meant to illustrate is how we can come to grasp the essential features of human sociality as an ontological reality, not just an arbitrarily posited and self-created convention. Sociality is not simply a feature of human life; it possesses causal powers and can be seen to be associated with certain kinds of what we can call "relational goods," or those goods produced jointly (i.e., by means of our sociality) and needed for sociality to exist in any vibrant and useful sense. Goods or ends can be seen as relational goods to the extent that they (1) can be seen to be essentially social in terms of how they are produced, insofar as they are dependent on cooperative, relational forms of action to be achieved; and (2) can be evaluated based on the extent to which those goods can provide the requisite self-development of the members of the community. The ends toward which we commit ourselves should be judged from within such a framework. Not doing so cleaves off our actual social reality and the processes that instantiate it from our cognitive and evaluative powers. In this respect, a critical social ontology still has in mind the basic principle laid out by Aristotle that society is an organization of its members who associate for some end or good.

Through understanding the concept of sociality, we can provide a ground for critical judgment. Recall that Hegel's position on this was that by grasping the conceptual dynamics of any thing, we will be able to engage in a critical engagement with the empirically existent forms that thing may take in the world. Objective-factual and normative-evaluative claims are therefore dialectically fused into a form of critical judgment once we see that we can contrast the existence of any thing with the extent to which it realizes or instantiates its immanent rational structures, processes, and end states.[13] We can distinguish this approach from the Kantian pragmatist approach because the social-ontological method raises the issue of the essential forms of sociality that must underwrite any valid claims about the means by which we shape social norms and institutions. The locus of examination must be on how pathological social formations can be understood to operate as the negation of a more positive, more emancipatory form of sociality. We do not post sociality as a fact that exists external or a priori to those social forms but instead see them as the immanent substance of what all social life actually is. The moment of judgment emerges once we can identify how capitalist society (or for that matter, any other form of society that can have rational self-awareness of its practices) promotes ends that negate the fuller forms of equal, interdependent sociality and the most developed forms of relational goods that can be articulated by that community.

Now we can see that mere mutual agreement with respect to norms is not enough. Because the life-world is an insufficient ground for conceptual development and the realization of the ontological domain of social reality and its possibility to secure freedom, it is only through certain kinds of social institutions and practices that the social-ontological can come to consciousness. For Hegel, this comes about through being a process of *Bildung* that occurs through institutions promoting the common interest, revealing to the subject the social-relational and interdependent structure immanent in our sociality. This means that the ontological reality of this social-relational interdependence is brought to rational awareness when we comprehend that it is a freedom-enhancing expression of our social being, that it is the most self-determining form of our essential substance (i.e., our sociality) that is shaped and formed in any given ontic form that we encounter and that our conceptions of judgment must be focused on how these ontic forms repress the vari-

---

13. Mark Tunick claims on this aspect in Hegel's metaphysical project that "Hegel looks at a practice he sees around him and develops an account of its purpose or rationale, an interpretation of the meaning the practice has, of its 'concept,' which he then uses to criticize manifestations of the actual practice that diverge from this purpose." *Hegel's Political Philosophy: Interpreting the Practice of Legal Punishment* (Princeton, NJ: Princeton University Press, 1992), 14.

ous ways our sociality can be reshaped to enhance our freedom.[14] For Marx, it was only through the class consciousness of working people that this cognitive realization could be achieved because they come to see the contradictions of a system that is organized for the benefits of the few but has the potential to deliver a common good—a common good that would be truly general and rational because it also nourished individual development and freedom. At the same time, Marx saw that capitalist social relations were ripe for this realization because society was becoming more interdependent as its creative powers grew. From Hegel, Marx was able to see that our social reality took on logical form: that they could express different relational, processual, and teleological features. Marx and Hegel see that the relational structure of social reality is the true essence of human reality; human action is essentially social and interdependent. This interdependence is the essential basis for the kinds of goods and social forms that any community articulates.

As such, we begin to see that the nature of freedom and the good can be construed as features immanent within any interdependent sociality. This is why Rousseau, and Marx for that matter, posit the notion that there is an objective basis for judging the kinds of institutions and practices that exist within and constitute any community. That objective basis can be understood as an objective common interest once we grasp that the good of each is dialectically fused to the good of all. The common good is immanent to the kinds of norms and practices that maximize the relational goods promoting the interdependent relational processes constituting our social reality. To understand which practices, which norms, which institutional formations are good in any critically useful sense of the word, we need to be able to endorse those practices not simply through some mutual agreement and justification. We must also, and more importantly, point to how such practices, norms, and so on can promote social-relational structures, processes, and ends that can fulfill the concept of our sociality as a shared form of reciprocal interaction promoting mutual development and common goods.

---

14. Stephen Houlgate therefore remarks, "This does not just mean that we sense that we ought to help others; it means that our practical activity must be habituated, by life in corporations and in the state, to being the actual pursuit of universal right and welfare." "The Unity of Theoretical and Practical Spirit in Hegel's Concept of Freedom," *Review of Metaphysics*, vol. 48, no. 4 (1995): 859–81, 878.

The Structure of Critical-Ontological Judgments

We can now explore how judgments can be understood in social ontological contexts. Ronald Beiner asks us to consider the idea of political
judgment as a kind of reflective reasoning where we adopt the distinction laid out by Kant. He suggests that these kinds of judgments be
seen as deliberation about rules in a set of given practices. He uses the
game of chess as an illustration. "In chess," he argues, "as in politics,
I am faced with particulars; that is to say, I do not deliberate about
rules, which are general or universal, but about application rules."[15] The
reason for this, Beiner explains, is that we are not making determinative
judgments about how to make a chess move; rather, we make rather
reflective judgments. Since a determinative judgment would be one where
we seek, in a Kantian sense, to subsume a particular under a universal, a
reflective judgment is about the application of general rules to particular
situations. There is no single right answer that can be derived from a
priori categories. In a determinative judgment, we can say that X is what
it is because it can be subsumed under a universal category. Hence, I
know that the computer on which I am typing this page is a computer
because it has characteristics that fit under the universal category of a
computer. I can judge this to be a computer in a determinative sense.
But in a reflective judgment, we do not make this kind of move. Instead,
we make judgments based on inference, moving from the particular to
the universal. Continuing with his chess example, Beiner argues, "the
concept of a good chess move does not determine the identification
of such a move in the way that, for instance, the concept of an even
number determines the identification of such a number. The latter
provides clear cognitive criteria, the former does not."[16]

Beiner's Kantian construction of political judgment is problematic
mainly because he continues in the postmetaphysical frame of thought,
where formal rules can be separated from the social content to which
they are applied. The problem is, as I have been suggesting all along,
that the strong powers of reification can infect and colonize reflective
powers of judgment. This interpretation of political judgment, based
in Arendt's Kantian move, removes social content from consideration.

15. Ronald Beiner, *Political Judgment* (Chicago: University of Chicago Press, 1983),
132.

16. Beiner, *Political Judgment*, 134.

In relying on reflective judgment, it may seem that we are liberating subjects to question and generate new forms of critique and demands against forms of power. But this is rooted in assumptions based in an early modern civic context.[17] The problem of critical political judgment must be able to call into question the social totality to achieve coherence. Critical-ontological judgments give us a way to think in terms of how the social totality mediates and shapes the particular; it provides a means of connecting the particular and the totality. Critique becomes coherent when the subject can connect how the various modes of social ontology come together to constitute the whole. But this also requires a capacity to judge whether the social scheme in question manifests pathologies rooted in defective features of the scheme and therefore creates blockages or distortions in our subjective ontological capacities.

Critical-ontological judgments, on the other hand, entail the capacity to achieve judgment with *ontological coherence*: a kind of insight into the manifold of social reality that will enable us to inquire into the dynamics of the relations, structures, processes, ends, and purposes that constitute our given social context as well as insight into the social totality that provides the context for it. Critical-ontological judgments are not deductive judgments or, in Kant's sense, determinative judgments. Instead, they operate in a different conceptual framework in that they critique immanently the prevailing social forms. It is immanent, however, in a double sense. First, it takes the social facts that are present consciousness on their own terms before, second, interrogating their relational, processual, and teleological dynamics. But in this process of critique, the reification of consciousness is pressed to its limits: the prevailing conceptual justificatory frames can only be undermined by working through the relations, processes, and purposes that any given social scheme manifests. This brings to consciousness alternative forms of relations and alternative social purposes and ends. Once there is consciousness of the relational, practical, and purposive dynamics of my social world, it becomes a terrain for questioning the valdity of those dynamics, raising issues of domination, exploitation, and freedom as features of those structures and processes. I may continue to accept features of my social reality and world until I confront

---

17. For a good example of this, see Miguel Vatter, "The People Shall Be Judge: Reflective Judgment and Constituent Power in Kant's Philosophy of Law," *Political Theory*, vol. 39, no. 6 (2011): 749–76.

the reality that they do not fulfill the normative assumptions I deem worthy of my obligation.

This is why grasping our ontology as social beings is also crucial. Only when I comprehend myself as an associative, relational being, where the common goods of my associational practices with others enhances our collective lives together and that my own self-determination depends on these common goods, then new criteria of judgment begin to open up for us. Political judgment has to have this ontological coherence in view because without it, we abandon the possibility for meaningful and reasoned social critique and transformation. Critical-ontological judgments inquire into the various shapes taken by our inherent sociality. The question of critical-ontological judgment centers on the purposes that organize our social reality. Critical-ontological judgments inquire into the extent to which the social reality that I inhabit either realizes personal and social goods that enhance freedom or instantiates defective forms of life. The ontological shape of our sociality is the primary object domain for these judgments. There is no relapse to a traditional, that is, precritical substantive ethics. Instead, the ontology of our values—the social forms they constitute and support or maintain—is at issue.

The move toward reflective judgment has had a deleterious effect on how we think about political judgment more generally. Arendt's turn to this idea in Kant was motivated by a phenomenological bias that saw consciousness as structurally separate from the objects of experience. From this, the linguistic turn was simply a means to abstract us even more from the actual objective dimensions of our reality. But as I labored to show above, this can be countered by a shift in perspective once we adopt a richer and, I think, more satisfying conception of reason as having a metaphysical structure. With this in mind, we can begin to inquire into the structure that critical-ontological judgments will take. This is what the Hegelian turn in critical thought embraces: the capacity of reason to see itself not as regulative of our experiences but as constitutive of the world itself, as embodied in the actual structures of social reality.

Critical political judgment, or critical practical reason more generally, as I have been arguing, contains a certain metaphysical structure that can account for the objective, ontological structures of social being. Let me return to my discussion about the metaphysical structure of reason. My thesis is that any valid form of reason has a metaphysical structure, which means that a statement must be considered valid if it can contain the conceptual structure of the object toward which it is directed. Hence, our status as concept users needs to be seen in relation to how the concepts we use are resonant with the object domain. More concretely stated, a dialectical-critical theory of consciousness overcomes the dichotomy of subject and object as well as that between fact and value. In this process, we see that the nature of practical reason becomes a means by which we have a more critical and socially transformative form of political agency. Unlike reflective judgment, critical-ontological judgment seeks to extend our critical reflection into the systemic processes that shape and generate our social reality. In the vein of immanent critique, it also exposes more rational, emancipatory forms of life that can emerge out of those that are defective and dominating.

Questions of political judgment necessarily interrogate the objective social world, but they also have to engage the fundamental question of all politics: that of the binding of any law, norm, custom, or institution in conscience. They are directed toward concrete institutional, social-organizational concerns that contain questions about the norms, values, and practices we share with others. This takes the form, as Stephen Toulmin has observed, of a *gerundive* in the sense that we must think about how any given social norm, institution, or practice relates to our own sense of obligation.[18] The form of relation takes the gerundive in the Latin sense of the term *obligandum est*, or the question: "is it worthy of obligation?" or "does it necessitate obligation?" The statement *X obligandum est* raises the question of what reasons may obligate me to perform, participate in, or whatever, *X*. This is only the entrance point to a critical structure of reasoning because it requires that we have the ontological field open as a kind of grammar to guide the structure of our reasons.

So any norm, practice, institution, or social convention can be opened up by the interrogative gerundive statement:

Does φ warrant my obligation?,

where φ indicates any given (ontic) social practice, norm, institution, or whatever. The question of obligation is tethered to the metaphysical

---

18. Stephen Toulmin calls these "gerundive concepts" and defines them as "concepts—logical, ethical and aesthetic alike—we can class together as 'gerundives,' thereby opposing them to such logical categories as 'properties' and 'subjective relations.' The name 'gerundives' is appropriate because they can all be analyzed as 'worthy of something-or-other.'" *An Examination of the Place of Reason in Ethics* (Cambridge: Cambridge University Press, 1968), 71 and *passim*.

structure of reasons and to the ontological ground, both of which set the framework for critical judgment. To think in this way is not a basic feature of speech-acts, as Habermas and others have assumed. Rather, it reflects on the ontological structure of the relational and purposive ends constituted by the norm in question. We cannot simply allow for consciousness and the pragmatics of language alone to supply us with the requisite material for judgment. What is needed is a coherent grasp of the ontological shape of sociality in which my subjectivity is embedded and which constitutes the prevailing reality. Once we think in these terms, we are in a space of reasons rooted in social ontology, and we can allow critical reason to discern the contradictions between the given reality that we experience and the repressed potentiality of new forms of social reality hidden within.

This is one reason to emphasize interrogative gerundive statements, because they frame our thinking in a particular way, specifically, to ask for reasons that will need to call into question the framework of rationalizations and habits of thought and custom that may be larded on to any practice social form or institution. To call into question φ therefore imitates a series of other questions that need to be satisfied. So if I am asked about the wrongness of murder, I may respond that it is simply wrong to murder someone. But this is not a reason, it is a habit of mind. I might respond that God forbids it, but this throws us back on to the precritical, inflated metaphysical problem where reasons are not given and only convention or custom decide. I may reply that it encourages or sanctions aggression, or some other reason. Here we get a bit closer to a more satisfying reason: murder is wrong because our purpose is not to end the lives of others but to live cooperatively. This may seem simplistic and does not take into consideration the difference between killing and murder, for instance. But it is resonant with the kinds of reasons that are social-ontological in nature: they rely on reasons that are nonabstract but achieve validity based on the ontology of our sociality. A critical metaphysics of our sociality reveals not a static, unchanging framework for ethics but a concrete generative ground for our ethical life.

What happens in examples of this kind is a series of layers of reasons—but reasons that are only really rationally satisfied when they reach the social-ontological framework. In this sense, to call into question φ we are not simply calling into question φ *simpliciter*, we are also, more importantly, calling into question the structures of rationalizations and reified "reasons" that have accreted to back up the practice or institution of φ. In this sense, we are questioning the standard by which reasons are considered valid. In this sense, Toulmin is correct when he argues:

> To question the standard is to question the theory—to criti-
> cise the theory as a whole—not to ask for an explanation of
> the phenomenon ostensibly under discussion (the properties
> of light-rays in outer space). So again in ethics: if I ask of
> the behavior prescribed in any standard of conduct, "Is *it*
> really right?" I am going outside the moral code; and my
> question is a criticism of the practice as a practice, not a
> request for a justification of a particular case of promise-
> keeping (or whatever it may be).[19]

The question of the standard is precisely what the ontological ground provides: we can now orient judgment in a critical direction when we understand that freedom is not a regulative concept over our activities or conduct but a constitutive feature of our social reality. Freedom or justice are not regulative ideals or principles, they are features of socio-relational structures, normative frames of consciousness, ensembles of practices, and institutional logics and social ends and purposes. These are our own products, and it is only when this is grasped that reification can be overcome, alienation undermined, and critical-practical reason gain firm footing. As such, the sterile split between fact and value becomes a more radical proposition to transform social reality into a realm of freedom and this, in social-ontological terms, means critiquing the kinds of social relations, social structures, norms, practices, and ends that make up the pattern of the shapes of our social world.

Before I get to a more concrete discussion of this topic, it is important to continue the argument of how critical-ontological judg-ments can be formulated. As I suggested already, the gerundive asks us to inquire into the legitimacy of any given institution, practice, norm, and so on. This requires nesting other questions that proceed from this interrogative gerundive form. What I needed is for my judgment not to rely on some abstract, regulative value to satisfy me. Rather, I need to see how the given norm, practice, or institution fits into the larger social

---

19. Toulmin, *An Examination of the Place of Reason in Ethics*, 149.

totality. As an example of this nesting structure, consider the following example. If I were to ask myself about the validity or legitimacy of any particular institution, I would have to inquire into its social-ontological structure. In the case of a norm, I would have to ask about how the given norm is nested in a larger framework of social reality, and so on. As I argued in the previous chapter, this means considering the various modes of that institution.

In this respect, asking:

(i) Does institution X warrant my obligation?

would necessarily entail that I inquire:

(ii) What function or end, ψ, does institution X realize?

Because ψ is a purpose or end, it is a teleological judgment that comes to the fore. For now, I can begin to see a structural connection between the ends or purposes of institution X and the actions I perform. Only then can the various modes of social ontology be employed in a coherent way. Once I ask about the purpose of institution X (or norm or practice φ), I can begin to see how my relations with others are shaped by this ensemble of norms and practices. I begin to question the purpose of what X realizes and, in so doing, call into question the reasons for my φ-ing. I can only frame proper answers to these kinds of questions by grasping the social totality that mediates the institution in question.

This leads me back to a discussion of the ontological framework for practical reasoning. The gerundive form of ethical reflection puts us into contact with the fundamental ontological ground in the sense that we must begin to ask ourselves what kinds of purposes, ends, relations, processes, norms, and practices—all of which are fundamental features of any social scheme—either maximize the basic principle of ontological ethics or negate it. An ontological framework for our social being leads us to the possibility of achieving what I call an ontological coherence with respect to normative concerns by linking our normative values and practices to the kinds of social reality they instantiate. The key to ontological coherence is to have practical reasoning take up the concerns of the constitutive relations and processes that undergird our social reality and open them up to critical reflection. This has the benefit of checking the slide into reification or relativism by inquiring into how the structures of social being shape our reflective capacities. Unlike the Kantian position that seeks epistemic validity of norms through consensus or justification of reason by reason exchange, the ontological framework relies on a thick Hegelian view of the possibilities of cognition to achieve valid forms of knowledge by penetrating the essential and constitutive structures of being.[20]

This does not grant us a timeless objective standpoint for critique and judgment, but it does offer a means by which we can penetrate the phenomenological structures of consciousness and grasp the actual fundamental processes and structures responsible for the ontic shapes of our social being. An ontological ethics works in this key: it seeks to reach into the generative mechanisms of our social world and the norms and values that we use subjectively to operate within it. It puts the cognitive grasp of our norms into critical contact with the ontological social schemes to which they are constitutively related. The key moment of critical judgment now can be seen as to how we can expose the asymmetry between the ontological potential of our social arrangements and the actual ontic forms they take. Our ethical life, our political institutions, and our individual moral capacities for reflection must be judged from the viewpoint of how they manifest and sustain interdependent relational structures, nonexploitative or extractive social processes, and common ends and purposes. We can call this the basic principle of critical social ontology and critical practical reason.

Ultimately, there is no way to have critical judgment in this context without the ontological ground and the principles it entails. Recall that I argued that the ontological ground is not a *substantive* criterion for judgment but an *ontological* criterion: it provides the requisite categories for grasping when a norm, practice, social purpose, and so on warrants my obligation toward it and, *ex hypothesi*, when it requires my disobedience

---

20. Kevin Thompson has described this as "ontological justification" which he describes as: "an establishing of the fundamental orders and constitutive processes of being. . . . [T]he warrant of a concept, claim, or belief to be what it purports to be is vindicated if and only if it is shown to be a moment that is either itself the result of a conceptual unfolding of some object or is a moment in a differential relation included in such a progression." "Systematicity and Normative Justification: The Method of Hegel's Philosophical Science of Right," in Thom Brooks and Sebastian Stein (eds.), *Hegel's Political Philosophy: On the Normative Significance of Method and System* (Oxford: Oxford University Press, 2017), 44–66, 60.

from it as well. To not do so would mean becoming an agent of that scheme's defectiveness, and therefore any rational agent must seek to make rational what has been irrationally constructed. The condition here was that a valid social scheme, relation, norm, practice, or purpose is valid if it provides the goods (material, cultural, psychological, etc.) needed for self-determining social agency. This means that the roles and institutions achieve validity when they can be shown to provide association members with mutual benefits. Families are good, valid forms of life if they are organized for the mutual benefits of their members. Once it can be shown that one member of the association has burdens placed on them for the benefit of any one or the rest of the association, it loses its validity. The purpose of the association becomes extractive rather than free, unequal rather than just. This is not a judgment based on convention, tradition, or whatever but on the associational essence of the species.

Phenomenology, Ontology, and the Structure of Critical Agency

Now we can see that valid reasons for any norm or practical question need to have an ontological basis. The ontological ground entails that valid judgments have the entire structure of a given social practice, institution, or norm in mind; that a social scheme, norm practice, or institution is valid to the extent that it has ends that satisfy the reciprocal, nonextractive, and common good of the members of association and those affected by it. Monogamous marriage is justified because of the free association between members of the marriage; they must be structured by free relational logics, that is, have the development of rational agency as their end. Families that are not shaped in this way affect the members of that association and those outside of it because it will produce individuals who may reproduce the defective values of inequality, misogyny, or whatever outside that immediate association.

What this points to is a theory of defective forms of relational schemes that derives from the concept of the purpose of our collective forms of activity as a species. Rousseau was correct in this sense when he argued that only by combining our activities and powers could we achieve higher forms of goods. Associations are to be judged in terms of how their structures exhibit forms of dependence and control or interdependence and cooperation, particular goods or common goods, and the development of its members or their instrumental use for the few. Immanent critique becomes possible only when we can think in critical metaphysical terms. Only when we can follow the link between our phenomenological experiences and the kinds of social-ontological processes, structures, and so on that constitute that experience. The life-world must be pierced; we must be able to proceed from appearance to essence. To fail in this is to collapse back onto the hall of mirrors problem described in the first chapter. A critical social-ontological perspective grants us dimensionality to our reflections. It explodes the reified, one-dimensionality of the life-world and allows us to think in terms of process, structure, and purposes.

Hence the phenomenological must give way to the ontological in any form of critical reflection and practice. The phenomenological can capture the ontic status of the object domain and the life-world, but if restricted to that level, it will be unable to generate rational social critique. Instead, it will be suspended in the abstract, afloat in the very practices and norms that the logics of the prevailing social reality continue to reproduce. Lukács rightly saw the problem: "The question then becomes: are the empirical facts—(it is immaterial whether they are purely 'sensuous' or whether their sensuousness is only the ultimate material substratum of their 'factual' essence)—to be taken as 'given' or can this 'givenness' be dissolved further into rational forms, i.e., can it be conceived as the product of 'our' reason?"[21] The "givenness" to which he refers is the phenomenological experience of the ontic, the realm of the "understanding" in Hegel's parlance. The key, as I have been arguing, is to move beyond the phenomenological membrane of consciousness in the cognition of "rational forms," to the constitutive ontological modes that generate that reality and, once comprehended, can be transformed from pathological forms into free forms of life.[22]

The move from the phenomenological to the ontological is also a means to undermine the reification of consciousness. Once we begin

21. Lukács, *History and Class Consciousness*, 116.

22. Compare my thesis here with what I see to be the problematic discussion by Albena Azmanova, which is unable to escape from the phenomenological and postmetaphysical paradigm, *The Scandal of Reason: A Critical Theory of Judgment* (New York: Columbia University Press, 2012), 180ff. I see it as essential to stress the thesis that cognition requires some capacity to grasp the totality as an social-ontological category to properly articulate rational critique.

to see the interdependence of our concepts, norms, practices, institutions, and the broader social reality we inhabit, we are moving into the realm of judgment. We are beginning to gain *ontological coherence*. But the same grammar of thought required to de-reify the ontic world is simultaneously the conceptual terms that can provide consciousness with requisite means to perceive the defective, nonrational, and contradictory nature of these social forms. Our ontology as relational beings, the purposive structure of human praxis, the shared cooperative nature of social institutions, the teleological ends toward which all of these are oriented bring to consciousness the question of the best way these should be organized, thereby potentially undermining the givenness of our social world. Inequality, exploitation, oppression, domination now have an ontological coherence that make them objects of critical consciousness and transformative praxis.

To take a more recent example of events, think of the transformation of feminism in early twentieth-century culture in this regard. What was once a radical impetus to transform social relations away form patriarchy and toward a more common and interdependent form of social equality has morphed in the popular culture and consciousness to the "power" of women to become independent, become entrepreneurs, and ape the kind of competitive, accumulative forms of power that are typical of capitalist market societies. In this sense, the values of a society constituted by processes of accumulation and competition come to recode previous emancipatory expressions of feminism. The point here is that the undergirding, constitutive ontological logics of society will continue to shape our understandings of social struggles, or equality and freedom unless they are unmasked at a deeper level. The ontic is unable to escape the ontological pull and unless the deeper structures and processes of the social totality are brought into view and critiqued, our evaluative and normative categories and practices will succumb to those deeper logics and their pathologies. To push beyond the ontic means to penetrate the essential constitutive ontological modes that undergird the reality we experience. Once the realm of the ontic is pierced by critical reason, ontological coherence becomes possible.

This is why holistic thinking and critical social ontology are essentially linked. To think only in terms of a part is to miss the capacity to question the reasons, the power-relational nexus that produces the shapes of the social world we inhabit. This emphasis on the totality as a means to grasp political judgment, however, is insufficient on its own. The main reason for this is that we have to understand how our interaction with the social world is itself shaped by it in the first place. There needs to be an account of how our phenomenological interaction with the world is to pass over into a comprehension of the whole. As I see it, this can only happen by using the ontological criteria I outlined in the previous chapter. When we learn to think in ontological terms, we begin to grant critical-cognitive shape to our phenomenological experiences in the world. We are not, I will argue, thinking or reasoning from some "external" or "privileged" position but from a point of view of genuine immanent critique. Experience requires theory for it to become mediated. This means that the connection between the phenomenological experience of the social world and the ontological account of its being are connected in crucial ways.

Phenomenological access to others is insufficient for critical awareness and critical cognition. More is needed and demanded. One of the core features of reified consciousness is the inability to perceive contradictions in one's social reality. This stems from what Antonio Gramsci referred to as the "episodic" character of consciousness where the experience of one's world is fragmented, limiting comprehension of the whole.[23] Indeed, as Neil Postman has insightfully argued: "The fundamental assumption of [our] world is not coherence but discontinuity. And in a world of discontinuities, contradiction is useless as a test of truth or merit, because contradiction does not exist."[24] Critical consciousness must overcome this. We can only grasp contradictions in our social world—and contradictions are indicative of what is irrationally constituted—when we have the totality in view. Lacking this, we cannot achieve the necessary critical depth for understanding how our experiences and the immediate world of our values, concepts, and practices are tied to larger forms of social process and structure. Marx's *Capital* can be seen to follow such an epistemic method: beginning with the commodity, the object immediately present to consciousness, it proceeds chapter by chapter into more ontologically substantive—but nevertheless decreasingly phenomenologically accessible—structures and processes until capitalism as a system can be grasped.

---

23. See Antonio Gramsci, *Prison Notebooks* (New York: International, 1971).

24. Neil Postman, *Amusing Ourselves to Death: Public Discourse in the Age of Show Business* (New York: Penguin, 1985), 110.

Likewise, critical social ontology seeks to thematize the totality for the purpose of social critique. It moves beyond "reflective judgment" in that it seeks a dialectical link between the particular and the universal. This is an operation of consciousness that cannot be accessed through phenomenological means, only through the objective point of view that seeks to understand how relational structures, processes, and purposes are organized. Experience must be mediated by critical thought; critical thought has a metaphysical structure in that it must resonate with the embodied structures and processes that give shape to the world. To experience racism, class domination, inequality, or some other form of power imbalance is not enough. It is also necessary to understand the processes at work giving rise to these phenomena; all social facts are rooted in some process, some objective form of activity that has its own norms and practices. More often than not, these forms of power can be traced to some unequal form of resource control—material, economic, status, and so on—that warp our collective-intentional and social-structural reality.

Ontological Coherence:
Overcoming Reification and Relativism

The basic line of reasoning of the critical social ontology approach can now be stated in more concise form. Critical judgment uses social ontology as a ground for explaining and evaluating the social forms that make up the existent reality. It does this, as I have shown, from the viewpoint of a mediated form of phenomenological awareness about the world that brings the subject from the realm of immediate to mediated experience. But its process is strictly immanent: it asks the subject to reflect on his or her social world from the perspective of obligation and the extent to which the reality in which he or she is embedded warrants that obligation. The operation of critical-ontological judgments pushes us to inquire into how the existent reality realizes certain ends or purposes and how these ends and purposes are themselves teleologically constitutive of the relations, norms, practices, and institutions that sustain them.

But it also mediates this reflection further because it starts not from the Cartesian point of the atomized self but from the social-relational basis of all human life. Once this basic substantive ontological feature is brought into consciousness, the forms or the shapes this social-relational essence takes become the focal point of critical reason. Since this social ontology is constituted by a structure of interdependent social relations that are dynamic and oriented toward relational goods and ends, which are in turn re-created through the collective-intentional rules of the community, we can see that any social forms that distort this structure can be seen as pathological. Ontological coherence is achieved when we can grasp the levels of social being that are the infrastructure for any social fact or institution. Ontological coherence is also much richer than a merely empirical description of my social world: it entails a critical-diagnostic and normative mode of reflection. Once we grasp that all forms of social reality around us are generated by us not as mere individuals but as cooperatively interlaced practical beings, then judging these forms becomes a matter of cognizing how these associational forms of life are structured and oriented. Because these forms of life are generated by norms and maintained by systems of value, peering beneath these justificatory frameworks entails questioning the extent to which these associations promote ends and goods that are truly for the common interest of the members of that association. The instrumental use or abuse of any member of a cooperative enterprise violates the basic principle of sociality.

This places us in a different framework for judgment than claimed by formal or substantive theories of ethics and validity. Hence, in some traditional societies, domestic violence may be seen as tolerable or perhaps justified or necessary based on traditional gender and family roles, whereas same-sex relationships would be seen as deviant from the point of view of a traditionally rooted substantive ethical life. But a critical theory of judgment that achieves ontological coherence overcomes this issue by grasping the social-relational and teleological features of these ontic social forms and their deviation from a potential social-relational ontology that maximizes reciprocity and common goods. Domestic violence becomes defective because relations of hierarchy, subordination, and control are anathema to the fuller purpose or end of familial relations: that of the mutual development and support of each family member. Same-sex relations become rationally valid from this point of view (i.e., they qualify as freedom-enhancing) because—as long as they are not abusive or whatever—they manifest forms of reciprocity and common interest that support self-determining individuality, the rational purposes of familial association. We need this ontological coherence to ground our judgments and discourse; it provides access to the totality, not as an abstract concept but as the ensemble of systematic relations and practices that are constitutive of social reality. Formalism also runs into problems when we are unmoored from the deeper social-ontological features involved in the ratification of norms. Hence, communities can sanction tax cuts on corporations and increases on themselves if they are under the normative sway of economically conservative norms and values.[25]

Overcoming reification and relativism is thus a first step for critical judgment to play its necessary function of social critique. The theory of reification I refer to here is broad: it refers to a defect of consciousness where the subject is immediately related to social reality. In this sense, reification measures the extent to which the subject has been operationally constituted by the prevailing norms and value orientations of society without having called into question the standards by which those norms and practices have been instantiated. Reification becomes an increasingly stubborn problem when it can filter into the very conceptual categories and collective-intentional rule sets that shape the self and the subject's cognitive and evaluative capacities.[26] Combatting and dissolving reification is only possible when we are open to questioning the basic value orientations that shape the social reality of which we are a part. That is because, as I have been suggesting, values are themselves ontological in a social sense in that they enact, constitute, and guide social actions, norms, practices, and the shapes that the ensembles of these practices take on. This must be a political act or the result of a political challenge to the culture that perpetuates the forms of social power that pervade our lives. For this reason, combatting reification must be a central role of any political critique of power. For reification to become the object of political critique once again, it is necessary to understand the inherently social-ontological structure of Lukács's argument.

With this in mind, I return to how we can reconstruct a theory of critical judgment from the reflections I have laid out here. As I see

---

25. See the interesting example explored by Edward T. Walker, "Legitimating the Corporation through Public Participation," in Caroline W. Lee, Michael McQuarrie, and Edward T. Walker (eds.), *Democratizing Inequalities: Dilemmas of the New Public Participation* (New York: New York University Press, 2015), 66–81.

26. I have explored this theory of reification in more depth elsewhere. See Michael J. Thompson, "Reification and the Web of Norms: Toward a Critical Theory of Consciousness," *Berlin Journal of Critical Theory*, vol. 3, no. 3 (2019): 5–35.

it, the essence of critical judgment must be expressed in an expanded form of thinking that can encompass the social totality as the basis for understanding any particular expression of social or political power. Reification becomes increasingly difficult to combat the more it penetrates into cultural and personality structures. But the reality it creates is always open to critique because it is a false totality—that is, it is an irrational totality because it does not serve universal ends and purposes. The contradictions generated by such an irrational system are the necessary cracks that force us back to retheorize the totality. In this sense, we must ask about the purpose and end of the social totality—we must inquire into the validity of ends and purposes of our lives as interdependent, cooperative social beings. This is precisely, I think, what Lukács urges in his critique of reified consciousness. His idea of "expressive totality" may seem to us now politically out of date, but I want to suggest that it has been dismissed too soon without proper theoretical treatment.

Lukács argues that it is only when working people discover that they are the "subject-object" of history that reification will be overcome. Put in a different way, it means that once working people grasp that the social world is rooted in praxis, specifically praxis as labor that is controlled and directed by capital, that they will see the defective shape of the capitalist world. This kind of consciousness, though, is not a contemplative form of consciousness but an active one. Lukács has in mind the need to change the practical relations we have with one another and with nature, and this means, as I have been arguing, a transformation of the normative structure of consciousness that orients our activities. As Lukács puts it: "the consciousness of the proletariat must become deed. . . . namely, since consciousness here is not the knowledge of an opposed object but is the self-consciousness of the object *the act of consciousness overthrows the objective form of its object.*"[27] What this means is that consciousness must become a new self-consciousness that sees the immanent ontology of our sociality and how this has been shaped and formed according to the interests of others, directed and oriented toward private needs, ends, and purposes as opposed to those of all. A rational universal is therefore discovered through a new form of

---

27. Lukács, *History and Class Consciousness*, 178. As Iring Fetscher notes: "The self-awareness of the proletariat therefore fulfills the same process in reality which Hegel had attriobuted to spirit: it leads to a breakthrough to freedom." *Marx and Marxism* (New York: Herder and Herder, 1971), 87–88.

self-consciousness. But this self-consciousness that allows us to know ourselves as social beings, as practical beings, and as members of a totality entails a new way of thinking and judging—a way of thinking and judging that can serve as the basis for critical rationality.

For this reason, Lukács maintains that three aspects of critique must be in play. First, we must become aware of the contradictions that plague the system as a whole. If we are able to do this, then it is necessary, second, for us to have "an aspiration toward totality, that action should serve the purpose, described above, in the totality of the process." What this means is an ability to grasp the truth of the totality—"the truth that in the dialectical totality the individual elements incorporate the structure of the whole."[28] In this sense, we need to be able to see any particular contradiction or norm or practice as part of a total process. Last, if we are to be able to judge any given norm or practice, "it is essential to relate it to its function in the total process."[29] If we can do these three things, then the hold of reification can be loosened. I suggest that thinking in terms of relations, processes, and ends or purposes is the grammar needed to think the totality as an ontological reality. Once we see this, we can begin to grasp how uncritical practical activity helps re-create and sustain the false totality generating the contradictions in the first place and push us toward embracing a "critical practical activity."

This may seem overly philosophical, but we can make it more concrete by casting it in terms of a social ontology. Once we gain self-consciousness as social beings, whose existence is interdependent on and in relations with other beings; that these interdependent relations are embedded in processes of change and activity; and, finally, that these processes and practices have ends and purposes, we can glimpse the essential structure of any given social reality in ontological (as opposed to empirical) form. The totality of social reality begins to expose itself. I go to work each day to bring home money to pay my bills and purchase things. As isolated "facts," these things taken independently render critical reflection inert. Once I ask about the purposes or ends of that work or the things I purchase, or about the kinds of relations that are needed to bring about the things for which I work or purchase, and

28. Lukács, *History and Class Consciousness*, 198.

29. Lukács, *History and Class Consciousness*, 198.

the other institutions, norms, and practices that uphold such a social reality, I begin to inquire into the legitimacy of such a system. Is it rational? Does it exist for the benefit of all? Reification only begins to break down at such a point, when the question of the ontology of my social world and my place in it is raised to consciousness. This is why Lukács argues that "Marxist theory is designed to put the proletariat into a very particular frame of mind."[30]

Once we see this as an alternative mode of critical judgment, we can also see the severe errors of the postmetaphysical, discursive, and phenomenological approaches to judgment that are current in theory today. Relying on thinkers such as Arendt, Habermas, or Honneth cannot get us past the blockages posed by reification. Indeed, as I see the matter, such theoretical projects do little more than refract reified consciousness back onto the judging subject. Indeed, their emphasis on a noumenal conception of intersubjectivity shears off the deeper normative, practical, and social-relational structures and processes that constitute our social reality. After all, this is what Marx really meant by the term "material": that our sociality has a thick ontology of practices, norms, processes, and relational structures and these structures are embedded in a social totality with its own imperatives. Without access to this totality, as Lukács importantly points out, there is no way to overcome the pathology of reification and come to terms with the deeper, core dynamics of our social world and how it shapes its members. Perhaps a return to this concept and its critical implications for culture and political judgment can help us return critical social theory to its original Enlightenment political aspirations for a rational, free form of sociality. Perhaps it can also enable progressive social movements to disclose a rationally valid emancipatory interest to overcome the dehumanizing, reifying tendencies of capitalist modernity.

---

30. Lukács, *History and Class Consciousness*, 262.

Chapter 8

Obligation and Disobedience

The Practice of Critical Judgment

> Let every man make known what kind of government would command his respect, and that will be one step toward obtaining it.
>
> —Henry David Thoreau

If the critical social-ontological theory of practical reason that I have been defending has any political salience, it is in its relation to one of the most central questions in political philosophy: that of our obligation to the state or the norms of the community more generally and the extent to which we as members of the political association should dissent from the prevailing social norms and institutions. I want to suggest that a satisfying answer to this question can be approached from the critical-ontological theory of evaluative reason I have been developing in the previous chapters. Political judgment will be of little use if it cannot provide some guiding framework for dealing with this crucial and fundamental issue. My thesis here will be that we do not have duties to those norms, practices, or institutions, to laws and states that are oriented toward social ends or purposes that do not have common ends as their orientation or, to use a term of Maurice Hariou, their "directive idea."[1] A common end is not a substantive purpose or value—such as,

---

1. Maurice Hariou, "La théorie de l'institution et de la fondation," in *Aux sources du droit: le pouvoir, l'ordre, la liberté* (Caen: Presses Universitaires de Caen, 1986), 98–100.

all people must believe or do *X* or conform to belief or practice *Y*. Rather, the common good or common interest is an ontological property of our associations that finds its legitimacy in the principles of non-extraction, nonsubordination, reciprocity, and commonality. A common good is an evaluative claim that rests on the subtheoretical primacy of how our sociality forms structures and purposes that either enhance our free interdependence or distort our relations and practices toward dependence or other forms of exploitation and domination.[2] The validity of these forms of sociality derive from the premise that they articulate self-determining forms of life, or forms of life that are concretely free and derive their legitimacy from the ontology, of kinds of social reality that such forms of life instantiate.

These principles are conceptual, but they are to be understood as constitutive concepts: concepts that do not regulate, but are the generative formulae for, the structures and practices of our associations with others. The rationality of any association therefore resides in that association's capacity to realize these principles as concrete, actual forms of sociality. Critical political judgment therefore requires that our obligation or nonobligation to institutions and norms be based on the criteria of validity laid out in chapter 7. I submit, however, that the essence of political obligation and nonobligation, or dissent, is intrinsically bound up with the ontological structure of the social reality that we inhabit as reflective members of society. Nonobligation is warranted when the ontological shape of any aspect of our society violates what we can call the *basic principle of legitimacy*: that is, when it is constructed, sustained, or organized for purposes and ends that enhance particular interests at the expense of common interests and that engender social relational and associational structures that are subordinating or extractive instead of being reciprocal and nondominating. These are ontological properties of objective social relations, processes, and ends that violate the very purpose of living in associations with others.

This thesis will almost certainly be met with worries about communitarianism and conventionalism. But these worries are misplaced. As I have been stressing, there is a fundamental difference between formal,

2. Michael E. Brown insightfully notes, "It is not adequately described by reference to shared values, shared meanings, and commonly accepted norms. These presuppose the very solidarity they are said to explain." *The Concept of the Social in Uniting the Social Sciences and Humanities* (Philadelphia: Temple University Press, 2014), 37.

substantive, and ontological ethics. Whereas substantive ethics asks us to have obligations to norms that are rooted in convention and what is accepted by the community, formalism asks us to obey abstract principles or decision procedures. The former obviates any critique, and we fall into the problem of ethical relativism, whereas in formal ethics, we are open to the problem of reification or the problem of the constitutive power of prevailing social logics to infiltrate our epistemic and evaluative capacities. An ethics based in ontology avoids these pitfalls because it does not subscribe to a concrete, ahistorical content to value, nor does it rest with formalism. A critical social-ontology can help provide the foundation for a basis to judge obligation and nonobligation, to provide criteria for legitimate, rational grounds for following a norm, rule, law, or institution or to disobey and transform it.

In many ways, the project of modernity has been a sustained confrontation of formal and substantive ethics. But my claim has been that a critical social ontology is a more robust option than either and is rooted in a coherent structure of political thought. The thesis is that our moral-evaluative categories must be understood as instantiating actual social forms of life in the world; that there are certain essential, species-specific properties of human life that guide how we can judge the various shapes our social schemes take. Key to this argument is an ontological thesis about human life: that it is essentially relational and practical and developmental or processual. Individuals are therefore a function of the forms of social life they inhabit, which shape and form them. Individual capacities can be understood as expressions of how their associational lives have been structured. Social schemes, or those organized forms of relations and practices, need to be understood as dynamically shaping their members. The social-ontological thesis becomes a critical stance once we are able to judge social schemes as organized for common purposes—that is, those that are mutually beneficial for the members of those affected by the scheme—as opposed to ends or purposes with only particular benefits as their end.

As I will argue here, a social-ontological account of political judgment can only be deemed valuable if it can grant us critical insight into the question of the legitimacy of the social world. I have been arguing that a satisfactory approach to the question of valid normative claims in general must be seen as rooted in the ontological structures that shape human relations of socio-interdependence and the kinds of ends and purposes toward which they are organized. This is a kind of critical reflection that allows us to comprehend the social totality within which judgment must operate. In this sense, I believe critical practical reason rooted in critical social ontology helps meet the criteria set by John Dunn: "The only way in which presumed moral obligations might be conclusively whipped in under the aegis of rational action is by constructing and vindicating a comprehensive theory of what, theoretically, ethically, factually, etc., it is rational for men to believe."[3] By connecting our cognitive and moral-evaluative capacities with the social-ontological structures that shape our social being, we can approach this question with more critical nuance. At a higher level, there is also the need to show how judgment, as I have been reconstructing it, relates to the most crucial question in actual politics: that of legitimacy and dissent. The crucial question I want to explore here is this: what are the foundational criteria for our rational obligations toward our social world—construed broadly as the norms, practices, and institutions that constitute it—and what criteria obligate us to dissent from the social world? As I see it, this is the fundamental question of all political judgment and is best answered by applying the social-ontological framework I have been exploring.

The thesis I seek to defend here is that a critical conception of political judgment must be able to show us that I am only obligated to those forms of social life (norms, practices, and institutions) that serve common interests; that we have a moral and political imperative to dissent from and transform those social schemes—and the attendant norms, practices, values, and so on that accompany and help constitute them—that violate the needs and requirements of the purposes of our associational social ontology. In stark contrast to the postmetaphysical approach critiqued in the first half of this book, critical social-ontology can shatter reified forms of thought by discerning how any particular is embedded in the social totality. It can do this because it provides a comprehensive approach to social reality, one that can encompass the thick relational, processual, and purposive aspects of human sociality and activity. The key insight here is both critical and normative: it provides us with a means to give substantive cognitive content to our ethical life. It can provide criteria for legitimate forms of social life and a means to discern those aspects of social reality that do not command our obligations. In the end, it offers criteria to answer, in a critical and engaged

---

3. John Dunn, *Political Obligation in its Historical Context* (Cambridge: Cambridge University Press, 1980), 247 and *passim*.

fashion, one of the most central questions in political philosophy: what obligates me to my social and political world? And, the flip side of the same question, when do I have an obligation to dissent as well?

Crito's Question, Rousseau's Solution

Should I obey a law or not? Do the norms or practices of my community or a given institution have normative weight on my conduct or should they motivate me to dissent from them? In the *Crito*, Plato has Socrates confront this fundamental question of our obligation to obey the state and its laws. At the center of Socrates's reply is a thesis about the relation of the individual to the community, one that must be dispelled before moving forward. Socrates does not escape his death sentence and chooses to follow the law because he believes himself to be an organic and integral part of that community. In this sense, his private interest in extending his life does not outweigh the obligation he has to follow the laws of the community. It is an argument for a noncritical form of group membership. As Socrates frames the argument:

> "Observe then, Socrates," the laws (οἱ νόμοι) would no doubt say, "that if what we say is true, what you are now undertaking to do to us is unjust (οὖ δικαία). For we brought you into this world, nurtured you, educated you, and gave you a share of all the good things we could to you and all the citizens. . . . But we say that whoever of you stays here, seeing how we administer justice and we govern the *polis* in other respects, has thereby entered into an agreement with us to do what we command. And we say that he who does not obey does a threefold wrong because he disobeys us who are his parents, us who nurtured him, and because after agreeing to obey us he neither obeys us nor convinces us that we are wrong."[4]

For Socrates, the individual is little more than a particle of whole, one who wrongfully sees himself as apart from the organic structure of the community. He again creates the rationale of the laws:

---

4. Plato, *Crito* (Oxford: Oxford University Press, 1966), 51c–e.

> Are you not intending by this thing you are trying to do
> to destroy us, the laws, and the entire *polis*, as far as you
> are able? Or do you think that the polis can exist and not
> be overturned, in which the decisions reached by the courts
> have no force but are made invalid and annulled by private
> persons (ὑπὸ ἰδιωτῶν)?[5]

For Socrates, the reason to reject Crito's offer to escape his death
sentence is that group membership entails duties on the part of the
individual to the political community. But this conception of the political community (τὸ κοινὸν τῆς πόλεως) is communitarian and has an
anthropological basis as its legitimacy, according to Socrates. Membership
is natural, and it has automatic duties that accord with it. It is also an
argument for a substantive ethics rooted in the norms and conventions
(semantic valences of the term οἱ νόμοι) and therefore the laws that
quash any effort at critical reflection let alone critical action.

   In this sense, Socrates's question about the legitimacy of obligation
and disobedience obviously fails any test of modernity. Group membership certainly does constitute a distinct social ontology, but the question
of disobedience must hinge on the extent to which the social scheme
of which I am a member has a more nuanced theory of the common
interest. Indeed, my thesis is that Socrates's answer to this question is
only partly correct. There is little doubt that as a rational agent, I should
have duties and obligations toward memberships that constitute my good
as an individual and that, as Socrates implicitly argues, are only possible
given our relational and processual ontology. What is lacking here is
a conception of the individual that is more than either a "private" or
"particular" self (ἰδιώτης), but one that has self-consciousness of the
relational and associational goods that warrant one's obligation. More
directly, each person has the capacity and the duty to call into question
the relations, processes, and purposes of our society and the institutions
of which we are members. Obligation and disobedience are therefore
dialectically related terms: they correspond to the attitudes we should
have toward those kinds of social schemes that manifest our good as
associational members or the corruption of those relations for particular,
nonuniversal ends and purposes. The relevant question that concerns us
here is: what are the rational, legitimate criteria for our obligation to
any social norm, institution, or whatever?

5. Plato, *Crito*, 50b.

I think this answer to the question posed by Plato in his dialogue finds its first real voice in Rousseau. Rousseau's answer to this classical question is the starting point for modern theories of dissent and obligation because he sees that our associational life must be structured at once for the good of each member and the association as a whole. He agrees with Socrates about the unjustness of one who acts for particularist interests or ends (ἰδιώτης), but he disagrees that the association can ever be considered legitimate or deserve our obligation if it goes against the interests of its members. Socrates's answer sounds, at first, like a similar argument to Rousseau's proposition that the criminal must "be forced to be free." But this would hold only if the transgression was in fact done for particularist reasons—say, committing crimes of theft, corruption, or some other act for selfish rather than public reasons. Socrates's transgression is not of this kind but calls into question a social scheme that exists not to develop and benefit the members of the association but to enforce conformity and stasis. For Rousseau, obligation is a question of legitimacy and legitimacy is a question of the extent to which the political association is organized for and has as its ends the common good of its members. Before defending this thesis, I deal with the relative parts of this argument, specifically the relation between the common good and the individual.

The Common Interest
and the Structure of Democratic Reason

Rousseau's difference from Socrates highlights an important contrast between the communal understanding of the common good and its modern variant. The principle is nevertheless Aristotelian in basic respects. In stark contrast to liberal political philosophy, the ontology that undergirds the republican idea of political life is that the association of each with the other is not purely voluntaristic but is rooted in the natural features of the species. The good that we can attain as particular individuals pales in comparison what can be achieved in cooperation with others. Not just psychological and emotional needs are satisfied by our associational relations with others; the material, technological, and cultural goods that can be enjoyed are also products of association. This associational ontology is therefore central to the idea of obligation insofar as it can be argued that our obligation should be only to those institutions and norms that are constitutive of those common goods.

What this means is elusive. A theory of critical-practical reason, as I outlined it in chapter 7, holds that valid reasons have a metaphysical structure. In other words, only those reasons that can capture and express social-ontological content are valid. The main reason for pointing to the connection between the common good and political judgment is that it can be asserted and defended that, as Thomas Aquinas had once put it, only those legal-political forms of authority that serve the common good are worthy of "binding us in conscience." Aquinas gives a rudimentary account of what the common good consists. Only just laws can bind us in conscience; just laws are oriented toward the common good. Justice and the common good are mutually reinforcing properties of legitimate law. There are three criteria delineating what a just law actually is:

> Now laws are said to be just both from the *end*, when, that is, they are ordered to the common good; and from their *author*, that is to say, when the law that is made does not exceed the power of the lawgiver; and from their *form*, when, that is burdens are laid on the subjects according to an equality of proportion and with a view to the common good. For, since one man is a part of the community, each man, in all that he is and has, belongs to the community; just as a part, in all that it is, belongs to the whole.[6]

The three features of the common good are therefore that of the end, author, and form, and we can see that violating these criteria constitute tyranny, or the violation of any common good that members of the association are not bound to obey or respect.[7]

Here we see the building blocks for the basic principle of legitimacy. It is rooted in an Aristotelian social ontology that sees the developmental capacities of individuals as a function of the political

---

6. Thomas Aquinas, *Summa Theologiae*, 2 vols. (Chicago: Encyclopedia Britannica, 1952), II, I, Q. 96, Art. 4.

7. Raffaele Laudani comments on Aquinas: "Laws that are not made for the well-being of its subjects and to protect the 'common good' and only in the personal interest of those who hold political authority are therefore 'tyrannical' and consequently do not have to be followed in any case." *Disobedience in Western Political Thought: A Genealogy* (Cambridge: Cambridge University Press, 2013), 27.

structure of the community as a whole. The "natural law" is resonant with the natural ontology that Aristotle and Cicero had laid out.[8] Even here, despite its conventional and communitarian overtones, there is a rudimentary theory of critical judgment. If we presuppose that our essential relationality and sociality is placed into different structures of relations, and these structures are governed by certain laws and norms, it becomes a central issue of concern to grasp the purpose of these structures and the forms of life to which they give rise. If an association placed burdens on some of its members to benefit others, it violates the criterion of the form; if that association is constructed and organized to produce benefits for particular members, it violates the criterion of the end; and if some make rules for the association when they have no authority to do so, it violates the criterion of the author.

We can extend this into Rousseau's often misunderstood conception of the general will to see how this thesis makes a kind of return in democratic form. For Rousseau, the general will is essentially a subjective and objective concept. At once it is constitutive of our individual consciousness and intentionality even as it is also a property of public life.[9] The essential idea orients conduct and personal interest toward common ends and purposes, seeing that man's essentially cooperative status in society depends on members of that society cognizing the common good as their own individual good as well. Legitimate forms of obligation, our duties as members of the political association, derive from this very orientation: citizens have obligations to only those political forms and social norms with this common good as its end.[10] Particular interests

---

8. Aquinas writes: "As Augustine says, quoting Tully, 'a nation is a body of men united together by consent to the law and by community of welfare.' Consequently, it pertains to the very notion of a nation that the mutual relations of the citizen be ordered by just laws." *Summa Theologiae*, I, II, Q. 105, Art. 2.

9. Luc Boltanski and Laurent Thévenot therefore argue that Rousseau "adopts the Jansenist use of the term 'general' to refer not to the entire set of human beings, or to citizens, but to the state reached by each person when, shedding his or her singularity and sacrificing all particular interests, he or she comes to know what is good in general, and succeeds in desiring the common good." *On Justification: Economies of Worth* (Princeton, NJ: Princeton University Press, 2006), 110.

10. Jules Steinberg properly argues that "Rousseau first approaches his task by arguing that it is improper to speak of citizens having a moral obligation to obey the law in any state where the laws express only the selfish interests of a ruling class." *Locke, Rousseau, and the Idea of Consent* (Westport, CT: Greenwood Press, 1978), 83.

are therefore different from individual interests governed by the general will: in the former, self-interest is narrow and nonuniversal; in the latter, self-interest is expanded, incorporating personal interest with the associative goods and interests of the community.[11] The reason for this is simple: our ontology as associative, cooperative beings becomes the central concept in the general will. As such, political legitimacy becomes rooted in the interests of a public governed by the general will.[12]

The general will now has a rational structure that can be used to judge valid political reasons. Not unlike Aquinas, Rousseau gives some features of the general will and uses these features to allow us to see when the state is legitimate and when it is not. These are not formal features of discursive reasoning. Rather, they are features of a kind of collective intentionality that allows citizens to become a democratic people. According to this, we can say that any norm, value, institution, or law must be thought through the following constitutive rules:

1. The rule of *equality*: no individual places unequal burdens on any other member of the community either for their own benefit or for the benefit of the community as a whole.

2. The rule of *generality*: any end of the general will be applicable to all needs that the citizens hold in common and that all members of the community and their needs are to be considered and taken into account.

---

11. I have defended this thesis along social-ontological grounds elsewhere. See Michael J. Thompson, "Autonomy and Common Good: An Interpretation of Rousseau's General Will," *International Journal of Philosophical Studies*, vol. 25, no. 2 (2017): 266–85.

12. J. G. Merquior argues on this point that: "Characteristically, the whole contractarian tradition in modern political philosophy was an attempt to cope with the *problem of justifying obligation*—a problem to which the incipient change in the relationship between law and custom added a new breadth and poignancy, that could not possibly have been known to the ancient and medieval theorists of rulership. Rousseau's doctrine of the general will deserves to be considered as the profoundest theoretical enterprise in this connection, since his was the only social contract theory to *equate legitimate law with the will of the public*." *Rousseau and Weber: Two Studies in the Theory of Legitimacy* (London: Routledge and Kegan Paul, 1980), 62.

3. The rule of *nonservitude*: no one gives himself to any other member of the community, corporate or individual, or is subordinated by their interests or wills.

The common good can be seen as constituted by these collective intentional rules. Social practices and institutions articulated by this rule set would manifest a world, Rousseau argues, where the individual and common good are both maximized. For him, it would solve the problem of how the individual can live in an association and the member and the association benefit.

We can now see how the foundation of the general will opens up a new structure of normative thinking in political theory. Hegel and Marx, for instance, develop their own distinctive theories amid this structure of thought, one where the concept of freedom is understood as the concrete social forms that join individual development with the structure and dynamics of group membership. We can see that the ontological is a fundamental consideration for political legitimacy because any association of which I am a part must meet the standards not of Socrates's polis-community but the solidaristic requirements of a kind of membership that is mutually beneficial for group and each member. This membership must not violate the expanded individuality of reciprocally related membership. Solidarity is the consciousness of my membership in a relational structure. It should be taken to neither imply nor entail convergent interests or communal group interest. No common good can ever be achieved by violating the rights of this kind of individuality.

As I have been suggesting, human associations are not rooted in nature but are products of inherent natural potentialities that we possess. A crucial logic to our status as social beings is the dialectic between part and whole, between private and public, and between individual and common goods. Being part of an ontological structure that allows for the dynamic reciprocity between these two dimensions of our structure—as opposed to a hierarchy between them (as in substantive ethics) or a disjuncture between them (as in liberalism)—entails being able to judge when the social schemes I am a part and that form my life are governed by such reciprocity. It informs not only the legitimate ends of society but also my duties toward as a part of it. As such, we can create and shape our social schemes as we see fit, and those that satisfy the criteria of common goods in this associational sense should be seen as warranting and deserving of our obligation and duties.

What we can call democratic reason should be deeper and more comprehensive than theories of public reasoning and deliberative democracy have proposed. For one thing, the theories of deliberative democracy focus on the procedures that can guide public debates. Validity is to be understood in terms of the formal features of dialogue, rather than in terms of the content of the reasons being offered. The strength of this approach, it is claimed, "seems to depend on whether the popular opinion being appealed to is the product of a properly conducted deliberation."[13] A core idea is that ensuring practices such as reciprocity, openness to the arguments of others, a general agreement as to the acceptance of reasons, and so on will establish a framework for deliberative judgment. More technically, the framework of deliberation serves as more than a mere regulative device for deliberation. It also has pragmatic implications for the validity of the outcomes of such deliberations. Douglas Walton emphasizes this point when he argues: "According to this pragmatic approach, an argument can be seen as a contribution to an orderly, goal-directed conversation between two parties. It can be judged to be rationally acceptable to the extent that it made a collaborative contribution to moving the conversation toward its goal."[14]

This falls into the same trap I discussed in chapter 3. Namely, the reliance on pragmatic mechanisms to judge the validity, let alone the rationality of public deliberations, tells us nothing about the content of the claims being adjudicated nor of the outcomes that are agreed on. Indeed, the approach of deliberative theorists is in real danger of merely reproducing the background assumptions and conceptual frameworks that

---

13. Douglas Walton, "Criteria of Rationality for Evaluating Democratic Public Rhetoric," in Benedetto Fontana, Cary J. Nederman, and Gary Remer (eds.), *Talking Democracy: Historical Perspectives on Rhetoric and Democracy* (University Park: Pennsylvania State University Press, 2004), 295–330, 304.

14. Walton, "Criteria of Rationality," 311. Also see James Bohman, *Public Deliberation: Pluralism, Complexity and Democracy* (Cambridge, MA: MIT Press, 1996), and Amy Gutmann and Dennis Thompson, *Democracy and Disagreement* (Cambridge, MA: Harvard University Press, 1998). For a more elaborate defense and discussion of this "dialogical" view of democratic reason, see Douglas Walton, *The New Dialectic: Conversational Contexts of Argument* (Toronto: University of Toronto Press, 1998).

already exist. The problem of what I have termed ontological coherence does not come into play and remains repressed, and the significance of this is that such deliberative theories do not provide for a means to undermine and explode the powers of reification on consciousness. Since reification recodes the agent's cognitive and evaluative capacities, these become generative of the conceptual and pragmatic mechanisms of deliberation. The danger of merely refracting the prevailing social reality back through such discourse thereby renders this approach vulnerable to the pressures of the internal validity of norms that have been taken up by each subject by the processes of socialization. In short, deliberative theories of judgment that ignore—indeed, that explicitly define themselves against—any ontological dimension to our understanding of what constitutes democratic reason, is open to the pathology of the reification of consciousness and the reproduction of social pathologies as well as the deeper social structures of reality that are constitutive of most public problems and require critical consciousness and transformation.

The key idea here is not that pragmatic theories of public deliberation need to be dispensed with, but that the criteria for evaluating democratic reasons cannot be captured through this framework. Instead, the criteria for what we can call democratic reason must be sought in the *content of the reasons themselves*, not the formal or pragmatic structure of deliberation. If we must judge valid reasons based on the social ontological criteria I have been elaborating, then the question of democratic forms of reasoning mesh with the question of democratic forms of life—or the ontological structures of sociality that are freedom-enhancing—as opposed to those that are merely agreed on. What counts as a criterion of validity rationally, in this sense, may not necessarily hold in terms of deliberative agreement. But the standpoint of critique must necessarily push the terms of public reasoning toward arguments that best capture or approximate ontologically valid arguments; the terms of debate in any deliberation must be held accountable to the richer context of validity that ontological coherence sets forth. Indeed, even more, these social ontological criteria for validity are not substantive criteria and hence are pliable in the face of social circumstance. There is no objective stance outside of public deliberation where some pristine truth resides; instead, the thesis here is that the thin account of public, democratic reasoning as deliberative and pragmatic, must be deepened and expanded for it to serve the ends of truly democratic reasoning. The social ontological framework provides us with a context of criteria for grasping defective dynamics of social reality even as it prompts us to inquire about how our relations, practices, and collective purposes and ends can be debated and transformed. It provides a deeper, more critical structure for the formulation of public reasons and their rational validity.

As I have been suggesting, one important way of grasping these social ontological categories for critical reason is the inquiry into the kinds of ends or purposes our social relations and collective practices serve. Rousseau asks us to see as rational and valid only those social institutions that have common ends as their goal, rather than particular ends. This is not a substantive prescriptive argument but a social ontological one where our practical reasoning reflects on the purposes of collective forms of cooperation, association, and practices. Common goods are therefore not transcendent values, nor are they premodern or precritical reservoirs of commonly held beliefs or values. Instead, they are immanent to the actual practices we engage in as associational beings, and once they take the form of nonsubordinating, nonextractive, mutually reciprocal forms of relations that promote the development of each member of the association, we have articulated a social reality worthy of our obligation. Recall that Rousseau makes this clear in the *Social Contract* as he builds toward his thesis of the general will.[15] The social-ontological thesis returns, but as a property of the goods and powers that we as an associational, cooperative species can manifest. The ontology of our social practices and relations therefore produce associational goods, or those goods that are only possible via cooperative forms of activity with common purpose.[16]

What this means is that critical political judgment becomes centered on the relative rationality or defectiveness of the associational

---

15. The quote is informative: "men cannot create new forces; they can only bring together ones that already exist, and steer them. So, their only way to preserve themselves is to unite a number of forces so that they are jointly powerful enough to deal with the obstacles. They have to bring these forces into play in such a way that they act together in a single thrust." Jean-Jacques Rousseau, *Du contrat social*, in *Oeuvres Complètes*, vol. 3 (Paris: Éditions Gallimard, 1964), 360.

16. Steinberg notes that: "Rousseau envisions a political community based upon a general will as one based upon a 'shared community of purpose,' insofar as proper citizen activity is concerned. In other words, a state embodies a general will to the extent that each discrete citizen seeks to promote the common good when enacting law and does not attempt to promote private interest." *Locke, Rousseau, and the Idea of Consent*, 85.

structures, practices, and goods that any social scheme instantiates. Any member of an associational structure or social scheme can and must inquire into the validity of these schemes and the relations, processes, and ends that make them up. If we know what criteria and what ontological forms are worthy of our obligations, it follows that this provides criteria for critical judgment and the criteria for dissent: now we can see that only those social schemes that promote the ends of collective purposes, that are oriented toward the good of each member of the community, deserve our obligations, and those that do not promote these ends command our nonobligation. The key idea is that the good be seen in ontological terms: as social ends that cultivate the developmental, capacity-enhancing potentialities of each individual. Hence, the good must cease to be viewed in purely subjective and formal terms. The common good should be seen as a criterion for what ends, relations, and processes warrant obligation and which ones do not. The common good as a social scheme is what should circumscribe the domain of critical political judgment.

Self and Social Relations: On Expanded Autonomy

A new way of approaching the concept of autonomy can be glimpsed now. Political judgment has little to offer us if there is no sense of how individual reflection and autonomy fit into the structure of critique. Any member of an association must be able to judge how association is shaped and what purposes or ends it is put to. Autonomy is that capacity to reflect on these ontological properties of the social scheme one is embedded in. The concept of autonomy is generally criticized for being undersocialized: the subject is not to be viewed as a monological, self-reflective agent but one who, according to the Kantian pragmatist paradigm, comes to see valid norms via the process of intersubjectivity. In this model, the validity of norms passes from the self-legislating subject's subjective realm to the intersubjective social realm, where agreement and consensus become the ground for normative validity. For various reasons, I have argued that this model is insufficient and that a social-ontological account of normative validity needs to be sought. This affects our conception of autonomy at the same time because the oversocialized conception of human agency pushes out the individual's capacity to reflect critically on one's social world.

Expanded autonomy differs from the Kantian understanding in that although it is a property of the subject, its form and content are shaped by the social-relational ontology of social reality. Critique becomes possible once each member of the association can see that association as a group enterprise, once each member is self-conscious of the social-relational substance shaped in that social scheme in specific ways. Expanded autonomy therefore places the subject in self-conscious relation to the relational structures that ensconce him. The cognitive dimension of Rousseau's concept of the general will is an exemplar of this expanded subjectivity, as is Hegel's theory of rationality in the *Philosophy of Right*. For both, the individual is a social-ontological entity, dynamically suspended in a web of relations with others. But each person is rational to the extent that they can cognize this membership and have self-consciousness of the purposes of the relations we have and form with others. There is, then, a central dialectic between individual self-consciousness and the collective group consciousness that enables social reality to emerge and sustain itself. Any social scheme is constituted by members with both capacities; only when the former capacity is satisfied does a social scheme become valid and rational. Lacking this, we descend into conventionalism and reification.

In this sense, the expanded autonomy of the social ontological approach should be sharply distinguished from the postmetaphysical phenomenological approach of Arendt's conception of "enlarged mentality." Recall that for Arendt, this referred to the capacity of each person to see the world through the eyes of the other. The "political" for Arendt rests on this conception, where each sees that one's existence is dependent on that of the other. But this approach shears off the thick ontology of our relatedness with others and the structures of relations and power and their ability to shape consciousness. Expanded autonomy captures this thicker reality: it seeks to understand how our associational life and the cooperative practices that instantiate our reality is ontically shaped and how this diverges from other social schemes that could potentially enhance our freedom as processual and relational beings. Any practical reasoning that happens outside of this social-ontological nexus will either rest on a vague notion of conscience or collapse into nihilism. We need to be able to hold the two dimensions of human ontology in our heads: to grasp at once the ontic status of the world as we find it on one hand and, on the other, question how the world either cripples or enhances our potentialities as humans. We must be able to hold this in view because without it there is no judgment, merely existential emotion. Throughout the course of the second half of the twentieth century and into the twenty-first, this has proven to be a corroded framework for practical reason and political activity.

In place of this, a critical social ontology can show us our essential relatedness with others; it can highlight how the existing social reality suppresses and even debases our human capacities; it can provide a ground for our critique of power and domination to achieve articulation. What Hegel referred to as "objective *Geist*" and what Marx referred to as "materialism" can be seen as social-ontological structures that give shape to our social being. Why do we live this way? How does a given institution or norm violate the purposes of associational life? These are valid questions for political judgment. It is something that each individual member of the political association must ask if they are to be considered rational and in possession of critical, rational agency. In this sense, Weber's account of moral conviction rings decidedly hollow, a shriek from the declining bourgeois world:

> However, it is immeasurably moving when a *mature* man— no matter whether old or young in years—is aware of a responsibility for the consequences of his conduct and really feels such responsibility with heart and soul. He then acts by following an ethic of responsibility and somewhere he reaches the point where he says: "Here I stand; I can do no other." That is something genuinely human and moving. And every one of us who is not spiritually dead must realize the possibility of finding himself at some time in that position. Insofar as this is true, an ethic of ultimate ends and an ethic of responsibility are not absolute contrasts but rather supplements, which only in unison constitute a genuine man—a man who *can* have the "calling for politics."[17]

Here the individual acting on conscience appears in its last gasp. For Weber, the pursuit of an "authentic modernity" was collapsing into the "iron cage," the demise of the ethic of responsibility and routinization of administrative forms of rational authority. What the ethic of

---

17. Max Weber, "Politics as a Vocation," in H. H. Gerth and C. Wright Mills (eds.), *From Max Weber: Essays in Sociology* (New York: Oxford University Press, 1946), 127.

responsibility needs to achieve critical force is a kind of moral-evaluative reasoning rooted in the actual conditions of human life and the contradictions our forms of life place on our development and free sociality.

In this sense, expanded autonomy denotes the capacity for each person to think in terms of his or her group membership, instead of terms of an abstract ethic of responsibility. Indeed, the ethic of responsibility becomes more concrete once I can ground ethics in ethical life and ethical life in the tension that exists between what is and can be; between the ontic expression of reality as we find it in the world and the potential being that can be once this world is transformed according to common goods and common interests.[18] Only when I can see that my individuality is enhanced by making by relations-with-others rational (i.e., free, developing, mutually affirming relations) can judgment be in play against the ontic structures and processes of the prevailing reality. New shapes for our sociality must be forged based on the search for this expansion of the individual's self-understanding as a social-relational being.[19] The abstract formalism of Kant's categorical imperative becomes a more concrete expression of the individual's capacity to reflect about

---

18. Tracy B. Strong sees in Weber a turn toward what political theory should be searching for: a form of politics with no grounding and, after Arendt, one without a "banister." As he puts it: "The passage in Weber is further noteworthy in that it comes precisely at the moment that Weber considers the justification for the acts of a person who truly has politics as a vocation. It is an act that brings a world into existence; it succeeds in that those who are not 'inwardly dead' are moved by it, presumably to act differently than they had been. This *existential Lutheran justification*, as I have called it, is explicitly non-utilitarian; it clearly makes no reference to natural law, or to the public good, or to individual glory, or to historical destiny, or to God's plan, or to the necessities of the universe. It rests on nothing but itself. No banister. Most centrally, it makes no appeal to a moral justification for policies." Tracy B. Strong, *Politics without Vision: Thinking without a Banister in the Twentieth Century* (Chicago: University of Chicago Press, 2012), 373.

19. Indeed, this is the Rousseauvian alternative to the existentialist conception of conscience and responsibility. As Marshall Berman argues, Rousseau "held up to modern men the ideal of a life that would be at once more individual and more communal, a life in which every man could best 'expand his being and multiply his happiness by sharing them with his fellow men. . . . Rousseau's one clear hope was that, if modern men responded to his ideas, they might very gradually reform their society from within through the education of future generations." *The Politics of Authenticity: Radical Individualism and the Emergence of Modern Society* (New York: Atheneum, 1970), 182–83.

the valid relations, processes, and purposes that constitute the social world he or she inhabits. Even in the case of intersubjectivity, discourse is still dependent on how each person thinks and judges. The idea that we can have an ethics without ontology only leads us back to the empty formalism that is cannot provide some framework for an individual's practical reflections.

The fear in modern technological-administrative societies, as I have been arguing, is that individuals will become increasingly folded into forms of conformist norms and belonging, if not to techno-administrative norms, or according to smaller group norms and forms of identity that spin off and circumscribe their group affiliation. In any case, an individual's reflective capacities are reified and contingent according to the group context in which they are embedded. But when each member is capable of reflecting on the ontological shape of any social scheme, then each can call the validity of that scheme into question and critically engage it. The ontological ground holds open the capacity to judge how the social scheme shapes and structures our lives and underpins the values, norms, and practices that shape our world. Social schemes organized for the good of a subset of the community, or those that exhibit extractive or subordinating relations and do not fulfill the rational ends of any association—that is, the maximization of its benefit to its constituent members—do not require our obligation. In fact, they require our nonobligation; we should dissent from and disobey the dictates of that kind of social form.

Critique, Obligation, and Disobedience

The thesis of expanded autonomy is central to the concept of critical judgment. In the view I am developing here, I maintain that rational individuals—that is, those who can cognize defective social purposes and social schemes—are obligated to disobey those institutions that do not maximize common interests. This concept is in need of unpacking. First, it is not at all clear how one would have an "obligation to disobey" any duty. But I believe we can defend the thesis that rationally committed social agents must have such an obligation because for them to live a free life, they must also live within free (i.e., rational) social schemes that promote the freedom of all. Since a free way of life is lived interdependently with others, any rational agent must see that to not disobey is, *ipso facto*, to sustain a defective social norm or relation or practice. Second, it seems to me to be an act of basic rational responsibility for any person to insist on the rational ends of the institutions that shape their lives. To do otherwise would deny one's rational rule following and force them to succumb to heteronomous and defective forms of social authority. If no rational argument can be given for its purpose, an institution, law, or norm should not be obeyed; a rational argument must be judged, as I have been arguing, in the social-ontological basis that it enhances common and individual goods and serves the ends of social freedom.

It is important to bring the various strands of my argument together to defend this thesis. As I have been suggesting, the ontology of the human species is essentially relational and processual. Each person develops his or her capacities and perfectibility only in a shared framework of cooperative relations with others. As such, the social and political community should be viewed as an association with the most rational purpose of cultivating the common good for all members. This is true not only of the state but also of civil society and nonformal intimate relations. The actual forms of relational life that come to the fore in our various social schemes may not be constructed with the good of the association in mind. It may be constructed to amplify the power of a subset of the association or to extract benefit, labor, surplus, or whatever from those members. It may be that certain social schemes are shaped by those imperatives of power and no longer have our development and perfectibility as their purpose or end. It is crucial for the defectiveness of the ontological shapes of these social schemes to be brought to consciousness and, once they are, for them to be transformed.

This theory of disobedience or dissent differs from many of the prevailing theories of this question. One difference is the thesis that we have obligations to those laws and norms that have been decided based on a democratic decision procedure. Peter Singer makes the argument that one root of obligation "stems from the fact that participating in a decision-procedure, alongside others participating in good faith, gives rise to an obligation to act as if one had consented to be bound by the result of the decision-procedure."[20] Obligation to "laws in a democracy apply only when no rights essential to the functioning of

---

20. Peter Singer, *Democracy and Disobedience* (New York: Oxford University Press, 1974), 133.

a fair compromise decision-procedure have been infringed."[21] But this is far too abstract to really count as a legitimate means for obligation. Dissent cannot be merely a reaction to imperfect decision procedures, although that is a very legitimate grounds. I think we need to expand the conception of dissent to include not only law and state institutions but also the other norms and practices that pervade modern society. Cultural practices and norms have become increasingly tied to forms of social power and control. They, too, must be included in any theory of obligation and disobedience.

This critique carries over into those theories of obligation that hinge on the concept of membership. Mere membership cannot be sufficient grounds for obligation. Michael Walzer, for instance, claims, "Obligation, then, begins with membership, but membership in the broadest sense, for there are a great variety of formal and informal ways of living within a particular circle of action and commitment."[22] According to this view, our membership in a social group becomes a criterion for obligation. But this does not provide us with any criteria for critical judgment or a sense of what kinds of norms, institutions, laws, and so on should be seen as legitimate and worthy of our obligations. Margaret Gilbert, for one, argues that "according to a central everyday conception, a political society is constituted by an underlying joint commitment to accept certain rules, rules that count intuitively as political institutions.[23] Those who are parties to the joint commitment are the members of the political society in question, or, if you prefer,

---

21. Singer, *Democracy and Disobedience*, 133–34.

22. Michael Walzer, *Obligations: Essays on Disobedience, War, and Citizenship* (New York: Simon and Schuster, 1970), 7.

23. More formally, Gilbert rests her argument on what she calls "absolutely conclusive reasons" which take the form: "X has an absolutely conclusive reason for performing some action, A, if and only if a consideration C that speaks in favor of A is such that given C, rationality requires that X do A, whatever else is true." There is no reason given for this other than X is a member of a group or some kind of joint activity. As I have been stressing, this cannot be sufficient because the ends or purposes of that joint activity may be obscure to me, may not be for my benefit, may entail becoming an agent of some harm to others, and so on. There is simply no critical criteria for judgment to be found here. See Margaret Gilbert, *A Theory of Political Obligation: Membership, Commitment, and the Bonds of Society* (New York: Oxford University Press, 2006), 31ff.

they are its core members."[24] From this Gilbert proceeds to make a claim for political obligation: "the members of a political society have obligations of joint commitment to support and comply with its political institutions whatever they are. Thus, if a given imperator has the standing to command them they have an obligation of this kind to do what he says. They may also have such an obligation to take the punishments it metes out."[25]

Such a position does not seem defensible. If I have an obligation, as my argument has been suggesting, it can only be rationally supported if they are obligations toward rational social schemes—toward those social schemes that maximize the common good of its members and the development of their free agency as members. Radical disobedience to a law or institution must have in view an alternative social scheme that would be worthy of our obligation. It must be able to possess what I called ontological coherence, or grasp what kinds of alternative social relations, processes, norms, and ends should replace those that are defective.[26] For Gilbert, the basis of political obligation is that of political membership, full stop. Merely being a member of a joint action imposes commitments and obligations. I am obligated to stop at a stop sign even if no one else is on the road, just as I am obligated to go to war if the state commands me to. My own selfish reasons cannot factor into the relevant decisions as a member of the political community when it comes to obligation. Gilbert has to maintain that unjust wars, for example, may override an obligation to obey the command. As she argues: "It may be that in joining the army and going out to the field of battle she will play a significant role in an unjust, aggressive war

---

24. Gilbert, *A Theory of Political Obligation*, 238–39.

25. Gilbert, *A Theory of Political Obligation*, 256.

26. I therefore disagree on this point with Robin Celikates: "although the motivations behind these forms of protest will often be substantial, their justification follows a procedural rather than a substantial logic, pointing to problems with the 'input' and organization or process of democratic opinion- and will-formation rather than with the 'output' or decisions these processes ultimately lead to." "Democratizing Civil Disobedience," *Philosophy and Social Criticism*, vol. 42, no. 10 (2016): 982–94, 989. As I see it, this leaves us without a ground for critical judgment and social transformation. There must be ontological ballast to our judgments; they must be able to articulate more than democratic inclusivity, but go further into the deeper structures and processes of the social reality.

that has been undertaken by her political society. Or the way in which the war is being conducted may be unacceptable, though the war itself is just. . . . It may be that her only honorable course is to default on her obligation."[27]

If this is the case, Gilbert has ruptured her own argument for membership being a prima facie reason for political obligation. Taking the example of possible reasons for defaulting on her obligation to go to an unjust war, Gilbert implicitly argues for the critical-social ontological thesis I suggest here. Indeed, if the purpose or end of the war is unjust or the means by which it is carried out is unjust, then it obviates the obligation. I think we should go further and say that it *obligates our disobedience*: the common interest of any association must have as its consistent aim the cultivation of those practices and uses of power (in the case of the state most specifically).[28] Since the resources needed to conduct war are socially generated associational goods, any unjust war can only be sustained via our own noninterference. But this need not only be in the case of unjust war. Any social scheme that does not have the associational good of its members as its purpose seems to me to violate this criterion as well. Families or other intimate relationships that are organized for the good of one at the expense of the other(s) involved, economies that serve the benefit of the few at the expense of the political community, and so on—all operate under the same logic. They are associational social schemes that do not have interdependence, mutuality, reciprocity, nonsubordination, and common goods as their aim. They do not deserve our obligations and thus exit from and transformation of those schemes is a demand of reason.

---

27. Gilbert, *A Theory of Political Obligation*, 259.

28. In his defense of the premise that there exists no right to disobedience, Joseph Raz concedes that there does exist a moral imperative to disobey in "exceptional" circumstances: "In support of a just cause it may be less harmful than certain kinds of lawful action (e.g., national strike, or a long strike in a key industry or service). It may be wrong not to resort to civil disobedience and to turn to such lawful action first, or give up any action in support of a just cause. The claim that civil disobedience is justified only when all else has failed or is certain to fail, like the claims that it should be open and non-violent, etc., reflects a failure to conceive its true nature." *The Authority of Law: Essays on Law and Morality* (Oxford: Clarendon Press, 1979), 275. Of course, the problem of judgment is sidestepped: there are no criteria given for judging when a case is exceptional and when it is not. I believe that critical practical reason can provide criteria for this kind of judgment.

If Frances is unsure whether to follow a law, to conform to a norm or custom—she must look at the what that law, norm, or custom actually realizes and what kinds of relations and practices it exhibits as part of its structure. She may think, for instance, that it is a good thing to arrive at work on time, do her job well, be respectful to her managers, and so on. These norms and practices are embedded in the functional requirements of the system, and in and of themselves deserve no obligation from Frances. She may begin to ask: what role do I play in this organization? What are the purposes of this institution, of the practices and norms that I follow? How does it make me relate to others, to myself? These are central questions of judgment, and they find their distinctively political meaning (as opposed to moral meaning) in how these forms of life shape one's being and potentialities. Should she have obligations to a parent or emotional partner who is abusive and emotionally exploitative?

For disobedience to be justified, there must be some sense that it is done in the interest of what is just and that not being disobedient would entail the agent's participation in some act of injustice. Its basic underwriting principle is the need to abstain from, diminish, and reshape social schemes that subordinate members of the association, extract benefits from them, and use them for the gain or expediency of the few. Its essential purpose is the democratization of that which is oligarchic or tyrannical; its goal is the reconstruction of our social schemes to maximize the realization of common goods, mutual benefits for members of the structure of nonsubordinating associations. In modern societies, these unjust social schemes appear more and more as the introjection of the prevailing purposes and relations of the given reality absorbed by the self; more and more it conceals the deeper forms of domination, misuse of common power, and the alternative schemes to which associational, cooperative forms of labor and practice could be put. Obligation is reserved only for those forms of life, those actions, laws, norms, and institutions that do maximize common powers and, *ipso facto*, the individual as well. Not just disobedience but social transformation is necessary, for one must entail the other if it is rationally adjudicated.

Disobedience and dissent must be seen to disrupt the reifying tendencies of modern forms of rationalized power and domination. The shattering of reification is a central task of critical practical reason and the social ontology that frames it. Critical theory's most robust insights have been precisely concerning this problem: how routinized and rationalized forms of social power have been able to embed themselves in the life-world of citizens. The reality and effects of these forms of power can be crowded out by conventional or reified norms of thinking and acting, thereby blocking critical reflection. Thoreau made this a central part of his defense of civil disobedience. For him, the state did not obligate his allegiance and duty because it was engaged in two highly problematic purposes when he was writing: the legal-constitutional protection of the institution of slavery and the war against Mexico.

At a more fundamental level, what Thoreau refers to as the "undue respect for law," where individuals follow the norms and legal strictures of society without asking about the purposes those strictures serve, is one of the core defects of uncritical obligation. As Thoreau puts it:

> A common and natural result of an undue respect for law is, that you may see a file of soldiers, colonel, captain, corporal, privates, powder-monkeys, and all, marching in admirable order over hill and dale to the wars, against their wills, ay, against their common sense and consciences, which makes it very steep marching indeed, and produces a palpitation of the heart. They have no doubt that it is a damnable business in which they are concerned; they are all peaceably inclined. Now, what are they? Men at all? or small movable forts and magazines, at the service of some unscrupulous man in power?[29]

Thoreau's thesis implores us to have critical awareness of the ends and purposes toward which our regimented and tacitly accepted norms and practices orient us. The result of rationalized forms of coordinated social order is that it negates rational reflection and critical judgment and displaces it with the rationale of the prevailing logic. Thoreau shows that lacking critical judgment means the extension of domination and power; it means our own entanglement with the instrumental purposes of the powerful. Disobedience to these norms and institutions does not constitute an antilegalism, as William Scheuerman has suggested, but a fundamental opposition to those forms of law and state-sanctioned

---

29. Henry David Thoreau, "On the Duty of Civil Disobedience," in *Walden and Civil Disobedience* (New York: Harper Perennial, 1958), 253.

power that cannot demonstrate their rational character, that is, their orientation toward common goods and social freedom.[30]

In opposition to Gilbert's defense of obligation, I must assert once again the thesis that critical social-ontology seeks to make explicit: that we must scrutinize the ends and purposes of the social schemes of which we are a part; we must judge these ends and purposes according to the kinds of goods they produce; and the kinds of goods that are valid and warrant our obligation are mutually beneficial to the members of that social scheme and all those affected by it. If one participates in a social scheme that detracts from the common good, to one's own good as an individual or to another, then the scheme and all of its constitutive norms and practices obligate one to disobey it. Thoreau has this in mind when he argues:

> If the injustice has a spring, or a pulley, or a rope, or a crank, exclusively for itself, then perhaps you may consider whether the remedy will not be worse than the evil; but if it is of such a nature that it requires you to be the agent of injustice to another, then, I say, break the law. Let your life be a counter friction to stop the machine. What I have to do is to see, at any rate, that I do not lend myself to the wrong which I condemn.[31]

The key issue critical social-ontology deals with is the cognitive and evaluative criteria for knowing how injustice appears in everyday life and the institutions that surround us. Joint membership cannot be a sufficient criteria for obligation, as Gilbert has argued. Rather, the ontological shape that any scheme takes is of crucial concern for critical consciousness. Given our irreducible associational status, group membership counts only as a criterion against some form of nihilism or illusory libertarianism. It grants us no criteria for gauging the relative justness or unjustness of any social scheme. Returning for a moment to the question put to Socrates in the *Crito*, we can say that the law condemning him to death had no legitimacy: no law can be considered valid that would seek to eliminate those who think differently.

30. William E. Scheuerman, "Recent Theories of Civil Disobedience: An Anti-Legal Turn?," *Journal of Political Philosophy*, vol. 23, no. 4 (2015): 427–49. See the critical response to this thesis by Celikates, "Democratizing Civil Disobedience."
31. Thoreau, "On the Duty of Civil Disobedience," 259.

Prima facie group membership tells us nothing about the validity of the ends of the association, nothing about how relations are shaped and structured, and nothing about how the social scheme in question does or does not realize common goods or ends that warrant obligation. We are back to Socrates's position that the implicit agreement he has apparently made with the polis is sufficient to consider his obligation to the community and its authority over his obligation. As I have been saying, I think this is unacceptable. Disobedience is a logical and rational outcome of a system that is not organized for common goods and purposes; even more, it is the obligation of individuals who are members of that association. Rational individuals have no obligations to those forms of association and attendant norms, values, and practices that do not have the common good of all members of the association as part of their ontological structure.

An interesting case study of this idea of disobedience is the film by Florian Henckel von Donnersmarck, *Das Leben der Anderen* (*The Lives of Others*, 2006), in which a dedicated Stasi officer named Wiesler (played by Ulrich Mühe) begins a gradual process of disobedience to his duties to the state. While secretly surveilling a writer named Dreyman (Sebastian Koch), Wiesler comes to realize that Dreyman will be writing an article for a West German publication on the rise in suicide deaths in East Germany. Leading up to this, Wiesler has come to experience the arbitrary exercise of power in the Stasi ranks and becomes disillusioned with the purposes and activities of the institution. He begins to see that the principles of socialism, in which he believes, contradict the actual behavior and aims of his superiors who seek only narrow personal gain and care nothing for the principles in which Wiesler believes. He does not interfere in Dreyman's writing of the article, and its publication exposes the rise in suicides in East Germany, thereby revealing the failed sociality of the state. Wiesler comes to see this as a justified act and begins to hinder the surveillance of Dreyman from within.

The film documents this change in ethical conscience on the part of Wiesler as he realizes that the social scheme of which he is a part no longer has a valid, rational end. The move toward disobedience turns not on some vague phenomenological engagement with the other—indeed, Wiesler is curiously mediated in his relationship with Dreyman by electronic surveillance and can only listen to what is happening, there is never an intersubjective engagement between the characters. Rather, Wiesler's ethical transformation occurs because he sees that Dreyman's activity and purpose are justified; they express a genuine concern with the public good and the justness of the state. Wiesler therefore sees that the scheme of which he is a part no longer has validity, and he begins to withhold his findings to protect Dreyman, finally leading to an outright act where he sabotages the entire investigation to protect Dreyman, accepting a demeaning demotion until the fall of the Berlin Wall several years later.

A core idea the film explores is how conscience can become activated. It is interesting that Wiesler's interaction with Dreyman is totally anonymous, there is no intersubjective interaction between them. Critical consciousness is activated by the gradual awareness of the defectiveness of the main character's social scheme: both the Stasi as an agency and the East German government as well. The moment of disobedience becomes gradually revealed as the character puts more of his experiences together and realizes the irrationality of the form of life that ensconces him. As a case study in disobedience, von Donnersmarck's film is superb. The cognitive realization of the defectiveness of the social scheme's critical consciousness leads to more than mere dissent—it leads to outright disobedience. But this disobedience has its roots in the transformation of conscience based in *ontological coherence* Wiesler can achieve by working through the contradictions between the ontic form of life he lives within and the ontological principles he finds just and that are being actively negated by the actually existing reality.

The Ends of Political Obligation: Common Good and Social Freedom

Critical political judgment using a critical social ontology therefore clarifies a modern conception of radical politics and conscience that the postmetaphysical and pragmatist approaches have decidedly glossed over. Erich Fromm once noted that "If a man can only obey and not disobey, he is a slave; if he can only disobey and not obey, he is a rebel (not a revolutionary); he acts out of anger, disappointment, resentment, yet not in the name of conviction or a principle."[32] Conviction and principle, in this sense, cannot be construed in Kantian, formal terms. Rather, as I have been suggesting, we must inquire into the ontological

---

32. Erich Fromm, *On Disobedience: Why Freedom Means Saying "No" to Power* (New York: Harper Perennial, 1981), 5.

shapes that our social reality takes; we must be aware of how our own ontology as relational, processual, and purposeful beings are constituted by the prevailing structures and purposes of my society and its various institutions. The dialectic between the phylogenetic ontology of each of us as members of a relational and processual species and the ontogenetic social facts of our actual lives is the field of critical political judgment.

Therefore, disobedience and obligation must go hand in hand. Any act of disobedience must be rooted in a principle that can ontologically ground a new social scheme or some amendment to the already existing social scheme. It makes no sense to simply disobey without an alternative principle that can constructively guide an alternative social reality. Unlike Melville's Bartleby, we cannot simply "prefer not to." Such an act is not a rational political act unless one seeks the transformation of that practice or institution. Thoreau's thesis—that each must let it be known what kind of government would command his obligation—is a crucial dimension of disobedience. Critical political judgment must move in this field of reasons. It must operate with an concrete grasp of social ontology as the field of contestation. Power and domination is the power to shape social reality; it is the power of some to construct institutions, norms, and shape our forms of cooperation to their interests and ends.

If we are to reset the project of social justice and radical democracy, this will only be realized via a rational-radical approach to the problems of modern domination and alienation. The need for normative coherence in an age of reification is real. The thesis is that our values should be viewed in social-ontological terms, that values are indeed ontological means that we need to understand what properties of social life, what social schemes will best fit and amplify our powers are cooperative, interdependent beings. Valid social relations and valid social purposes can be judged in this regard; we must see the good as a social-ontological property of the social-relational structures of our associational life. As I have suggested, disobedience becomes necessary when the structures, processes, and purposes of my society defy or violate the reciprocal dynamic between self and society, between the person and the community. Associations and their attendant norms and practices are only valid when they satisfy such criteria and satisfy common purposes and ends without violating the criteria of nonsubordination and nonextraction between members. Critical, rational judgment does not require a "banister," but it does require a conceptual grammar rooted in social-metaphysical reasons that can reconcile the diremption of subjective consciousness from our social being.

Given the irreducible fact of human sociality and its propagation into distinct ontological forms and shapes, we can see that obligation is a core normative component to the particular forms of social life we inhabit. Disobedience from any ontic social scheme is necessitated once ontological coherence can establish it as organized in some way for particular instead of common ends and goods, which engenders social-relational structures that entail nonreciprocal and dominating relations. I think this was at the core of thinkers such as Rousseau, Hegel, and Marx—to mention only a few who made use of an social-ontological ground for rational, legitimate social relations. Freedom as an ontological and objective, realized category must be understood in these terms. Social and individual freedom are interdependent concepts; they are mutually enhancing and determinative. How we organize our social relations and their purposes, the processes our sociality takes, and the norms and practices instantiating them should be at the core of critical judgment and the aim of social transformation.

Democratic Individuality, Solidarity, and Social Transformation

Critical judgment therefore has as one if its primary roles the resuscitation of a radical, rational form of democracy that can lead to concrete social transformation. Part of the power of the critical social-ontological account I have offered here is that it can work toward overcoming the implicit nihilism that sparked the move toward the postmetaphysical turn. Critical political judgment must be able to forge the basis for what Raffaele Laudani has called "destituent power," or an understanding of "conflict as a process of continual and generally open-ended withdrawal from the legal, political, economic, social, and cultural stumbling blocks" that essentially prevent the articulation of genuinely democratic forms of political life.[33] Laudani correctly sees "destituent" power as dialectically related to "constituent" power, or the power of people to

---

33. Laudani, *Disobedience in Western Political Thought*, 4. Also see the important discussion by Frances Fox Piven, *Challenging Authority: How Ordinary People Change America* (Lanham, MD: Rowman and Littlefield, 2006), 19ff.

construct legitimate forms of rule and sovereignty. Both are needed, as Laudani indicates, because the capacity to construct our own institutions also implies our capacity to dissent from them, to exit them.[34] Social power is not eradicable; it can be shaped in different ways, but there is no point where it can be eliminated as in some pure libertarianism or anarchism.[35]

Essential here is the dialectic between the ontic and the ontological, the phylogenetic and the ontogenetic, what is potential and what is existent. Enhancing collective and democratic forms of power and diminishing domination and exploitation is therefore the core project of reshaping and reorganizing social relations and institutions. This is a politics with vision that overcomes any need for external or transcendent values or principles. This form of vision is derived from the immanent critique of our practices and the alternative ways our relations with others, the purposes we set for our collective and personal lives, and the norms and practices to which we commit ourselves can be arranged and organized. The vision is embedded in the potential capacities and powers that can be developed via alternative modes of social reality and new forms of sociality. The ontological conception of judgment depends on this dialectic between what is and what can be because it needs to posit an actual essential structure of human life. This structure is not a preordained nature, nor is it some kind of static natural law. Instead, it points to the ontological modes discussed earlier: it maintains that humans can make new and better forms of life based on how our essence as relational, processual, and practical beings are organized.

Domination and subordination, alienation and reification, and other pathologies can be overcome only by rearranging the relational-practical structures within which our development as selves is processed. The postmetaphysical view was born out of the fears of the post–World War II world. It was a response to the collapse of religion and other forms of normative authority and permanence that were erased with the birth of the atomic age, the realization of genocide, and the banality

---

34. See Raffaele Laudani, "Lo spazio atlantico della disobbedienza; Modernità e potere destituente," *Filosofia politica*, vol. 1 (2008): 37–60.

35. Laudani argues: "Despite carrying clear libertarian instances, destituent power is not anti-institutional per se, because, on the contrary, it makes the assumption of the nonartificial and ineradicable presence of power and its institutions." *Disobedience in Western Political Thought*, 4.

of bureaucratic, welfare-state capitalism. But the cure was too drastic. In receding into intersubjective pragmatism, Kantian noumenalism, or Heideggerian existentialism, political philosophy gradually has retreated from the more trenchant form of critique that was rooted in the social-ontological tradition and the kind of radical republicanism that it supported.

This requires that we grasp the concept of political judgment as being linked with the nature of democratic individuality. Just as Hegel's distinctive theory of human reason as being constituted by intersubjective norms and structures of relations mediates the individual's consciousness, so does critical political judgment make us cognizant of the relational-practical essence of our lives with others. A genuine sense of solidarity becomes possible once abstract individualism is overcome and a concrete individualism rooted in expanded autonomy can come to fruition. Solidarity is the self-consciousness of our essential interdependence with others; it is the conviction that each group member must defend and have in view this interdependence as a core normative and descriptive feature of healthy, free sociality and self-development.[36] Solidarity is a form of obligation on the part of individuals with one another: it is a commitment to our interdependence and the common norms, practices, and goods that enhance and maintain it. Solidarity as the self-consciousness of our interdependence is an expression of expanded autonomy—autonomy, in this sense, is in no way the negation of solidarism but its essential prerequisite. In this sense, it is also an objective criterion for disobedience and dissent. It provides the rational normative context of meaning for judging which forms of life warrant our obligations and which do not. Genuine individuality, in this sense, is therefore a prerequisite for rational social solidarity, which must be viewed as the highest, most rational form political organization. Democracy must track this form of sociality. It must be rooted in the kinds of reciprocal interdependent sociality that solidarity manifests. In this way, individuality and society are reconciled dialectically, and one does not become absorbed or shattered by the other.

---

36. See the classic discussion by Léon Bourgeois, *Solidarité* (Paris: Librarie Armand Colin, 1902) and the more recent discussion by Peter Baldwin, *The Politics of Social Solidarity: Class Bases of the European Welfare State, 1875–1975* (New York: Cambridge University Press, 1990), 1–54.

In the end, political theory can only retrieve its sense of purpose if it can engage a vision of what a just, free form of social life can emerge. This requires engagement with the concrete life practices and institutional structures that form our social reality. Our ethical life—the constellation of values, norms, and practices that generate our world—should be seen as constitutive of our social world. These values, norms, and practices are sustained by those who have refused to judge them. They have been shaped and made ambient by those who seek to maintain power over others and over the community as a whole. Disobedience can only come from judgment; judgment can only come from critique. Vision about alternative ways of shaping our social and political lives must come from this kind of critical reflection. The opening of the possibility for something new, for expanded forms of social and personal freedom can only be liberated from the prevailing forms of social reality that frustrate and stall them.

Human progress is a matter of the historical change of these social forms, of how the human community has reworked and reordered its internal relations and the avowed ends and purposes for the collective efforts of society as a whole. Shattering the web of norms that ensconce us in a destructive and inhumane form of life can only begin once we have grasped our ontology as social and developmental beings and once we have the power of critical judgment to call into question the social schemes that shape and organize our sociality, our powers, and the texture of our lives. If the form of thinking about human affairs and human potential I have explored here has any value, it will be judged by the extent to which a new kind of political vision can be shaped and a new horizon of historical possibility is finally grasped.

Bibliography

Abensour, Miguel. *Democracy against the State: Marx and the Machiavellian Moment*. Cambridge: Polity Press, 2011.

Alexy, Robert. "A Theory of Practical Discourse." In S. Benhabib and F. Dall-mayr (eds.), *The Communicative Ethics Controversy*. Cambridge, MA: MIT Press, 1990, 151–92.

Aquinas, Thomas. *Summa Theologiae*, 2 vols. Chicago: Encyclopedia Britannica, 1952.

Arendt, Hannah. *The Origins of Totalitarianism*. New York: Harcourt Brace Jovanovich, 1951.

Arendt, Hannah. *The Human Condition*. Chicago: University of Chicago Press, 1958.

Arendt, Hannah. *Between Past and Future*. New York: Penguin, 1961.

Arendt, Hannah. *On Revolution*. New York: Penguin Books, 1963.

Arendt, Hannah. "Truth and Politics." In P. Laslett and W. G. Runciman (eds.), *Philosophy, Politics and Society*, 3rd series. Oxford: Basil Blackwell, 1969, 104–33.

Arendt, Hannah. *On Violence*. New York: Harcourt Brace, 1970.

Arendt, Hannah. *The Life of the Mind*, vol. 1. New York: Harcourt, 1971.

Arendt, Hannah. *Responsibility and Judgment*. New York: Schocken Books, 2003.

Arendt, Hannah. *The Promise of Politics*. New York: Schocken Books, 2005.

Aristotle. *Rhetoric*. Oxford: Oxford University Press, 1975.

Aristotle. *Politics*. Oxford: Oxford University Press, 1990.

Aristotle. *Nicomachean Ethics*. Oxford: Oxford University Press 1994.

Athens, Lonnie. *Domination and Subjugation in Everyday Life*. London: Routledge, 2015.

Austin, J. L. *Philosophical Papers*. Oxford: Oxford University Press, 1961.

Azmanova, Albena. *The Scandal of Reason: A Critical Theory of Political Judgment*. New York: Columbia University Press, 2012.

Baldwin, Peter. *The Politics of Social Solidarity: Class Bases of the European Welfare State, 1875–1975.* Cambridge: Cambridge University Press, 1992.

Balibar, Étienne. "From Philosophical Anthropology to Social Ontology and Back: What to Do with Marx's Sixth Thesis on Feuerbach?" *Postmodern Culture,* vol. 22, no. 3 (2012): 1–35.

Barber, Benjamin. *The Conquest of Politics: Liberal Philosophy in Democratic Times.* Princeton, NJ: Princeton University Press, 1988.

Barker, Ernest. *The Political Thought of Plato and Aristotle.* New York: Dover, 1947.

Baum, Manfred. "Freedom in Marx." *Radical Philosophy Review,* vol. 10, no. 2 (2007): 117–31.

Beiner, Ronald. *Political Judgment.* Chicago: University of Chicago Press, 1983.

Beiser, Frederick. *Hegel.* New York: Routledge, 2005.

Benhabib, Seyla. "Communicative Ethics and Current Controversies in Practical Philosophy." In S. Benhabib and F. Dallmayr (eds.), *The Communicative Ethics Controversy.* Cambridge, MA: MIT Press, 1990, 330–69.

Benhabib, Seyla. *Situating the Self: Gender and Postmodernism in Contemporary Ethics.* New York: Routledge, 1992.

Bentley, Russell. "Rhetorical Democracy." In Benedetto Fontana, Cary J. Nederman, and Gary Remer (eds.) *Talking Democracy: Historical Perspectives on Rhetoric and Democracy.* University Park: Pennsylvania State University Press, 2004, 115–34.

Berdahl, J., and P. Martorana. "Effects of Power on Emotion and Expression during a Controversial Group Discussion." *European Journal of Social Psychology,* vol. 36 (2006): 497–509.

Berman, Marshal. *The Politics of Authenticity: Radical Individualism and the Emergence of Modern Society.* New York: Atheneum, 1970.

Bernstein, Basil. *Class, Codes and Control: Theoretical Studies towards a Philosophy of Language,* vol. 1. New York: Shocken Books, 1975.

Bernstein, Richard J. *The Pragmatic Turn.* Cambridge: Polity Press, 2010.

Böhler, Dietrich. "Transcendental Pragmatics and Critical Morality: On the Possibility and Moral Significance of a Self-Enlightenment of Reason." In S. Benhabib and F. Dallmayr (eds.), *The Communicative Ethics Controversy.* Cambridge, MA: MIT Press, 1990, 111–50.

Bohman, James. *Public Deliberation: Pluralism, Complexity and Democracy.* Cambridge, MA: MIT Press, 1996.

Boltanski, Luc, and Laurent Thévenot. *On Justification: Economies of Worth.* Princeton, NJ: Princeton University Press, 2006.

Booth, William James. "The Limits of Autonomy: Karl Marx's Kant Critique." In R. Beiner and J. Booth (eds.), *Kant and Political Philosophy: The Contemporary Legacy.* New Haven, CT: Yale University Press, 1993, 245–75.

Bourdieu, Pierre. *Language and Symbolic Power.* Cambridge, MA: Harvard University Press, 1991.

Bourgeois, Léon. *Solidarité*. Paris: Librairie Armand Colin, 1902.

Bratman, Michael E. *Shared Agency: A Planning Theory of Acting Together*. New York: Oxford University Press, 2014.

Breen, Keith. "Violence and Power: A Critique of Hannah Arendt on the 'Political.'" *Philosophy and Social Criticism*, vol. 33, no. 3 (2007): 343–72.

Brown, Michael E. *The Concept of the Social in Uniting the Humanities and Social Sciences*. Philadelphia: Temple University Press, 2014.

Bubner, Rüdiger. *Polis und Staat. Grundlinien der Politischen Philosophie*. Frankfurt: Suhrkamp, 2002.

Cassirer, Ernst. *Rousseau, Kant and Goethe*. New York: Harper, 1963.

Caterino, Brian. *The Practical Import of Political Inquiry*. New York: Palgrave Macmillan, 2016.

Celikates, Robin. "From Critical Social Theory to a Social Theory of Critique: On the Critique of Ideology after the Pragmatic Turn." *Constellations*, vol. 13, no. 1 (2006): 21–40.

Celikates, Robin. "Democratizing Civil Disobedience." *Philosophy and Social Criticism*, vol. 42, no. 10 (2016): 982–94.

Cicourel, Aaron. *Cognitive Sociology: Language and Meaning in Social Interaction*. London: Penguin, 1972.

Cobb, Jonathan, and Richard Sennett. *The Hidden Injuries of Class*. New York: Norton, 1972.

Coward, Rosalind, and John Ellis. *Language and Materialism: Developments in Semiology and the Theory of the Subject*. London: Routledge and Kegan Paul, 1977.

Dahms, Harry. *Modern Society as Artifice: Critical Theory and the Logic of Capital*. London: Routledge, forthcoming.

Dallmayr, Fred. *Polis and Praxis: Exercises in Contemporary Political Theory*. Cambridge, MA: MIT Press, 1984.

De George, Richard T. "Social Reality and Social Relations." *Review of Metaphysics*, vol. 37, no. 1 (1983): 3–20.

De Greu, C. K. W., and P. Van Lange. "The Impact of Social Value Orientations on Negotiator Cognition and Behavior." *Personality and Social Psychology Bulletin*, vol. 21, no. 11 (1995): 1178–88.

Dent, Nicholas. *Rousseau: An Introduction to His Psychological, Social and Political Theory*. Oxford: Basil Blackwell, 1988.

Deutscher, Penelope, and Cristina Lafont, eds. *Critical Theory in Critical Times: Transforming the Global Political and Economic Order*. New York: Columbia University Press, 2017.

Dewey, John. *The Quest for Certainty*. New York: Putnam and Sons, 1929.

Diggins, John Patrick. *The Promise of Pragmatism: Modernism and the Crisis of Knowledge and Authority*. Chicago: University of Chicago Press, 1994.

Donati, Pierpaolo. "The Common Good as a Relational Good." *Nova et Vetera*, vol. 7, no. 3 (2009): 603–24.

Donati, Pierpaolo. "Social Capital and Associative Democracy: A Relational Perspective." *Journal for the Theory of Social Behaviour*, vol. 44, no. 1 (2013): 24–45. Donati, Pierpaolo, and Margaret Archer. *The Relational Subject*. Cambridge: Cambridge University Press, 2015.

Duckett, J., and K. Fischer. "The Impact of Social Threat on Worldview and Ideological Attitudes." *Political Psychology*, vol. 24, no. 1 (2003): 199–222.

Dunn, John. *Political Obligation in Its Historical Context*. Cambridge: Cambridge University Press, 1980.

Durkheim, Emile. *The Rules of Sociological Method*. New York: Free Press, 1938.

Durkheim, Emile. *Professional Ethics and Civic Morals*. Glencoe, IL: Free Press, 1958.

Elder-Vass, Dave. "Social Structure and Social Relations." *Journal for the Theory of Social Behaviour*, vol. 37, no. 4 (2007): 463–77.

Ellul, Jacques. *The Technological Society*. New York: Vintage Books, 1964.

Faye, Emmanuel. *Arendt et Heidegger: Extermination nazie et destruction de la pensée*. Paris: Éditions Albin Michel, 2016.

Feenberg, Andrew. *Technosystem: The Social Life of Reason*. Cambridge, MA: Harvard University Press, 2017.

Feldman, Stanley, and Karen Stenner. "Perceived Threat and Authoritarianism." *Political Psychology*, vol. 18, no. 4 (1997): 741–70.

Ferrara, Alessandro. *Justice and Judgment*. London: Sage, 1999.

Ferrara, Alessandro. *The Force of the Example: Explorations in the Paradigm of Judgment*. New York: Columbia University Press, 2008.

Fetscher, Iring. "Marx's Concretization of the Concept of Freedom." In E. Fromm (ed.), *Socialist Humanism: An International Symposium*. New York: Doubleday, 1965, 238–49.

Fetscher, Iring. *Marx and Marxism*. New York: Herder and Herder, 1971.

Forbes, Ian. *Marx and the New Individual*. London: Unwin Hyman, 1990.

Forst, Rainer. *The Right to Justification: Toward a Constructivist Theory of Justice*. New York: Columbia University Press, 2011.

Forst, Rainer. *Justification and Critique: Towards a Critical Theory of Politics*. Cambridge: Polity Press, 2014.

Forst, Rainer. "Noumenal Power." *Journal of Political Philosophy*, vol. 23, no. 2 (2015): 111–27.

Freyenhagen, Fabian. "Honneth on Social Pathologies: A Critique." *Critical Horizons*, vol. 16, no. 2 (2015): 131–52.

Friberg-Frenros, Henrik, and Johan Karlsson Shaffer. "The Consensus Paradox: Does Deliberative Agreement Impede Rational Discourse?" *Political Studies*, vol. 62, no. 1 (2014): 99–116.

Fromm, Erich. *The Sane Society*. New York: Henry Holt, 1955.

Fromm, Erich. *The Crisis of Psychoanalysis*. New York: Henry Holt, 1970.

Fromm, Erich. *On Disobedience: Why Freedom Means Saying "No" to Power*. New York: Harper Perennial, 1981.

Gabel, Josef. *False Consciousness: An Essay on Reification*. New York: Harper and Row, 1975.

Gadamer, Hans-Georg. *Wahrheit und Methode. Grundzüge einer philosophischen Hermeneutik*. Tübingen: J. C. B. Mohr (Paul Siebeck), 1975.

Gadamer, Hans-Georg. *Philosophical Hermeneutics*. Berkeley: University of California Press, 1976.

Gadamer, Hans-Georg. "On the Possibility of a Philosophical Ethics." In R. Beiner and J. Booth (eds.), *Kant and Political Philosophy: The Contemporary Legacy*. New Haven, CT: Yale University Press, 1983, 361–74.

Gaines, B., J. Kuklinski, P. Quirk, B. Peyton, and J. Verkuilen. "Same Facts, Different Interpretations: Partisan Motivation and Opinion on Iraq." *Journal of Politics*, vol. 69, no. 4 (2007): 957–74.

Garsten, Bryan. *Saving Persuasion: A Defense of Rhetoric and Judgment*. Cambridge, MA: Harvard University Press, 2006.

Geiger, Ido. *The Founding Act of Ethical Life: Hegel's Critique of Kant's Moral and Political Philosophy*. Stanford, CA: Stanford University Press, 2007.

Gilbert, Margaret. *Living Together: Rationality, Sociality and Obligation*. Lanham, MD: Rowman and Littlefield, 1996.

Gilbert, Margaret. *A Theory of Political Obligation: Membership, Commitment, and the Bonds of Society*. Cambridge: Cambridge University Press, 2006.

Goff, Tom W. *Marx and Mead: Contributions to a Sociology of Knowledge*. London: Routledge and Kegan Paul, 1980.

Gould, Carole. *Marx's Social Ontology: Individuality and Community in Marx's Theory of Social Reality*. Cambridge, MA: MIT Press, 1978.

Green, Philip. *American Democracy: Selected Essays on Theory, Practice and Critique*. New York: Palgrave Macmillan, 2014.

Grice, Paul. *Studies in the Way of Words*. Cambridge, MA: Harvard University Press, 1989.

Gutmann, Amy, and Dennis Thompson. *Democracy and Disagreement*. Cambridge, MA: Harvard University Press, 1998.

Habermas, Jürgen. *Philosophical-Political Profiles*. Cambridge, MA: MIT Press, 1983.

Habermas, Jürgen. *The Philosophical Discourse of Modernity: Twelve Lectures*. Cambridge, MA: MIT Press, 1987.

Habermas, Jürgen. *Moral Consciousness and Communicative Action*. Cambridge, MA: MIT Press, 1990.

Habermas, Jürgen. *Postmetaphysical Thinking: Philosophical Essays*. Cambridge, MA: MIT Press, 1993.

Habermas, Jürgen. *Between Facts and Norms: Contributions to a Discourse Theory of Law and Democracy*. Cambridge, MA: MIT Press, 1996.

Habermas, Jürgen. *On the Pragmatics of Communication*. Cambridge, MA: MIT Press, 1998.

Habermas, Jürgen. *The Inclusion of the Other: Studies in Political Theory*. Cambridge, MA: MIT Press, 1998.

Habermas, Jürgen. *Truth and Justification*. Cambridge, MA: MIT Press, 2003.

Hahn, Songsuk Susan. *Contradiction in Motion: Hegel's Organic Concept of Life and Value*. Ithaca, NY: Cornell University Press, 2007.

Jonathan Haidt. "The Emotional Dog and Its Rational Tail: A Social Intuitionist Approach to Moral Judgment." *Psychological Review*, vol. 108, no. 4 (2001): 814–34.

Hariou, Maurice. "La théorie de l'institution et de la fondation." In *Aux sources du droit: le pouvoir, l'ordre, la liberté*. Caen: Presses Universitaires de Caen, 1986, 98–100.

Harris, Neal. "Beyond Recognition: A Critique of Contemporary Social Pathology Diagnosis." Ph.D. diss., University of Sussex, 2019.

Hartmann, Nicolai. *The New Ways of Ontology*. Boston: Henry Regnery, 1949.

Hegel, G. W. F. *Wissenschaft der Logik*, 2 vols. Frankfurt: Suhrkamp, 1969.

Hegel, G. W. F. *Grundlinien der Philosophie des Rechts*. Stuttgart: Reclam, 1970.

Hegel, G. W. F. *Enzyklopädie der philosophischen Wissenschaften*. Frankfurt: Suhrkamp, 1986.

Heidegger, Martin. "On the Essence of Truth." In *Martin Heidegger: Basic Writings*. New York: Harper Torchbooks, 1971.

Heidegger, Martin. *Sein und Zeit*. Tübingen: Max Niemeyer, 2001.

Heidegger, Martin. *The Essence of Human Freedom: An Introduction to Philosophy*. New York: Continuum, 2002.

Henrich, Dieter. "Logical Form and Real Totality: The Authentic Conceptual Form of Hegel's Concept of the State." In R. Pippin and O. Höffe (eds.), *Hegel on Ethics and Politics*. Cambridge: Cambridge University Press, 2004, 241–67.

Hinchman, Lewis P., and Sandra K. Hinchman. "Existentialism Politicized: Arendt's Debt to Jaspers." *Review of Politics*, vol. 53, no. 3 (1991): 435–68.

Honneth, Axel. *The Struggle for Recognition: The Grammar of Social Conflicts*. Cambridge, MA: MIT Press, 1995.

Honneth, Axel. *Disrespect: The Normative Foundations of Critical Theory*. Cambridge: Polity Press, 2007.

Honneth, Axel. *Reification: A New Look at an Old Idea*. New York: Oxford University Press, 2008.

Honneth, Axel. *The Pathologies of Individual Freedom: Hegel's Social Theory*. Princeton, NJ: Princeton University Press, 2010.

Horkheimer, Max. *The Eclipse of Reason*. New York: Continuum, 1974.

Horstmann, Rolf-Peter. "Substance, Subject and Infinity: A Case Study of the Role of Logic in Hegel's System." In K. Deligiorgi (ed.), *Hegel: New Directions*. London: Acumen Press, 2006, 69–84.

Houlgate, Stephen. "The Unity of Theoretical and Practical Spirit in Hegel's Concept of Freedom." *Review of Metaphysics*, vol. 48, no. 4 (1995): 859–81.

Houlgate, Stephen. "Hegel's Logic." In F. Besier (ed.), *The Cambridge Companion to Hegel and Nineteenth-Century Philosophy*. New York: Cambridge University Press, 2008, 111–34.

Hyppolite, Jean. *Genesis and Structure of Hegel's Phenomenology of Spirit*. Evanston, IL: Northwestern University Press, 1974.

Irwin, T. H. "The Metaphysical and Psychological Basis of Aristotle's Ethics." In Amélie Oksenberg Rorty (ed.), *Essays on Aristotle's Ethics*. Berkeley: University of California Press, 1980, 35–53.

Israel, Joachim. *The Language of Dialectics and the Dialectics of Language*. London: Harvester Press, 1979.

Jaspers, Karl. *Reason and Existenz*. New York: Noonday Press, [1933] 1955.

Jaspers, Karl. *Philosophy*, vol. 2. Trans. E. B. Ashton. Chicago: University of Chicago Press, [1932] 1970.

Kahan, Dan M. "The Cognitively Illiberal State." *Stanford Law Review*, vol. 60 (2007): 101–40.

Kain, Philip J. *Hegel and the Other: A Study of the Phenomenology of Spirit*. Albany, NY: SUNY Press, 2005.

Katz, Jerrold J. *The Philosophy of Language*. New York: Harper and Row, 1966.

Kavoulakos, Konstantinos. *Georg Lukács's Philosophy of Praxis*. New York: Bloomsbury, 2018.

Kervégan, Jean-François. "Towards an Institutional Theory of Rights." In Italo Testa and Luigi Ruggiu (eds.), *"I That Is We, We That Is I": Perspectives on Contemporary Hegel*. Leiden: Brill, 2016, 68–85.

Kervégan, Jean-François. *The Actual and the Rational: Hegel and Objective Spirit*. Chicago: University of Chicago Press, 2018.

Knowles, Dudley. *Political Obligation: A Critical Introduction*. London: Routledge, 2010.

Koehler, J. "The Influence of Prior Beliefs on Scientific Judgments of Evidence Quality." *Organizational Behavior and Human Decision Processes*, vol. 56 (1993): 28–55.

Kolb, David. *The Critique of Pure Modernity: Hegel, Heidegger and After*. Chicago: University of Chicago Press, 1986.

Kosman, Aryeh. *The Activity of Being: An Essay on Aristotle's Ontology*. Cambridge, MA: Harvard University Press, 2013.

Kuklinski, J., P. Quirk, J. Jerit, and R. Rich. "The Political Environment and Political Competence." *American Journal of Political Science*, vol. 45, no. 2 (2001): 410–24.

Lakoff, George. *Moral Politics: How Liberals and Conservatives Think*. Chicago: University of Chicago Press, 2002.

Lane, Robert. "The Fear of Equality." *American Political Science Review*, vol. 53, no. 1 (1959): 35–51.

Lara, María Pía. *Narrating Evil: A Postmetaphysical Theory of Reflective Judgment*. New York: Columbia University Press, 2007.

Larson, D. "The Role of Belief Systems and Schemas in Foreign Policy Decision-Making." *Political Psychology*, vol. 15, no. 1 (1993): 17–33.

Laudani, Raffaele. "Lo spazio atlantico della disobbedienza; Modernità e potere destituente." *Filosofia politica*, vol. 1 (2008): 37–60.

Laudani, Raffaele. *Disobedience in Western Political Thought: A Genealogy*. Cambridge: Cambridge University Press, 2013.

Lichtman, Richard. *The Production of Desire: The Integration of Psychoanalysis into Marxist Theory*. New York: Free Press, 1982.

Livergood, Norman D. *Activity in Marx's Philosophy*. The Hague: Martinus Nijhoff, 1967.

Lederman, Shmuel. "The Actor Does Not Judge: Hannah Arendt's Theory of Judgment." *Philosophy and Social Criticism*, vol. 42, no. 7 (2015): 727–41.

Lord, C., L. Ross, and M. Lepper. "Biased Information and Attitude Polarization: The Effects of Prior Theories on Subsequently Considered Evidence." *Journal of Personality and Social Psychology*, vol. 37, no. 11 (1979): 2098–109.

Lukács, Georg. *History and Class Consciousness*. Cambridge, MA: MIT Press, 1971.

Lukács, Georg. *The Ontology of Social Being*, vol. 3, *Labor*. Trans. D. Fernbach. London: Merlin Press, 1980.

Marcuse, Herbert. "The Obsolescence of the Freudian Conception of Man." In *Five Lectures*. Boston: Beacon Press, 1970, 44–61.

Markell, Patchen. "The Rule of the People: Arendt, *Archê*, and Democracy." *American Political Science Review*, vol. 100, no. 1 (2006): 1–14.

Marx, Karl. *The Economic and Philosophical Manuscripts*. In Erich Fromm, *Marx's Concept of Man*. New York: Frederick Ungar, 1964.

Marx, Karl. *Theses on Feuerbach*. In L. Easton and K. Guddat (eds.), *Writings of the Young Marx on Philosophy and Society*. New York: Doubleday, 1967, 400.

Marx, Karl. *Grundrisse*. London: Penguin Books, 1973.

Marx, Karl. *Capital*, vol. 1. New York: Vintage, 1977.

Marx, Karl. "Wage Labor and Capital." In *Collected Works*, vol. 9. London: Lawrence and Wishart, 2010.

McCarthy, George E. *Dreams in Exile: Rediscovering Science and Ethics in Nineteenth-Century Social Theory*. Albany, NY: SUNY Press, 2009.

McConnell, Grant. *Private Power and American Democracy*. New York: Vintage, 1966.

Mead, George Herbert. *Mind, Self and Society*. Chicago: University of Chicago Press, 1934.

Merquior, J. G. *Rousseau and Weber: Two Studies in the Theory of Legitimacy*. London: Routledge and Kegan Paul, 1980.

Meyers, Peter Alexander. *Abandoned to Ourselves*. New Haven, CT: Yale University Press, 2013.

Mishra, Pankaj. *Age of Anger: A History of the Present*. New York: Farrar, Strauss and Giroux, 2017.

Mouffe, Chantal. "Radical Democracy: Modern or Postmodern?" In A. Ross (ed.), *Universal Abandon? The Politics of Postmodernism*. Minneapolis: University of Minnesota Press, 1988, 31–45.

Neuhouser, Frederick. *Rousseau's Theodicy of Self-Love: Evil, Rationality, and the Drive for Recognition*. New York: Oxford University Press, 2008.

Neuhouser, Frederick. *Rousseau's Critique of Inequality: Reconstructing the Second Discourse*. New York: Cambridge University Press, 2014.

Nussbaum, Martha. "Aristotelian Social Democracy." In Aristide Tessitore (ed.), *Aristotle and Modern Politics*. Notre Dame, IN: University of Notre Dame Press, 2002, 47–104.

Palermo, Giulio. "The Ontology of Economic Power in Capitalism: Mainstream Economics and Marx." *Cambridge Journal of Economics*, vol. 31 (2007): 539–61.

Parsons, Talcott. *The Social System*. New York: Free Press, 1951.

Pettit, Philip. "Democracy, Electoral and Contestatory." In I. Shapiro and S. Macedo (eds.), *Designing Democratic Institutions*. New York: New York University Press, 2000, 105–47.

Pinkard, Terry. *Hegel's Phenomenology: The Sociality of Reason*. Cambridge: Cambridge University Press, 1994.

Pippin, Robert. *Hegel's Idealism: The Satisfactions of Self-Consciousness*. Cambridge: Cambridge University Press, 1989.

Piven, Frances Fox. *Challenging Authority: How Ordinary People Change America*. Lanham, MD: Rowman and Littlefield, 2006.

Plato. *Crito*. Oxford Classical Texts. Oxford: Oxford University Press, 1966.

Postman, Neil. *Amusing Ourselves to Death: Public Discourse in the Age of Show Business*. New York: Penguin, 1985.

Putnam, Hilary. *Ethics without Ontology*. Cambridge, MA: Harvard University Press, 2006.

Raz, Joseph. *The Authority of Law: Essays on Law and Morality*. Oxford: Clarendon Press, 1979.

Raz, Joseph. *The Practice of Value*. Oxford: Oxford University Press, 2003.

Renault, Emanuel. "Critical Theory and Processual Social Ontology." *Journal of Social Ontology*, vol. 2, no. 1 (2016): 17–32.

Rickert, Edward J. "Authoritarianism and Economic Threat: Implications for Political Behavior." *Political Psychology*, vol. 19. no. 4 (1998): 707–20.

Ritter, Joachim. *Metaphysik und Politik. Studien zu Aristoteles und Hegel.* Frankfurt: Suhrkamp, 1969.

Robinson, R., D. Keltner, A. Ward and L. Ross. "Actual versus Assumed Differences in Construal: 'Naïve Realism' in Intergroup Perception and Conflict." *Journal of Personality and Social Psychology*, vol. 68, no. 3 (1995): 404–17.

Rodgers, Daniel T. *Age of Fracture.* Cambridge, MA: Belknap Press, 2011.

Rokeach, Milton. *The Open and Closed Mind.* New York: Basic Books, 1960.

Rorty, Richard. *Philosophy and Social Hope.* New York: Penguin, 1998.

Rosen, Stanley. *The Idea of Hegel's Science of Logic.* Chicago: University of Chicago Press, 2014.

Ross, Nathan. *On Mechanism in Hegel's Social and Political Philosophy.* New York: Routledge, 2008.

Rousseau, Jean-Jacques. Preface to "Narcisse." In *Oeuvres Complètes*, vol. 2. Paris: Éditions Gallimard, 1961.

Rousseau, Jean-Jacques. *Du contrat social.* In *Oeuvres Complètes*, vol. 3. Paris: Éditions Gallimard, 1964.

Rousseau, Jean-Jacques. *Discourse sur l'origine et les fondemens de l'inégalité parmi des hommes.* In *Oeuvres Complètes*, vol. 3. Paris: Éditions Gallimard, 1964.

Ruderman, Richard S. "Aristotle and the Recovery of Political Judgment." *American Political Science Review*, vol. 91, no. 2 (1997): 409–20.

Ruggiu, Luigi. "Reason and Social Ontology." In Italo Testa and Luigi Ruggiu (eds.), *"I That Is We, We That Is I": Perspectives on Contemporary Hegel.* Leiden: Brill, 2016, 86–105.

Ryle, Gilbert. "Final Discussion." In D. F. Pears (ed.), *The Nature of Metaphysics.* London: Macmillan, 1965, 142–64.

Schaff, Adam. *Marxism and the Human Individual.* New York: McGraw-Hill, 1970.

Scheuerman, William E. "Recent Theories of Civil Disobedience: An Anti-Legal Turn?" *Journal of Political Philosophy*, vol. 23, no. 4 (2015): 427–29.

Schrag, Calvin O. *Communicative Praxis and the Space of Subjectivity.* Bloomington: Indiana University Press, 1986.

Schwartz, Jonathan Peter "Political Judgment Confronts Ideology: Hannah Arendt's Contribution." *Polity*, vol. 50, no. 3 (2018): 485–511.

Searle, John. *The Construction of Social Reality.* New York: Free Press, 1996.

Searle, John. *Freedom and Neurobiology: Reflections on Free Will, Language, and Political Power.* New York: Columbia University Press, 2007.

Searle, John. *Making Sense of the Social World: The Structure of Human Civilization.* New York: Oxford University Press, 2010.

Sève, Lucien. *Marxism and the Theory of Personality.* London: Harvester Press, 1975.

Sidanius, Jim, and Felicia Pratto. "Racism and Support of Free-Market Capitalism: A Cross-Cultural Analysis." *Political Psychology*, vol. 14, no. 3 (1993): 381–401.

Simmel, Georg. *The Sociology of Georg Simmel*. Trans. Kurt H. Wolff. New York: Free Press, 1950.

Singer, Peter. *Democracy and Disobedience*. Oxford: Oxford University Press, 1973.

Smith, Vardaman R. "Marx's Social Ontology: His Critical Method and Contemporary Social Economics." *Review of Social Economy*, vol. 42, no. 2 (1984): 143–69.

Solt, Frederick "The Social Origins of Authoritarianism." *Political Research Quarterly*, vol. 65, no. 4 (2012): 703–13.

Spinoza, Benedict. *A Theological-Political Treatise*. Trans. R. H. M. Elwes. New York: Dover, 1951.

Stahl, Titus. "Verdinglichung als Pathologie zweiter Ordnung." *Deutsche Zeitschrift für Philosophie*, vol. 59, no. 5 (2011): 731–46.

Steinberg, Jules. *Locke, Rousseau, and the Idea of Consent: An Inquiry into the Liberal-Democratic Theory of Political Obligation*. Westport, CT: Greenwood Press, 1978.

Steinberger, Peter J. *The Concept of Political Judgment*. Chicago: University of Chicago Press, 1993.

Stern, Robert. *Hegelian Metaphysics*. New York: Oxford University Press, 2009.

Strawson, P. F. *Analysis and Metaphysics*. Oxford: Oxford University Press, 1992.

Strong, Tracy B. *Politics without Vision: Thinking without a Banister in the Twentieth Century*. Chicago: University of Chicago Press, 2012.

Sunstein, Cass "Deliberative Trouble? Why Groups Go to Extremes." *Yale Law Journal*, vol. 110 (2000): 71–119.

Sunstein, Cass "The Law of Group Polarization." *Journal of Political Philosophy*, vol. 10, no. 2 (2002): 175–95.

Taylor, Charles. *Hegel*. Cambridge: Cambridge University Press, 1975.

Taylor, Charles. "The Motivation behind a Procedural Ethics." In R. Beiner and J. Booth (eds.), *Kant and Political Philosophy: The Contemporary Legacy*. New Haven, CT: Yale University Press, 1993, 337–60.

Tetlock, Philip. "Cognitive Style and Political Belief Systems in the British House of Commons." *Journal of Personality and Social Psychology*, vol. 46, no. 2 (1984): 365–75.

Thompson, Kenneth. "Organizations as Constructors of Social Reality." In G. Salaman and K. Thompson (eds.), *Control and Ideology in Organizations*. Cambridge, MA: MIT Press, 1980, 216–36.

Thompson, Kevin. "Systematicity and Normative Justification: The Method of Hegel's Philosophical Science of Right." In T. Brooks and S. Stein (eds.), *Hegel's Political Philosophy: On the Normative Significance of Method and System*. New York: Oxford University Press, 2017, 44–66.

Thompson, Michael J. "A Functionalist Theory of Social Domination." *Journal of Political Power*, vol. 6, no. 2 (2013): 179–99.

Thompson, Michael J. "Hegel's Anti-Capitalist State." *Discusiones Filosoficas*, vol. 14, no. 22 (2013): 43–72.

Thompson, Michael J. "Philosophical Foundations for a Marxian Ethics." In M. Thompson (ed.), *Constructing Marxist Ethics: Critique, Normativity, Praxis*. Leiden: Brill, 2015, 235–65.

Thompson, Michael J. "Capitalism as Deficient Modernity: Hegel against the Modern Economy." In Andrew Buchwalter (ed.), *Hegel and Capitalism*. Albany, NY: SUNY Press, 2015, 117–32.

Thompson, Michael J. "False Consciousness Reconsidered: A Theory of Defective Social Cognition." *Critical Sociology*, vol. 41, no 3 (2015): 449–61.

Thompson, Michael J. *The Domestication of Critical Theory*. London: Rowman and Littlefield, 2016.

Thompson, Michael J. "Collective Intentionality, Social Domination, and Reification." *Journal of Social Ontology*, vol. 3, no. 2 (2017): 207–29.

Thompson, Michael J. "Autonomy and Common Good: An Interpretation of Rousseau's General Will." *International Journal of Philosophical Studies*, vol. 25, no. 2 (2017): 266–85.

Thompson, Michael J. "The Two Faces of Domination in Republican Political Theory." *European Journal of Political Theory*, vol. 17, no. 1 (2018): 44–64.

Thompson, Michael J. "The Metaphysical Infrastructure of Hegel's Practical Philosophy." In M. Thompson (ed.), *Hegel's Metaphysics and the Philosophy of Politics*. New York: Routledge, 2018, 101–41.

Thompson, Michael J. "A Theory of Council Republicanism." In J. Muldoon (ed.), *Council Democracy: Towards a Democratic Socialist Politics*. London: Routledge, 2018, 108–27.

Thompson, Michael J. "Reification and the Web of Norms: Toward a Critical Theory of Consciousness." *Berlin Journal of Critical Theory*, vol. 3, no. 3 (2019): 5–35.

Thompson, Michael J. "Critical Agency in Hegelian Ethics: Social Metaphysics versus Moral Constructivism." In J. Gledhill and S. Stein (eds.), *Hegel and Contemporary Practical Philosophy: Beyond Kantian Constructivism*. London: Routledge, 2020, 256–87.

Thoreau, Henry David. *Walden and Civil Disobedience*. New York: Harper Perennial, 1958.

Tomasello, Michael. *Becoming Human: A Theory of Ontogeny*. Cambridge, MA: Harvard University Press, 2019.

Toulmin, Stephen. *An Examination of the Place of Reason in Ethics*. Cambridge: Cambridge University Press, 1968.

Tugendhat, Ernst. *Self-Consciousness and Self-Determination*. Cambridge, MA: MIT Press, 1986.

Tugendhat, Ernst. *Vorlesungen über Ethik*. Frankfurt: Suhrkamp, 1993.

Tunick, Mark. *Hegel's Political Philosophy: Interpreting the Practice of Legal Punishment*. Princeton, NJ: Princeton University Press, 1992.

Tuomela, Raimo. *Social Ontology: Collective Intentionality and Group Agents*. New York: Oxford University Press, 2013.

Vatter, Miguel. "The People Shall Be Judge: Reflective Judgment and Constituent Power in Kant's Philosophy of Law." *Political Theory*, vol. 39, no. 6 (2011): 749–76.

Vollrath, Ernst. *Die These der Metaphysik. Zur Gestalt der Metaphysik bei Aristoteles, Kant und Hegel*. Wuppertal: Alois Henn, 1969.

Vollrath, Ernst. "Handeln und Urteilen: Zur Problematik von Hannah Arendts Lektüre von Kants 'Kritik der Urteilskraft' unter einer politischen Perspektive." In H. Münkler (ed.), *Bürgerreligion und Bürgertugend. Debatten über die vorpolitischen Grundlagen politischer Ordnung*. Baden-Baden: Nomos, 1996, 228–49.

Walker, Edward T. "Legitimating the Corporation through Public Participation." In C. W. Lee, M. McQuarrie, and E. T. Walker (eds.), *Democratizing Inequalities: Dilemmas of the New Public Participation*. New York: New York University Press, 2015, 66–81.

Walton, Douglas. *The New Dialectic: Conversational Contexts of Argument*. Toronto: University of Toronto Press, 1998.

Walton, Douglas. "Criteria of Rationality for Evaluating Democratic Public Opinion." In Benedetto Fontana, Cary J. Nederman, and Gary Remer (eds.), *Talking Democracy: Historical Perspectives on Rhetoric and Democracy*. University Park: Pennsylvania State University Press, 2004, 295–330.

Walzer, Michael. *Obligations: Essays on Disobedience, War and Citizenship*. New York: Simon and Schuster, 1970.

Warren, Mark E. "Can Participatory Democracy Produce Better Selves? Psychological Dimensions of Habermas's Discursive Model of Democracy." *Political Psychology*, vol. 14, no. 2 (1993): 209–34.

Weber, Max. "Politics as a Vocation." In H. H. Gerth and C. Wright Mills (eds.), *From Max Weber: Essays in Sociology*. New York: Oxford University Press, 1946, 77–128.

Weidenfield, Matthew C. "Visions of Judgment: Arendt, Kant and the Misreading of Judgment." *Political Science Quarterly*, vol. 66, no. 2 (2013): 254–66.

Weissman, David. *A Social Ontology*. New Haven, CT: Yale University Press, 2000.

Wiener, Norbert. *The Human Use of Human Beings: Cybernetics and Society*. New York: Da Capo Press, 1954.

Wiggins, David. "Deliberation and Practical Reason." In Amélie Oksenberg Rorty (ed.), *Essays on Aristotle's Ethics*. Berkeley: University of California Press, 1980, 221–40.

Wilkes, Kathleen V. "The Good Man and the Good for Man in Aristotle's Ethics." In Amélie Oksenberg Rorty (ed.), *Essays on Aristotle's Ethics*. Berkeley: University of California Press, 1980, 341–57.

Winfield, Richard Dien. "Ethical Community without Communitarianism." *Philosophy Today*, vol. 40, no. 2 (1996): 310–20.

Wittgenstein, Ludwig. *Philosophical Investigations*. Oxford: Blackwell, 1953.

Wolin, Richard. *Heidegger's Children: Hannah Arendt, Karl Löwith, Hans Jonas, and Herbert Marcuse*. Princeton, NJ: Princeton University Press, 2001.

Worrell, Mark P. *Dialectic of Solidarity: Labor, Antisemitism and the Frankfurt School*. Leiden: Brill, 2008.

Yeomans, Christopher. *Freedom and Reflection: Hegel and the Logic of Agency*. New York: Oxford University Press, 2012.

Zaretsky, Eli. *Political Freud: A History*. New York: Columbia University Press, 2015.

Zerilli, Linda. *A Democratic Theory of Judgment*. Chicago: University of Chicago Press, 2016.

Index